THE GENTLEMAN'S COMPANION

Volume I

The Exotic Cookery Book

Volume II

The Exotic Drinking Book

CHARLES H. BAKER

Published by Echo Point Books & Media
Brattleboro, Vermont
www.EchoPointBooks.com

ISBN: 978-1-62654-112-2

Cover design by Rachel Boothby Gualco,
Echo Point Books & Media

Editorial and proofreading assistance by Christine Schultz,
Echo Point Books & Media

Printed and bound in the United States of America

The Gentleman's Companion

VOLUME I

THE EXOTIC COOKERY BOOK
OR, AROUND THE WORLD WITH KNIFE, FORK, AND SPOON

By *Charles H. Baker, Jr.*

INCLUDING:

A Company of *Hand-Picked Receipts,* each one *Beloved & Notable in its Place,* collected faithfully on *Three Voyages & a Quarter Million Miles around the World, & Other Journeys.*

NOT FORGETTING:

Certain *Valuable Words to the Wise, Gleaned* from Divers Chefs *in Many & Strange Places;* & the *Home Formulae for Construction of such Intriguing Exotics as Hell-Fire Bitters, Key West Old Lime Sour, Herb Vineagars;* to Say Nothing of Various *Strange and Delicious Sauces & Bastings for Fish, Flesh, Fowl, & the Wilder Games.*

The Author discovered that gathering material for an exotic book on cookery was pleasant as well as technically informative.

DEDICATION

Contrary to current routine this volume is not dedicated to Publisher, Wife, Friend, Mistress or Patron, but to our own handsome digestive tract without which it never could have seen light of day.

"GENTLEMEN," said Mr. Peregrine Touchwood, "Man is a Cooking Animal; & in whatever Situation he is found, it may be assumed as an Axiom, that his Progress in Civilization has kept exact Pace with the Degree of Refinement he may have Attained in the Art of Gastronomy. . . . From the Hairy Man of the Woods to the Modern *Gourmet,* apportioning his Ingredients & blending his Essences, the Chain is Complete!"

Introduction to:

The Cook & Housewife's Manual,

Med Dods,

Edinburgh, A.D. 1826

CONTENTS

A FOREWORD

IT WAS all of fourteen years ago during a first adventure around the world that we made the agreeable discovery that all really interesting people—sportsmen, explorers, musicians, scientists, vagabonds and writers—were vitally interested in good things to eat and drink; cared for exotic and intriguing ways of composing them. Diplomats and colonial officials were pungent gourmets.

We soon discovered further that this keen interest was not solely through gluttony, the spur of hunger or merely to sustain life, but in a spirit of high adventure. It was intrigue of the unexpected in herb or spice or sauce; the titillating savour of exotic ways of putting flesh to fire or greens to bowl.

Sportsmen boasted of a new Malay curry as proudly as they would pelt a ten foot tiger. Explorers took the same agreeable thrill in discovering a succulent *Calalou* as in sourcing the Congo.

Diplomat, artist and scientist beamed on a special Black Sea *Bortsch* from Odessa as he might on an international pact; a Brazilian basket of deep fried whole shrimp became as vital as a tube of madder lake to painting a Rio beauty's shawl; a Tahitian fish salad with lime and coconut dressing took rank with making health contagious instead of grippe.

But most important of all, ***these people who cared for superior food were equally interested in the history of those exotics, their traditional background, their romantic origin!***—something this volume has endeavoured to possess.

That was all we needed to start us on this pleasant madness of receipt collection. Being a passionate collector of divers and amazing addenda from all over the world, it was a relatively simple matter to hang a field note book and pencil among other burdens as we threaded our way from bazaar to eating house to bistro to coffee shop.

Thus an agreeable and mounting collection has lived with us faithfully three voyages and a quarter million miles around the world, across Europe; in Asia, Africa, the British and Dutch East Indies; the Philippines, Hawaii and the three Americas. It has snupped Bahamian and other island dishes through the whole sweep of the West Indies, and various coastwise Americana through ten thousand additional sea miles sailing our own deep water ketch *Marmion* from Key West to New England's north shore. We eagerly delved back into bygone years in canoe and under tent among the Florida Keys, the river and lake region of central Florida. We recorded a few choice memories from twenty-five years spent in the deep south: Florida, Virginia, South Carolina, Tennessee.

This initial volume—barely half the collected list!—represents our final selection of exotic savouries. Each one is beloved and notable in its place and, something not yet found in parallel efforts—lists ingredients which at most can take no longer than seventy-two hours to possess in any part of America. In moderate proportion it is a collection of lusties. Certain dishes do appear to list many ingredients, but if readers will take pause to note each of these, a vast proportion are found on any sanely stocked kitchen shelf.

In a way this collection was begun for fellow men, by a man. Having traveled far too much for our own good we had come to indorse womanhood mainly for her beauty, grace, discretion and charm. Having lived in many cities we had learned to flee from Women-with-Brains, Women-who-Did-Things; had learned to cleave, rather, to thoughtful young eyes and lovely smiles who sat back quietly and let us talk and prove ourself to be a monstrous clever fellow. Owning every book on cookery extant in English—and a few in foreign tongue—right from the golden age of Louis XV, through the cooking renaissance of Brillat-Savarin and clear up to our present incomparable Henri Charpentier, there had been a score of immortal chefs. Yet with possible exception of the late Madame Poulard, French sorceress of the omelette pan, what now remembered woman had ever dared create anything beyond the already written word of former male cookery masters? What delectable dish had even been named for a woman, except those by a man chef for some lovely and famous patroness?

Yes, it terrified us to think what might happen if we surrendered our collection of stout dishes for a squad of critical female readers to compare to their own floating islands or quaint tapioca affairs. Away with floating islands, a pox on sago depressions! And by gad sirrah we didn't need any pink paper panties on our roast fowl either. No sir. This exotic cookery business of ours wasn't to woo any promoter of strawberry socials, women's auxiliary luncheons, or the demure young bride. Our mission was not promoting fancy pastries for profitable sale, coy desserts for diverting the attention of brides. All these questionable depravities had already been done only too well by every woman's cook book in Christendom.

In our lawless way we doubted if any lady would give a rusty bobbie pin if we had eaten South India curry in Trichinopoly, *enchilladas* in Taxco, corned beef and' in Dinty Moore's in Shanghai. Or what did they care if we had gorged on *arroz con pollo* in Barranquilla, a lordly *rijstafel* in Soerabaja, beefsteak and kidney pie in St. Albans, or earthenware bowls of scalding and immortal onion soup at L'Escargot in its sixteenth century spot near Les Halles, Paris' vast central markets?

Why should any nice lady care if we'd consumed small Korean shrimp in Seoul, bird's-nest soup in Formosa; sampled frozen coconuts in Bangkok or sat crosslegged in Kyoto during the cherry blossom festival eating *sukiyaki* and sipping endless thimblefuls of hot saki served by laughing dolls in bamboo patterned kimonos? What weight could it possibly carry in the world of women that we had explored twenty-one courses of a Mandarin dinner—including hundred-year-old eggs, candied duck, *Fishes Dipped in the Six Perfumes,* and a huge Mandarin host who could belch louder than Sir Walter Raleigh—across the narrow Pearl River channel from Shameen, in Canton? It certainly wouldn't matter a jot that we had been introduced to *blinis* and sour cream with good black Russky caviar shipped in via Harbin, while we sat across from a Manchu princess of the blood who smoked funny long White Russian cigarettes, sat between red lacquer columns of Erik Nyholm's Buddhist *Temple of the Propitious Pearl* which broods on the very top of Western Hills—has brooded there in fact for five hundred years—sat there sipping chilled chablis and eating *blinis* and watching the steel coin of Old Buddha's summer palace lake while the dying sun lashed Peking's stark Tartar Wall through her eternal age-old haze of red dust—when Peking *was* Peking.

What would they care about things consumed on the terrace in front of the nipa-thatched Manila Polo Club, when the peak of Mariveles stood notched and black against the afterglow? Or about the time our bride and I sat until the small hours before dawn with Walter Spies, watching the legong dancers, listening to the gamelans, and running through his own harmonizations of Balinese music for five pianos—and consumed mild Bali curry of cucumbers and eggs and eggplants, sprinkled with freshly grated coconut and crumbled Bombay duck, which last is no duck at all, but an odd dried species of Indian fish which for reasons not pertinent to mention rises to the nets of dark strange fishermen of the Malabar coast near Goa?

Why should we fancy up a volume for this drove of feminists whose whole day was spoiled, setting sun of which found them unpossessed of some new disguise for bread pudding when—but how could *they* know it?—any male with the digestion of a titmouse would rather top off a good dinner with a sound spot of Stilton cheese-and-port than the duckiest little prune whip born of egg whisk?

No, to our wry and ungarnished male mind it seemed high time some loyal brother actually did something for his random fellow man.

Then a perfect howl went up. Widely scattered lady acquaintances told us, rather bluntly we thought, just where we rated in the family of reptiles. Our friend Coe Glade, leading contralto for Chicago and San Francisco's opera, first viewed us coolly through improbable huge dark eyes and tartly informed us that she owned national renown for composing Sunday morning breakfasts. Another cool lady volunteered advice that she had just completed a three months' course at *Le*

Cordon Bleu in Paris, and she guessed we hadn't troubled to do that! Ernest Hemingway's wife Pauline proved to us how beach birds should be stuffed.

Then came climax. A very handsome girl advertising genius, who had resided fourteen years in Havana, fastened on our lapel in the Stork Club and supposed all the way through a six course meal that we knew all about *Moros y Cristianos*—Moors and Christians, or black beans and rice. That we had included *Pollo Piña, Camagüey*—which was fowl of discreet age and rearing after being smothered in sun-ripe pineapple pulp, the peel of small green limes, raisins and a gift of white rum. She imagined that our knowledge of muskmelons impregnated with *Anis del Mono*—which is Spanish anise liqueur of the monkey head label—and chilled colder than cold, would fill a whole chapter. How about *langostinos* boiled in sea water the way they did them out Matanzas way with a green sauce of mayonnaise, lime, garlic salt and Nepal pepper? . . . Well, and so we were getting up a man's cookery book were we. And what now, precisely, did we intend doing about it? Furthermore, because of our questionable stove-side conceits for male *amateurs* she imagined all smart American women from Seattle to Key West now had to put on sackcloth and ashes, admit gullible feminine mediocrity, and bow down forever to pink quivery things that leer out of ice boxes at you and taste like pink soda pop with a dab of vanilla cotton batting on top. So, and so, and so! . . .

Our head was bloody but unbowed. We hung on grimly, waiting for the bell—and the check—when a great light exploded across our groping brain. We suddenly realized that *all* America was seething in a thumping renaissance of good cookery, master and mistress alike. In spite of prohibitions and depressions, wars and rumours of wars; in face of rubber stamp personal mediocrity with which all ruling gentlemen seemed bent on moulding their citizens, this slow rebirth in one of the truly fine arts quickly became the most cheerful and tolerant gleam on the whole current horizon.

Why, now, when we really stopped to think of it, the entire American scene was fairly waving with grills, salad tongs, coffee biggins and duck presses! Ladies had sloughed off gardening gloves for asbestos grilling gauntlets. Perhaps the base betrayal of the prohibition era had blessed us in disguise, spurring all men and women into knowing what *was* fit for primate nourishment and thirst! No longer would it be smart to boast ignorance in proper food and wine. Strong men openly strutted their pet species of crêpes suzettes, and other strong men clapped them on the back.

It was incredible. It was like wrist watches. Before our naive entry into the last European war any American gentleman caught wearing one of those useful time pieces was in danger of audible ridicule in company, suspect, if not in bodily peril. A scant dozen years back any Yankee male friend guilty of tossing salad, poaching a filet of sole or whipping up a deep dish apple pie was in contempt—held to be a hair different from his normal fellow; a foppish gazing-stock, an irregular queer fish whom all orderly men looked upon with that mortified disbelief they would feel should a favourite maiden aunt remove her upper plate at a White House banquet.

Dark eyes so charmingly opposite us had caused the light to break —that ladies as well as gentlemen at last were racing into this new and healthful sport of random cookery. This combined battle of the pots was why American shops were designing, discovering, infinitely smarter and more colourful utensils; why the once-trite corner grocery was fairly burgeoning with bayleaf, soya sauce and basil. No local yokel stared now when asked for mango chutney, wild rice or tarragon vinegar. We bet that even those dwelling in truly isolated sectors could post a letter to the nearest city and get our hickory salt and Nepal pepper within a couple of days.

Mentally we started waving the star spangled banner for this national rebirth of good taste. Our mind's eye saw a vast and orderly company, men and women, marching rank on rank with grilling racks at shoulder arms. It all made us feel very proud and confident and homey. We sipped a leisurely dry Amontillado sherry to the brown eyes opposite. We were very proud of our countrymen, but especially so of our countrywomen—woman. We raised the thin stemmed crystal. Then just as we were going to speak of all this the waiter stood between us and thrust menus at us, with the gift only waiters seem to have.

But our feminine gourmet of the dark eyes didn't even glance at it. She smiled up at the waiter with more charm than the situation called for and said, "Bring me a prune whip, please. With lots and lots of nice thick cream on top. If you haven't got one tell them to make one!"

Then she looked back at us blandly. "Now," she said, "remember you were going to tell *me* things about all kinds of strange things to eat."

THIS VOLUME, then, is a company of hand-picked receipts we have met during world wanderings, or which have been added to the collection through grace of friends and correspondents with dilatory or permanent domicile in odd and intriguing spots of the globe. Although we don't list the eternal Frenchman's live snails, or hundred-year-old eggs, or sea-slugs—*bêche de mer*—or bird's nests of swallow spittle, or deep fried octopus, or creamed rattlesnake, or alligator tail, we have at one time or another and for one reason or another eaten all of these.

In this primary volume it seemed more neighbourly to cleave those select exotics that have most appealed to the American side of our palate; those which require ingredients neither rare nor too difficult of source. In this process half were rejected. All the residuary list has been eaten with gusto by ourselves. Each has stood the test of time *in situ,* and we can affirm that none is any chancey addendum supplied by some local armchair explorer whose travels abroad have taken him as far toward the mysterious East as Coney Island.

We therefore invite you to cruise with us on the magic carpet of your own kitchen saucepan, and share the rare flavours from many far off places. It is our further earnest hope that such trusting and gustatorial readers will find half as much pleasure in recreation of these dishes as we had in their original consumption!

CHAPTER I

A DESIGN *FOR* COOKERY

Relating where *Imagination & Daring* take Their Part; why *Suspect the Lean & Hungry Chef;* & brief Instruction on *Measurements & Heats;* & finally an *Invitation to The Blender.*

CREATION of an Exotic Cookery Book of this sort presupposes not only the ability to read on the part of its readers, but the additional attributes of intelligence, imagination and a hustling spirit of adventure.

With bookshop shelves groaning beneath their burdens of routine cookery books there can be no place here for formulae or instruction on such items as the making of brown or white foundation sauce; what basting is; what is meant by marinate, lard and score; just as we assume vocabulary including such essentials as au gratin, brochette and sippet; or truss, toss and skewer; or when we say "faggot" no bundle of inflammable dry twigs is indicated but a clutch of sweet herbs. With a selected list of exotics having already cut down original strength by half through lack of space, it would not be reasonable to bleed elected receipts further by inclusion of elementary matters of this type. And in passing it is profitable to note that, besides the host of books on general cookery compiled for housewife or amateur, there are several small limply bound volumes for the professional chef, dealing tersely with hundreds of sauces, egg dishes in 1000 ways, the chef's reminder, and so on.

This then is solely a book of succulent exotics easily created from basics buyable in any man's home town, not a general primer on making raw food palatable.

FROM the start every amateur chef might do well to approach his kitchen with a gleam of imminent adventure in his eye! Preparation of a fine exotic dish can be exactly like a latter-day Columbus sailing to new and unknown worlds. It required imagination to make Queen Isabella part with her jewels. It took daring to sail westward in those top-heavy high-pooped sailing ships, equipped with doubtful compasses and having no valid assurance what lay before them; or what mysteries and thrills hid behind that setting sun.

There can be the same adventure in cookery, explorations of a milder and more healthful sort. Preparing a worthy dish is like painting a fine portrait, composing a nocturne or setting down a sonnet. There is constant chance of putting something *individual* into the deed, letting the chef dominate the receipt.

The herb shelf is a three-manual pipe organ, the sauce cabinet is a palette of varied colour, a simple black pepper handmill can be an unpurchasable violin of overtone. No reader should be too bound by the written word. Take the essentials, then set sail on private adventures of amateur cookery common to no one. With a very little experience we can vary any receipt this way or that, to reflect our own personality, taste, or climate.

The best exotics all over the world are not found in any cookery books. The Hawaiian, Javanese, Spaniard or Russian who first did them well had never even heard of cookbooks; in all probability could not read one if he had. Time and later chefs caught up the original dish, garnished and improved it. Tribes and provinces approved it. It became individual, and in its own peculiar way brushed with immortality. The trouble with too many chefs, amateur and professional, is that they forget that every elaborate salad came from green shoots; that larded pheasant was first grilled on a sharpened stick. In other words, there is a limit to fancy trimmings. It takes no biochemist to mark this dead line. *It comes when the trimmings become so pungent that they confound the worthwhile flavour of the basic dish.* And especially in delicate fine items like small game, fish, shellfish and certain inner quadruped importances like sweetbreads, too much fancying up is likely to approach debacles we too often find abroad—like drowning a brace of partridge in vast seas of red sauerkraut!

Receipts here should be followed in basis, then slightly varied to suit the vagaries, whims and moods of the chef. Toss in a spoonful of vanity to impress the lovely audience of the moment, a dash of daring, a pinch of conservatism and a cup of confidence. And so, fellow adventurers in gastronomy: Good hunting!

JUST WHY the LEAN & HUNGRY CHEF IS SUSPECT

". . . *Beware the lean and hungry chef,*" is an old proverb, and nothing could be more true. In other words when cooking any dish: Taste, *taste, TASTE!*

No chef, male or female, amateur or professional, can ever create without tasting his way through the dish so as to catch and preserve each little nuance of flavour, bouquet, texture, piquancy. No professional worthy of his basting spoon can taste his way through life without building up certain comfortable and ample layers of *en bon point* around the equator. Sometime explore the kitchen of any truly fine restaurant and ask to see your chef; or aboard a fine ship, or in a southern plantation house. A lean and hungry chef cannot be plying his craft and the truth is not in him.

DISREGARD the CULT of MYSTERIOUS BOASTERS

BUT THIS chef inspection must not be permitted to cast the amateur down. Just like plumbers, ship navigators and professional hunting guides, all professional chefs dearly love to twine an aura of mysterious and solitary knowledge about their work. Both God and the prophets are on the side of their own private kettle! Your hesitant questions will fetch evasive answers. You will be left feeling of somehow having violated one of the more important social niceties in the mere process of asking—of being guilty of being a mental pygmy, an amateur childishly poking its untutored nose into the affairs of elders. This, dear reader, is—if we may be pardoned the idiom—a clutch of horsefeathers.

Nonsense! It took us twenty-five years to learn that navigating a small ship—or a large one for a' that—was a matter of arithmetic, trigonometry and horse sense; not one of the black arts. It took us thirty to discover that any citizen with brain enough to hurdle grammar school can, with a little imagination and gambling spirit, turn out as good or better food in limited quantity at a time than the average professional chef. And one of the main reasons is that he cooks for fun, not for pelf. It is a high spot in the week when all the blackamoors depart and we have kitchen and grills to ourself. It is a joy, not a grim profession. The amateur is not frayed with the burden of daily routine. It is far easier for him to conjure up that slight *Umph!* which can salvage an average dish from its mediocrity and enshrine it among the company of the culinary elect.

WITH IMAGINATION RELY on FOUR BASIC PRINCIPLES in COOKED DISHES, & REMEMBER to KEEP THEM HOLY

Proper and accurate measurements.
Proper cooking temperatures.
Proper length of cooking time.
Proper time for serving.

It is amazing how often we catch ourself being careless with measurements; have oven or water too hot or cold; produce food inaccurately timed, or see it served dreadfully warm when it should come sizzling directly from broiler. . . . *Have hot foods hot as hades; cold foods arctic cold!*

A FINAL PLEA for the AMATEUR NOT to ATTEMPT too many DISHES at a GIVEN TIME, SINCE a FEW THINGS of MERIT CAN OUTSHINE a PLATOON of MEDIOCRITY . . . and a WARNING on LIABILITY of GUEST-HELPERS

It took us years of good-natured misjudgment to learn that few guests are worth their blasting powder in kitchen. Most of them seek only the easy and amusing tasks, dirty endless tools and merely succeed in delaying matters. Especially women with a little knowledge are a major cross. Give them a copy of the Old Testament to run through. It will engage their attention, keep them silent, improve the mind.

From many years' trying experience take warning from us, and assume from the start that if things are going to taste right and come out on time, *we must do the whole show without help or interference.* It is wiser to attempt a one- or two-dish meal of importance, than a seven course affair which not only will prove mediocre nourishment but a fair ticket to the booby hatch.

The elder Strauss certainly never tried setting down three or four Viennese waltzes at the same time, and most certainly didn't have a duet of well-meaning ladies jot his notes down for him if he had! Be firm on this and in the end such a routine will be recognized as just and right, and command due respect.

TEMPERATURE CHART for the OVEN and DEEP FAT KETTLE

This is important, especially when roasting large meat and poultry items, or deep frying items of some size which tend to cool boiling fat. Oven thermometers come with all good stoves these days, and an accurate deep fat thermometer is very easily found in any decent hardware store.

Very Slow Oven	250° Fahrenheit
Slow Oven	300° Fahrenheit
Medium Oven	350° Fahrenheit
Medium Hot Oven	375° Fahrenheit
Hot Oven	400° Fahrenheit
Very Hot Oven (mainly for wild ducks)	450° to 500° Fahrenheit

Certain technical institutions list more heats than this, but no chef born of man could use them due to variables: Temperature of meat when put in oven; efficiency of oven in question, as no two are exactly alike. If the temperature needle swings a few degrees over those given here, don't let it spoil the fun. We aren't running a high tension chemical laboratory anyway. Preparing pleasant dishes is 80 per cent sanity and 20 per cent technicality, after all.

TELLING OVEN HEATS without THERMOMETERS of any SPECIES

An English friend discovered this for us, and in England they still do many things the old way, and not one family in a dozen has anything like a cooking thermometer in the house.

Simply put a piece of white paper in oven.
Look at it in 5 minutes.

Slow Oven: Paper golden brown in 7 minutes.
Medium Oven: Paper golden brown in 5 minutes.
Hot Oven: Paper dark brown in 5 minutes.

TIME TABLE for COOKING MOST MEATS

Beef: Rare, 15 minutes per pound; well done, about 20 minutes.
Fowls: 20 minutes per pound on the average.
Lamb: 30 minutes per pound.
Pork: 30 minutes per pound.
Veal: 30 minutes per pound.

DEEP FAT KETTLE COOKING TEMPERATURES

Food	*Time to Cook*	*Temperature*
Doughnuts, crullers, fritters & small mixes	3 to 5 minutes	370° Fahrenheit
Fishballs, oysters, croquettes & uncooked things generally	1 to 2 minutes	395° to 390° Fahrenheit
Chops & cutlets, breaded	5 to 8 minutes	400° to 390° Fahrenheit

SEASONING, a PLEA to MAKE IT LIGHT at the OUTSET of a DISH

This is a thought so obvious that many an amateur chef has ignored it to his shame, and straightway become hoist by the petard of his own salt shaker. For Einstein in all his glory, nor the combined genius Edison and Steinmetz, could never lift over-salting out of a dish once ruined. . . . And this applies ***especially to liquids which are to be*** *boiled down, reduced, for quite a while in their cooking.* A dish of black bean soup may be mildly salt at the outset, but when thick may taste like the Dead Sea.

Countless experienced and otherwise sound cooks still make this mistake.

The same caution applies to pungent peppers, sauces and herbs in cooked dishes. It is so easy to add the needful dash just before serving, so impossible to subtract an overdose when once in, or to dilute with additional raw materials and still have the dish be recognized by its own author, when done.

HERBS in HOT and COLD DISHES

We have found that herbs, dried herbs especially, may be used at least three times as freely in a chilled, uncooked dish like salad, as can be used in cooked affairs. Heat extracts the volatile oils and flavours from the herb leaves. Overseasoning results from too generous herb donation to soups, roasts, and the dressings of fowls; whereas in a French dressing the taste is so slightly drawn out by the liquids that quite a lot makes only a reasonable flavour difference in final estimate by taste.

A WARNING on the USE of WINES in COOKERY

Nothing adds such delicate zest to many soups, fish, shellfish, crustacean and amphibian items, as a little wine. But except for white or red *unfortified* wines actually used in cooking, poaching or basting food, *NEVER ADD to the COOKING DISH until JUST BEFORE DISHING up at TABLE.*

This means sherry, port, Madeira and Marsala—*ALL FORTIFIED WINES, whether DRY or SWEET!*

Why? . . . Well, a fortified wine means one which has been raised in alcoholic content through later addition of suitable amounts of brandy—which last of course runs far higher than wine in proof—around 35 per cent alcohol, against from 10 to 15 per cent. . . . Under any heat this alcohol vanishes in steam, takes most of the taste and lovely aroma with it. What remains in the cooked dish is most depressing. It tastes like dregs from an old cask boiled down with a raccoon pelt, and has never been known to endear any chef to a gourmet's heart.

A FINAL DUET of ADVICE, concerning the VIRTUES of USING BUTTER & SUGAR in COOKERY

Here too is an ancient secret, ignored by too many chefs of all degree—probably by its very obviousness. Butter added to all sorts of fish, flesh, vegetables and sauce picks up the basic nature of the whole dish and endows it with an additional richness which we've found improbable in any other fatty agent. It is not economical in pennies, but if an amateur chef's reputation isn't worth thirty cents worth of dairy butter every other Thursday we had better go back to some other and more balanced form of indoor amusement.

When we said sugar in cookery we did not limit ourselves merely to obviously sweet dishes, but to many, many others. The ancient Chinese have always recognized this virtue and although we cannot over-eat their candied Peking duck we render credit where credit is due on other things. As a strict matter of fact there was no civilized cookery anywhere in the world until the middle of the 18th Century—except in China. . . . A little sugar on steak to be broiled, on pork; in the boiling water for the tenderizing of green peas, corn on the cob, carrots, lima beans; in green salads—but here have a care that the dressing is not made to taste sweet, a common American fault by those who should be advised. Sugar is something for each amateur to experiment with. It has the fine faculty of amplifying and framing the main delicate flavour of certain foods, much as odd products of a non-scented nature are used to fetch out the true worth of a fine perfume essence.

HEAVEN'S GIFT to the AMATEUR CHEF—the *WARING BLENDER*

The world is so full of indirect commercialism in these civilized days that many publishers of standing actually hesitate to mention a thing of merit by name, for fear of being thought a sponsor with a material interest in the item involved; or for fear of giving offense to some other lively manufacturer producing something of similar nature.

We debated the question all through composition of this volume, and of *The Exotic Drinking Book*, and have decided to speak our own mind without fear. Certainly no one hesitates extolling genius in Alexander Graham Bell, Simon Lake or Dr. Alexis Carrell, for their telephones and submarines and antiseptics, and we fail to see why Mr. Fred Waring should be ignored in these pages when his contribution to food and drink preparation is just as vital in its own especial way as the previous three gentlemen have been to a very testy and bewildered world.

Mr. Waring has always appeared to us as a gentleman, a scholar, probably the best golfer in modern musical circles, and a maestro of a cleverly melodic musical school all his own which many other internationally known bandsmen and radio staffs have flattered through out-and-out imitation, without too much credit to the originator. Besides these minor talents Mr. Waring proved himself a still more able citizen by pouncing on an invention designed primarily to agitate fluids and ice—with a nicely controlled violence and centripetal activity which does things in sixty seconds to a Daiquiri which it took Messrs. Harry Stout and Jennings Cox (originators of this peerless drink) five or six minutes of progressive effort and fatigue to produce.

But what it was able to do to food was something we wager even its parent never dreamed of at the start. For reducing green groceries such as spinach, carrots, celery and the like, to health-giving pulps or vitamin drinks for aged and young, it has no peer. For purees or any fine blending it is a pearl beyond price.

Wherever our antique English or French cookery books coyly say, "Rub through sieve," or "Pound fine in a mortar," we turn a superior shoulder and toss the whole assembly in the Waring Blender, and presto, the job is done—if not to complete fineness at least to a point where final putting through sieves and other reducers is simply a matter of gentle gravity aided by a helpful spoon, and not a major muscular task. To get what we mean we can only suggest rubbing a gallon of our Barranquilla Black Bean Soup through a sieve, then next time turning the whole puree problem over to the rapidly turning blades of Mr. Waring's brain-child, and draw personal conclusions as to whether labour has been saved or not.

Of course, this Blender is too well known to all American hosts to need either explanation or introduction, but for benefit of new arrivals to these relatively free and lucky shores we submit the following non-technical information.

There is a metal covered, liquid-proof, non-tarnishing chromium base of decent modern line and sound electrical engineering, which houses a motor with vertical spindle, of high rpm, and requiring rare and modest oilings in well indicated spots.

The top half of the Blender is a strong heavy glass mixing unit of 32 ounce working capacity, resembling a four-leaf clover in cross section, and which is in fact like a big sloping sided tumbler or bar glass. This whole unit lifts off base for pouring.

Through the Blender bottom runs a special high speed bearing and a short vertical spindle on which triple tempered steel blades are mounted. The lowest pair drive substances upward; the center pair are actually knives and do much of the cutting up; the top pair draw the substances down into the whirling blades again—like a miniature airplane propeller. When glass mixing unit is set on base the motor shaft automatically engages the base of Blender spindle.

This Blender is no toy. It is made for heavy and constant usage. Clubs and hotels toss in jiggers of spirits, juices, big lumps of ice, and away she goes. No damage to anything. It makes fruit pulp and puree and mixes all sorts of things from shrimp cocktail dressing to tropical Daiquiri Cocktails until—if so desired—the latter may be dished out with a spoon like snow from a Sun Valley ski-run. There is, literally, nothing else remotely like it.

Since Mr. Waring is a gentleman of shy and retiring demeanor, we will not attempt to agitate his nervous sensitivities by frequent allusion to this speedy labour saver by its usual family surname, but simply by the two-word title *The Blender*. And those who read, mark, learn and inwardly digest its uses will call us thrice blessed for time and labour saved, entirely aside from any mechanical thoroughness in the job it does.

BASIC STOVE-SIDE MEASUREMENTS to REMEMBER

1 Pinch or a few Grains	:	Slightly less than 1/8 Teaspoon
2 Teaspoons	:	1 Dessertspoon; 1/3 Oz. Avoirdupois
3 Teaspoons	:	1 Tablespoon; 1/2 Oz. Avoirdupois
2 Tablespoons	:	1 Oz. Avoirdupois
8 Tablespoons	:	1 Gill; 1/2 Cup; 4 Oz. Avoirdupois
16 Tablespoons	:	1 Cup; 1/2 Pint; 8 Oz. Avoirdupois
4 Cups	:	1 Quart; 32 Oz. Avoirdupois

DON'T FORGET the OLD, OLD RULE

1 Level Tablespoon: ½ Oz. of Butter, Milk, Salt, Sugar or Water. Plenty accurate enough for average usage.

A COMPLETE TABLE of WEIGHTS & MEASURES GIVING WEIGHTS in OUNCES and CORRESPONDING MEASUREMENTS MAY BE FOUND in the *APPENDIX* on PAGE 209, together with OTHER PERTINENT LORE.

Due to many old English receipts, and in fact many old-time American cookery notes, diaries and the like, listing proportions in ounces this table has been included for readers who wish to explore such green pastures.

SYMBOLS of MEASUREMENT USED in this VOLUME

1 tsp	:	1 Teaspoon
1 tbsp	:	1 Tablespoon
1 pt	:	1 Pint
1 qt	:	1 Quart
1 gal	:	1 Gallon

ALL MEASUREMENTS in this VOLUME *ARE LEVEL*

CHAPTER II

HORS d'OEUVRE & CERTAIN FIRST COURSE IMPORTANCES

Eighteen, or so, *Exotic Whets both for Pre-Solid & Pre-Liquid Use* which Can Cause One to be Honoured Among Men; A brief *Dissertation on the Regal Caviar;* West Indian Sauces for *Cocktails of Seafoods;* together with a *Brace of Stiffeners* for the *Failing Spine.*

SCHOLARS eagerly inform us that the French word "hors d'oeuvre," literally translated means "outside the work;" but like most scholars and literal Gallic translations this weighty disclosure leaves much to the imagination. As near as we can learn it probably was idiom for certain dishes which, by character or type of service, were more or less apart from the main routine of a meal.

An appetizer, or whet, is anything that inspires a desire or relish for food. The amateur should hold this thought constantly in mind in order not to be gradually drawn in to the mounting wave of questionable taste now sweeping America—that of stuffing guests with ten times more hors d'oeuvre, canapes and the like than he should have, and sending him brimming with cocktails and with all appetite quit, to face the really important thing of the evening: dinner.

An hors d'oeuvre which in quantity or type destroys appetite or dulls the delicate taste buds is a mischievous thing, the enemy of all fine gastronomy, and should be smitten hip and thigh. Do not let us be deceived in this thing. No matter a host's wealth, rank, manners or morals; in spite of all excellence in materials served, the truth is not in him if either through solid or liquid whets he destroys appetite.

The grand pre-revolutionary Russian, our modern Dane, Swede or Norwegian, will muster an array of hors d'oeuvre, or smörgåsbord, in variation and tonnage to preclude all hint of their being appetizers as we think of the word. Hors d'oeuvre to these gentlemen meant many tasty dishes to compose a major part, and often all, of any given meal. As such it has its own virtue and tradition, being a definite section of the meal, not just an appetizing first course.

After considerable dining abroad we have definitely come to the conclusion that the American host tends to burden his hors d'oeuvre tray too heavily, and also is leaning more and more toward that risky piece—the canape. Either go whole hog or none; either trot out the whole gamut of smörgåsbord table and make dinner a slight minor addition to the feast, or serve barely enough fresh, smart, piquant and daintily garnished appetizers to titillate the appetite into a small frenzy for courses to come.

In conception and purpose the canape is a pretty little item but, being married as it is to odd bits of bread or toast foundation the very construction of the thing makes its virtue almost impossible except when guests are quite few in number. During recent years our house seems to have instituted a Christmas afternoon business where people drop in for carols, wassail bowl—hot and cold—and other seasonable thoughts. It has gradually amplified in scope; and starting harmlessly enough we found ourselves last year confounded by a list of one hundred invited, and nearer two hundred arrived. So this last Christmastide we prepared. Allowing five average varied canapes per guest, that made an even thousand to compose. Professional sources tend, we had found, toward fancy colours and all the crisp flavour of cotton petit point, with three Filipinos working, by the time the last canape was ready the toast under Number I was already soggy and tough as saddle leather. It just cannot be done in quantity unless a whole platoon is flung into the work. With so many frantic varieties extant, we dodge them.

One thing worthy of remembrance is that hors d'oeuvre of all kinds should, in all ways possible, be pleasing to the eye as well as the palate. A few brightly garnished, fresh, crisp appetizers are worth a burden of hours-old, drab, careless affairs—regardless of merit in raw materials. And in this connection may we add a single re-emphasis on the old truth: ***Serve hot dishes hot, and cold dishes cold.*** Lukewarm items lose all charm and character.

The most civilized thought in liquid accompaniment to such dishes leans always toward the dry type of cocktail, or fortified wine. Our true gourmet will accept the briefest course of hors d'oeuvre, accompanied by not more than two dry cocktails, or vermouth, vermouth and bitters, or dry sherry, and ***no tobacco at all if his will is valent.*** He will view costly additional outlay on tray after tray of needless canapes with a wistful air, willing by whatever gods he may afford that the tariff of all this costly display of extra provender might reasonably be applied against a bottle or two of truly fine vintage instead of the good—but seldom exceptional—wine American hosts usually choose.

This then is our earnest prayer:

> In serving hor d'oeuvres, make them few; make them good. Make them hot or make them cold. And finally, make them attractive to the eye.

It is all so very simple, yet like most simple and virtuous matters we find it constantly being neglected for more mediocre, costly and indiscreet practice.

> WORDS to the WISE, No. I: On the Validity of spelling 'Recipe' 'Receipt.'
>
> There are already enough pink ribbons tied around cookery terms without giving the French every credit for fair cookery routine. It may be Palesteen or PalesTINE; quinneen or quinNINE, but dwelling as we do in an English-speaking country it is only just to adopt the Anglicized formation of the word. We have a volume dated just after 1650 calling it 'receipt.' What was good enough for Charles I, is good enough for us!

FIRST COMES IMPERIAL CAVIAR, the GRANDEST of THEM ALL, BEING the SALTED EGGS of RUSSIAN STURGEONS

Various nations and places have their own special whets but there is only one caviar. Gourmets, without urging either of themselves or the sturgeon, all agree upon this. Caviar, regardless of rarity or price has stood the test of time against all and sundry comers.

There are two general types: Red and black—the former usually being salted eggs of salmons or other fishes, and lacking in aristocratic merit. In turn the black kind, which is made from eggs of the Russian sturgeon, is prepared in two ways: Fresh, and canned or extra salt.

Fresh caviar has relatively large, resilient, pleasant-appearing eggs; while the so-called salted—canned—type is usually made up of smaller eggs packed together in a more or less wilted and unhappy mass. Actually all caviar is salted but the fresh is not salted so strongly; eggs are firmer and each more or less individual and separated from its neighbour. Its high tariff, especially during recent times, is due to two reasons: the world at large is becoming conscious of its merits; and fresh caviar must be kept refrigerated *at all times* to prevent deterioration. This means by ship, train or plane; and it is a fair journey from the Volga to America.

CONVEYING the THOUGHT that DRESSING up CAVIAR IS FAR WORSE than GILDING LILIES

Except with traditional sour cream—*smetana*—as given elsewhere in the Chapter, *caviar should never be mixed with any sort of dressing agent.* By this we mean fresh caviar when served *as caviar* for hors d'oeuvre—not casual salt caviar used as flavour or trimming for some other food item.

Mayonnaise, for instance, on fresh Mallosol or Beluga caviar is in exactly the same taste as painting a picnic scene on Mr. Heifetz' pet Stradivarius. Caviar is its own excuse, has its own flavour, its rare delicacy. Clouding the pungency of that flavour with other dressings immediately alters the picture. A fine thing is fine, for and of itself. To the gourmet rarity or high price never enter the picture. Ostentation with caviar, trimming it up with fancy blendings, brings a slight shudder.

THERE ARE FIVE RULES about CAVIAR, which ARE JUST as EASY for Us as for the ROYAL CHEF to the LATE TSAR

1. All caviar must be very, very cold; not merely cooled. *Chill directly on ice for at least three hours.* Chill it in its dish of service; packing the

latter in fine ice when fetching to table or buffet. Never turn well-chilled caviar into serving dish at room temperature.

2. Serve it with quartered lime or lemon on one side, a teaspoon or so of *finely* chopped onion on the other. Persian limes, now visible on many good fruit counters, are much the best. They are very delicate, large, void of seeds. If not available locally, just write any friend in southeast Florida, as they bear the year round.
3. Please don't do elaborate things with accompanying bread. Just have thin, crisp, dark brown toast with crusts trimmed off before putting to fire. A little butter is optional, and sweet butter is always best. Butter may be sweetened by working regular butter between thumb and fingers under cold faucet to reduce salt. Press out between palms or butter paddles to extract surplus waters.
4. To our palate Mallosol or Beluga caviar averages best, seems to ship best. Prefer large black eggs, moist-appearing, each grain undamaged and undefiled, round and solid looking. . . . However the smaller grained canned caviar is far better than no caviar, and the red type is also good—actually being preferred by several friends. . . . We also have friends who prefer the works of Mr. E. Phillips Oppenheim to *Seven Pillars of Wisdom.*
5. Never allow metal to touch fresh caviar for longer than a moment. Handle or mix with wood, glass or ivory tools, serve from china or crystal—*never silver.*

THE USE of GRATED or CHOPPED EGG with CAVIAR Is of DOUBTFUL PROFIT, but CONSIDER a TRIFLE of GRATED *FRESH* COCONUT

No addition to caviar of this kind can be anything more than a colourful trimming, for certainly egg yolk and white has nothing caviar hasn't. It cannot add or bring out one iota to the sturgeon eggs. . . . We found finely grated fresh coconut meat served by the smartest hostesses in the tropical ports of the East. We use it here when we afford caviar, and find the delicate oily taste seems to point up the caviar a trifle. Fresh coconuts are found everywhere in America these days. It's merely a suggestion.

CAVIAR SERVICE IS a HAPPY CHANCE for ARTISTIC GESTURE

Here is the real chance for the artist with hot stylus and block of clear ice! What could be more ravishing than a fine crystal bowl nesting on a fish of ice; a turtle. Or fill the large pan beneath the freezing space in a refrigerator; add colouring matter, blossoms, glass coloured fish, and what not; then freeze. We've seen sculptured eagles, baskets, ships, animals, fish, and flowers, with caviar bowls enthroned therein in chilly magnificence.

CAVIAR, *MID-OCEAN COUNTRY CLUB,* BERMUDA; an EXOTIC from the GULF STREAM

During an article-seeking voyage to this pleasant island we became involved in one especially memorable dinner, by friends, after eighteen holes of golf in a half gale of wind, and some excellent dry Amontillado sherry. . . . Simply fry out large rounds of bread in very hot olive oil—deep fat kettle is best. Drain on paper and spread on a thick layer of chilled caviar; season with lime and a dash of Mr. McIlhenny's immortal Tabasco Sauce or Hell-Fire Bitters, noted on Page 28, and affix thereon a *very thin* slice of mild Bermuda onion trimmed to exact size of toast. Grate fresh coconut on top, and serve. . . . Those we first found had crossed anchovies as a penthouse touch, but this last was sheer swank, adding nothing to the caviar itself.

CAVIAR with *BLINI,* or RUSSIAN PANCAKES, *ERMITAGE RUSSE,* PARIS

Blini differ from the usual American product of Aunt Jemima for two principal reasons—they are made to rise with yeast overnight, and usually contain a trifle of buckwheat flour; their small size—2½" to 3"—and composition marry perfectly with caviar and sour cream. *Blini* by seven, mix before eleven! We first discovered really fine blini at Ermitage Russe, in Paris one spring. They probably weren't much better than any good *blini* in any good Russian spot; but it was spring and the horse chestnuts had lighted their white candelabra, and we were very much in love. And when Rumanian—they would import a Rumanian into a Russian place!—Dino Ionesco played minor things on his czimbalom our hearts tore apart, and there we were drinking cold Krug *'19*, and in love and eating the best *blini* and caviar in the whole beautiful world!

TO MAKE the *BLINI*, that WAY

Soften a cake of yeast with 2½ cups of warm milk, stir in 2 cups sifted white flour and work smooth. Stand in even warm temperature for 8 hours, then work in 2½ cups buckwheat flour. Break two eggs, separate whites. Beat yolks and first work in 4 tbsp butter, then add to flour; donate ¼ tsp salt, ½ tsp sugar, and let stand 3 hours longer. Finally work in beaten egg whites, pause another 15 minutes, then pour batter off top without stirring again. . . . *Blini* must be delicate and thin, so batter should be consistency of cream.

BLINI with CAVIAR & *SMETANA, ERMITAGE RUSSE*

Brush *blini* with a little hot butter. Serve one to each guest, heap with good black caviar, and cover the succulent little black mound with a double tablespoon of *smetana*, or sour cream, first chilled and whipped for a moment to keep from straying away.

BLINI ROLLS, *au CAVIARE, à la KASBEK*, from PARIS in 1926

Paris again, but this time at Kasbek over in the Montmartre direction and in a dim cave with red checkered tablecloths lighted through the wooden tops, from underneath. Music again with the Caucasian girls singing and dancing, and a seven-stringed Russian guitar played by a man who used to play for Nicholas in the grand gone days in St. Petersburg. . . . Brush *blini* with butter, then sour cream, then spread with caviar. Roll and skewer with toothpicks every inch and cut across with sharp knife, showing caviar in spiral layer. Lemon and a bit of onion pulp were the side additions, and a fine still white Burgundy—Bâtard Montrachet *'11*, and the same girl who sang *Brown Eyes* for them in English to the Russian guitar. Heigh ho!

THOUGHTS on the SOURING of CREAM not yet HAVING ATTAINED that SOMETIMES DESIRABLE STATE

The souring process may be aided and abetted. Simply heat cream or rich milk very slowly until it barely starts to simmer. Then just before cool stir in a little vinegar or cream of tartar. It thickens promptly. We prefer lime or other citric juice due to the more delicate flavour. A tiny bit of salt is optional.

POACHED EGGS STUFFED with CAVIAR, *à la MOSCOW*

Here is a swank dish which can be an hors d'oeuvre, *served hot* or a fine entree. This receipt was brought to us by a friend who was for three years stationed in Russia, through causes not connected with cookery, and has proven a scholarly dish. . . . Poach eggs, chill well. Prick yolks and drain out soft part. Stuff yolk cavity with caviar, then roll carefully in flour, then lightly beaten egg, then fine dry bread crumbs. Fry to delicate golden brown at 380° in lots of deep fat in kettle or skillet. Garnish with deep-fat-fried fresh parsley—which *only takes a few seconds* to cook; and garnish with quartered lime or lemon. . . . Delicious! And must be served sizzling.

CANNIBAL CANAPE, a REFUGE for the LISTLESS and LUSTLESS

Here is something suitable for certain bachelor, or other, crises when the soul and frame lie supine, like a fine fruit withered on vine; sparkless, without virtue or activity. Served with, let us say, The *Maharajah's Burra Peg,* Peking *Tiger's Milk,* or Wilson's *South Camp Road Cocktail* from Jamaica—all evident in *The Exotic Drinking Book*—a gentleman even in this sorry plight might again be able to hold up his head among the rugged.

So: dice a little cold *lean* beef very fine indeed, touch with lime or lemon juice; with salt and plenty of tabasco or cayenne, to taste. Cut rye bread rounds, thin, and toast dry. Brush lightly with garlic or cut onion. Spread toast with sweet butter, add meat. Consume.

AULD KILKENNY *PICKLED EGGS,* from an ANCIENT IRISH RECEIPT

This piquant variation of trite hardboiled eggs should be revived oftener. It makes a good hors d'oeuvre, is delightful with cold fowl or joint, summer cold cuts and for garnishing a fine salad. Alternated with pickled walnuts, beside meat, they are especially delicious.

To 1 doz freshly created eggs we need 3 cups vinegar, 2 tsp ground ginger, 1 tsp of allspice broken with spoon; 2/3 tsp broken peppercorns, ½ tsp or so of salt. . . . Hardboil eggs for 20 minutes; peel shells. Mix vinegar and spices and boil slowly for 15 minutes. Fill mason jars with *entirely cold* eggs, pour pickle liquor over them. Screw on tops and stand for 4 weeks or so. But remember, gentlemen, the eggs *must* be fresh, really fresh. Pickling a storage egg is chemically impossible as, for example, a 1920 vintage flapper.

BARBADOS PICKLED FISH, from the BRITISH WINDWARD ISLANDS

This tasty was gathered into the fold during a cruise through the West Indies in 1929, and was produced by the smart wife of a resident British official living in Bridgetown. It made a fine appetizer, and would garnish any exotic green salad, or even a pick-me-up similar to Tahiti's own fish salad addition, *I'a Ota,* via Charles Nordhoff from Papeete, West Indian *Conch Salad* or *Souse,* all noted in the Index.

To a couple of pounds boned boiled fish we pour over the following marinade: Enough vinegar or lime juice to cover fish, and liquid put in saucepan. Toss in 6 or 8 whole cloves or 3 pinches ground; 2 pinches ground ginger, ½ tsp mace, ½ tsp hot dry mustard, 3 bayleaves crushed between the palms; 2 finely chopped onions, salt and hand-ground black pepper to taste. Then a dash or two of Angostura bitters. . . . Bring this marinade to a slow boil, simmer 20 minutes, turn over cooked fish. Stand in refrigerator 3 hours. . . . A little Key West *Old Lime Sour,* Page 169, is our favourite addition for a true West Indian touch.

SMOKED SAILFISH, SMOKED MARLIN SWORDFISH & KINGFISH: SMOKED EELS, GEESE & TURKEYS

All these smoked delicacies, sliced thin, and served as is, add an exotic touch to the hors d'oeuvre tray. The first three may be had through correspondence with any friend in southern Florida, the last is a new revival of a fine old Colonial whet; the other two hail from Germany, and are imported by some of the finer shops in cities. The first three are quite modest in tariff.

SPANISH *GAZPACHO,* a POTENT GARLIC SPREAD which MAY BE DARED in COMPANY with TRIED & TRUE FRIENDS, ALL of WHOM ARE GUARANTEED to STAY PUT for the EVENING, a SPECIALTY of SPAIN & CUBA

One afternoon we motored around the bay at Gibraltar to Algeciras for a little variation of native food after the fairly awful choice available in Gib itself. Here before the recent revolution everything was at peace; the little old town went along about its business as it had for centuries. We dined on a terrace with the sun at our back, and lighting the Rock, while files of stately white herons flew eastward toward some unknown destination. *Gazpacho* came first, with thimbles of *Anis del Mono,* or "Anise of the Monkey Head." We were among friends who did likewise. We later found it in Havana, too. In Mexico.

Actually this garlic spread is much like other Latin things under different names. The only hard-to-get item is a little cumin seed, and a few days notice with our druggist will do this. . . . Toss the following into a mortar, for two persons: 2 cloves garlic, 2 pinches salt, hand-ground black pepper, 2 pinches cumin. Pound until garlic is crushed into paste, then olive oil is worked in until we have a smooth cream. . . . Spread this on slices of peasant bread, cover then with a thin layer of imported canned tomato paste or pulp—*not* canned tomatoes of usual type—and on top of the whole a couple of tbsp of finely chopped pimentos. A little vinegar, lemon juice, or water is often sprinkled on to help in softening the bread. Serve in a dish nested in finely crushed ice as it should be served very, very cold indeed.

VIRGINIA HAM WHETS, OUR OWN GIFT to the GOURMET WORLD ABROAD

Even in a book of exotics we have to list outstanding Colonial masterpieces of gastronomy; and Virginia Ham, especially the peanut fed variety from the Smithfield region are honoured abroad as jewels of price. Our first introduction to Virginia Ham was attending school near Charlottesville; hams smoked on the neighbouring farms. In later years sailing north and south on *Marmion* we never missed going into Pender's store in Norfolk, and picking out a squad of big black mellow hams, with the peanut oil fairly blooming out of them!

Cut cooked ham into paper thin rosy curls and serve with no further garnishment. Another way is to chop ham fine, mix with grated egg and a little good mayonnaise, and stuff into tender celery.

VIRGINIA or WESTPHALIA HAM, Simla Style, from an Indian Adventure

Simla is a hill station where certain lucky folk, officers' wives, and young gentlemen with fierce and predatory glances, go during the hot rainy Monsoon season of India. Life is quite gay through varying reasons, and many smart hostesses try out new and varied touches of exotica at the dinner table. Once during a bridge and poker adventure small rounds of butter-fried toast surmounted with round-cut wafers of ham, and spread over with good fine-cut mango chutney, were introduced. It made an instant success, and as good chutney is buyable in any good small town grocery these days, we include it here. Virginia Ham is by far the better.

Oddly enough this delicious ham, avocado pears, turkeys, grapefruit, dried beef, yellow rat cheese and canvasback ducks, form a septet of strange bedfellows—but here are about all the credits your European high-toned chef will grant the States!

KIPPERS in BLANKETS for HORS d'OEUVRE, a Grand Breakfast Enlivener, or a Midnight Snack

This was snupped from a famous London Snack-Bar in Piccadilly during a recent summer spent in England. . . . Trim kippered herrings into neat strips about 1″ wide and as long as width of two bacon rashers. Wrap with thin sliced smoked bacon, or curls of Virginia

Ham, pin with toothpicks and grill until bacon curls. Serve on hot buttered thin toast, crusts trimmed off, and the upper side rubbed slightly indeed with garlic. Garnish with finely snipped parsley.

MUSHROOMS, *SMETANA,* or MUSHROOMS in SOUR CREAM, *HOTEL MAJESTIC,* SHANGHAI; another HOT HORS d'OEUVRE

Those of us who weep for the Shanghai that was will remember the Majestic, originally a palace created for a fabulously wealthy Chinese; later adapted to a small hotel. We remember having missed ship once in Shanghai, and after Martinis in the little cocktail lounge that was hand-painted like a trellis beneath a deep evening sky winking with electric stars, we went in to a superb meal. Out of deference to a White Russian member of our little group the host commanded this dish, which was noted down for later investigation.

Take 1½ lbs small mushrooms, cut them up and brown them carefully in 3 tbsp butter. Next mince 2 fairly large onions finely and cook gently until clear brown in another tbsp butter. Add salt and cayenne to taste. Warm 1½ small cans of beef bouillon in saucepan, turn in everything, and simmer slowly until mushrooms are very tender. . . . Take a little of the hot juices, work in 2 tbsp flour until smooth as cream, stir into the rest. Add 2 cups sour cream and simmer 5 or 6 minutes longer. Serve quite hot.

A *DAUSSADE,* or *PAIN DAUSSÉE,* BEING A LUSTY ONION WHET from MARSEILLES

Both onion and garlic are used far more generously abroad than here, and for better or worse we list this onion specialty which is so good alone, or served along with soup. . . . Take one of those round crusty French, Italian or Mexican loaves; cut it in the longest slices possible. Freshen some butter and spread. Slice a big mild onion and rub through coarse sieve—or put in The Blender—with a little sour cream, a tsp or so of tarragon vinegar, hand-ground pepper to taste, and plenty of salt. Work into a smooth heavy cream, spread on buttered slices, and cut these into crosswise fingers ¾" wide.

The Marseilles *Anchoïade à la Provençale* is a similar process using a little onion pulp, a few boneless anchovies, 2 tsp tarragon or red wine vinegar, a crushed small garlic clove and cayenne to taste. Add 2 tbsp or so olive oil and work through sieve or make smooth in The Blender, or pound in a mortar. Spread the result on slices of peasant bread and grill under broiler until edges of bread start to brown. Must be served sizzling.

PORK SKIN SNACKS, *à la VEDADO CLUB, HABANA*

As far as we are concerned Cuba has some of the finest chefs in the western hemisphere. Like the cookery of Mexico, New Orleans, and other once-Spanish possessions, succeeding creole chefs have built local refinements and trimmings on the parent root—resulting in many exotics both unexpected and piquant. . . . This Pork Skin Snack is one of the most amazing. We ran onto it the other year when our friend Gardinar Mulloy was winning the tennis championship of Cuba. . . . Just have your pet butcher trim off an area of fresh pork skin and thin layer of fat attached to same,—no meat at all!—cut it into 1½" squares and brown in deep fat at 370° Fahrenheit. Serve like potato chips and you have a new taste thrill. A great favourite at the very swank Club Vedado. Used mainly as a pre-liquid whet. The Cubano name is *chicharronés*.

GARLIC POPCORN, *HABAÑERO*

We carry along with garlic up to a certain point, for no cookery worth a passing glance can possibly ignore that ancient and valuable lily. Ancient Chinese, centuries before Christ, prescribed it for high blood pressure, and our finest modern specialists have fallen into line three or four thousand years later! If used properly its aroma is not dangerous. There is nothing quite like it for pointing up certain basic flavours in a dish. . . . First pop the corn, or get it *freshly popped,* and undecorated with ancient heated butters from the gentleman on the corner. To 1 cup butter allow 1 finely chopped garlic clove. Simmer these two *very gently* for 5 minutes, put through fine sieve to eradicate the chopped lily, then pour the aromatic fluid over our bowl of fresh popcorn, tossing diligently the while to insure equitable distribution. . . . Fine for soup croutons, but be sure and administer to soup at moment of service, or they will be soggy and tough. Also a smart pre-liquid thirst producer.

SARDINES *à la RUSSE,* being an Hors d'Oeuvre from Maisonette Russe which Is in Paris

Not too long ago it was the thrill of a lifetime to take a smart and veiled lady to places with an air of intrigue and vague mystery. We hope that some of our readers with romantic leanings have not forgotten Maisonette Russe, on Rue Mont Thabor. Here the lighting was dim enough to suit any minor connivance, the food was expensive but good, the music swooning and packed with the plaints of sobbing lovers of the tragic and departed day of old Imperialistic Russia. With our chablis, then, came the following:

Prepare fairly thick golden toast with crusts trimmed off. Mount sardines on top, brush with lime or lemon juice, sprinkle with finely grated yellow orange peel, and broil under fierce heat to do the job promptly. Another touch is a pinch of caraway seed added to each portion. The quicker the job the crisper the toast.

SARDINES, *à la SRINAGAR,* or *à l'INDIEN*

One trip out to India we stayed a while with a college mate, Byron Spofford, who was American Commercial Attache for India, Burmah and Ceylon under Hoover. Spofford's houseboat in the Vale of the Kashmir was something to fire the spark of envy in any man's heart, drifting from Srinagar down the lotus-starred reaches of Dal Lake in the cool clear July air, with the three-mile-high peaks soaring above everything; lazing in the Shalimar Gardens built for the pleasure of a Mughal Emperor three hundred years ago! Cocktails and pale hands in the violet dusk, while the Kashmiri boys sang in the cook-boat trailing aft. . . . An especial favourite appetizer was: Pound sardines and mango chutney in ratio of 2 to 1, rub through sieve to extract coarse portions. Grill squares of trimmed white bread, and spread. May be served hot or cold; hot is rather the best, we found.

SPOFFORD'S COPENHAGEN CANAPE of SALMON, from DENMARK

After leaving India Spofford went with American Minister Ruth Bryan Owen to Denmark where appetizers are a major event in everyone's life. The following is a great favourite there for small cocktail parties. . . . Cream equal amounts of butter and *freshly* grated horseradish. Cut graham bread thin, trim into size 1" x 2". Spread well, establish thereon a pair of narrow strips smoked salmon, then 4 short ones laid across. Spot a caper in each enclosure thus formed and bestrew edge with finely chopped parsley.

SEAFOOD WHETS of MISCELLANEOUS & DIVERSE CHARACTER

Voyagers to the volcanic island of Martinique will remember the street vendors of Fort de France, usually negresses with brilliantly coloured head kerchiefs, who sell those small white-hot cooked tidbits called *Bouchée*. Martinique is a torrid spot requiring torrid foods, and there it was we found this.

A *BOUCHÉE* of CRABS, SHRIMPS, LOBSTERS or any FINELY CHOPPED MEATS, *MARTINIQUE*

Take cooked, minced, meats and moisten with lime juice. Season with salt, dry mustard, 2 dashes Angostura, pinch of grated nutmeg, and as much tabasco or Hell-Fire Bitters, noted below, as the palate can take. Next fry some fine crumbs in very hot olive oil, and mix with seasoned meats, 1 part to 3. . . . Cook in either of 2 ways: Hollow out soft rolls, leaving crust and thin layer of white; brush with olive oil, brown in hot oven. Then pack with meat, cover with curry or cream sauce, dust with crumbs, dot with butter and brown again. . . . The street vendor often sells them this way: Form into small balls, dip in batter, then crumbs, and brown in deep fat at 370° Fahrenheit.

NOW the FORMULA for the JUSTLY FAMOUS "HELL-FIRE" BITTERS from the STRANGE BRITISH ISLAND of TRINIDAD, sometimes CALLED "CAYENNE WINE"

This valuable English receipt was, to our knowledge, first recorded by Dr. Kitchiner in 1817. It is to be found in some slight variation throughout the British Colonial world, and on the tables of canny gourmets who had tasted the condiment, and took the formula home with them. We found it in Port of Spain on a West Indian cruise down to South America in 1929. We find that by adding a certain amount of strained lime or lemon juice, and allowing the business to ferment, that the mixture gains charm in the seasoning of food.

Cut up as many round red bird pepper, or hot red pod peppers, as is necessary to fill a pint bottle loosely. Over this pour as much sherry, brandy and strained lime juice, as the vacant air spaces will take. Donate 1 scant tsp of salt, and ½ tsp quinine powder. Now stand for 2 weeks on kitchen shelf, uncorked. It is then ready for use. Some stout boiler-plated Britishers even put a dash or 2 in their gin and bitters! The original British mixture used the wine-brandy blend, but ignore the citric fermented juice. . . . Cayenne Wine: means the result of substituting 2 tsp—about ¼ oz—of Cayenne pepper for the fresh red peppers, in the above routine, omitting the quinine.

SIMILARLY HOT SEAFOOD ITEMS of CRABS, SHRIMPS & the LIKE—or BEEF TONGUE, or MEATS—CALLED *EMPAREADADOS,* GUAYMAS, MEXICO

We have two different friends recently fishing out of Guaymas for striped marlin and other large and ill-tempered fishy citizens. They fetched back photographs of swordfish enough to satisfy anyone, and one or two notes on food from a vast *rancho* where they visited, rode, hunted and explored, in Sonora. Among them is this characteristic appetizer, which can vary with larder and taste. Seasoning may be mild or torrid. . . . These also can vary with type of bread used, and the chef's imagination. Slice bread thin, trim to 1½″ squares or rounds; dry but do not brown in oven. Dip these quickly in milk, spread on any finely ground, well-seasoned *cooked* filling such as crabmeat, shrimp, pork, beef, lobster, or *Tongue;* and the latter can be in a single slice. Cap with another cut of bread; press together; dip in lightly salted batter. Place carefully in wire basket and fry in deep fat at 370° to a tempting golden brown. Serve sizzling. They always draw forth exclamations of delight.

AND, FINALLY, WE PRESENT a BRIEF COMPANY of FIVE EXOTIC SEAFOOD COCKTAIL SAUCES from HERE & THERE: & in the LAST, a BRACE of LIQUID STIFFENERS CALCULATED to RECTIFY the FRAIL & FAILING SPINE

SAUCE No. I, *à la MARMION;* BEING OUR OWN PET ORIGINATION

If all the seafood hauled in over *Marmion's* rail were laid end to end, it would reach quite a distance; and in all the varied preparation and consumption several original items have stood the test of friends and time. . . . To ½ cup chili sauce add 2 tbsp tarragon vinegar, ½ tsp paprika, 1 cup mayonnaise, ½ tsp hot mustard, ¼ tsp celery salt, tabasco to taste and a speck of crushed garlic with husks removed. Toss into The Blender, or beat with fork until well mixed. If garlic vinegar is on hand, don't add fresh garlic pulp. Chill well.

SAUCE No. II, SEA ISLAND GEORGIA STYLE

Sailing south in the Fall of 1935 in *Marmion* we flirted with the edge of a November hurricane, crossed the bar at Fernandina with waves breaking in 23 feet, and coasted up back of a friend's dock on Cumberland Island, in the Andy Carnegie estate, and found notable bourbon, a half acre mint bed, and many fine fresh shrimp in the tide creeks just waiting for our 5 foot cast net. Served chilled, this local sauce went instantly into the log. . . . Sour cream, 4 tbsp; ½ cup mayonnaise, 2 tbsp chili sauce, lime or lemon juice, 3 or 4 tsp; rub in a little sweet marjoram between palms. Put in The Blender or use egg beater. The sour cream adds the "touch;" marjoram points up the delicate whole. . . . Excellent for cold boiled fish.

SAUCE No. III, from PORT of SPAIN TRINIDAD, *au Angosture*

The British Island of Trinidad is known for its perpetually renewing lake of asphalt called La Brea, and as being fountainhead of immortal Angostura Bitters, invented to ward off fever in 1824 by Herr Doktor Johann Gottlieb Benjamin Siegert—one time army surgeon under Bluecher. The secret formula is alleged to have passed into the hands of only seven human beings. Correct or not—we list on Page 152 of *The Exotic Drinking Book*, a formula which has been known in England for many years which does well enough—it is only natural that this Trinidad Cocktail Sauce should include these famous bitters. It was brought to us by a pilot who flies the big Brazilian Clipper for Pan-American Airways and who always just manages to spare our chimneys when setting the big 40-passenger ship down into a northeast breeze here after her run from the Caribbean.

To the juice of two large limes add paprika to colour, 2 dashes Hell-Fire Bitters or tabasco, 2 tsp *freshly* grated horseradish, ½ tsp worcestershire, ½ cup ketchup or chili sauce; then add salt and Angostura until highly noticeable. . . . Especially good with oysters. Mix and chill well.

SAUCE No. IV, being the TASTIEST POSSIBLE EXOTIC from FARAWAY SEOUL, KOREA, where WE VISITED in 1932 & 1931; and which MASTERPIECE WAS DOUBTLESS THOUGHT up by a CUNNING JAPANESE CHEF

This delicate sauce is a marvel for cold lobster, shrimp, boiled salmon, crabmeat and the like. Take some really good mayonnaise and with a *wooden* fork crush up enough pickled walnut to suit personal taste. Metal forks tarnish in the astringent walnut juices. Rub through a sieve of coarse mesh; add paprika for colour if desired. Incidentally the Japanese are wizards at preparing any sort of fish or seafood, we've found. Chill well.

SAUCE No. V, from the DAY BOOK of a ROVING BRITISH ARTIST FRIEND who WANDERS about the WORLD on SMALL SHIPS in SAIL

This gentleman we met just before his last voyage on an old Maine gaff-headed schooner from here to Tahiti, the Fijis, Dutch East Indies and Philippines. This sauce he noted down in Apia, British Samoa. It sounds whimsical but is a new taste thrill, so fear not the spiritual addition at the end!

To 1 cup mayonnaise add ½ tsp worcestershire, 1 tbsp lime or lemon juice, ¼ cup chili sauce, dash tabasco, sour cream 2 tbsp, salt to taste and lastly *1 tsp gin per serving portion!* A dash of Angostura is optional.

TWO STIFFENERS for the BREAKFAST, or OTHER, ZERO HOUR

To extract the juices from clams, conchs, and other allied shellfish proceed as follows: *Hard Clams* or *Quohaugs*—pronounced *Ko-Hogs* down east, please!—or soft clams, known also as "steamers." . . . Cover clams with water—that will run about 6 cups per peck. Cover tightly and steam slowly. When clams are open the job is done. Needless to say we must use scrubbing brush and clear water first—removing all sand and other flotsam. This makes strong juice; salt and dilute to taste, if need be.

For *Conchs*—simply cut up skinned conch white meat; cover with water, boil 20 minutes or so; drain off juice; salt.

TO CLARIFY CLAM or CONCH BROTH

First strain broth through cloth, then stir in either: a little lightly beaten egg white, a handful of chopped *lean* raw beef, or crushed *washed* egg shells. Put on stove, whisk well. When boiling 15 minutes, skim again; let cool, then strain again—being careful not to agitate sediment in bottom of saucepan. . . . Now for the *Clam Juice Stiffener, No. I:*

We take equal parts clam and tomato juice, and to each 1 qt mixture add: small bit crushed garlic, 2 tsp scraped onion pulp, ½ tsp celery salt, 2 tsp worcestershire, 1 tbsp lime or lemon juice, 2 tsp freshly grated horseradish; dash tabasco, dash Angostura, 1 tsp sugar. Whip well or turn into The Blender; rub through coarse sieve. Chill well on ice, or shake with ice in cocktail shaker.

CLAM JUICE STIFFENER, No. II, Culled, Oddly Enough, from a North Cape Cruise—and, of all Things, Norway

To 3 cups clam broth add 1½ to 2 tbsp lemon juice, 1 tsp fine confectioner's sugar, ¼ cup ketchup or chili sauce, 1 tsp worcestershire, 2 tsp finely and freshly grated horseradish and the same of onion pulp. Salt to taste, and at the last sprinkle on a pinch to each glass of pounded caraway seed. Turn into The Blender with a handful of ice, or whip well to blend before chilling on ice.

> THE *STOMACH* is the Mainspring of our *SYSTEM*—if it be not sufficiently ***wound up*** to ***warm*** the *HEART* & ***support*** the *CIRCULATION,* the whole business of *LIFE,* will, in proportion, be ineffectively ***performed.*** We can neither ***think,*** with precision,—***walk*** with vigour,—***sit down*** with comfort,—nor ***sleep*** with tranquility.
> ***Ancient Proverb***

CHAPTER III

SOUPS *FROM* FAR & WIDE

Being Fifteen Exotic Soups, both Delicate & Virile, Ranging from an Enchanting Thing of Mallorcan Almonds, spiced, with Cream; through a Grecian Soup of Amiable Fowls with Eggs, Sour Cream & White Wine; to a Succulent Portuguese Affair of Shrimps & Things called *Sopa de Camarão, á Portuguesa.*

FOR CENTURIES soups have made the reputations of chefs; ever since chefs came into kitchens from camps. Kings have bestowed titles, treasure and broad acres because of soups. Men have come from half around the world to eat a certain soup in a certain place.

Unfortunately, until recent years, most decent soups meant hours slaving with the stock pot. In Europe and other lands where labor is cheap and through other household duties a fire is constantly burning in stove, home made soups from home made stocks were tasty and thrifty at the same time. But thanks to Brillat-Savarin and immaculate American industry we can purchase at any small store bouillons or consommes of beef, veal or chicken at tariff which, from a plain matter of budget, make the time and trouble of stock making both needless and unprofitable. Only in making certain soups of delicate fish, or in poaching fish, is anything like the old methods made necessary.

After virtually paddling our way around the world with a soup spoon we have discovered one worthwhile fact about foreign practice that America might note to her profit: granting good raw materials in each case, American failure in comparison with exotic chefs lies in a very simple factor—our seasoning with spices, herbs and other products strikes too much of a level. We season very delicate soups too much with tastes other than the one main ingredient; in hot or spicy or highly seasoned soups we strike too low a note, being afraid to risk the original. Also it is possible that we forget that sugar is a seasoning as well as sweetening; and once again we mildly suggest that our wide fear and ignorance of garlic and onion—a ridiculous state of affairs caused by careless chefs who fail to discard solid parts of the lily after flavour is extracted—finds us at sorry disadvantage through granting this handicap to foreign technique.

And here again, in Soups, the unpardonable sin after tastelessness is that of mediocre heat. A hot soup must be steaming; a cold soup—of which we list two, and which America neglects to her sorrow—must be chilled as thoroughly and carefully as we would a fine champagne. A lukewarm fluid in plate is the brand of a mischievous cook and careless host; a dual condition which is both signal insult to guest intelligence, and to the good foodstuffs being spoiled.

SOPA de ALMENDRAS, á MALLORQUIÑA, being a FINE THING of GRATED ALMONDS, HERBS & SPICES in CREAM, from VALLDEMOSA in the ISLAND of MALLORCA

The use of almonds in the cookery of southern Europe is something worth remembering here where we consume them mainly in salted state, for their flavour under heat becomes notable. This soup was discovered on our second visit to the Spanish island of Mallorca, and while on pilgrimage to secure some Seville orange seeds from the tree in the monastery garden where George Sand and Chopin passed a season long ago, in Valldemosa.

Take 2 cups of blanched almonds and put 1½ cups of them through fine blade of food chopper; turn into mortar, add 2 tbsp icewater to keep oil from forming. Work to smooth paste, reserving ½ cup in chopped form. . . . To 1 qt—4 cups—chicken or veal broth add 1½ tbsp *finely* chopped lean ham, 2 pinches powdered clove, ¼ tsp mace, ¼ tsp nutmeg, salt and cayenne to taste. Add bouquet of bayleaf, stalk celery with leaf left on, a sprig thyme and the same of basil—all tied with thread; or use 2 pinches each, powdered herbs. . . . Simmer slowly 20 minutes; strain through fine sieve. Add pounded almonds, simmer 20 minutes more. Lastly stir in ½ cup reserved chopped almonds, boil up once, stir in 1 tbsp sherry and serve very hot with big tbsp cold whipped cream on top.

WORDS to the WISE, No. II, on the VIRTUES of CAYENNE in ALL WHITE CREAM SOUPS

The finest chefs ignore black pepper in white cream soups. The flavour often does not agree with the tempo, and the resultant black specks of pepper, they feel, lowers the visual attractiveness of the dish. The same applies to delicate bisques of shrimp or tomato.

ANDALUSIAN COLD "SOUP-SALAD," or *SOPA-ENSALADA FRIA á ANDALUZ*

We consider this one of the best dishes in this whole volume. We find it pleasantly startling to discriminating guests and the best hot-weather soup we've found anywhere in the world. Oddly enough instead of coming to us via Ernest Hemingway or our bull-liquidating friend Sidney Franklin, or from some other Spanish habitué, it is from memory and pen of Tom Davin—formerly head of the American Museum of Natural History publications and now book editor for Sheridan House.

1 qt tomato juice, or the sieved pulp of fresh or canned tomato
Enough croutons, or sippets, of butter fried bread
2 or 3 hardboiled eggs
1 small fine minced cucumber
1½ tsp worcestershire
1 mild onion chopped very fine
1 tsp dry mustard
1 lime or lemon sliced thin
1 clove well crushed garlic
1 lemon or 2 limes, juice
2 tbsp olive oil
1 sweet green pepper chopped fine
1 dash or so tabasco
Salt & hand-ground black pepper

Work egg yolks and olive oil into smooth paste in wood salad bowl. Add crushed garlic, seasonings, lemon juice; then work tomato pulp in, add cucumber, green pepper. Stir briskly. Chill on ice 3 hrs. . . . Cut egg whites into strips, put on bottom soup bowls with chopped pepper, thin slice lemon and possibly 3 strips scarlet pimento. Pour in soup, *add 2 ice cubes to each bowl;* dust on hot croutons. Consume with dry white, chilled wine.

RUSSIAN CROUTONS, Eminently Suitable for Many Soups

Our Russki chef, instead of frying these in butter as the Frenchman does, slices bread thin, trims crusts, brushes with melted butter and sprinkles with *a little very sharp* grated cheese. He then browns in hot oven. The slight tang of cheese points up the soup taste.

GARLIC POPCORN, Noted under Hors d'Oeuvre on Page 25, & Served Hot & Crisp just before Fetching to Table, Is also Pertinent & to be Admired for Soup Trimming

AND NOW a POLISH COLD SOUP of TART APPLES, Claret, Lemon Rind & Currant Jelly

This exotic chilled companion dish was brought to us by a much-travelled friend who motored through Poland. . . . Slice 8 *tart* cooking apples, cover with cold water; add yellow rind 1 lemon cut into fine strips, 1/2 tsp cinnamon, 1 to 1 1/2 tbsp sugar, 1 or 2 pinches powdered clove and a little salt to taste. . . . Simmer slowly until apples are tender and rub through sieve.

Put on ice and chill 3 hrs. Then add chilled *strained* juice of 2 average small limes or 1 lemon, and a bottle of *chilled* claret or still red Burgundy. Melt 2 tbsp currant jelly and stir in rapidly just before serving, again with 2 ice cubes in each plate. Dust with fine toasted breadcrumbs. Lovely when the mercury climbs!

BLACK BEAN SOUP, Barranquilla, which Is in Colombia

Colombia means emeralds, mahogany, coffee, gold and oil. And up the Magdalena River the white men who seek those things, and others, built the amazing modern city of Barranquilla huddling among the foothills beside an old Spanish city. We found this black bean soup in a small restaurant in Old Town. It ranks close to being among the first six soups in the world, to our notion.

To 1 cup black beans soaked in water overnight and drained, add a fresh qt slightly salted water, a hambone or chunk of smoked hock,

4 bayleaves, 4 whole cloves, 1/4 tsp celery seed, 2 coarse celery stalks chopped fine—leaves and all; a big red Spanish onion and 1 clove garlic—these last fried gently first in 1 tbsp butter or olive oil until tender. . . . Start all these to simmering, then point up the torridity with 1/4 tsp dry mustard, 1 tsp chili powder, and 2 dashes tabasco. Discard bone and celery leaves. Put in The Blender or rub through sieve. Then serve piping hot in plates first garnished with 2 slices cold hard egg; and 2 slices lime or lemon, cut thin. If more thickening is wanted, melt out 1 tbsp each of butter and flour, work smooth with some of the hot soup, then stir in. . . . This black bean soup varies in all Spanish settled countries. It can easily make a one-dish meal, served with coarse bread and a big green salad. A spoon whipped cream and 1 tsp sherry is optional, as a final garnish.

BAHAMA CONCH CHOWDER, *à la CAT CAY,* as FIRST PREPARED for Us by THAT COLORADO CLARO GENTLEMAN, JIM ARAÑHA, of BIMINI on BOARD GOOD SHIP *MARMION,* CIRCA 1933

We rate proper conch chowder as third best soup in the world, with Green Turtle 1st, and Parisian Onion Soup tied with Petite Marmite for 2d place! In fact if any forthright French chef ever got his hands on a sweet-meated Bahama or Florida Keys conch they would be shipped to Paris every trip the *Normandie* made, in dry ice! Yes, these succulent shellfish are the tenants who vacated those lovely pink shells our dear old Aunt Euphorbia Fittich used to hold open the parlor door, or to center up the mantel between glass domes of wax flowers. To serve eight hungry mariners cruising any of these warm tropical waters; for a one-dish meal:

12 conchs, skinned, pounded like veal with mallet, cut 1 1/2" sq
3 big mild red or white onions
Piece salt pork 1 1/2" x 2"
Salt & hand-ground pepper
2 tsp sugar
4 cups milk, fresh or evaporated
1/4 cup sherry, Madeira or Marsala
2 small sweet peppers
4 bayleaves
1 tsp thyme
3 cups cooked diced potatoes
2 tbsp each, flour & butter
1 clove garlic, crushed

Cook onions and pork until former are tender; discard pork. Cover conch meat with water then add everything *except* milk, potato, thickening of flour-butter, and the wine. Simmer until sweetly tender, add milk and diced potato, stirring latter in gently; thicken with butter-flour roux if desired, adding wine at the last. Serve with pilot biscuit, dried in oven.

This chowder must be tried to be appreciated, and every yachtsman coming to Florida should read, mark, learn and inwardly digest conchs in all forms. Jim Arañha has for some years been our bait cutter, chef, entrepreneur, mentor and shoal-water guide. He not only put on a performance of Hamlet for us, being head of the Bimini library and culture society, but uses longer words than Bernard Shaw, and was assistant lightkeep at Great Isaac Reef as well as at Great Stirrup Cay. Look him up in our name.

A GRECIAN SOUP of MATURER FOWLS, EGGS & LEMONS, to SAY nothing of WINE & OTHER SUBSTANCES: SNARED in ATHENS in 1931 & REJOICING in the TITLE: *SOUPA AUGHOLEMONO,* as near as OUR QUAINT SPELLING CAN MAKE IT

We had occasion, once, to look up a favourite female cousin who was ratting around in Ur of the Chaldees, and then became placed in some shared authority in Greek Archeological Museums. This soup not only finds outlet for fowl of an age discouraging to patience, teeth and digestion, but strikes a totally new note in the realm of chicken soups. Further, at the Hotel Grande Bretagne it mighty nigh saved our miserable life after a freezing, snowy day prowling the Acropolis, in company with a young, tireless, handsome, agile and elusive lady from Greenwich, whose name and genius it is not pertinent to mention.

Cut up the oldest, fattest hen available, cover with cold water and fetch *very slowly* to the boil, meanwhile contributing 2 bayleaves, a pinch each of thyme and basil; and half a lemon rind, a clove of garlic, a modest dose of salt and cayenne. While gaining heat search kitchen and add anything like 2 small onions, a clutch of celery stalks,

2 carrots, and 1 tsp sugar. When meat falls from bones put through sieve, but while at boil adding a bit of water as needed from time to time to keep a good strong broth. Now put strained broth in saucepan, add ¼ cup dry rice, juice 1 lemon, simmer until rice is quite soft; also point up with salt and cayenne as needed. Stir in two beaten egg yolks, evenly. Serve at once, floating 1 tbsp sour cream on top, dust with croutons and pinch nutmeg at the last.

A SOUP of PLUMP & GENTLE FOWLS of DISCREET AGE, and RED *RIPE* BANANAS, *á SANTIAGO*

Proceed as in the Grecian dish, and when broth is done and you have a qt proceed as follows: Reserve breast and trim into shreds the size of matchsticks, cutting with the grain. To the rich broth add 2 red bananas, stood in sun until well ripened; simmer 10 minutes slowly, and rub through sieve or put in The Blender. Serve hot with a pinch of nutmeg on top.

This number was collected during a visit to Santiago and subsequent to an afternoon's visit to the factory of Bacardi, being escorted thither by a late member of that illustrious family. It was, all in all, a memorable day. For several reasons.

A FINE RICH SOUP of CALVES' KIDNEYS, from the THRESHOLD of the ALGAUR ALPS in BAVARIA, and KNOWN as *NIERENSUPPE*

This unusual thought came from Oberammergau, home of the famous Passion Play and the Anton Lang Christus. It is a lusty of fine seasoning and full flavour. . . . Slice a pair of calves' kidneys into small bits; remove any useless sections. Chop 3 spring onions fine and brown gently in 3 tbsp butter. Contribute 2 bayleaves, and a pinch each of thyme, marjoram and rosemary—all rubbed between palms. Add chopped kidneys, ¼ tsp mace, and smother. When light brown add 2½ tbsp flour worked smooth with juice; toss until flour is lightly brown. . . . Turn into saucepan, add 4 cups beef broth or stock, salt and pepper to taste, simmer ½ hr until good and rich. Now beat yolks 2 recent eggs with 1/4 cup sour cream. Draw pot off stove and when it stops simmering stir in this egg-cream mix thoroughly to bind; then at last 1 tbsp sherry or Madeira. . . . Garnish with chopped parsley and butterfried bread cubes of 1/4" size.

AND NOW the ONE & ONLY ONION SOUP from L'ESCARGOT, on Rue Montorgueil, near *LES HALLES*—Paris' 12th Century Markets

This truly fine restaurant was administered, during our last stay in Paris, by M. Lespinasse, once chef to Baron G. de Rothschild, and the King of Egypt. There is more atmosphere compressed into its small space than almost any other spot in all Paris—right from the clean sawdust-covered floors, the big gilt carved snails affixed at the doorway, and the painted ceiling, we were reverently informed, had once been property of their late beloved client the immortal, the divine, Sarah Bernhardt. Great men of all nations beat a pathway to its doorway, and Onion Soup there is something to mention in low, respectful tones. The atmosphere here is completely different from the neighbouring dives and "atmosphere" spots where slumming fancy gentlemen and fancier ladies rush in to rub elbows with labourers and stall-keepers from the abattoirs and markets. And so, *bon chance, mes amis!*

WORDS to the WISE, No. III, on the IMPERATIVE NEED for NUMEROUS ONIONS of PROPER SIZE & TYPE for THIS MASTERPIECE

American chefs are so hoist by the bootstraps of economy that Onion Soups they father are puny, watery, emasculated affairs not worthy of the name. Even Onion Soup in cans is better. Here in America we have gone, on urging of friends, to find similar dilute apologies in restaurants whose products they spoke of in bated breath. . . . To our modest mind any soup tied for second choice out of all the world, deserves decent treatment. THEREFORE: *USE RED ONIONS: USE EIGHTEEN to SERVE SIX!* Discard extra pulp if need be, but gain essence through strength.

MOST ONION SOUPS ARE RUINED through FIVE MAJOR SINS

1. We use entirely too few onions; should use big red onions.
2. We forget olive oil, substituting butter. Incorrect.
3. We use too much salt entirely. Spoils flavour.
4. We omit sugar entirely. And this is a real secret!
5. We use pre-grated, stale rank Parmesan cheese; not freshly grated from a hunk on our kitchen shelf.

THEREFORE to SERVE EIGHT:

Start 8 cups or so of rich beef broth to heat in saucepan. Slice from 14 to 18 red onions thinly; on bias, to avoid rings. Cook cut onions *very gently* in ¼ cup French olive oil and when getting clear and tender, add 4 tbsp butter. Onions must never be brown, black or crisp —but limpid as a maiden's eyes, tender as her generous heart! . . . Season now with salt, pepper, sugar; the last a good 2 tbsp.

Meanwhile trim bread rounds to fit heated earthenware casseroles, toast lightly. Portion out onions and their succulent juices equitably among the 8 casseroles; almost fill with stock. Then like a miniature, pungent raft float on the toast, load it with a big tablespoon of grated fresh Parma cheese. Put on covers and pop in oven for a quarter hour at 375° Fahrenheit; and serve sizzling.

A LUSTY RED ONION SOUP from OUR OWN PUERTO RICO, with an ENHANCING TOUCH of EGG BINDING, and VINEGAR—merely a TOUCH—SPICED with TARRAGON

To serve 8 proceed exactly as above, ignoring casseroles and toasted bread floated atop. . . . When onions are tender, add stock, simmer up in saucepan. Now beat up four fresh egg yolks with 2 tsp tarragon vinegar, and stir briskly into the fragrant pot to thicken. Dish out of tureen with ladle, and use olive-oil-fried bread sippets or croutons on top—no cheese. A wonderfully rich and satisfying one-dish meal, this.

WORDS to the WISE, No. IV, BEING a PLAINTIVE URGE to PRIME WEEK-END GUESTS with EITHER of these ONION SOUPS, *for SUNDAY MORNING*—or other—*BREAKFAST*

There is something about soup made from this invaluable lily that cools the blood, eases the mind, fetches body and soul within nodding distance once more. Try it. We have seen more than one house party salvaged from certain disaster by homely wisdom of this sort!

A SOUP of OYSTERS from ST. JACQUES CAP FERRAT, which Is Neither in Nice, Villefranche, nor Monte Carlo, but between and adjacent to Them All

One brightly enameled blue-sky day we wound up the Grand Corniche drive to tarry with an Editor Friend who, for reasons of his own, saw fit to engage a villa and other useful equipment in this charming spot—the whole thing hanging like a pretty swallow's nest not too high above the incredible blue of the Mediterranean. Among this villa's useful equipment was a *Niçoise*—a plump, merry chef no higher than a fence picket. And he afforded oyster soup, and we whose oyster experience was more or less limited to Grand Central Station, and our Atlantic and Pacific Coast gamut of milk stews and pan roasts, found in the dish good reason to take pause.

Choose small sweet oysters similar to our southern coast, rather than grand ones. The touch of garlic is unexpected and new, the clove picks up the brisk aria and the grand finale comes through the hint of tart dry white wine. It makes a meal for two diners, as meals right well should, on occasion.

Lightly brown a crushed garlic clove and 2 minced medium onions in 3 tbsp butter; discard garlic husks. Put 1 qt rich milk into double boiler to heat, add onions and cook until very tender and put oysters liquor in a saucepan to heat, together with a little salt, cayenne, and a bayleaf. Just *before* oysters are curled turn into the milk-onion pot. Stir in ½ cup dry white wine. Cook oysters a minute longer and serve with a ring of fine chopped parsley on each plate, with scarlet petals of paprika in center. No worcestershire!

AN INTRIGUING SOUP of SHRIMPS, CALLED *SOPA de CAMARÃO*, from the ANCIENT & ROMANTIC PORT of LISBON

Portuguese cookery of seafood ranks among the first four schools in the world, yet it is virtually unknown to America. Actually they discovered the salt codfish long before any Gloucesterman sailed out to the Grand Banks, and have dozens of ways for preparing it. It is similar to Spanish cookery, yet subtly different, although come of Spanish root. Portuguese adventurers were the first importers to Europe of Brazilian coffee, coconut and bananas. They carried their own ideas to the Far East before the British or Dutch were known out there. Even the Hindustani word for bread *pão*, or "pan" as it is pronounced; and Japan shrimp "tempura" style is a Portuguese inheritance. Rice is beloved still by Portuguese who fetched it in via the Orient; and other variations come from the Moorish invasion of Spain to Portugal. The main thing to remember is: Use olive oil, not butter, for the Lisbon touch. This will serve four.

1½ lbs uncooked *fresh* shrimp
1 crushed garlic clove
1 lemon or 2 limes, juice
2 or 3 bayleaves
½ cup dry white wine
8 tbsp olive oil, ½ cup
1 big mild onion, red is best
Dash tabasco or hot pepper
A little flour & butter
½ cup tomato pulp
Salt, to taste, put in last

First boil shrimp gently, starting in *cold* slightly salted fresh water, enough barely to cover. Remove heads and shell; reserve heads. Remove dark vein in tail. Fry out garlic and minced onion until tender; discard garlic. Now add tomato pulp, and all seasonings except wine and salt. Saute 5 minutes, then add shrimp stock. . . . While simmering pound up heads and shells, put in potato ricer, wet with stock and squeeze every drop of rich juice out. Repeat twice. Add this juice to pot, simmer until good and strong. Strain into saucepan, rub all pulps through sieve; add white wine; thicken to taste with a little flour browned in butter—equal amounts. Now salt, to taste. Boil up once more; serve with sippets of fried bread.

WORDS to the WISE, No. V, on the WISDOM of SALTING SOUPS NEAR TIME of SERVICE, rather than at the OUTSET

As mentioned elsewhere this thought is doubtless a needless caution, but we still have to remind ourselves now and then to observe it! Salt, once in, cannot be removed except by a miracle. A soup that tastes just salty enough at the start can, when reduced in quantity by boiling, be bitterer than the dead sea. Water boils away, salt remains.

A NATIVE TURTLE SOUP from MEXICO, GULF of CAMPECHE STYLE, or *SOPA de TORTUGA, á GOLFO de CAMPECHE*

Here is another exotic fetched to our verandah by one of those calm, cool-eyed gentlemen who tool the big Pan-American clippers this way and that over the blue Caribbean, Central and South America. This dish is pungent, and a veritable soup-stew adapted to a notable one-dish meal. Green turtle is best, of course, but failing a supply of this rarer species, either the loggerhead common to the American littoral from Georgia Sea Islands around the whole Gulf Coast to South America, or the hawkbill—the tortoise shell turtle—are fine. It will serve four well.

Take 4 lbs turtle meat, any small *hot* pepper, a clove of crushed garlic, small minced red onion, 4 chopped carrots and 4 stalks chopped celery, a little salt. Smother gently in lard or olive oil for 10 minutes. Then add quart of cold water and simmer until meat is very tender—not forgetting 4 bayleaves, pinch of thyme and 2 of basil. . . . Add 2/3 cup any red wine except port. Salt finally to taste. Serve with thin slices green lime, or lemon, cooked turtle eggs, or sliced hard eggs in plates. A little diced calipee, or yellow, lower-shell turtle fat, simmered in soup first, adds character. Hell-Fire Bitters will do as well as hot pepper pod. . . . *Basil is a tradition with cooked turtle dishes.* Green turtle meat is available in most large cities in America.

A DEEP SOUTH FRESH WATER TURTLE SOUP-STEW KNOWN as *CALIPASH*, & Easily Possible Anywhere on Lakes, Streams or Ponds in South Carolina, Georgia, Florida, Alabama, Louisiana or Texas, *à la SUSAN RAINEY*

Susan Rainey came into our plantation family life down in Central Florida when we were six or seven, and ruled the kitchen for fifteen years. Susan was South Carolina "Geechee," or descendant of field-hand slaves in the huge Gulla Country plantations of rice and indigo. She was very black, and muttered invocations against this threat or that, wore charms against bad luck, rheumatism, faulty teeth, snakes, corns and additional offspring. Her husband was local African Baptist shepherd of a flock of holy black sheep who could time the end of our Sunday chicken dinner to a split-second. Susan's ancestors, for two generations of po' times after de wah, had been forced to live off the land: Possums, coons, rabbit, doves, soft shell turtles and "cooters" —those striped headed hard shell turtles seen everywhere—all went into the cook pot. Armed with a vast iron stew kettle, and wearing a pair of our own abandoned tennis shoes properly razor-cut for toe-ease, she officiated at many strange, highly seasoned and tasty dishes when "dem fancy no'thern Yankee folks, he and she, done gawn up deah away fum we-all."

Ever since then we have marveled at white-man ignorance of such delicacies as cow peas, pigeon peas, turtle *Calipash,* Pine Bark Stew, and similar Afro-American carry-overs from African tribal days. The word "exotic" means, according to people who write dictionaries, anything "foreign or strange." That is why we list Susan's *Calipash* here. . . . Oddly enough the very word is exotic, from American Indian corruption of the Spanish *carapacho,* meaning the carapace or rounded shell of turtles; hence any stew cooked in the upper shell of terrapin or turtles. . . . It used to be a famous dish at our house, and the Pittsburgh Laughlins and the Chicago Piries used to come on state occasions to consume this dish.

Two average turtles will serve six. They should—for aesthetic reasons—be guillotined out of sight, let bleed, then with hatchet make a horizontal incision both sides between feet, to separate top of shell from flat lower portion. Reserve eggs, if any—and some of the fat. Scald feet to skin, using pliers for this operation to save temper. Put in kettle, cover with cold water, salt lightly, and add 8 or 10 cloves, 1 hot pepper pod or 3 dashes tabasco, 1/4 tsp mace, 1/2 tsp allspice. Simmer slowly and when tender trim off bones, dicing meat cross-grain to avoid strings. . . . Fry out, meanwhile, 1 medium diced onion, speck crushed garlic, in 1 tbsp butter. When tender add to meat and rich stock. Melt out 2 tbsp flour with same of butter to make brown roux, work smooth with soup, then stir well into the pot. The stew should be like heavy cream.

Meanwhile have upper shells scalded and neated up. Pour in stew, salted to taste. Add pinch sweet basil to each, 1 tbsp sherry each, same with 1 scant tbsp lemon juice and a trifle of grated yellow rind. Spread sliced turtle eggs, or hard chicken eggs, on top. Cover with any good pastry dough, prick to permit steam exit, and brown in oven at 350° Fahrenheit, brush with a little milk during last 10 min to glaze. Serve with any good white wine, chilled. Here's a deep south touch for any plantation owner!

A STUTTGART HOT SOUP of WINE & SNOWY EGGS, CALLED *SCHNEEKLOSSCHEN, à la THEODORE* of the *S. S. RESOLUTE* GRILL

Long before the ascendancy of Austrian paperhangers we made two trips around the world on German *schnelldampfers*. Much of the cuisine was heavy, all was nourishing, and some was amazingly and refreshingly delicate—of which this slightly sweet and snowy soup is a typical example. . . . Make a gentle white roux of 1 1/2 tbsp each butter and flour—do *not* brown. Work in a little milk to make smooth as cream. Stir into double boiler with 2 1/4 cups tart white wine of Rhine or Moselle type. Add 4 pinches cinnamon, the yellow peel 1/2 lemon. Cook 20 minutes, stir in beaten yolks 3 fresh eggs. . . . Meantime whip 3 egg whites with 2 1/2 tbsp sugar until stiff. Ladle into hot plates, float meringue on top in a snowy drift, dust with 1 tsp confectioner's sugar on each, and finally dust with pinch of cinnamon per serving. This is especially welcome to the invalid or convalescent weary of the usual. More white roux makes it thicker if that is the wish.

> "Don't give we-all no fancy sto'-boughten cookin book, Ma'am. Jes' han' me good vittles and turn me loose on a good stove—Ah said a *GOOD* stove!"
>
> From the *Kitchen Sayings* of *Cook Susan Rainey*, Zellwood, Florida, *Circa*, 1907

CHAPTER IV

FISHES *FROM THE* SEVEN SEAS

Swimming an Exotic Gamut Involving Fifteen or so Piscatorial Denizens Prepared in Fashion both Savoury & Tantalizing, such as a Bretonese *Brandade* of Salted Cods, Fishes Dipped in the Six Perfumes from Chinese Canton, Baked Snappers in the Manila Fashion with Chopped Cashews, and the Persuasive Way a Russian Prince of the Blood might Deal with a Dish of Tender Trouts. . . . To say nothing of Ten Discreet Companion Sauces.

IT HAS always found us a trifle sad that America, with inland and coastal waters teeming with a variety and excellence of fish denied Europe, should find foreign chefs taking far greater pride in its preparation. No country in the globe can show all the coral reef fishes of our Florida coast, which are parallel to identical species in the South Seas, and the whole spread from there to the salmon of Maine and Alaska, the rainbow and brook trout of our northern streams.

Yet in our fish cuisine, barring the lusty originality of certain thrifty New England chowders, the Afro-American tradition of Charleston, and the Creole inheritances of New Orleans, we simply fry, boil, bake or broil, squirt on a dash of lemon, cream or tomato sauce, and let it go at that.

By this we do not contend that any fish unaccompanied by sliced truffles and a ten-ingredient fancy sauce is invalid, but we do suggest that America should realize that lemon treatment is far more valuable *before* cookery than after, that piquant thoughts in basting or dressing can take a mediocre weight of edible fish and transform it into something men can write poems about.

We, through disposition of fate, have had a great deal to do with fishes—both in their capture, their culinary transformation, and their consumption. It began too many years ago when our male parent came barging out of a placid retirement addicted to botanical and literary pursuits, to re-enter the field of engineering in co-charge of Camp Four, on Upper Matecumbe Key, when the railroad was extended over those coral islands to Key West. In one of Kirk Munroe's Canadian sailing canoes we made daily excursion to the Great Barrier Reef where we took varied loot in the form of brilliantly coloured reef fish, stone crabs—the king of all crabs!—conchs, and Florida lobster. We have fished fresh water lakes and streams from Florida to New England, to British Columbia, and during later years have fished for big tuna and marlin and other game fishes both here and off Bimini and Cat Cay.

On trips around the world we have always been especially eager to try exotic ways of fish preparation. We've eaten deep olive oil fried squid in Naples, *bêche de mer* in Hongkong, skates in Nice—and avoid such marine diablerie in this account. We do, however, set down a chosen band of exotics out of thrice that total collected—each notable for some virtue or succulence.

BACALÃO á BILBAINITA, being a MOST SUPERB DISH of SALTED CODS in the FASHION of SPANISH BILBAO, on the BAY of BISCAY

To fellow patriots assuming that the salted codfish was exclusively part of the sacred Bostonian crest, let us hasten to explain that sturdy, hard-fisted sailormen from Bilbao, from Lisbon, and from French St. Malo—to say nothing of God knows how many Norse folk—sailed their craft to the Grand Banks of Newfoundland long before Pilgrim Fathers knew of their existence. In whatever land the Portuguese or Spaniard conquered, the salt cod—or *bacalão* in Spanish—swam merrily after. They have taken this rigid, unprepossessing fare and transformed it into a kingly dish. To those of us knowing dried cod in the form of fishballs we present a lusty exotic for that special Sunday morning breakfast.

3 lbs dry salt codfish
4 big red or white onions
2 small cloves garlic
1 to 1½ cups bread crumbs
Hot peppers, or tabasco; to taste
6 or 8 sweet peppers
4 lbs tomatoes
2½ cups olive oil
2 slices soft bread
3 bayleaves, tied together
1 cup flour

First the puree sauce. Brown 1/3 of the onions, tomatoes and minced peppers gently in 2/3 cup olive oil then simmer covered for 45 minutes. Rub through sieve, or put in The Blender. Keep hot. . . . Brown fish soaked overnight in a little olive oil and dredged in flour, until pale amber. Now brown remaining onions and peppers in rest of olive oil, when onions are tender add tomato reserved; also bayleaf and crushed garlic; add puree to this. Season to taste. Simmer 10 minutes longer. . . . Arrange baking dish as follows: First a substratum of puree and vegetables, then the *bacalão,* then the rest of the sauce. Cover with bread crumbs dotted with butter and brown in hot oven around 400° Fahrenheit.

A *BRANDADE,* which Is a BRETONESE CLASSIC also COMPOSED of SALTED CODS CREAMED with SHALLOTS, PARSLEY, LEMON, TRUFFLES & VARIED SPICINGS

The Breton fishermen besides being notable for their red sailcoth trousers, have many typical dishes, and like the Spanish and Portuguese to the south'ard, know how to do things with salt codfish. This dish was discovered by us personally in 1926 during a trip into France. At risk of censure for showing two dishes of the same type of fish, we present the *Brandade* as something typically French as onion soup, for instance.

1 lb salted codfish
½ to ¾ clove garlic
¼ tsp nutmeg
Hand ground black pepper
2 tsp parsley
3 cups thick cream
¼ cup olive oil; 1 scant cup same
1 tbsp lemon juice
1 tsp grated yellow rind
3 tbsp chopped truffles, or mushrooms
Rounds of fried bread

Choose a fine lusty bit of fish. Soak overnight in milk. Drain, break in flakes, put in cold water and poach 20 minutes, timing from first boil. Drain again, skin and bone. . . . Now heat the ¼ cup olive oil in saucepan. When smoking toss in flaked fish, crushed garlic. Stir vigorously with *wood* spoon until finely shredded. . . . Now warm the scant cup olive oil; and cream. Stir oil into fish one spoon at a time. When like stiff paste start adding cream same way. Final dish should be like a very heavy puree. Stir in spices, mushrooms already cooked, and lemon additions. Serve in timbale garnished with triangles of butter-fried bread, and pointed up with whatever sea fare the larder affords: Bits of shrimp tail, lobster, small lightly poached oysters and the like. Utterly delicious.

WORDS to the WISE, No. VI, PUBLISHING the VIRTUES of MILK rather than WATER BEING the PROPER OVERNIGHT BATH for SALTED CODFISH or HIS HALF-BROTHER, the FINNAN HADDIE

Milk, or half milk and water, seems to extract the saline content from such species of fish far better than water alone. And where the latter is used it is wise to change it now and then while the soaking process obtains.

FISHES DIPPED in the SIX PERFUMES, being a NATIVE CHINESE DISH from CANTON-SIDE

Exactly thirteen happy years before Canton knew the terror and the death that rained from the skies, we went there by steamer from Hongkong—the Hongkong, Canton & Macao Steamship Company—up through the Tiger's Mouth into Pearl River where literally millions of Chinese are born, live and die on their small river craft. Five hours from the formal British Colony of Hongkong to the heart of Mother China where human beings were crowded 35,000,000 to a single province. We stayed in Shameen through hospitality of a Shanghai-met French gentleman in the Cantonese silk business, and through him stumbled upon this dish in a Chinese Club on the other side of the river, where also tiny sing-song girls entertained us with what they quaintly contend to be singing, and we smoked our first and last five pipes of poppy dreams.

Cut up two pounds of fine white fish into average pieces. Dip first into lemon juice, and set to marinate in a little salted water containing 1 tbsp onion pulp, for 2 hours. Drain and reserve liquid; dust with a *little* powdered anise seed (from the drug store), then with cayenne, dip in lightly beaten egg and brown golden in lots of hot butter. Put on hot platter; take 3 tbsp butter, add to marinade, 5 tbsp soya sauce, ½ tsp sugar. Thicken with a little cornstarch, working in with hot liquid to avoid lumps. Simmer, pop in fish for 2 minutes, put sauce into boat and serve separately. Soya sauce may be increased or decreased, to taste. Mace in powdered form can substitute for anise, if latter is inconvenient. An odd taste thrill.

BAKED or ROASTED FISHES, being the Grandest Possible Way of Presenting a Noble Specimen of the Snapper, Kingfish, Wahoo Tribe; or other Large Mackerels

This generation of ours being considerably after the day of miracles, let us earnestly counsel amateur chefs that no fish from any sea can baste himself, and without basting the finest red snapper can become a tasteless unprofitable thing offering all the juicy flavour of a wad of cotton batting. When the unproven chef announces baked fish, all true gourmet's tremble for the dish! Therefore, to keep a fine five pound fish from drying in pan:

1. Grease pan well with olive oil or butter.
2. Dredge fish with a little flour.
3. Place not less than 4 slices salt pork or *fat* bacon over fish—and more are better.
4. Bake in medium oven around 350° to 375° Fahrenheit.
5. Baste every 10 minutes ***without fail.*** If still too dry add ¼ cup butter or olive oil as additional basting.
6. Baste, *baste, BASTE!* And one of those self-basting double roasters is a help, only keep oven heat nearer 375° if this is used, browning uncovered at the last.

BAKED FISH, MANILA STYLE, EMBRACING CHOPPED CASHEWS, LIMES, CHEESE of MILD DISPOSITION, NUTMEG, SHERRY & other ADMIRABLES

After a Sunday afternoon with Monk Antrim at the cockfights—and more of this gentleman later!—a quartet of us went over to the Polo Club, after two Quarentine Cocktails from hand of Monk's own priceless Chino bartender at the huge Manila Hotel. There, with chilled Chilean *Undurraga Rhin* in brown squatty saddlebag-fitting bottles, we had the following masterpiece, involving a fish much like our own southern coast red snapper. It would be equally suitable for pike, bluefish, a big rainbow trout or black bass.

A fine 5 lb fish, red snapper best
1 cup grated *mild* cheese
1 cup milk
6 tbsp butter
¼ cup sherry or Madeira
1 small garlic clove, crushed
3 cups cashew nuts, chopped
3 limes, juice; or 1½ lemon
1 cup bread crumbs, dry, fine
½ tsp grated nutmeg
1 small onion, scraped pulp
2 bayleaves, rubbed fine

One secret is that fish is painted inside and out with lime juice, salted lightly, and iced that way for at least 4 hours before cooking. Take *well* greased baking dish; dispose fish on bottom. Mix chopped nuts with cheese, garlic pulp and onion, moistening with milk to make stiff paste. Salt and cayenne to taste, and all seasonings. Then spread your fish with this toothsome blanket, and cover with dry fine bread crumbs. On this put generous walnuts of butter and brown in medium oven around 350° to 375° Fahrenheit, basting well. . . . Chopped almonds, Brazils, hazelnuts or pecans do equally well, but the cashew is traditional in the Philippines.

WORDS to the WISE, No. VII, concerning the VIRTUES of BAYLEAF in COOKING FISHES, ESPECIALLY THOSE BAKED or ROASTED

No chef has stood eye to eye with any fish about to be baked which would not gain character from addition of a bayleaf or two, both in stuffing and in basting liquid; and the same for fish chowders of every type.

A *PULAO* of PIECES of FISH, or SHRIMPS, which WE FOUND JOURNEYING from the GULF of MANAAR, on the NORTH COAST of CEYLON, to VISIT the WEIRD TEMPLES of MADURA, TANJORE & TRICHINOPOLY

This exotic will be found listed under Shrimps, where it justly belongs, under Chaptering for *SHELLFISH, CRUSTACEA, FROGS & TURTLES,* Page 80.

A MARTINIQUE *PIMENTADE* of FISHES, which HAS BEEN DESCRIBED as HOT as LOVE, FIERCE as the MAW of PELEE, TASTY as a YOUNG MAIDEN on a FLOWER-DRAPED BALCONY. From a VOYAGE to FORT de FRANCE in 1929.

Like Martinique *Bouchées,* listed under *Hors d'Oeuvres,* this dish varies with raw materials and the case-hardening of guest palates. . . . First marinate fish in lots of slightly salted lime or lemon juice, for at least 4 hours. Cover head, tail and trimmings with cold water, a pinch each of usual sweet herbs, speck garlic, bayleaf, couple of small onions, and stalk of celery. Simmer up slowly for 15 minutes. Strain off this court bouillon, put in fish. Add from 2 to 3 small round red bird peppers, or pointed pods, or several dashes tabasco. Add lime marinade liquid; poach fish slowly until tender. Keep warm and make sauce by reducing part of stock with 1/4 cup tart white wine. Garnish with quartered green limes or lemons. Onion may be omitted; but garlic, never.

WORDS to the WISE, No. VIII, on the KINDLY OFFICES of LIME or LEMON JUICE in PREPARATION of *ALL* FISHES for COOKERY

Either of these juices applied to fish removes strong scents and actually starts to tender the tissues through "cooking" action of citric acid. The trouble with America is that we too often apply citric juices to fish *after* cooking when it is far more valuable *before* cooking. . . . Add a little salt to marinade, let fish stand from 2 hours to overnight. . . . Refer to *I'a Ota,* Tahitian Fish Salad, from the notebook of Charles Nordhoof.

A WORD on the DELICACY of BOILED FISHES, and WHAT IS POACHING

If fine baked snapper is the most regal fish dish, the most delicate invite boiling or poaching. Here again amateur chefs have been left on a limb by the printed cookery word. The result in corrupted seafood is a crying shame; the discouragement to the amateur, worse still. The rules are few but *rigid*.

1. Don't try to boil any good fish in kettle. Fare forth to any decent household supply store and purchase a regular Fish Boiler. . . . Don't be parsimonious or crippled by false economy—*GET a BIG ONE*. For a large fish cannot go into a too-small Boiler, while a small fish is finely treated in a big Boiler. . . . Such a Boiler permits fish to be boiled whole; has a perforated shelf-like support holding fish off bottom.
2. Remove with infinite care when done, so fish does not break up. Delicate fleshed fish should be wrapped in cheesecloth to hold together.
3. *NEVER* let simmering stop once started, regardless whether water or Court Bouillon is used. Latter best.
4. Where we read receipts calling for a little vinegar in the fluid, substitute about ⅛ more of lime or lemon juice and forget the vinegar entirely. Much more delicate flavour.
5. Fish to 1 lb take 10 minutes; from 1 to 1½ lbs, 15 to 18 minutes; 1½ to 3 lbs, 18 to 28 minutes; 3 to 5 lbs, 28 to 40 minutes; 5 to 8 lbs, 40 to 60 minutes. . . . Bigger fish require more time, naturally. Done when meat leaves bone—but be sure about this for few things are more depressing than undercooked boiled fish!

POACHING FISHES, what IT IS

Chefs will vary in opinion here, but reduced to legible English Poaching means simmering *very* gently in any fluid elected, in a covered pan rather than a big boiler or kettle; preferably with a domed and tight-fitting cover so that steam may rise, collect and drop down—automatically basting fish. Liquid may be water, wine, milk, court bouillon. Poaching usually employs somewhat *less* liquid than boiling. It may also be done in a shallow pan.

It is, of course, done without cover in certain cases. The process actually is boiling, of course, but usually involves smaller, tenderer fishes, or smaller cuts of large fishes. We often poach trouts, or filets of sole, but never boil them.

A RUSSIAN DISH of BOILED FISHES INVOLVING also SHRIMPS, MUSHROOMS, BAYLEAF & SOUR CREAM

In 1926 we discovered Maisonette des Comediens Russes, on the Rue Vivienne. It is rather amazing, being operated by White Russian officers, and not only affording just about the finest Russian cooking anywhere in Paris, but with really Russian music, no swing or any of the varied abortions French or other foreign gentlemen quaintly assume to be American jazz; no dancing. Just Russian gypsy music, with a touch of Hungarian concertina work thrown in. It is very gay, especially after midnight. It made us very sad and sorry about the whole Revolution business, and those wonderful madly gay, fantastic days of the Tsar's court.

3 lbs fine fish fillets
½ lb chopped mushrooms
4 bayleaves, tied together
1 bunch beet or turnip greens
½ cup lime or lemon juice
1 cup cooked shrimp
4 tbsp butter
2/3 cup sour cream
1 to 1½ tbsp flour
Salt and cayenne to taste

Mix juice with another ½ cup salted water and marinate fish for an hour. Meantime cover greens with water, a little salt, bayleaf and cayenne. Boil 10 minutes, then put in fish and poach slowly. When tender put on hot plate. While fish poaches make sauce: Chop mushrooms fine; if they are large, peel off the top skin; and where there is a choice prefer the button type. Fry out in 3 tbsp butter. When tender melt out remaining tbsp butter with flour; work smooth and add to mushrooms. Next stir in sour cream. Simmer up once more. . . . Serve fillets on platter surrounded with shrimp, and mask with sauce. Be careful greens do not cling to fillets. Thin sauce with a little stock if too thick. A very delicately flavoured dish indeed.

WORDS to the WISE, No. IX, EXTOLLING the NEED for SAUCES other than the USUAL CREAM TYPE for BOILED FISH—MAINLY *MOUSSELINE* & SAUCE *PRINCESSE,* which ARE ESPECIALLY PLEASANT.

Mousseline is one of the immortals. No finer sauce exists for a delicate boiled fish. Simply mix 2 parts good Hollandaise Sauce with 1 part whipped cream. May be hot or cold.

Sauce *Princesse* is especially equitable with boiled salmons. It requires 1 cup Hollandaise, ½ tsp beef extract, 6 oysters poached in own liquor until edges curl; then minced. Mix well.

SARDINES or PILCHARDS, COOKED FRESH from the SEA, *à la MARMION*

Two summers ago we were fishing tuna with Ernest Hemingway in Bimini, and we gave Tommy Shevlin a bachelor party on *MARMION*. So next day we were tired and didn't go fishing, and Carlos, Ernest's *Cubaño* head gaffer on *PILAR,* threw a cast net over the side of the dock and hauled it in packed with about two bushels of wriggling silver sardines, and gave us a bucket full. And there was our breakfast! Small fishes like these abound from Maine to the Argentine, and just why men wait until some Norwegian cans them in olive oil to eat them has always escaped us, for when cooked fresh they may be eaten bones and all like smelts. . . . Simply scrape with back of knife—one stroke each side, and scales are gone. Toss a garlic clove in a skillet full of olive oil. When smoking hot either brown, lightly salted, as-is; or dip first in salted milk, then egg, flour, then brown. Serve sizzling.

ROASTED SHADS, *á SEVILLANA,* or as the SPANIARD DOES

An itinerant female cousin addicted to roving in far countries and doing water colours of what she sees, fetched this back to us scribbled on the back of a bright sketch of the chef! To us, American baked shad was delicious, but still a plain baked fish. For those who wish to voyage into the unexpected let's consider the combined taste advantages of wine, olive oil, a trifle of mushroom, and the liver of the fish itself.

1 3-lb shad, or 2 of 2 lbs
2 bayleaves, broken up
Salt & cayenne, to taste
¾ cup tart white wine
1½ limes, or 1 lemon, juice
1¼ cups finely minced mushrooms
2½ tbsp olive oil
2½ tbsp butter
Reserve shad livers from market

Score fish lightly on both sides to permit sauce to penetrate. Brush with juice and let stand 2 hrs. Then brush with oil, season well. Grease pan with butter, and any surplus oil. Brown in medium oven around 350° Fahrenheit for 25 minutes or so. Baste well. . . . Meantime chop livers, parboil, and rub through sieve. Same with chopped mushrooms, cooking in reserved liver broth. Mix liver puree and mushrooms, add white wine, turn into pan about the fish, ten minutes before done—basting constantly. Use this reduced wine-liver-mushroom basting for sauce.

A FAIRLY FANCY, yet EASY, RUSSIAN WAY of FRYING SMELTS, which WILL BE a DELIGHT to the EYE & a FILLIP to the JADED PALATE

Here is another from Maisonette Russe, in Paris. To us to whom a smelt was merely a small totally consumable fish, fried either in or out of batter, it opened our eyes to the possibility of fancy trimmings on certain occasions, with gourmets visible.

2 lbs fresh smelts, large as possible
18 to 24 shrimp, depending on size
2 tsp mushroom or walnut ketchup
1½ tbsp butter
1½ tbsp flour
1 cup flour, for added duty
2 tbsp fine dry breadcrumbs
3 cups veal stock
2 tbsp lemon or lime juice
½ tsp dry hot mustard
Salt & cayenne, to taste
3 beaten egg yolks
½ small clove garlic
2 tsp chopped parsley

Large smelts are essential, as they have to be filleted with razor-sharp knife, and bone taken out. And the piquant frying sauce is what makes this dish; additional seasonings are up to the chef. . . . First melt out the butter and brown the crushed garlic gently; discard latter. Work 1½ tbsp flour into a smooth roux, add to heated stock. Chop up shrimp into lemon juice and add to stock. Put in all seasonings and the added 3 tbsp butter. Simmer very slowly for 15 minutes. Keep this rich sauce in reserve; chill well then paint fillets thoroughly, skewer together with short bits of toothpick to make like whole fish. Dip first in flour then in beaten yolk, and fry in deep olive oil or other fat (except butter) at 370° Fahrenheit. Serve the remaining sauce in a silver boat, heated well, for those who wish it.

FILET of SOLE, *HABAÑERO,* a Delicious Solution for Poaching Fillets of any Sweet & Tender Fish, a Classic from the Habana Yacht Club that We Discovered in 1930

Poach fillets in half tart white wine, half lightly salted water. Brush with lime juice mixed with onion pulp, ½ cup to 1 tsp latter. Brown fine-chopped almonds in a little butter. Season fillets, spread on chopped nuts evenly and thinly. Brown under quick broiler flame. Dust with chopped parsley and a trifle of fresh grated Parma cheese. Serve with dry white wine of the Rhine or Moselle type; with Undurraga *Rhin,* or better still, with still white Burgundy.

CHINESE FRIED TROUTS, or "The Small Water Angels of Soo-Chow"—Being a Compound of White Wine, Ginger, Egg Batter, and the Juice of Lemons or Limes, from the Beautiful Lake City of the Same Name, where Dwell the Loveliest Chinese Maidens in the Whole Wide World

May we repeat the fact that long before our European ancestors stopped wearing bear skin kimonos the Chinese had an intricate and civilized cookery? In the white race the first civilized cookery was in Italy; then France. Many Chinese culinary dishes startle the western eye and palate. Maybe they are right; maybe we. However, besides the American born Chop-Suey which is unknown as a native Chino dish, there are many receipts worthy of our attention as exotics—as this one.

Take 6 small trout, properly drawn. Dry with a cloth; brush with lemon juice mixed with onion pulp and a *trace* of crushed garlic. Make batter of 5 egg whites, ½ cup tart white wine—using Japanese *saki* if no Chino rice wine handy, for they are much the same—½ tsp sugar, salt. Beat stiff. Roll lightly seasoned fish carefully and brown golden in deep lard or olive oil at 370° Fahrenheit. The final exotic touch is a slight dusting with ground ginger just before service.

HOW a RUSSIAN PRINCE of the BLOOD ONCE COOKED A DISH of SMALL TROUTS, with WHITE WINE, VERY OLD RUM INDEED, SWEET HERBS, a FEW SHRIMPS, & a TOUCH of SHERRY OR MADEIRA

This is a very old receipt from St. Peterburg before the fall of the Tsar, and when food was something besides basic nourishment under five year, or other, plans. It is fancy but delicious, and all ingredients are easily found, provided we have the necessary 1 doz trout! . . . Take fish heads, tails and trimmings, add 2 doz raw shrimp, a minced onion, salt, 2 bayleaves, a stalk of celery and half cover with water. Cover tightly and simmer slowly until shrimp are done. Shell shrimp tails, remove the top-side dark vein. Pound heads, put in sieve and drain stock through several times; then reduce this enriched fluid gently by half. About ½ cup of strong stock is needed. . . . Mix 2 cups dry white wine, 2 tbsp Jamaica rum, and 1 pinch each: basil, savoury, thyme, crushed bayleaf, 1 tsp chopped green mint. Put lightly salted trout in bowl and cover with wine-herb marinade for 2 hrs. . . . Use big pan to cook fish without bending, poach in the wine marinade about 2 minutes. Mince shrimp tails, toss them in butter. Put poached fish on platter carefully, rub sauce through sieve, add shrimp and 1 tbsp fine chopped parsley for garnish, and pass in gravy boat. If sauce is too thick, reduce slightly before adding shrimp. A very delicate and lovely dish.

AND NOW a COMPANIONATE LIST of THIRTEEN ADDITIONAL EXOTIC FISH SAUCES with which the AMATEUR CHEF MAY BECOME HONOURED among MEN, & without MAY BE HOIST by the TRITE PETARD of SALT & PEPPER UNADORNED

1. *Babcock Sauce,* a tested classic, and mainly for boiled fish: 1 cup strained clam broth, ½ tsp hand-ground *black* pepper, ¼ tsp salt—no more! Then ½ tsp hot mustard, 3 tbsp butter, 1 tbsp flour. . . . Do not use white pepper, or finely ground black. If no hand pepper mill, crush up whole peppercorns in bowl, as visible pepper is part of the tradition. . . . Melt butter and make roux with flour and mustard. Season, stir in clam juice slowly, heating very gradually. . . . When it boils note chronometer. Draw off in precisely 2 minutes, no more!
2. *Four Savoury Butter Sauces:* Very finely chopped mixed pickle, a little fine-chopped watercress, butter to suit. . . . Anchovy paste, dash tabasco, butter to suit. . . . Finely chopped parsley, little lemon or lime juice *strained,* butter to suit. . . . Anchovy paste, finely minced capers, butter to suit. . . . Mix all of these well until butter is creamed and light. If sweet butter is used, add salt to taste.
3. *A Piquant Fish Sauce from Dijon, which is in France:* This is very admirable with baked fish, as it is derived from such bastings founded on butter-in-pan. . . . Put fish bastings through coarse sieve, add a trifle of fine-chopped chives, shallot, or spring onion top, a pinch of basil. Add a little water and reduce slowly until very thick. Then donate 2 tsp mild French mustard, 2 cups white cream sauce, 1 doz finely chopped capers. Simmer up once more and it is ready.
4. *Old Key West Lime Sour:* This is a native classic from the Florida Keys, from the Bahamas. It is good in fish sauces, on fish itself in small quantities; good for salad dressings for fish and green salads. . . . To 2 cups strained lime juice add level tsp salt. Stand in warm kitchen 2 wks; cork then and keep in cool place, as it is ready to use. Queer scent, exotic taste!
5. *A Sauce for Broiled Fish, from Nantes, also in France:* Rub 6 sardines through a sieve, cream with 4 tbsp butter, juice 3 limes or 2 lemons, tsp fine-chopped parsley, ½ tsp scraped onion pulp. Brush over fish when it comes out sizzling.
6. *A Shrimp Sauce Suitable for Boiled Fish:* Much in favour abroad, and varies the usual caper sauces found everywhere. . . . Take enough white sauce to fill boat; stir in 1½ tsp anchovy paste, juice ½ lemon

or 1 lime, strained; 6 shrimp tails broken small; Cayenne to taste. Small cubes of lobster will also do well, small chopped oysters, sliced hard eggs. Let sauce simmer up once, then serve. White sauce for fish should be made on base of ½ milk and half fish stock or court bouillon.

7. *A Viennese Sauce for Boiled or Grilled Fish of Size:* Make roux of 1½ tbsp each butter and flour; don't brown. Add 2/3 cup hot sour cream. When worked smooth add 1½ tbsp tarragon vinegar, salt to taste. Now add 2 tbsp or slightly more *freshly* grated horseradish. Now ½ tbsp chopped capers. Simmer all together once, and serve very hot.
8. *Pepper Sauce for Boiled Fish, Mainly:* Here's one we found at a fine seafood restaurant in Nice, in 1931. . . . Pound 1 tsp whole peppercorns finely, simmer in ½ cup tart white wine. Reduce until nearly dry, then turn in 2 cups cream sauce based on half cream and half court bouillon. Boil up once; strain.
9. *Dr. Kitchiner's Piquante Sauce for Fish, & all other Flesh:* This classic dates back to 1817, and the immortal Doctor. . . . Pound yolks 2 hardboiled eggs with 1 tsp French mustard; pepper and salt, and 2 tbsp olive oil. Mix well and add 3 tbsp tarragon vinegar. Now add your preference of these: 1 tbsp mushroom ketchup, walnut ketchup; or walnut pickle, or a few fine-chopped capers. Rub through a fine sieve. . . . To our private thought a little cayenne and onion pulp would aid.
10. *A Cubaño Green Sauce from a Favourite Haunt of Ours in Matanzas, and Utterly Delicious on all sorts of Delicate Fish, Lobsters and the Like:* To ½ cup of thick sour cream add 1 cup good mayonnaise. Now comes 1 tbsp watercress or spinach for colour, fine-chopped of course. Next a speck of garlic pulp, enough green lime to suit tartness of taste; tabasco, a dash. Whip thoroughly and rub through sieve, or toss in Blender. Should be very cold for cold fish. Rub through fine sieve in all cases. . . . A tsp green tarragon, chervil or basil is also wonderful. Dry herbs are permissible but not so delicate or attractive to the eye in this receipt.

EXPLODED OLD WIVES' TALES No. I, on the BETRAYAL in USING RED WINES either in FISH COOKERY, or in FISH SAUCES

Now and then we have stumbled—especially in rather ancient foreign books on fish cookery and modern American efforts neither based upon authority, nor personal culinary experience—upon dishes commanding the use of red wine in fish cookery. Eschew such snares like the plague. Except for infrequent French *Matelotes* of fish where red wine is traditional, use unfortified white wines, tart preferred, in fish cookery. . . . Where sherry and Madeira are indicated for flavour, *add immediately before serving, never before,* for reasons explained.

"Health, Beauty, Strength, & Spirits—& I might say the Faculties of the Mind, depend upon the Organs of the Body—*one of the most Important of which is the Stomach*. . . . When these are in Good Order, the Thinking Part is Most Alert & Active; the Contrary when they are Disturbed. . . ."

Dr. Cadogan, England, 1757

CHAPTER V

SHELLFISH, CRUSTACEA, FROGS & TURTLES

Not Forgetting Smothered Conch, *Ernest Hemingway*, the true Norfolk Oyster Roast, Peppery Stuffed Crabs from Pointe à Pître which is in Guadeloupe, Devilled West Indian Crawfish, *Cat Cay*, Old Scottish Spiced Lobster, Shrimps dealt with on the Kona Coast of Hawaii, and a Duet of Turtles.

THIS IS another favourite chapter, not alone because we are so fond of seafood ourselves but due to the amazingly varied flavours the amateur chef can effect through slight changes in seasoning, through broiling *au naturelle* and without that perennial American habit of boiling in plain water first, through cooking certain crustacea in oil *with the shells on,* through roasting oysters in their own succulent juices and not merely frying or stewing these sweet bivalves.

Possibly the most important thought to hold with regard to these strange seagoing bedfellows is to remember that, with a few rare exceptions, their charm is in the delicacy of their flavours—so let none of the native virtue be subdued by over-seasoning; but where there is high seasoning—like certain stuffed crabs—make the seasoning truly high and peppery. And the second grain of counsel is that when cooking seafoods American chefs tend to use too much water and too little hot fat, as will be explained anon.

Here again we purposely concentrate on Caribbean or Latin-American exotics, since the French school especially is billed on menus in any metropolitan restaurant; but particularly so due to the constantly growing fleet of American yachtsmen and winter visitors now visiting those sunny tropical shores where we too have spent so many happy months during the last ten years—on ships great and small. Each one set down here is featured for mighty good reasons. Each guarantees its own unique and exotic taste experience. Some are old classics. If we have been able to discover something here and there which is new, or little known, we take joy in the fact.

IT IS of INTEREST to NOTE that FIVE EXOTIC COLD SEAFOOD COCKTAIL SAUCES, VARYING the TRITE THEME of KETCHUPS and CHILI SAUCES, MAY BE FOUND OUTLINED at some LENGTH under *HORS d'OEUVRE* on PAGE 29.

A NASSAU CURRY of CONCHS, that LOVELY & FLAVOURFUL SHELLFISH COMMON to the FLORIDA KEYS, the BAHAMAS & WEST INDIES, & already TOUCHED upon as an EXOTIC CHOWDER

Pound the white meat of 8 conchs until tender; cut into pieces 1" x 1½". Fry out 1 big mild minced onion in 2 tbsp fat, until tender and clear. Work 2 tsp curry powder into ½ cup rich milk, fresh or evapo rated. Add to onions, and also toss in bayleaf, pinch thyme, 4 cut up tomatoes. Everything goes into a big covered skillet or iron kettle and simmers in its own pleasant juices until conch tenders. Add a trifle of coconut milk or water from time to time, to keep fluid enough. Serve with freshly grated coconut kernel, slivers of smoked sailfish, smoked haddock or salmon—first flaked small and oven-dried. . . . After personal experience with this receipt we recommend cucumbers peeled and cut in ¾" cross-sections rather than the tomato, which spoils the typical curry appearance, and adds nothing typical of curries, either old or new. This dish nourishes six to eight.

SMOTHERED CONCH, *ERNEST HEMINGWAY*, as PREPARED by CARLOS then HEAD GAFFER on GOOD SHIP *PILAR*, while SAILFISHING off SOMBRERO LIGHT in the GULF STREAM; and WHICH FED SIX

This delicious Key West–Florida Keys favourite can easily be prepared in any deep heavy frying pan, dutch oven or kettle. Prepare 8 conchs as above, this time parboiling in a little water to tender, while preparing other ingredients. Fry out 6 slices fat salt pork with 2 medium sized sliced onions, 4 or 5 medium tomatoes cut in eighths, juice 1 small lime, 3 bayleaves and a dash or so of worcestershire. Drain off conch broth, reserving for future stiffeners; add 2 tbsp butter before covering tightly and smother slowly until tender. Add 2 tbsp sherry just before serving, and have oven-crisped pilot biscuit in quantity. One red pencil pod or red bird pepper is optional, but nice.

EULOGY to STONE CRABS, which ARE without DOUBT the REGAL EMPEROR of the WHOLE CRAB TRIBE, before DISCUSSING THEIR COOKERY

The Florida or West Indian Stone Crab is a big fellow growing rarer every hour due to merciless pursuit by market fishermen everywhere from Daytona southward to Cuba. In the old days market men kept only the larger claw, releasing the crab; now both claws are wanted, and the crab—instead of growing another mandible and meantime feeding himself one-handed, is a sacrifice to the nut-like delicacy of his own tender flesh. These stone crab claws are huge, a glorious colour scheme of pale cream yellow, scarlet touched as to pincers, and finally tipped in shiny jet black. The epicure's traditional way of eating stone crab is with drawn butter; cold with Hollandaise or with a simple French dressing made of salt, hand-ground black pepper, olive oil, a dash or 2 of Key West Old Lime Sour, and lime juice. We list an assorted array of drawn butters for this and other marine citizens which we've collected during our wanderings about the world—to vary the rather trite plain drawn butter we see everywhere.

TEN VARIATIONS of the ETERNAL DRAWN BUTTER THEME for CRABS, STEAMED CLAMS, CRAWFISH, LOBSTERS, PRAWNS, *LANGOSTAS* & *LANGOUSTES,* SHRIMPS & SUCH VARIED CITIZENS

To each One-Half Cup of Drawn Butter Add:

1 tbsp lime or lemon juice; 1 tbsp lime or lemon juice plus 1 tsp chili sauce; 1 tsp each lemon juice and scraped onion pulp; 10 capers

chopped very fine and 1 tsp caper vinegar; 1 tsp lemon or lime juice and same of freshly grated horseradish. . . . Add speck garlic to butter before melting, then discard the lily and add 2 tbsp walnut pickle liquor; work 1 tsp anchovy paste to cream with same amount of lime or lemon juice, adding cayenne; snip 1 tsp chives very fine with scissors and add same of lime or lemon juice; speck fresh garlic pulp and ½ tsp Key West Old Lime Sour, see Page 169; 1 tsp lime or lemon juice, oil twisted from curl of lime peel and dash tabasco. . . . These were culled from seven different countries.

In all cases whip up flavourings thoroughly with melted butter.

DEVILLED STONE—or MORRO—CRABS, *á ZARAGOZANA,* sometimes CALLED *CANGREJOS de MORRO, RELLEÑOS*

Now and again in travelling about we find that all fine native restaurants need not be in the basilicas of ancient churches nor in buildings once occupied by irregular royalty or Mme. Sarah Bernhardt. Now and again they are bright, new, frighteningly moderne as to chromium plate; but when there is a fine chef they are invariably crowded. Such is Zaragozana in the old city of Habana, where we were taken by a friend fourteen years in Cuba—and, *amigos,* what sea food! What red snappers; what *langostinos* and *langostas,* those slender graceful clawless lobsters of Cuba's rocky coast! . . . Although we eat only the claw meat of Stone or Morro Crab, in this case the shell—which affords so little meat in usual cases as to be unprofitable—is retained as a vessel for the fragrant receipt.

First rub empty shells of crabs boiled in sea, or salted, water, with cut garlic clove and olive oil, and set aside.

Next pick meat from claws and that easily salvaged from shells, but do not chop up fine; leave in reasonably large bits. To each cupful of meat allow: 2 tbsp lime juice, 1 tbsp chopped capers, 1 tsp onion pulp, plenty of tabasco or hand-ground black pepper to make hot; salt—then stand on ice.

Now for the extra stuffing. For each cupful meat allow: ¼ cup fine diced avocado pear pulp, *not too soft and ripe;* ¼ cup fine chopped mushrooms; ⅛ tsp dry mustard; 1 pinch each of mace and basil, well rubbed between palms; 1 tsp melted butter; ½ beaten egg yolk; 1 tbsp *Carta de Ora* Bacardi Rum; enough fine crumbs to mask, and a little olive oil.

Mix marinated crab meat thoroughly with this stuffing. Pack into shells. Cover with crumbs, moisten with olive oil and brown in medium oven around 350°. The avocado is the typical *Cubaño* touch. Heat breaks down pulp and rich nut-like flavour permeates the whole business. . . . Also wonderful for all other kinds of crabs, lobsters and crawfish. Should be seasoned highly, please remember.

PEPPERY STUFFED CRAB, *à la HOTEL des BAINS,* GUADELOUPE, FRENCH WEST INDIES, which CONFOUND THEIR MORE CONSERVATIVE AMERICAN COUSINS

Here on this volcanic double French Island we journeyed up into the high mountains where we found a charmingly seedy little French Hotel maintained by one M. Dole, who then—and we hope now—for bedroom, sitting room and verandah took tariff at one dollar twenty-five per day with red wine and meals. There was a ravishing view of green ex-volcanoes cooling their toes in blue sea; ancient casked rum was ten cents a noggin, and to top it off there were a trio of big square pools in varying depths and delicately framed between feathery bamboos and mahogany trees just above the place, where warm mineral spring water flowed perpetually. We had this crab with a slim waistless bottle of *Berncasteler Doktor* Moselle.

6 to 8 empty hard crab shells	1 cup milk, fresh or evaporated
1 small clove garlic, crushed	1 hot pepper; or 4 dashes tabasco
1 tbsp chives or shallots, chopped	Salt, to taste
2 tbsp butter, melted	2 tbsp strained lime juice
½ cup fine dry crumbs	Soft bread, several slices
1½ tbsp lean bacon, minced fine	3 dashes Angostura bitters

Meat from shells and claws

Figure two parts crab meat to one of soft bread. Moisten latter with milk and bitters mixed. Fry out garlic, shallots and pepper, with bacon. Mix everything thoroughly, stuff shells previously painted with olive oil. Cover with fine crumbs, dot with butter or olive oil, brown around 375° Fahrenheit. Seasoning is always to taste, of course; but should be very peppery.

A WORD on the VIRTUES, HABITS & CULINARY SUCCULENCE of the FLORIDA, or WEST INDIAN, CRAWFISH; also CUBAN *LANGOSTINOS*, & HAITIAN *LANGOUSTES*

The former is known also as "spiny lobster." It has no claws and frequents rocky holes along the coral reefs, and tidewater creeks under shelving banks or mangrove roots. They are plentiful from Bermuda southward through the whole vast sweep of the islands; while the smaller, tenderer, slenderer *langouste* tribe is found the world over. Both species are guiltless of claws, but are otherwise comparable to any usual lobster. Muscular tensile strength is determined by age, so choose smaller specimens, especially for broiling. Crawfish are much tenderer when broiled, grilled, or deep-fat fried as-is, and *not* boiled first.

EXPLODED OLD WIVES' TALE No. II, on the FALLACY of PLUNGING LOBSTERS, or for that MATTER *any* CRUSTACEAN, into BOILING WATER

We are glad to announce that what we, in our modest and fumbling way, found to be true twenty-five years ago when doing our own cooking on a canoe trip down the east coast of Florida, is now confirmed by none other than the incomparable Henri Charpentier—probably our greatest living chef, and luckily for America, long domiciled on these shores.

Never plunge, toss, slide or push lobsters or crawfish into boiling water. Sudden contact of fleshly tissue with this scalding bath sets up an aggravated and permanent case of rigour-mortis. Once-tender muscles toughen; tough muscles become adamant. . . . Rather take kettle filled with sea, or salted water—preferably with slight acidulation of vinegar or lemon juice—and gently lower the victim into it.

Lobsters, crawfish, crabs, *can not feel.* It is not cruel. The slowly mounting heat lulls them to rest, and they emerge rosily tender as they went in.

It's the same as making a stew. Hot or boiling water toughens meat fibres instantly.

WORDS to the WISE No. X, NOMINATING SEA WATER as PROPER FLUID for BOILING LOBSTERS & CRAWFISH, if THEY MUST BE BOILED

Lobster meat boiled in fresh water is relatively tasteless flesh; in plain salted water it is better, as salt permeates every fibre; but boiled from a start in *cold* sea water is best. Just enough salt, plus an impressive list of blessed chemicals such as iodine, which physicians, chirurgeons and such professional leeches assure us is beneficial to the human machine. . . . Most important of all is that salting is correct.

DEVILLED CRAWFISH or LOBSTER, *CAT CAY,* being an Excerpt from *MARMION'S* Log

This is another dish created by our Afro-Portuguese pilot, chef, and big fish gaffer, Jim Arañha—mentioned elsewhere in this volume. We weren't fishing tuna or marlin that day because Hemingway had gone to meet Grant Mason's very decorative wife on the Pan-American Airways Plane. We'd gone ashore to visit with Charlie Cook—or "Cookie"—Lou Wasey's major domo on that tiny island paradise on the west Bahama reef. Then we picked up a basket of crawfish by the sunken concrete ship, landed on Piicquet's Rocks to hunt sea bird nests while Jim concocted this chef d'oeuvre which would make Prunier's head chef blanch with envy!

Boil 4 medium crawfish; split shells and mince to ½" cubes, reserving shells. Scald 2 ripe tomatoes and skin. Take heavy iron pan or saucepan, melt 4 tbsp butter, add 1½ tbsp mild mustard, 1 tsp worcestershire, 2 bayleaves, juice 2 small limes, 4 tbsp chopped up mango chutney—Ah there's the touch, shipmates!—a scant handful of chopped peanuts. Add cut up tomatoes, crawfish; saute *very* slowly covered. Add a few bits soft bread, 2 tbsp sherry. Stuff the half shells, previously rubbed with garlic, with this savoury blend, and either brown under broiler as-is, or dust with Parma cheese, freshly grated, before doing so. We've never tasted anything better anywhere.

WORDS to the WISE No. XI, EMPHASIZING the CARDINAL SIN of MINCING LOBSTER or CRAWFISH too FINELY, & on the MERITS of BROILING UNBOILED, and DEEP-FAT FRYING UNBOILED

The delicate flavour of this sort of meat becomes dissipated and invaded with foreign tastes further than is good, when chopped very small. Cubes ½" thick and up to ¾" long—possibly longer—are best. . . . This applies to newburgs and all allied dish as well as Lobster *Thermidor, l'Americaine,* and as above.

If truly native taste is to be retained don't forget when broiling such specimens to broil raw, not after boiling away half the taste first in water! . . . This goes for all but the largest and toughest specimens. Split, brush with lime juice, rub with garlic, paint with olive oil, salt and put to coals. That's all.

When deep-fat frying, either crawfish or lobster retains its characteristic delicious flavour much better when not boiled first, and much flavour thus dissipated—see the duet of Batters, listed later in this Chapter.

Any Broiled Lobster is especially worthy when garnished with Dr. Kitchener's Piquante Sauce or *Cubaño* Green Sauce, listed under *Fishes* on Page 63; or the Devilling Spread, below.

CRAWFISH or LOBSTER, BROILED or GRILLED *en BROCHETTE,* a TASTY ROUTINE from the CHEF at CAFE de PARIS, across the little PLAZA from the CASINO, in MONTE CARLO, 1932

Cut lobster into ½" thick cross-sections if small; into cubes ½" x 1" x 1¼" if large. Marinate well moistened in liquid: ½ white wine, ½ olive oil, for an hour. Rub brochette with a trace of olive oil, with a garlic clove and arrange things in sequence: 1 small mushroom top, bit of lobster, bit of lean-fat smoked bacon or Virginia ham, and so on again—ending with a final mushroom. Brush with olive oil, grill over coals, dust with salt and cayenne. Put in platter, moisten with savoury butter. Fetch to table flaming from 1 tbsp pre-heated brandy, set alight.

ONE DUET of THOUGHT on the FRYING of CRUSTACEANS & FISH. CRAWFISH, or LOBSTER or SHRIMP or FISH, Is DELICIOUS FRIED in BATTER—RAW—of which THESE ARE TWO EXOTIC EXAMPLES: ONE from NAGASAKI, JAPAN, 1931; ONE from PORT ANTONIO, JAMAICA, 1933

The Japanese have always been magicians with frying delicate sea foods that adapt typical Japanese genius to suit western palates. They fry in peanut oil, sesame oil, or lard. We find olive oil best, due to its added flavour, with lard a close second. . . . To 1 cup good mayonnaise add 1 tsp very finely chopped chives or spring onion tops and a speck of crushed garlic, and mix well. To 2 cups crumbs, dry and fine, add 2 tbsp finely chopped roasted and blanched almonds or pistachio nuts. Dip lobster first in mayonnaise, then crumbs, then brown in deep fat at 370°.

The Port Antonio Batter: Having friends possessed of a plantation in the rainbow-garlanded, lush windward mountains, we came to know Port Antonio first in 1929, when yacht made harbour. . . . Sift 1 cup flour and 1 tsp salt in bowl. Now mix in 2 tbsp *finely* grated fresh coconut kernel, *not* the shredded dry kind which has all the flavour of cork life preserver filling. Make depression in top; work in slowly 4 egg yolks, well beaten, and 3 to 4 tbsp olive oil. Mix well; add a little warm milk until like thick cream. Stir in 1½ egg whites, *not* beaten. Dry seafood well, dip in batter, fry in deep fat at 370° also.

A PROPER DEVILLING SPREAD from the BRITISH ISLAND of JAMAICA, & which Is EXCELLENT on CRAWFISH, LOBSTER & ALL VARIETIES of SEAFOOD; both as a CONDIMENT & a SPREAD PAINTED on before the FINAL FEW MOMENTS of BROILING or GRILLING

To 1 tsp dry mustard and the same of worcestershire, add 1 tbsp drawn butter, 2 tbsp ketchup or chili sauce, 1 tsp scraped onion pulp, a speck of crushed garlic, the juice of 1 small lime and salt to taste. The final touch is 1 dash angostura. . . . Wonderful on big fish steaks like kingfish, swordfish and the like.

FROGS' LEGS, *à la PALAIS de la MÉDITERRANÉE,* which Is on the *PROMENADE des ANGLAIS,* in NICE

Contrary to many friends we have discovered a surprising number of delightful dishes in large well-lighted places as well as in musty 16th Century buildings all stuffed with history and mystery. Gould's incredible Palace-Casino is typical. We found a small friendly *bar-maitre* who knew Mood Indigo Cocktails; there was a girl with us who was very eager, very young, very near-sighted and very pretty. Her ankles were very pretty. The champagne was very cold; the frogs' legs—*Jambes des Grenouille*—were also very pretty. This should nourish eight guests to perfection.

2 lbs of frogs' legs, jointed;
2 doz legs, 1 doz pairs
6 finely chopped spring onions
¼ clove of crushed garlic
1 cup chopped button mushrooms
Salt and cayenne, to taste
4 oz butter
3 tbsp tart white wine
2 cups of good cream sauce
1 tbsp chopped parsley
2 bayleaves
2 tbsp sherry or Marsala wine

Dip frogs' legs in milk, dust with salt and cayenne, dip in a little flour. Heat butter, turn in onion, garlic and bayleaves, chopped mushrooms, and then brown frogs' legs to a delicate gold colour. Take them out and reserve on a hot plate. Add wine to saucepan, simmer up, poach frogs' legs 5 minutes longer. Put this cooking sauce through a sieve, after taking out the mushrooms. Stir into hot cream sauce and put mushrooms back again. Stir in the sherry or Marsala. Serve with sauce poured over frogs' legs, and dusted with chopped parsley for garnish.

OLD SCOTTISH SPICED LOBSTER, which Is an HONOURABLE & ANCIENT CLEIKUM CLUB RECEIPT from the TIME of MEG DODS

Meat of 2 boiled lobsters or crawfish, cut into slices, should be put into saucepan and browned lightly in 1 tbsp butter. Then put into 3 cups rich chicken broth or stock. Season with 3 tbsp walnut ketchup, or same amount pickled walnuts crushed with liquor to equal amount; 1/4 tsp worcestershire, 1/2 tsp each powdered clove, nutmeg and mace; salt and cayenne to taste. Now donate 2 tbsp tart red wine—an unusual thought—and simmer it all very slowly for 10 minutes. Serve on toasted and buttered trenchers of bread. . . . Personally we prefer white wine in seafood cookery, but when a Scotsman does anything there's probably a sound reason for it!

RAW OYSTERS after the BORDEAUX FASHION, or CHILLED OYSTERS with SIZZLING SMALL SAUSAGES

Just why this enticing and contradictory oyster feature hasn't become better known in the States is baffling. Not only is it a superb midnight snack, but makes a fine first course at dinner. Instead of cocktail sauce have a small very hot garlic-rubbed dish put in center of oysters on half shell, containing four sizzling hot tiny spiced sausages such as we call "cocktail" sausage. Garnish only with salt, cayenne, lemon. . . . *Voila!* Oysters cold as the poles, sausage hot as hades—and just watch the guests exclaim with favour!

EXPLODED OLD WIVES' TALES No. III, on the MAJOR SIN of WASHING ANY SORT of OYSTER out of SHELL

Next to scouring out a well-seasoned, fragrant salad bowl with hot water and soap, what could be worse than washing a fine raw oyster? Regardless of what dear old Aunt Besorah Fittich may say about germs and cleanliness—either eschew oysters entirely or else please let's not dissipate most of their delicate flavour down the drain!

WORDS to the WISE of DUAL IMPORT, BEING No. XII of the SERIES, on EATING ALL OYSTERS SUDDENLY from TIME of SHELLING, and NEVER FRAMING THEM on the FLAT SIDE of SHELL

Oysters shelled hours ago become anemic caricatures of themselves. If at all possible get them unopened in shell; serve either right from shell into pot—or on shell, chilled and fresh.

The man with soul so dead that he will bed down a neat self-respecting raw oyster on its convex, flat shell—thus permitting all the native liquor to waste itself in a welter of cracked ice, is an improperly adjusted citizen who might well be watched that he does not buy a red headed bride big purple hats, or put ice in vintage still champagne!

THE NORFOLK, VIRGINIA, OYSTER ROAST, *MARMION,* from a STORMBOUND WEEK SPENT aboard KETCH in NORFOLK, while a SIXTY MILE GALE WALKED PAST outside the CAPES

With downcast lash and delicately tinging cheek we submit this original dish as an exotic, generated from what to do with a bushel of unshucked oysters, five hungry shipmates and a good yacht stove! . . . Also half a dozen Smithfield Virginia hams swinging from the galley carlins, as we rocked at anchor in the tide-set, suggested trimmings. . . . First open oysters and save liquor, and, unless an adept, better leave this to the oysterman to save wrists and temper. Wash deep halves of shells, rub each with a touch of cut garlic clove, and center up with ¼ tsp scraped onion pulp. Put strained liquor—to avoid sand, gravel and other littoral addenda—in saucepan. To each cup add juice 2 limes or small lemon, double dash tabasco, and reduce by 1/3. Stir in 1 tbsp Virginia Dare Scuppernong Wine—made not too far away from where we were by our grand friend Paul Garrett—adding a little salt to taste. Thicken with a little flour and butter. Sauce should be thick, piquant. . . . Put oysters in half shells; mask with sauce, center with 2—¼" cubes of rosy Virginia ham. Pop under broiler until edges barely curl. Serve with Virginia Dare dry white wine, or Chablis.

WORDS to the WISE No. XIII, on the HARMONIOUS WEDDING of OYSTERS & Chablis

We can't say why, with all the fine dry white wines on earth,—and perhaps no one can say why—but really well chilled Chablis was simply intended for oysters in any form. It is limpid, delicately amber, suave, dry. But watch the year; '19, '21, '23, '26, or '28 are good. A poor Chablis is nothing, being both tartly sharp and of small rank or discretion.

OYSTER PAN-ROAST, *DIABLESSE,* from the LOG of FRITZ ABILDGAARD (ALONE in the CARIBBEAN) FENGER, SAILOR, AUTHOR, EXPLORER, RACONTEUR, NAVAL ARCHITECT & GOURMET

Fritz, whom thousands of Eastern yachtsmen know, not only sailed his tiny rudderless canoe *Yakaboo* right spang from Trinidad to the Virgins, alone and across wide and dusty tide channels, but along with mate—wife—and boatswain—son—spent some years on schooner *Diablesse*—both these voyages being set down in a pair of books *Alone in the Caribbean* and *The Cruise of the Diablesse,* which appear constantly in reprint. Fritz and ourselves have swapped lies, drinks, swizzles and food receipts for some years. His oyster pan-roast is a classic which has been copied but never equalled.

Shell oysters and put in bowl, saving deep halves of shell. Wipe these dry and rub with cut garlic clove. Take a tin pie plate, or other shallow oven dish; fill level with ice cream salt or other coarse salt. Press shells down in this bed. Put oyster in each. Melt out plenty butter, add a little worcestershire and lots of Harvey's sauce, to taste; salt and paprika for added colour. . . . Pour this basting over oysters, mask with fine buttered crumbs, and brown in hot oven until edges curl—around 400°. . . . Fenger's final advice is: "That rock salt does all sorts of good things coming through the garlic and all the rest, and just why God only knows. So don't skip it. Besides it keeps the oyster shells from capsizing in a seaway. Eat as fast as they come out of oven. Good chow!"

TORCH-BEARER OYSTERS, being a PRIZE RECEIPT of CERTAIN DISTINCTION which MAY not IDLY BE IGNORED, HERE or ANYWHERE

Three years or so ago Dorothea Duncan, Food Editor of the Washington *POST,* won herself a trip to Bermuda through invention of this thought, donated by the Oyster Institute of America through unanimous decision of its judges. . . . Now we do not know precisely just what the Oyster Institute of America is, or what interest they may have had—singularly or collectively—in the certainly brilliant lady Duncan. But we do know that her oyster conception is exotic enough to take position with all comers, far and near. We have noted it as a smart modern course for an amiably questing bachelor to serve, *à deux* and *chez lui,* with the electrics darkened and only the candles and the blue-blazing oysters borne to the table with ceremony and dignity befitting the occasion.

Allow 6 large or 8 small oysters to each person, and dry between towels. Oysters should be freshly opened. Next put in cocktail glasses set in cracked ice. Chill very cold. Next add a small amount of rum barely to cover: Bacardi 4 parts, Jamaica 1 part is good proportion. Set afire and bring in flaming. Garnish with quartered limes or lemons, not thinly sliced; salt, pepper, tabasco, or other flavours to taste. Too much doctoring, however, destroys the rum taste and aroma.

AN AL FRESCO DISH of UNSHELLED SHRIMPS, Browned in Brazilian Style from Rio de Janeiro

We have discovered that upon arrival in Brazil every North American is politely confronted with five circumstances by the native patriots: Brazil is larger than the continental United States, Rio has the loveliest harbour in the world, Brazil grows more coffee than any country in the world, the Amazon is the biggest river in the world, and the Brazilian ladies are the handsomest in the world. Much as we would like to discuss these matters we find that all—with possible exception of the gallant last—are strictly true.

Oddly enough, whereas the rest of South America claims to stem from Spanish discovery and settlement, Brazil is Portuguese. This shrimp dish too is Portuguese. Right today we can find the very same cooked shrimp in big baskets for sale in the streets of Lisbon or Oporto; to be eaten like popcorn on the spot, or while strolling down the avenue. It makes a rather hilarious dish to serve on a cruising yacht, on beach picnics, or when camping in shrimp territory. And, as with all crustaceans cooked in shell, we get a peculiarly delicate and satisfying native flavour retention which is lacking when they are boiled first. Rules for this dish: lots of room, plenty of paper napkins, a dish for discarded shells.

Serve heaped in a big wooden drugget, or basket; eat with fingers, discarding heads and tail shells; and of course the dark vein as well. Cook as follows: get as many shrimp as we estimate guests can eat, then 1/3 more. Have enough olive oil to fill our biggest frying pan, or deep fat kettle—and this once please don't use *any* other fat except olive oil. Heat oil to 370° Fahrenheit; chop 3 or 4 cloves of garlic and throw in with first batch of shrimp. Discard when dark brown, and renew with fresh garlic as needed to disburse flavour. When shrimp are redly done drain on paper towels, dust with salt and pepper; and there we have it.

CHINESE FRIED SHRIMP from Happily Renamed TAIWAN, in Formosa; Noted During Voyages there in 1931 & 1932

Shrimp dishes, especially deep-fried or in curries, are delicious all through the Far East—from Japan to Bombay. This dish is very simple, requires a touch of the garlic lily again which Henri Charpentier, the incomparable, lists as one of the cornerstones of fine cookery—but with no deleterious aftereffect we can assure you.

Soak 2 lbs of shelled *raw* shrimp tails in enough water to cover, to which has been added the juice of 2 limes or 1 lemon, and a sprinkling of salt. Make furrow with thumb-nail, and remove the dark sand-filled vein—*which should be done in cooking any larger shrimp: not needful with small ones.* Contrary to popular superstition this vein bears no harmful substance; merely samples of terra firma consumed with the little beastie's food. Marinate 1 hour. Drain and fry in a little very hot lard with ½ clove of garlic for 2 minutes. Add 1 cup tart white wine—like Chinese rice wine or *saki*—1 scant tbsp brown sugar, 1 tsp salt. When tender drain; and serve with a sauce made from this pan gravy diluted with equal amount of soya sauce. The sugar may be cut down slightly so as not to shock the American palate too much; also soya content may be reduced by half if guests do not admire its potent taste.

SHRIMPS DONE in KONA COAST of HAWAII STYLE

Here we offer a native dish from Kona Inn, near Kailua on the

"Big Island" of Hawaii, where big marlin swordfish, huge Pacific sailfish, and other large and violent fishes are sought after by American anglers with rods and reels. If there is a lovelier, more peacefully drowsy spot in all the world than the Kona Coast of Hawaii we have yet to find it. Made to order South Seas transplanted north of the Equator—blue water, wide beaches, rustling palms, delightful population.

Fry raw shrimp tails until very light golden red in a pan with butter, a speck of crushed garlic and a big onion sliced; salt and pepper to taste. . . . Now the sauce of coconuts. Grate kernel of 1 fresh coconut in its milk; simmer up 5 minutes gently, put whole business through cloth and squeeze out the rich cream at last. Add to pan along with 1 tbsp soya sauce per pan. . . . Drain shrimp, strain sauce and thicken with flour worked smooth. Put shrimp in buttered earthenware—or other—oven dish; mask with sauce and finally with grated white kernel of a second coconut. Brown delicately under broiler or in a very hot oven.

WORDS to the WISE No. XIV, a CREOLE CHEF'S THOUGHT on the SAVOURY BOILING of SHRIMPS

New Orleans, France and the Far East; and possibly Charleston—there we find shrimps vital and important items of food, deliciously prepared not just fried, or boiled and dumped into a cocktail glass with a dab of warm ketchup. . . . Creole chefs contend seasoning must go in first *while cooking,* not applied to the surface of flesh afterwards when it is too late to penetrate the fibres. . . . Salt water stoutly and to 1 qt add: 2 bayleaves, 6 whole cloves, ¼ tsp tabasco or small hot pod pepper, 2 coarse chopped celery stalks, 1 pinch each thyme and basil; ¼ to ½ clove garlic—optional and to taste. . . . Note the changed expression of guests when this routine produces a shrimp cocktail, or boiled shrimp for any purpose.

A *PULAO* of SHRIMPS, or PIECES of TENDER FISH, which WE FOUND JOURNEYING from the GULF of MANAAR, on the NORTH COAST of CEYLON in 1926

The cookery of southern India, Ceylon, and the Malay Peninsula, sometimes is much milder than the torrid eye-watering curries of Bengal and the Punjab country. This receipt asks for several ingredients but all of them are easily found, so try not to skip any!

To 4 cups raw shrimp allow a boiling medium consisting of milk from 2 coconuts, in which grated kernel has been simmered 10 minutes then strained through a cloth; finally squeezing rich milk out from kernel. Add juice 1 green lime, a little salt, ¼ clove garlic. Simmer shrimp until red, drain; break off tails and shell, and remove the dark vein in the tail. Crush heads and shells and put in a sieve; pour shrimp water through several times to collect richness.

Now melt 1 cup of butter in a saucepan and fry out 3 big mild onions until golden and tender. Add ¼ cup chopped blanched almonds, ½ tsp ground cinnamon, same of mace, ¼ tsp powdered ginger, ½ cup raisins, 1 tsp curry powder, 1½ tsp whole peppercorns and salt to taste, and the cooked shrimp. While this is cooking slowly, covered, put 1 cup thoroughly washed rice—Patna type preferred due to its solid blunter grain—into the shrimp stock. When almost tender add ¼ to ½ tsp saffron, purchasable at all good grocery or drug stores. . . . Turn shrimp and trimmings onto a hot platter. Cover with rice, which has meantime absorbed all the delicious coconut-shrimp stock. Serve grated fresh coconut, grated dry smoked fish or Bombay duck, and chutney for side dishes to be passed to each guest.

CONSIDER SHRIMPS HAPPILY MARRIED with CHOPPED HAZEL NUTS, & OUR OWN PRIVATE TASTE DISCOVERY in COOKERY: FRENCH VERMOUTH of the DRY TYPE

This receipt may be varied by using chopped almonds, pistachios, piñons, or pecans. It is quick and easy, and very flavourful. . . . Fry 1 lb fresh shrimp tails that have been marinated 2 hours in ½ cup of blended lemon juice and olive oil, in 3 tbsp butter, along with ½ clove garlic. Reserve this marinade. When done, discard garlic. Put shrimps on a hot dish. Add ½ cup finely chopped nuts to hot butter in the pan; add lemon-oil marinade, perhaps adding more lemon juice to tart taste. Now 2 dashes tabasco and 1½ to 2 tbsp dry French vermouth.

Simmer 5 minutes and turn over shrimp. We've added 2 tbsp tomato paste with good results, on occasion.

BROILED TURTLE STEAKS, *á ISLA de PIÑOS,* Being a Receipt from an American Pineapple Planter in Estates there before Our Government Returned the Island to Cuba

Steaks may be from green, hawkbill or loggerhead turtles, but not too thick or too aged—½" to ¾" thickness is correct. Rub with cut lime vigorously so as to get oil from peel into steak, rub with a cut clove of garlic, sprinkle with salt and let stand in squeezed juice of lime for 1 hour. Brush with lots of olive oil and broil like any steak over coals or under broiler, seasoning to taste.

SMOTHERED TURTLE in the MISSISSIPPI *CAJUN* STYLE, a Luscious, Easy Classic from the Vast Delta Country

The Cajuns are strange people, a blend of Portuguese, Indian, and heaven only knows what else. They fish, shrimp, trap fur in the maze of bayous and marshes of the big Delta. Priests wade into the water and bless their shrimp boats at start of season. They know how to cook turtles. Our only recommended addition is a small can of chopped button mushrooms.

Trim 2 lbs steaks into 1½" squares, season well with salt and hand-ground black pepper, squeeze on some lemon or sour orange juice and stand a while. Add plenty of chopped onion, a sweet pepper chopped well, 3 or 4 tomatoes cut into eighths, 3 bayleaves, a crushed garlic clove, and mushrooms. . . . Moisten well with stock made by boiling salted turtle trimmings, and smother very slowly in tightly covered skillet until turtle is tender. Serve with big mounds of rice. This will nourish 4 hungry folk.

A NATIVE TURTLE SOUP from MEXICO, Gulf of Campeche Style; and a Kindred Dish, which Is Actually a Stew of Fresh Water Turtles Done In their own Shells, & Known as *CALIPASH* by Our Afro-American Plantations, Will Be Found on Page 45, under *SOUPS*

ARCHBISHOP ALFRIC: "And what, Good Cook, is thy Profession worth to the Community?"
COOK: "Holiness, without me all People would have to Eat both Greens & Flesh Raw."
ARCHBISHOP ALFRIC: "But might not they Readily Dress such Viands Themselves?"
COOK: "Ah yes, Holiness, but in Such Case all Men would be Reduced to the Role of Servant."

Literal Version from *Archbishop Alfric's COLLOQUY,*
England, 10th Century

CHAPTER VI

POULTRY & *THE* INNER DRESSINGS *OF* FOWLS

Dealing Briefly with Ducks, Geese and Turkeys, but Being Concerned mainly with Chickens; Remembering *Rijstafel,* which Is in Reality a Lordly Curry Ceremony from Lovely Java, *Arroz con Pollo* from Panama, the *Small Water Angels of Soochow;* Tortola Chicken Baked in Coconuts, a Louisiana Jambalaya, not Forgetting a Guadeloupe Dish Called *Poulet aux Pistaches de Terre et Bananes, à la Morne sans Toucher.*

DURING all our collection of poultry receipts we long ago decided not to enter into the technique of frying, roasting and the like, but try, rather, to offer a totally new list of dishes; each notable for this special reason or that, and all possible anywhere within reach of a decent grocery store.

Ducks, geese and turkeys are touched upon very lightly and that part of the text is devoted mainly to a few pertinent words of cooking technique, on bastings or sauces that have delighted us in times past. Guineas and pigeons we feel, have always felt in fact, are more correctly game than tame barnyard fowl, and for that reason are treated in the GAME Chapter following.

Those receipts immediately following this paragraph all possess some marked nuance of flavour, a touch of herb, of fruit, a certain basting, this or that seasoning, completely elevating them above an everyday question of cooking in frying pan, on grill, or in oven. Seasoning, as always, may be varied from mild into the very torrid classification, to suit individual taste and digestive apparatus; therefore we suggest that the amateur approach each dish still fired with a spirit of adventure and vary the overtones to harmonize with mood and larder. Our one bit of advice in poultry cookery of the usual sort is to remind readers that the usual fault is dryness. Therefore in roasting or grilling, brush well with fat, baste diligently. All items about to be fried should be blotted or wiped dry in order to avoid those miniature and painful volcanic eruptions of hot fat caused by water drops exploding into steam.

All items to be boiled should be started in cold water, simmered gently; and bear in mind that if they are boiled *beyond* the point of being tender they will be stringy, sodden and lack flavour.

If broilers have passed the adolescent and tender birthday usually associated with such cookery, a few moments of gentle steaming will work wonders, before putting into the fat.

ARROZ con POLLO, the OLD TRADITIONAL "RICE with CHICKEN," NOTED in the UNION CLUB, PANAMA CITY, during ONE of OUR DOZEN or so TRIPS to the ISTHMUS

Cristobal on the Atlantic and Balboa on the Pacific—those are the model towns under Uncle Sam's jurisdiction in the "Zone," and they lie like neat, prim, starched maidens, cheek-by-jowl with the modern evolution of the civilization left by the Conquistadores for better or for worse in Colon and Panama City. There in Old Panama the ruined cathedral tower points up an accusing finger denouncing its sack and burning by Morgan's men. Culture and lotteries, courtly Spanish girls with big gazelle eyes whisk by in shiny motor cars and guarded closely by their duennas; while a block away is the so-called Coconut Grove section with ladies of all nations behind their grilled windows. . . . In the Union Club, perched high on stilts above the huge Pacific tides is where the cream of Panamanian society gathers. They have a good chef there. His *Arroz con Pollo,* although basically still the old favourite from Spain, has local and tropical touches. It will nourish from four to six guests.

2 plump chickens of tender years
6 thin slices dead ripe pineapple
2 tbsp lime or lemon juice
½ cup fine bread crumbs
1 tsp, scant, of tabasco sauce
Salt and pepper, to taste
2 pinches saffron
4 to 5 cups of Spanish rice
½ cup raisins or currants
4 tbsp tomato paste
1 orange, sliced quite thin
1 cup butter
½ cup sherry wine
½ cup guava jelly for garnish

Cut chicken into pieces, brush with lime juice, season with salt and pepper; let marinate in this lime juice and seasoning both for 2 hrs to seal in flavours. Now fry gently in butter, and when tender add tomato paste, raisins, wine and other seasonings. Stir once, cover tightly and keep warm but do *not* cook again. . . . On a large hot platter make a ring of Spanish Saffron Rice, and in the center of this pleasant atoll pile the chicken. Turn sauce over chicken also. Meanwhile cut up ripe fresh pineapple slices into 1" square bits and fry out for 5 minutes with the crumbs—using canned fruit if no really ripe fresh ones at hand; but discard the juice entirely. Turn this over the chicken, garnish with thin slices of orange, mounting a crimson jewel of guava jelly on each slice. . . . Scarlet pimento also garnishes well.

TO MAKE SPANISH SAFFRON RICE

Take 1 cup rice; pick out any dark grains or foreign substances, but do not wash. Put 2 tbsp olive oil in the top of a double boiler, place directly on a slow fire and gently fry out 1 finely minced onion with half a bisected garlic clove. When tender, discard garlic, turn in the cup of rice, ¼ tsp saffron, ½ tsp salt. Stir well and add just enough beef or chicken broth to cover. Cook uncovered in a double boiler until tender, adding more broth as needed. Stir gently with a *wooden* fork to keep from breaking grains. When tender, turn into a shallow pan and dry in a *warm*—not hot—oven. Rice should be quite dry.

CHICKEN BAKED with PLUMPED RAISINS, VARYING NUTS, WINE & LIMES, *á GUATEMALTECAN*

We collected this one in hauntingly beautiful *Antigua Vieja,* set like a neglected white gem 7000 feet up in the Guatemalan mountains, when we and our then recent bride were making pilgrimage down the west coast of Mexico and Central America. There in Antigua we found an amazing half deserted city of broken marble and stone and stucco, cracked and rent palaces and churches, huge crumbling dwellings of long-dead Spanish aristocrats, all stricken by the earthquake of 1773. The whole place was like a city under a spell, most buildings being inhabited by Indian families; sometimes with several packed in a wing, in a single room, of a house; and cooking fires blackening wonderful frescoes, or a carved white marble frieze! Once the richest city in the New World, in all this strange contrast we found a hushed and tragic charm brooding over the place, with the volcanic peaks of *Agua* and *Fuego* soaring a mile higher still, back of the place, from whence the fire and boiling water came to smother Antigua over a century and a half ago. But a few good Spanish names still carry on gallantly. We have a German acquaintance who operates a small inn, in what was once the cloister of a nunnery. He knows these people well. This dish came from his place; a memory of a luxurious and by-gone era.

2 plump young chickens	2 limes sliced very thin
1/3 cup chopped blanched almonds	3 large onions, sliced thin
1 sweet pepper chopped fine	1 doz large stuffed olives, sliced
1 cup butter	½ cup raisins or currants
3" piece cinnamon bark; 2 bay-leaves	Enough bread crumbs to stuff
1 dash Angostura bitters	Salt and pepper to taste
	½ cup sherry or Madeira wine

Wipe chickens inside and out, then stuff with the mixed raisins, onions and chopped pepper—this last peeled by scalding, and seeds removed. Season highly and add enough bread crumbs to fill the cavities. Sew up neatly, brush the birds with a little lime juice, dust with salt and pepper, and brown lightly in a pan of hot butter. . . . The next step is to cover the bottom of a buttered oven dish with sliced limes, add two dashes or so of Angostura; then come the successive layers of almonds, coarsely sliced almond-stuffed olives—or ripe olives—then the stick of cinnamon broken into bits, 2 bayleaves, and finally the chickens. Put in all the frying butter. . . . Cover tightly and roast these comely twins in this fragrant atmosphere very slowly until tender, at around 275°. A few minutes before taking out remove the cover, sprinkle on the wine. Peanuts, Brazil or cashew nuts, all lend distinctive variations to this dish. Chop them up coarsely.

SIZEABLE OLIVES STUFFED with CHOPPED BREASTS of CHICKEN, a TRIFLE of HAM, NUTMEGS, PARMA or ROMAN CHEESE, a TOUCH of SWEET WINE, then FRIED in BATTER in DEEP FAT

Whenever we get to Naples we always look up Pat Marighliano about sundown, when his job as head guide for American Express finds him weary and ready for food and rest. Then Pat searches out odd spots unknown to outlanders, where red mullets are cooked in mysterious ways, and shrimps, and succulent bits of cuttlefish deep-fried in boiling oil—all washed down with white dry Pomino wine from Tuscany, and then when we are full and tobacco comes out, there is always an old Italian with what was once a glorious tenor, perhaps in La Scala, and a guitar for him to sing by. And Pat orders tiny glasses for both of us and we take green Certoza in the hawk's-foot-and-ball pottery bottle, and he always gets blood red Alchermes, which is a cordial compounded for objects problematical but charming to our naive mind, and which embraces—among other things—spices like cinnamon, clove, and coriander, and perfumed with jasmine, or rose essence, or iris. And alcohol too, of course, in strength enough.

Then sometimes before we eat, the Madonna of the house fetches in a small basket to keep us busy while the kitchen affairs progress, and once in a basket we found these fried stuffed olives, which would make a delicious relief from the eternal pigs-in-blankets our hostesses seem to have lurking on every hors d'oeuvre tray these days! Better allow 6 olives for each guest present.

Cooked chicken white meat & ham to fill, both minced very finely
12 huge stoned Spanish olives
3 pinches grated nutmeg
2 tsp butter
1½ tsp freshly grated Parma cheese
1 beaten yolk to bind stuffing
Salt and pepper, to taste
Enough simple frying batter to cover

Take cooked chicken and lean smoked ham in these proportions: 2 parts chicken to 1 of ham. Mix well, season, and brown lightly in butter; add the nutmeg. Draw off fire and let cool. Now mix in beaten yolk, pack tightly in olive jackets, cap with grated cheese, dip in batter and brown in deep fat at 370°—olive oil being traditional, of course. Drain on paper or cloth. Serve sizzling hot.

THE LOUISIANA *CALALOU*, which Is Strictly a Catch-All Dish Inherited from West Africa through the Plantation Cooks of the Great Delta Country, Has Been Listed in a Succeeding Chapter under *MEAT DISHES both TEMPERATE & TROPICAL*, Page 143.

A GUADELOUPE DISH of JUVENILE FOWLS, Cooked *en CASSEROLE* with Bananas, Herbs, a Little Wine, Coconut Milk & Chopped Peanuts, & which Was Called: *POULET aux PISTACHES de TERRE et BANANES, à la MORNE sans TOUCHER*

Lovely Guadeloupe has been discussed elsewhere in this volume, also the place of the little Frenchman by the warm mineral springs far back in the hills out of Point à Pitre. In Guadeloupe as well as in Haiti, a *Morne* indicates a high mountain, for all high mountains in the tropics—especially with trade winds blowing—mean very prevalent fog or wind-cloud, hence the title "Gloomy."

This dish is very simple, and all ingredients are at the corner grocery in these days of enlightened cookery. . . . The basic requirement is for 2 fowls of discretionary and tender years, and plump as may be. Cut them into 4 major parts, each; brush with the juice of 2 limes, or 1 lemon, dust with salt and pepper, and brown delicately in

¼ lb butter. Now add 3 tbsp finely chopped smoked bacon or ham, 2 tbsp chopped spring onion, 1 tiny red podded hot pepper, or 3 dashes tabasco, 4 bayleaves and ¼ tsp each of thyme and basil. About ½ cup sweet white wine comes next, the pot is covered, and set on a slow fire.

Now take a ripe husked coconut, puncture 2 of the "eyes" and reserve the milk. Crack open the nut, grate the white part of the kernel, add to the milk and simmer 5 or 10 minutes. Drain through a cheesecloth, wringing at the last to extract the rich creamy juice. Add this to the cooking pot, and recover. Cut up 3 red bananas, or yellow, and along with ¼ cup of chopped roasted peanuts, impart their gifts to the steaming delight. Simmer very gently until chickens are tender, adding a bit of water, wine or chicken broth, if it seems to dry out too much. Serve steaming hot, garnish with snipped parsley, and offer barley as a companion dish, or boiled rice.

JAMBALAYA, LOUISIANA BAYOU STYLE, & DONE with CHICKEN

This famous creole dish comes down to us from mixed Spanish-French parentage, seasoned and tempered by the Afro-American Parish plantation cooks of the Delta, or among the bayous where they raised sugar cane, rich black Perique tobacco that comes from no other spot on earth, rice, or tabasco peppers. This particular formula is from the notebook of a friend now living and writing on Royal Street in a lovely ancient house down in the old French quarter.

Like a *Calalou, Jambalaya* may be varied with the meats and vegetables on shelf; veal or tender lamb may substitute for chicken; but rice must always be included, and piquant seasonings are traditional. This dish will serve six guests.

Take 2½ cups of minced chicken and 1½ cups of boiled rice which is not quite done. Mix together in saucepan and reserve. Fry out gently 1 big minced onion, a tiny speck of crushed garlic, 1 cup sliced okra—optional—2 cups of skin-free cooked tomato, 1 chopped green pepper, 1 small head of chopped celery, and 1 bunch of snipped parsley, in 2 tbsp lard or butter. When onion colours slightly, mix with chicken—rice; add 3 dashes tabasco and ¼ tsp ground mace.

Butter a pottery oven dish well, turn everything into it, cover with lots of bread crumbs fried a couple of minutes in 1 tbsp of butter, and brown in medium oven around 350°.

THE TRUE EAST INDIAN *MULLIGATAWNY,* which MORE OFTEN IS ACTUALLY a STEW & NOT a SOUP; which IS a CURRY, yet NOT STRICTLY a CURRY; & IS MADE of FOWLS, COCONUT MILK, HERBS, CURRY & LENTILS

We picked this up on our first trip out to India, and we guarantee it to produce the finest mid-afternoon siesta imaginable. Out at the bungalow at Juhu Beach, 14 miles above Bombay, where the Arabian Sea bathes tawny level sand wide enough for morning polo games, it was a great Sunday favourite. For 4:

Joint 1 chicken and cut into small pieces. Heat ⅛ lb butter and lightly brown 2 medium sized minced onions, and ½ clove crushed garlic, until they are golden brown—then discard the more potent lily, if so desired; your Indian cook always leaves it in! . . . Mix 1 tbsp curry powder with 1 tsp salt, then work smooth with a little of the hot butter, and add to onions. Brown chicken in butter drained off the onions, reserve edible meat, and put rack and all bones into a good sized kettle. Add onions to this, and the enriched milk of a coconut as described in second receipt before this one. Put on slow fire, add 2 bayleaves, the lentils previously soaked overnight in cold water, lots of black and cayenne pepper until quite hot, add 2 cups chicken broth or stock. Simmer for 1 hour, remove chicken racks, gristle and bits of skin, cook uncovered until soup-sauce is thick as heavy cream. Squeeze in the juice of 1 lime or ½ lemon, put the meat back. Simmer up once more and serve with a side dish of rice prepared in the true Oriental fashion noted on Page 96 under *Rijstafel.*

POLLO MOLÉ en PIPIÁN, à la RESTAURANT PAOLO, BEING an IMPORTANT MEXICAN DISH of DEBUTANTE FOWLS, PIÑON NUTS or BLANCHED ALMONDS, PEANUTS, SWEET PEPPERS & SOUR CREAM, to SAY NOTHING of GRATED ORANGE PEELS & SPICE

Here is another dish that beckons to the pleasant depravity of the siesta, after *almuerzo*—the heavy Mexican noon meal—during or, rather, after which our right-minded citizen down there avoids all outdoor exercises, sunlight, and extra-mural distraction of every species. It may come as a surprise to readers that in Mexico City the best Mexican cookery is not to be found in public restaurants, or hotels or night clubs, but right in the homes of local citizenry. After midnight, for instance, there isn't a decent bite to eat to be found. Gentlemen and ladies are supposed to get home at sane hours. Butch's—an enormous place, once a marble galleried bank and now a restaurant run by an American negro—offers good ordinary food; some of the hotels are good enough in the same way that average American hotels are good, but only Restaurant Paolo in that huge city of a million folk affords truly fine cookery—and that had to be produced by an Italian, as far as we could learn! Here we found lovely *Mexicano* food with European tendencies, beautifully prepared and beautifully expensive. This one was retained for your approval. It is very similar to the various legion of Mexican *Molé* dishes, but contains only the simple sweet bell pepper as we know it.

Pipián is actually a flour made of toasted squash seeds, and used for thickening sauces. Our secret is to say nothing and use cornstarch. Not even the oldest Mexican gourmet can tell the difference! . . . Start the chicken simmering in slightly salted water, with 2 bayleaves. Cover tightly. When tender cut into small joints, discarding rack; reserve stock. . . . Now mince a medium sized onion, 2 tomatoes, 4 sweet peppers and 2 cloves of garlic. Add 2 tbsp chile powder. Fry until tender in 2 tbsp olive oil, lard or butter.

We need 1½ pints of chicken stock, so if not enough on hand add a little canned broth. Add this stock to vegetables, put in ¼ cup sour cream, and also donate a speck of bitter chocolate the size of a thumbnail, 2 pinches each of clove and nutmeg, plenty of black pepper, 2 small red pod peppers, or equivalent tabasco; add 1/3 of the finely chopped nuts, and grated yellow peel of an orange. Simmer 20 minutes, mix 2 to 3 tbsp cornstarch with a little hot broth, work out lumps and stir in. Simmer until reduced by ¼, put in The Blender or rub through a coarse sieve, put chicken back; simmer up once more and serve. This *Molé* sauce must be rich and thick.

A *PILAFF* of CHICKEN LIVERS, *à la Turc,* BEING a SIMPLE *PILAFF* CHARACTERISTIC of the NEAR EAST, and FOUND in the KING DAVID HOTEL, in JERUSALEM, shortly after NEW YEARS in 1931

There are as many kinds of *Pilaff* or *Pilaw* in Turkey and Persia as there are *Pulaos* in India, or Spaghettis in Italy! This is typical. Make a ring of Saffron Rice, similar to that mentioned on Page 87 under *Arroz con Pollo,* and into the center heap a saute made out of chicken livers, a handful of chopped ripe olives, a similar amount of cubed eggplant, a pimento, chopped cooked mushrooms. A touch of curry is optional, but we find that even better still is to add 2 tbsp sherry wine—which Mohammed the Prophet doesn't approve of!

POLLO PIÑA, BEING a DISH of CHICKENS SMOTHERED with RIPE PINEAPPLE PULP, LIME PEEL, BROWN SUGAR, a SLIGHT GIFT of BACARDI RUM, & other AMIABILITIES

We have a schoolmate now "in sugar" with one of the big *centrales* in Camagüey Province, Cuba. He reports this dish may be made with 2 cups of canned pineapple pulp, but best results come from picking a fresh fruit as ripe as possible—standing in direct sunlight until quite soft. It will serve from 4 to 6 hungry guests. Bacardi flavour in cooking is mild, and any brown rum may be substituted.

Have 2 broilers cut into quarters, wipe dry, brush with lime juice, dust with salt and pepper, then flour; finally browning gently in 2 tbsp butter with cover tightly on pan. . . . When tender turn in 1 medium sized minced onion, 3 tbsp currants, peel of 2 limes grated, 1 tsp brown sugar, 2 average sized tomatoes rubbed through a coarse sieve, salt and pepper to taste. Crush up the pineapple in a mortar or bowl; or cut up, add enough juice to cover blades, and reduce to pulp and stir in. Simmer until reduced by 1/4, put in The Blender or rub then add 3 tbsp *Carta de Oro* Bacardi, or 2 tbsp brown rum. Saffron Rice is the best possible side dish.

NOW a TRUE BOMBAY *PULAO,* which Is a Stew Dish Made of Chickens, Spices, Herbs, Raisins, Rice & other Things—Being Similar to Many Spanish or Mexican Dishes, yet Subtly Different

This name is derived from the Persian *Pilaw,* and it is mother to the term "Purlo," or "Purloo," that to our southern darky cook means chicken cooked with rice-and-things. At first glance it may seem to parallel tropical Americana recently listed here, but in actual result it is not so hot in pepper content, but somewhat higher in spice. Raisins, as is the case in Spain and Latin America, are typical additions to meat throughout the Near East and East, and it more than likely was Spain's luck to inherit their use via the Moorish conquest of the Iberian Peninsula. . . . This dish was cooked for us by the Mohammedan Head Bearer of a friend living in Bombay, after return from a hunt away back in the Mahratti hill country.

Mature fowls may be used, but be sure they are plump and fat. First set chicken to simmer in lightly salted water, just enough to cover, and when tender cut into joints, discarding racks. Cut up giblets and add to chicken. Now heat ½ lb butter and lightly brown 3 big thinly sliced onions; add 2 tbsp raisins, 5 or 6 whole cloves, 3 tbsp chopped almonds, ⅛ tsp powdered ginger, ¼ tsp mace, 6 whole peppercorns, ½ tsp cinnamon, and 1 crushed clove of garlic. . . . Turn in ¾ cup dry rice, and the stock from cooking chicken. Cover tightly, do not stir or rice grains will break; and lastly be careful to keep at low heat so as not to burn. Just before rice is tender all through take a little broth and simmer it with 2 pinches saffron, and add to *Pulao* for typical colour. A trifling amount of curry is proper, but not imperative. Personally we prefer to ignore it in the dish.

WORDS to the WISE No. XV, Being a ÇANNY MOHAMMEDAN BIT of ADVICE from HEAD BEARER ALI SIDDIQ, *PULAO* CHEF *par EXCELLENCE,* on WHEN & HOW to CUT up CHICKEN for SUCH DISHES

If we cut up chicken before boiling down for stock and to tender, the flesh falls to shreds too quickly. If we attempt to cut up after the dish is done, the flesh gets torn to bits. Therefore cut chicken into as small bits as possible directly after being first tendered, and it is removed from the stock pot. Always use a keen knife for this operation.

NOW a FEW NOTES on that SUPER CURRY KNOWN as *RIJSTAFEL* in the DUTCH EAST INDIES, & MORE PARTICULARLY in JAVA where IT REACHES ITS MAJESTIC PINNACLE, in CLUBS like the FAMOUS *CONCORDIA* on *WATERLOOPLEIN*, the *HARMONIE;* in HOMES of DUTCH OFFICIALS and COMMERCIAL PRINCES, in HOTELS such as the *DES INDES* & the *NEDERLANDEN*

This dish is a classic everywhere throughout Holland's far-flung island empire of the East Indies. Literally translated it means "rice table," but that explanation is only half truth because a true *Rijstafel* is one of those inconceivable things which must be seen to be credited. These stout Hollanders are probably the only European nationals who can thus stuff themselves frequently in a climate like an orchid house, and live. Yet they do, and thrive on it.

Our first sight of this business was in 1932. We had chartered a plane for ourself, and with Ruth Elder, another charming young lady who was then our fiancée, her mother, and other adventurous souls, had set out to fly as near to Bali as we could get from Batavia by the Koninklijke Nederlandsche Indische Luchtvaart Maatschappij plane —ending up in Soerabaja after a look-see at the startling stupa of gigantic Boeroboedoer outside of Semarang. At the *Oranje* in Soerabaja we met up with a gray haired septuagenarian named Whitney, as we now recall it, who built bridges for profit and was then retired. His hobby was catching fish—anywhere and everywhere. He had just popped up from landing big rainbow trout in the mountain torrents of New Zealand, to dangle his baits before the suspicious snouts of some odd sort of fish or other he had recently heard tore tackle apart away up the Barito River in Borneo, and having caught them to heart's content, was now taking the "pig boat"—really an immaculate little KPM steamer—to Bali where there was a fantastic tale about fantastic fish lurking in the steel blue crater lake nestling at the foot of the sulphurously active lava cone of *Goenung Batoer* at *Kintimani*.

We saw him later and found those furious fish were a species of catfish—but that is another story! anyway, we happened to be looking at a table of a dozen Hollanders wondering how in heaven's name they could stand such tropical heat in their high tight military collars, when from the kitchen door came a winding queue of some fourteen or fifteen barefoot boys, in brown patterned batik sarongs and head kerchiefs, each bearing some sort of ceremonial dish. "Ah! A *Rijstafel!*" cried our fishing gentleman. "You should see one the Dutch Governor gave for the Sultan of Djokjakarta. There were fifty-five boys in line!"

We watched, fascinated. All twelve Hollanders sat up straight and serious. Hollanders are not a dour race, as so many writers have falsely written. They are a gay, jolly and even boisterous race—but, by thunder, eating proper *rijstafel* is a serious affair to be treated seriously and respectfully!

RIJSTAFEL ROUTINE for an AVERAGE SERVICE of DUTCH CURRY

First the Number One boy appears with a big platter or bowl heaped with more and whiter rice than we dream can be piled on any one platter. . . . Each guest heaps his plate with a bigger heap than we dream any mortal can consume at a sitting. This milestone reached, conversation resumes, and the gentlemen resume sipping de Kuyper *schnapps,* gin slings perhaps, but more likely they will consume endless big sweating brown quart bottles of Amstel beer to lay the dust and cool the pipes before its torrid attack so imminently present.

After the Number One comes the file of boys, looking like an American college snake dance, only come bearing gifts in platters; and at their head proudly stalks the Number Two, bearing as his appointed duty a big bowl holding vast tonnage of chicken curry still steaming in its own perfumed juices. Each guest makes a crater in his mountain of rice and heaps it brimming full of curry, spreading the sauce evenly over the rice.

Now the condiments, which vary from several kinds of chutney to small ground up forcemeat balls of deceased piscatorial citizens whose demise—judging from their scent—must have been sometime in the fairly remote past, and which the average westerner can't stare down —met eye to eye. For this reason we list only those condiments and trimmings easily had from the corner grocery, or at most through a letter to some large-town fine grocery in New York, Chicago or San Francisco.

1. Mango chutney of 2 kinds, hot and hotter. Both Indian types.
2. Bombay Duck, which is no duck at all, but a small dried fish peculiar to the Malabar Coast of India. This is usually broken up small and spread on the curry, or munched—as the guest wills.
3. Finely shredded smoked codfish, bought in fillets, toasted crisp in the oven, boned and broken fine.
4. Small bits of diced eggplant, fried in oil and highly seasoned, to taste.
5. Chopped hardboiled egg, both yolk and white together.
6. Plain freshly grated ripe coconut kernel—*not* the shredded, tasteless species Aunt Clutie-Belle uses on her birthday cakes.
7. Finely chopped orange peel, yellow part only.
8. Finely chopped pomelo, or grapefruit, peel; yellow part only.
9. Finely chopped mild onion.
10. Finely chopped sweet green pepper.
11. Shredded, sun-ripe pineapple. Buy one as ripe as possible, then put in full sun until soft as can be without inviting decayed or spoiled spots in outer shell. Slice lengthwise after peeling, cut into eighths, then remove all tough portions, using only ripe, softer pulp.
12. Chopped blanched nuts: cashews, almonds or peanuts; roasted almost black.
13. Small plumped raisins or currants. Scald to plump.
14. Fried ripe bananas, cut in cross slices, and dusted with brown sugar, clove and cinnamon.

This, now, will give us a fair sized *Rijstafel* curry. There is no East Indian Emily Post to worry about manners or technique with these trimmings. Most folk spread everything evenly over rice and curry on the plate, then mix the entire outlay with a sort of mortar-spading motion using fork, or knife, or both.

Guests may ignore certain condiments; others take all, and in varying amount. Some of these items may appear strange, if not out and out whimsical, but each one has been included for a purpose; each one has, through the test of lusty fork work and time, become accepted as correct; each one through its own small virtue seizes upon the basic curry-rice flavours, and points them up to hitherto unsuspected eminence much the way ambergris—itself a rather unprofitable odour—can, even in trifling amount, make a perfume essence into something miraculously impossible hitherto.

A SIMPLE CURRY ROUTINE for the AMERICAN HOUSEHOLD

Our Filipino Number One, Esteban Lueña, was once chef on a destroyer in the tropics. He has just whipped up a simple buffet supper party for a few kindred curry addicts. . . . At one end of the main table there were hot plates, silver. In front of these was a large wooden bowl of hot cooked Patna rice—buyable through any good store at a few days' notice, and having a plumper better grain shape for curry. . . . In the center of the table was a smaller bowl or platter of cooked curry; meat, sauce and all.

From this point onward, starting with mango chutney came small dishes of condiments with a spoon in each. Everyone mixed and blended to his, or her taste; and a vast amount of ale was on hand to put out the resulting inward conflagration. To make a curry party perfect, Roman couches really should be provided, if pertinent in risk, for every diner promptly begins to nod drowsily soon after.

TO COOK a PROPER DISH of RICE for CURRY, or any other PURPOSE, for that MATTER

Just as America has the handsomest ladies and the fanciest bath tubs in Christendom, she has won an all time low medal for rice cookery. Just why this relatively simple task should result in a sodden, compact, almost plastic mass of broken rice kernels is something no one has yet explained. For true cooked rice production, here is the easiest Oriental method. When cooked, rice should be a pleasant sight; each grain firm, yet done all through; each grain amiably separated from its neighbour; white, gleaming, enticing.

1. Use Patna rice, due to the better shape of grain. Wash thoroughly in several waters until all loose starch is gone and water is no longer cloudy.
2. To 1 cup uncooked rice allow 3 qts briskly boiling water to which has been added juice ½ lemon and 3 tsp of salt. Lemon juice keeps the rice white in hard water.
3. Put rice in a little at a time. Never stir with a spoon. Use wooden fork and "lift" the grains if they tend to stick. After 10 to 12 minutes, test grain between thumb and finger to see if it is soft all through. Job takes from about 12 to 20 minutes, depending on type of rice being used.
4. Check boiling instantly by adding 1 pint cold water.
5. Put into a collander or coarse sieve, and when drained turn into a shallow pan *very lightly* greased with butter and put into a *warm,* not hot, oven. In this way grains will dry nicely, swell, and keep separated.

AND NOW ANOTHER BRIEF LIST of Curry Requisites Involving Preparation of the Actual Curry Itself

1. Always stir curries with a wooden spoon. The strong natural chemicals of the sauce cause metal spoons to taste.
2. Never stand a curry powder bottle where light can strike it, for in this way flavour departs. . . . Without in any way being commercial we cannot but mention that Captain White's Curry Paste, which any good grocery may import from England through his agents, is the next best thing to a home-ground, freshly made curry powder—which last is too complicated to be possible in the average American household.
3. Never use all lean meat in curry. This applies mainly when using lamb, and four-footed flesh. Plan 2 parts lean to 1 of fat. This adds richness and character.
4. Meat should be cut around ½" thick, and not over 1" square, so that curry flavour may penetrate all through.
5. Eschew potatoes in any self-respecting curry. They blot up flavour from other things. Any proper British Colonial curry-master views potatoes in curry with the same mortification as he would if dear old Aunt Carbona should unlimber toothpicks at a Court garden party.

6. The vegetables in curry may be varied: cucumbers and eggplant are traditional; hardboiled eggs—duck eggs especially—added soon before service, are also good. Onions are imperative, and no curry worthy of the name was ever made without at least a touch of garlic. In fact, our Filipino boy puts ½ clove in the rice boiling water with no noticeable aftereffects of an ostracizing nature.
7. Besides chicken, which is favourite with western palates, excellent curries may be made of breast of veal, veal cutlets, lamb, mutton, sweetbreads; lobster, shrimp, any form of white fish, eels, oysters, prawns, crawfish or *langoustes;* rabbit or hare; leftover fowl such as goose, duck or guineafowl; even crabmeat and small tender clams.
8. Roughly these are the basic proportions: 1 to 1½ tablespoons of curry powder, with ¼ lb butter, with 2½ lbs or slightly more, of combined meat and vegetables to be curried.
9. Always melt out butter, then work in curry powder until it makes a smooth paste, in order to avoid lumpiness.

NOW a MADRAS CURRY of YOUNG CHICKENS, which MAY BE USED as BASIS for *RIJSTAFEL,* which WE PICKED up in SOUTH-EASTERN INDIA in 1926, during a TRIP from the GULF of MANAAR to CALCUTTA

An expert can tell a Bengali curry from one of Madras, from that of Malay type. We aren't clever enough to pick out varying Indian currys, but find that Malay curries usually are slightly milder, and naturally tend to involve seafood more often than inland dishes. Most Indian curries include enriched coconut milk, made by simmering grated kernel in the milk of a ripe nut, then squeezing through a cheesecloth to extract cream—this taking the place of the almond milk used here.

1 plump, tender fowl, meat only
3 average onions, minced
2 tsp sugar; salt to taste
2 tbsp chutney, chopped up
1 handful of small raisins
¼ cup blanched almonds
½ cup cream or milk
Flour, enough to dredge pieces
½ clove garlic, crushed well
8 whole peppercorns
½ tsp powdered ginger
1 cucumber in ½″ cubes; a big one
1½ cups chicken stock or broth
1¼ tbsp curry powder

Melt butter, roll boned bits of chicken in flour and brown lightly. Take out and put in saucepan, and meantime brown onion and garlic gently in the butter also. Work curry powder smooth with some hot butter, stir in chicken stock, chutney, raisins, peppercorns and salt to taste. Cover and simmer gently. . . . Meanwhile fry finely chopped almonds in a little additional butter, and when light brown turn into stout bowl and pound to paste. Heat the cream and add almonds, stirring constantly, for 5 minutes; being careful not to burn. After curry has simmered for ½ hr add the almond-milk combination, and the onions. Uncover curry pot and simmer that way until gravy is thick and rich, bearing in mind that East Indian curry does not depend on flour or other thickening for the major part of its density of sauce, but on thorough reduction by cooking heat. Finally squeeze in the juice of ½ lemon. If it dries out too much, add a little chicken or veal stock. . . . Curry strength may be raised or lowered to individual preference. It is wonderful in hot weather.

A ROYAL RUSSIAN DISH of Saute Breasts of Tiny Chickens, *à la SMITANE,* as Served at the Bungalow of One Cossack Named Boydyenko in 1926, just Before, for Reasons Never Published, He Suddenly Resigned from a Position on the Advisory Staff of the Young Chinese Army

This dish is a delicate thing worthy of low lights, our best still white not-too-dry wine, and a charming companion *à deux*. . . . Only use small well-fed squab chickens, breasts only. Dust chicken lightly with salt. Poach delicately in plenty of hot butter and ¼ cup tart white wine, then when light brown place on hot silver platter and reserve. Meantime sauce should be under way. To make 1 cup:

Use just a trace of butter in a saucepan and gently cook 1 small sliced onion, 2 or 3 chopped spring onions, and a dash of salt and cayenne, until clear and tender. Add 1/3 cup dry white wine and 2/3 cup sour cream—or fresh cream warmed 15 minutes—with 1 tsp lemon juice. Simmer gently, uncovered; add salt and cayenne to final taste. When reduced to consistency of heavy cream, put through a sieve. Pour over chicken and garnish with crossed strips of scarlet pimento. May be served flaming by putting a little heated brandy in a ring around the silver platter, and setting alight.

CHICKEN *TORTOLA,* which Is as Good a Name as any for Chicken Baked in the Shells of Ripe Coconuts, Tropical Style

Just to the eastward of our own St. Thomas lies the British island of Tortola, with Road Town—which, by the way has no road!—its main town, and capital of the British Virgins. The outdoor and indoor sports of Tortola seem to be fishing, treasure hunting, begetting children—both black, white and khaki—and fishing. Their cuisine is slim. Finding this dish there was an accident and we report it in that location simply because a rambling yachting friend who pokes the bowsprit of his ketch in many strange spots had recently explored the rocky shores of Sir Francis Drake's Channel from Norman Island to Virgin Gorda—the "Fat One" mentioned by Christopher Columbus—and sent the formula back to us a scant week before it came in by mail from two spots in the South Seas!

Again basic indications point toward a fowl of tender years, although this is not essential. Cut into fairly small pieces and discard bones and skin. Fry out 4 rashers of diced bacon and brown chicken lightly; salting lightly, to taste. Take out chicken and reserve. . . . Now dice a big onion fine, do the same to a seeded green pepper, and along with a speck of garlic toss these items in the same hot grease until fairly tender—further adding 1 tsp brown sugar, 2 dashes tabasco, and salt to taste. Put this with the chicken.

TO OPEN the RIPE COCONUT SHELLS, a Tricky Proceeding, yet Simple if Instruction Is Honest

We've fixed this dish ourselves on several occasions when gourmets were impending as guests and can assure you that no man born of woman can take a saw and saw a cap off a batch of coconuts without hours of wasted time, blistered palms, slashed fingers, and discovery of additional vocabulary which, strictly, should be used only in prayer. . . . No, and even a vise won't hold them tightly without cracking, or popping them half way across the lot.

First puncture 2 "eyes" and drain milk into a bowl. Just hold coconut with end having the 3 "eyes" touching hard rock, concrete, or metal at a point ¼ of the way back. Strike smartly with a hammer on the top side, more or less vertically above the lower bearing point, and the nut will crack all the way around in a rough but clean circle.

Fill 2/3 full of the chicken-vegetable blend, introduce 1 bayleaf and 1 tbsp white wine into each nut. Season finally, to taste. Tie lids back on with a bight of string, and stand in a baking pan having 1" of water on the bottom. Put in a medium oven for 45 minutes, and serve one to each person. . . . Other vegetables also will do, such as okra, cut in slices, green corn off the cob, palm hearts, cucumber, egg plant, mushrooms, or what not. If sherry is used do not add until 10 minutes before service—removing the shell caps and allowing 1 tbsp to each coconut. This is one of the most attractive and delicious chicken dishes we know, for during roasting the coconut kernel donates a rich bouquet to the cooking chicken.

AND NOW WE PROGRESS to a BRIEF DISCUSSION of DUCKS & DUCKLINGS, a SUBJECT TREATED further in RESPECT to the WILDER VARIETIES under the CHAPTER on *GAME & HOW LONG to HANG IT*

To our odd and unruly male mind there has been a great deal too much discussion on the subject of duck cookery, and especially when tossed off on the subject of wild ducks—taken up in our next Chapter—the orators have neither been hunters nor frequent consumers of waterfowl. They have read all the alleged etiquette about cooking ducks, both pressed and unpressed; have believed the romance, taken it up and shouted it from the housetops, just as they have read about the Orient and believe every Japanese a risky knave and all John Chinamen gentlemen of honesty and highest honour; just as they have read about the tropics and incorrectly believe the Southern Cross superior to the Big Dipper as a constellation; believe the tropic night falls "like a sudden black curtain," whereas there is a noticeable twilight in Singapore, Galápagos or Kenya Colony, right on the Line.

Except when dining possibly three, or at most five, guests, no amateur in his right mind will attempt duck *à la presse* if he is solvent enough to hire it done, or order it done in some spot like Tour d'Argent in Paris, where through the numbering ceremony of M. Frédéric Delair, alas for twenty years gone to his fathers, a Rouennaise duck is dedicated to the diner, numbered, cooked, pressed and eaten and paid for. To our mind this once charming thought is a form of alimentary exhibitionism. Besides all this, when done personally, this pressed duck is a gory process, a smelly process, and one already too well described in a host of cookery books to be covered here.

In other words, insofar as the amateur chef is concerned, fried duck isn't quite cricket except in haste in camp; boiled duck would hardly be profitable, therefore roast duck—in varying style—is the only usual answer. Barring the external application of condiments, wines and seasonings during the cooking process, it is our thought that in sauces, garnishes and stuffings, that most pleasure lies. A duck under any name is a duck; like a proper goose it is always fat and greasy in cooking; very rich to eat. The main problem is to divert the mind from these attributes, excellent though they be—through such sauces and dressings.

BUT FIRST LET US OFFER a Semi-Mad Chinese Receipt We Picked up during Our Next to Last Stay in Hongkong, Titled *ANGELS in MELON CRADLES*

This dish is just mad enough to be good, and although we have not gotten around to trying it yet we inscribe it here in hope that an adventurous soul here and there will try it out. . . . A young fat duck is first rubbed inside and out with salt and pepper, then stuffed with the following dressing: bread crumbs, enough to fill cavity, and moistened to a fairly stiff paste with Chinese rice wine—*saki* will do—or any semi-dry white cooking wine. Add 4 tablespoons of blanched almonds pounded to a paste with 1 tbsp of ice water, and sprinkle the whole with 2 pinches of anise seed, also pounded. Lacking this use 1 tbsp anisette, or *Anis del Mono,* the fine Spanish anise cordial. Then mix in ¼ tsp ginger powder. Blend this stuffing well, stuff and sew bird up.

Cut a small watermelon in half, hollow out a depression to receive the bird half way. Put duck breast in depression, dust the back with 1 tbsp brown sugar and 2 pinches of ginger, then roast in hot oven around 375° to 400° for 15 minutes; turn and roast for same time on other side, basting every 5 minutes with a sauce made from 1 cup white wine, 1 tbsp brown sugar, 1½ tbsp vinegar, ⅛ tsp powdered ginger and 2 tbsp grated orange rind—yellow part only. . . . After bird is well browned, lift out of melon cradle. Reduce pan juices with heat, thicken slightly with a little cornstarch worked smooth with gravy, add 1 tbsp tart jelly and serve in separate boat.

EXPLODED OLD WIVES' TALE No. IV, on the FALLACY of STUFFING CHILLED BIRDS IMMEDIATELY before POPPING in OVENS

Even if sweet old Aunt Beryl always stuffs her birds right off the ice and ten seconds before roasting, ignore this sinful act. Stuff all roasting birds at least a couple of hours beforehand, overnight is better still. This permits seasonings and savours to be absorbed by the bird even before being aided with oven heat. Each chilled bird should thaw at kitchen temperature for a good hour before roasting, or it may prove underdone within when almost burned without—especially in larger fowl.

A DANISH ORANGE SAUCE for DUCK, direct from the AMERICAN MINISTERIAL OFFICES in COPENHAGEN in 1933

After our duck is roasted pour off all except 2 tbsp of the fat floating on top of pan gravy. Reserve this fat. Next strain out 1 cup of the gravy itself—no fat—and keep hot in a saucepan. Work 1 tbsp or so of flour into a smooth paste with same amount of reserved hot fat, and stir in well. Season to taste with salt and cayenne. Grate the peel of an orange, yellow part only, add 1/3 cup orange juice. Work this orange business into gravy, then add 1 tsp orange Curaçao, along with 1 tbsp melted bitter orange marmalade. This is delicious!

A FRENCH BASTING-SAUCE, Containing Orange also, together with Currant Jelly & Port Wine

Use 1 cup orange juice, 1 tbsp brown sugar, 1½ tsp vinegar, a grated yellow rind of 1 orange, as a basting sauce. When duck is done pour off *all* floating surface fat from the gravy. Melt out 1½ tbsp flour with the same of butter, work smooth and thicken gravy in the hot pan. Add 1 tbsp black currant jelly, and reduce this sauce in pan until quite thick and gummy, then add ¼ cup port wine, stir once and pour over the bird.

GOOSE AFFAIRS, which Are Much Similar to Duck, but Larger

Geese are cooked the same as ducks, only longer—actually an hour or more. Sauces and stuffings are similar for tame birds. Apple sauce is so traditional with goose that we list one here; and not a usual one either, but made of roasted apples.

FRENCH CANADIAN ROAST APPLE SAUCE for Roast Goose; Quebec, 1934

Peel, quarter and core enough tart apples to fill a baking dish. Impale each apple with 2 whole cloves. Boil up a syrup made of 1 cup brown sugar and ¾ cup of water. Stir in the juice of 1 lemon, add to apples, and bake ¾ hr at 350°. When apples are tender, sprinkle with 1 tbsp dark rum, dredge with plenty of added brown sugar, the grated yellow rind of 1 lemon, ¼ tsp ground clove and twice the same of cinnamon. Now—and here's the point!—pop under the broiler until the last sugar starts to caramel.

A RUSSIAN SAUCE for ROAST GOOSE, from a Memorable Christmas in the Year A.D. 1926, Dining at Samarkand—a New York Russian Restaurant We Weep to Think Is No More

A feast day to a Russian is a time for joy and song; sad and minor songs it is true; but lovely, stirring songs. Samarkand used to be, like the Russian Eagle, a meeting place of wistful émigrés; and late at night someone would tune up the seven stringed Gypsy guitar, and the music would begin. Or Kousnetzov—we hope the spelling is right—would stand and sing the Volga Boat Song in his magnificent bass. Christmas was a feast night for us. It happened to be our birthday. We had a charming companion, and there was wine, and roast goose brought in flaming, and vodka and strong tea in glasses flavoured with a dash of orange flower water or jam. . . . The sauce for the goose, old time Russian style:

Add 2 tbsp freshly grated horseradish to ½ cup cooking gravy, strained, ¼ cup of very thick white cream sauce and ¼ cup sour cream. Add 1 tsp finely chopped chives, 1 pinch of tarragon, ¼ tsp dry mustard, 1 tsp sugar, juice ½ lemon, 1 tsp grated yellow lemon peel. Heat for a few minutes and mix very well, but do not boil. Serve in a gravy boat.

GUINEAS

Guineafowl or guineas, of any age, we always have held to be far more properly under Game classification, than classed as domestic poultry. Both in flavour and action in life they are allied to their wild cousins in shooting cover or forest. For this reason receipts touching on their culinary treatment will be found under *GAME, & How LONG to HANG IT*.

A FEW THOUGHTS on that NOBLEST of AMERICAN BIRDS, the TURKEY

American cooks actually get European credit, as they should, for methods of cooking this native fowl. Abroad it is a fallacious tendency to smother the bird in sad seas of messy vegetable dressings; in pot roasts and God alone knows what else—entirely ruining all possibility of the delicate flavour of the bird itself coming through in its original taste form. When exotic cookery rides our own doorstep in the eyes of the rest of the world we must record it here.

First a few technical warnings: be sure and lard the sharp edge of breast bone, and the ankle ends, with strips or rashers of salt pork or bacon, fastened on with string or skewers. This prevents burning before rest of bird is done. Greased brown paper will serve also. . . . Roast face down for all but the last ½ hr, then turn over. . . . A plump turkey cooked in an uncovered roaster needs occasional basting. But please don't spoil the delicate natural gravy by adding a lot of uncooked starchy flour, when a slight amount is all we need. Just brown the flour out after working smooth with an equal amount of melted butter, then add. . . . Above all don't always overload turkey dressing with quantities of sage, admirable though that herb may be; and, finally, avoid all beef extract "enricheners" like the plague. Vary the process through composing new thoughts on stuffings. A little adventurous originality is half the fun anyway, if for no other reason because of the surprise and delight it brings to the guest in our house.

WITH REFERENCE to Duck, Goose, Guineahen, Pigeon & Turkey Stuffings & Dressings of All Kinds

Since this poultry, or fowl, department fell under two classes of bird—wild and tame, and since our dressing collection for wildfowl is far more unusual than for tame, and because wildfowl dressings will enhance any dish made with a tame subject, all stuffings and such like matters are listed under *GAME, & HOW LONG to HANG IT*. . . . Ducks, Geese, Guineahens, Pigeons and Turkeys are treated in proper order, and in considerable detail.

> "We can not expect Tranquility of the Nervous System, whilst there is Disorder of the Digestive Organs. . . . *As we can perceive No Permanent Source of Strength but from the Digestion of FOOD,* it becomes Important that we should attend to its Quantity, Quality and Periods of Taking it, with a view to Ensure its Proper DIGESTION."
>
> *Abernathy's Sur.*
> *London, 1817*

CHAPTER VII

GAME *OF ALL* SORTS, & *HOW* LONG *TO* HANG IT

Companionate and Lively Dishes concerned with Furred & Feathered Game; such as Hungarian Partridges Cooked in Grape Leaves, *à la Budapesth,* the Way of a Scotsman with Grouse, Queen Elizabeth's Roasting Marinade for Saddle of Venison, & *Pigeons from the Temple of Heaven,* which is in Peking, in China.

FROM the start this became a favourite Chapter, partly through having been lucky enough to cook and eat a good bait of game in such widely scattered spots as the Florida Everglades and Maine, Idaho and India, British Columbia and Africa. We further must own to a definite stimulation in cooking a dish founded on items we ourself have hunted and taken. Added to this is the fact that almost all wild flesh, due to lawless matters of unbalanced diet and personal habit, has a more pronounced natural taste than tame; and for this additional reason game readily adapts itself to the lure of the unexpected in cookery.

But before a culinary shot is fired we must prick one romantic bubble which has bobbed about credulous tenderfoot ears since the serpent guided Adam—*there are no receipts of Famous Guides here.* We have no wish to dissipate any rosy Old Guide's Tale hovering about the north country moose caller or our soft footed Seminole turkey hunting guide, but we must simply rise and affirm that, by and large, in spite of all the mystery they love to conjure up about their art, they are the most abortive bunch of skillet wielders in or out of captivity. Oh yes, we know all about Moosehead Joe's famous braised moose meat and Kootenai Jake's roast Canada honker, and Okeechobee Tigertail's fillet of alligator tail. We've guided hunters and been guided. We've eaten guide cooking for going on thirty years. We say that such gentlemen may be mental giants when it comes to decoying fur or feather into ballistic proximity; but not half a dozen of the whole tribe we've met had time to care a hoot about game cookery, or had imagination to do much about it if they had.

No, it is our rigid opinion that the most imaginative game dishes today are worked up by amateur sportsmen-chefs; and actually it's about time someone put up a smoke screen of mystery about himself to match Moosehead Joe's mating call on the birchbark horn; high time we amateurs entered our guide infested camps with some assurance on our side; not as a disciple to his Guru, but with determination in eye and bearing. Let us look those fellows squarely in the eye and demand that the grouse or duck or venison haunch gets done—so, and so, and so!—thereby conjuring up a mite of overdue guide-respect heretofore only possible through a two hundred yard running head shot in timber, or an incoming double on pintail with a fifty mile gale under their sterns.

In game cookery America can hold her head high; can foot it on an even basis with England and France, and outstrip the rest of the world. In other kitchen practices Europe can level her cultured and palsied finger at our juvenile age as a nation; but inasmuch as there was no civilized cookery of any kind before the first third of the 18th Century, except in China, America has equal game cookery tradition. As a matter of fact our forefathers were at that time nourished largely by a sporting bill of fare in a new land teeming with game, while Europe was already in the midst of game depletion on all common lands, with stocking confined solely to titled landowners under stark prohibition to the rest.

Of course Italy had her spaghetti, France her fragrant meat stews and Russia her sturgeons' eggs, but despite all those reports about humming birds' tongues for the emperor there was scant culture in any of it. Henry VIII ate his stag bloody-broiled and half seasoned, and even his most elaborate state banquets were notable solely for their huge helpings and the coarseness of preparation. Even in Elizabeth's time any gentleman caught using a fork was viewed with the distrust we would grant a world's champion boxer in a Lord Fauntleroy suit. We have, in fact, a lovely formula of Louis XIV for burning the feathers off a live and kicking goose, later roasting it—undrawn—and setting it before guests half raw, unsalted, and basted with a fluid made of sugar syrup, then a viciously expensive luxury, and *violet perfume!*

No, Europe's game cookery is synchronized with our own. Their first great chefs came from Italy, as everyone knows, then the French school rose to its exalted estate. But after considerable travel and nourishment in Europe, after some two years spent living on European-owned ships, we found their game cookery intricate and amazing—when the old way was so nice. All right-minded folk will admit that the main charm in most game is its very own natural tastes, yet long-named foreign chefs dearly love to drown all sorts of game from roebuck to ortolans—buntings to us—in barbarous seas of boiled cabbage, onions, turnips, and even sauerkraut. Corned beef and cabbage is our friend, Bubble and Squeak our brother. Sauerkraut is a noble and healthy conception, but Odsblood! not smothering the finest game that flies. America was too busy fighting Indians or wolves or both, to have time for fancying up game in pot. That is our start, and we have kept on. In other words game, having its own unique and often delicate flavours—like quail, pheasant and partridge—should not be submerged in a tidal wave of other, commoner, flavours; not any more than a Frenchman should take a sound *Château Latour '04,* and trim it up with a lacing of six day old moonshine. We think sauerkraut is nice—with pigs knuckles and salt beef and things, but please not on quail, pheasant, partridge, snipe and guineas!

It springs from no desire to wave the stars and stripes when we promise that no American, with the taste buds of a mouse trap, would permit this sort of vandalism, any more than Henri Charpentier would cover a chafing dish of *Crêpes Suzettes* with a pint of black strap molasses.

Game cookery is a matter for reason and common sense, not a clutch of threadbare traditions founded on semi-barbarous quirks in the dim past. For this reason most Americans cook their game reasonably hung, not semi-putrefied and undrawn. We have always had plenty of healthy ice, now have healthy refrigerators; while Europe has never been that lucky. We have eaten English-hung woodcock with the trail left in. We found them perfectly edible but faintly tinged with the bitterness of the gall sac, and, through having their alimentary equipment in quiet decay for some days, they afforded scents and savours not one-tenth so delicate or vital or pleasant as the natural bird itself, drawn and undecayed.

This entire matter of game hanging is too variable to cling to any set of rules, sane or insane. The whole affair is dictated by humidity, climate, the type of diet, and the whole or mutilated condition of the kill itself.

Hanging at best is primarily done in civilized society to effect a certain breaking down of tougher fleshly tissues, not due to shame through lack of refrigeration causing us to nourish on a carcass high along the road to mortification. Personally we find that game plucked and drawn just as soon as possible and hung as quickly thereafter as convenient in a chamber under dry cold is best. We have now in our own refrigerator drawer six ducks that have been amiably awaiting there since the season's opening November 20th last—and this is July 1st.

Anyone who can eat a bird hung by the neck until it drops to the larder floor, like consumers of 6 minute roasted duck, and boasts he can carve up its long-hung, bloody torso with relish, either lies in his teeth, has cannibal ancestry, or needs an operation on his nose.

NOW a TIME-TABLE for the HANGING of GAME

1. Always remember this must be varied to suit warmish weather, and excessive humidity, or both.
2. Hang where it is cool and dry as possible, without freezing the game solid.
3. Even while in the field be sure to cover torn, shot-wounded areas to shut out the flies. Once the flies touch such game it spoils in an un-

believably short time. Same for eyes and beaks, which also provide ingress to fly attention.

4. Be sure game is perfectly dry before hanging. Inspect night and morning for dew or dampness forming. This means have in shade, yet in circulating air.
5. Our proven practice is to draw as soon as possible, plucking all birds at same time. Deliver to the butcher where he will hang indefinitely alongside his other meats, under dry and ideal conditions—yet not freezing or frozen.

TIME-TABLE, Based on Dry Average Cool Fall Weather, not Refrigerated

Wild Duck: 4 to 5 days. Mild weather, 1 to 3, depending.

Wild Goose: About 6 days. Mild weather, 1 to 3, depending.

Grouse: 8 to 10 days. Mild weather, 2 to 4 days, depending. Our British friends hang from 2 to 3 weeks, dry & cool.

Guineahen: 3 to 4 days. Mild weather, 1 to 2, depending. A delicate fine bird; don't spoil him!

Partridge: 4 to 6 days. Mild weather, 1 to 3, depending. Delicate too! Especially Hungarians.

Pheasant: 8 to 10 days. Mild weather, 2 to 4, depending.

Rabbit: 2 to 3 days. Mild weather, consume at once. Actually rabbit gains little from hanging.

Wild Turkey: 4 to 5 days. Mild weather, 1 to 3, depending. The grandest bird of them all, delicate flavour, so watch closely to avoid risk of "going by."

Woodcock: 8 to 10 days. Mild weather, 2 to 4, depending.

Venison: 10 days to 3 weeks. Mild weather, 1 to 4, depending.

A FEW MISCELLANEOUS & ADDITIONAL THOUGHTS on All Types of Game

By "mild weather," we mean warm weather. So watch game closely, for a sudden hot spell will ruin the finest brace of grouse ever shot.

Inspect edges of dissected abdominal areas. To average Americans the first sign of telltale blue-green discolouration is the danger signal. Personally we always trim these out, if and when cooking after that.

Remember that all game except fat duck, goose, raccoon or bear is "dry" meat. It requires lots of frequent basting, careful larding, or it will come from oven or grill tasteless as fibre—be it ever so prime when it goes in.

To our mind venison is a somewhat over-romanced meat. Unless we bag something so adolescent that game wardens begin doing forcible things, it is likely to be tough. It is particularly dry to cook—so be wary of trying to grill steaks as though that old buck were prize sirloin. Lard roasts; or wrap with bacon or pork; or better still marinate well for several hours, and baste religiously every few minutes when roasting. Don't overlook the value of lemon, lime or sour orange juice in tendering game, removing over-strong tastes and adding savour. Don't ignore the wild sour orange descended from the bitter-rinded fruit Columbus fetched to the New World and now gone wild in the bush all over Cuba and Florida. It adds great zest.

Strong birds, in addition to this marinating needed by strong meats, have most of their bad taste in skin, and in the bones. If we must eat coots or fish duck, and such like scabrous provender, skin and bone both; soak in salt water overnight. We ate pelican once because we had to, boned and skinned and soaked. There's nothing fishier than a pelican except fish.

When broiling or grilling game, brush with some good fat like lard, bacon grease, or olive oil. Sear fiercely hot, then cook at milder heats until done. Butter will not stand the fire.

WORDS to the WISE No. XVI, on the FALLACY of WASHING GAME

Beyond wiping with a damp cloth no game seems to gain from washing in water, although everyone does it everywhere, thus sending much flavour down the drain. Wet down, game can easily change to quickly spoiling meat. The earliest game receipt in our collection, dating to 1650, clearly states:

"Wipe jointe or game fulle welle, but do not in enny conscience washe the same in water."

PROPER GARNISHES for GAME, & the CONSTRUCTION of TRENCHERS

Fried Bread Crumbs: To a cup of bread crumbs allow 6 tbsp butter. Heat butter quite hot, brown crumbs, drain on brown paper or towel; serving either on main game platter or in a gravy boat.

Other Garnishes: Fried smaller rounds of bread make traditional garnish for small game. Also natural forest touches are in order: holly leaves and berries, leaves, other bright berries, sliced oranges.

Trenchers: Take a fairly short loaf of crusty French bread, slice lengthwise

1" thick or just under. Brush with butter and brown briefly under broiler or over coals; or fry in very hot butter. . . . Use it for a base for supporting game, and game cuts. The trencher should be as long as the game itself. There is nothing so wonderful for blotting up the fine gravies and juices which otherwise escape on plate. . . . *The last thing to devour is the trencher itself!*

SMALL BIRDS of MIXED BAG VARIETY, in the ITALIAN MANNER, & DISCOVERED during a VISIT in CAPRI not so LONG ago

While it has always given us a mild turn to think of fine Italian gentlemen dining off helpless migrating songbirds, and we have never seen the hair-raising thrill of shooting larks decoyed to a stuffed owl, there is no valid reason why we could not adapt what we learned to such small birds as snipe, plover, rails, pigeons, wild doves, quail, or what not, although a quail should be cooked more in a manner where his own delicate taste is undominated.

1 doz small game birds, 2 per guest
¼ cup red wine vinegar; or cider type
6 rolled & pounded anchovies
1 can Italian tomato paste
Salt & cayenne, to taste
Enough olive oil to brown
½ cup veal or chicken broth
1½ cloves garlic, crushed
½ cup chopped ripe olives
Trenchers of bread, see above
Marsala or sherry wine, to taste

Heat oil quite hot and brown seasoned birds lightly. Make sauce by mixing tomato paste with the other materials, simmer up and pop the birds in; cover and cook slowly until tender—about ½ hr. Stir in ¼ cup of sherry or Marsala wine. . . . Have a pan lightly greased with hot olive oil, brown big 1" thick slabs of Italian bread on both sides. Place a pair birds side by side on each trencher, and pour the sauce over everything.

A *PILAU,* or *PURLO,* of SMALL DARK FLESHED GAME BIRDS DONE in the GULLA COUNTRY FASHION back of OLD CHARLESTON, from a PLANTATION OWNER'S NOTEBOOK

Blackbirds, dove, snipe, plover, pigeons, any or all will do, mixed or otherwise! Remember it is the piquant stuffing that sets off this dish dating away back into slavery time.

8 to 10 small birds
1 cup finely chopped celery
2½ cups rice, slightly underdone
1 medium sized minced onion
8 minced rashers home smoked bacon
6 beaten eggs, yolk & white
4 cups chicken broth, to cook rice
¼ cup vinegar & ¼ cup mild mustard
Salt & hand-ground black pepper

Wash rice in lots of water, then boil in broth until not quite done. Drain and turn into a shallow pan to dry in *warm* oven, not hot. . . . Meantime fry out bacon, and reserve the latter. Use grease to brown both the celery and onion, lightly. Drain, mix with cooked bacon, seasoning lightly. Mix these with the rice, stir in the beaten egg binder. Stuff the birds and sew them up. . . . Meantime mix vinegar-mild mustard basting. Season birds well. Brush birds in olive oil and brown in a fairly hot oven, around 375°, for ½ hr, basting frequently with the piquant fluid. Serve on a platter inside a ring of cooked rice, and pour the basting juices over everything. . . . We have varied this by using wild rice mixed with plumped raisins instead of the onion. Very gratifying.

ROASTED WILD DUCK GENERALLY, & Roast Pressed Wild Duck in Particular—sometimes Called *CANARDS SAUVAGES, à la PRESSE*

Routine for a proper roast wild duck, for pressed duck, is simple but as inviolable as the late Queen Victoria's moral code. Probably it should be all the more rigid through the amateur having believed the foolish romance tossed around regarding 6 minute ducks. Now we've shot and eaten a good many hundred ducks, during the 2 years we've spent in tents or "sleeping out." We've cooked them over charcoal, in ovens, frying pans, over coconut husk fires on Andros Island; in metal containers over alcohol, wood, kerosene and distillate stoves. Our claim is that no raw 6 minute duck, hung or unhung, and regardless of age, sex, diet, social or geographical habitat, ***ever*** smells nice!

We've had to make 2 fairly well known and professed raw duck addicts back water before witnesses by cooking them prime wild-rice-fattened young hen mallards in oven exactly as they commanded—around 450° to 500°, *and giving them 8 not 6 minutes.* The unholy flesh tasted like slightly muddy raw meat. They had a scent that never came from any lotus petal. Just why America embraced this raw duck fallacy is unknown. It must be that folk have read this wonderful twaddle in English books, thought it smart, and wanting to make themselves out monstrous clever fellows both in field and with duck press—have retold the tale. This whole belief is on a par with our juvenile American faith in European diplomacy, and our erratic worship of sparkling Burgundy wine.

We can assure everyone that no big duck—mallard, redhead, black duck or canvasback—ever dull enough to fly within gunshot can ever be cooked in 6 minutes! A tiny greenwing teal can be done in 9 or 10 maybe—*maybe,* we said—but anything from sprig size and larger: impossible. Charles Nordhoff eats raw fish in salad sometimes, and so do we. Ernest Hemingway eats raw conchs now and then, and so do we. But no one except some wide-eyed citizen toting a 2000 dollar gun with a 14 karat trigger, and who believes everything he reads, can really say he likes duck flesh bloody-raw after actually having sampled the article himself, and not just through reading the printed page!

ROASTED & PRESSED WILD DUCK, Cookery Routine for the Purist

1. Pluck, draw, singe and rub clean with a damp cloth. Do not wash, either outside or in.
2. Hang for 4 or 5 days in a cool dry place; see above.
3. Thaw to kitchen temperature before cooking.
4. Brush with some good cooking fat like olive oil or bacon grease—*not butter,* rub inside and out with salt and pepper, perhaps insert 2 stalks of coarse celery into cavity. Butter burns too easily at 500°.
5. Be sure oven is hot—between 450° and 500°—*before* ducks go in.

Allow 10 to 12 minutes for teal, 12 to 15 minutes for widgeon, scaup, sprig, and all medium sized ducks; 15 to 20 minutes for mallards and other big ducks—this last varying with age and sex, a big man-about-town aged drake being a tensile package as anyone can verify who has tried to carve one. . . . These cooking times insure a prime duck, not a bloody one. Sear 5 minutes, then open oven door to reduce to 450° or so.

6. Slice off breast from wing toward breastbone, amputating legs and ignoring wings. Put on a hot platter and cover to keep from drying out any more than necessary.
7. Squeeze juices from carcass in duck press, and add to any casual juice extracted in carving. The purist seasons juices with a little salt and cayenne, and serves as-is. . . . Other gourmets prefer reserving some of the duck's blood and adding it a little at a time to juices simmering in a chafing dish—this slow addition being required in order not to curdle. This seasoned handmade gravy is poured over breast and legs out of a boat. . . . Other sauce additions start in with either of these two foundation sauces and: add a little grated yellow orange peel, melted currant jelly, butter, sherry, paprika, worcestershire—all or any of these. We personally favour the taste and scent of orange peel and apricot pulp with wild duck, after trying everything mind can conjure up. Soak apricots overnight, boil, and rub through sieve.
8. Serve the best still dry red wine the purse affords; decant it properly 2 or 3 hrs before serving. *Do not warm before a fire*—that is another old hunter's tale—merely decant and leave with stopper out in the dining room. Nature will do the rest. Nature always does.

WORDS to the WISE No. XVII, URGING FINAL DIVORCE of ALL WOMEN from ALL CONTACT with GAME COOKERY, VERBAL or MANUAL

May heaven shield us for setting this down in cold print, but employ no female aid or advice when cooking game. A curry, for instance, is also strictly a man's business. Male. And the same order applies to game. Women, by and large, seem to lack the proper psychology or respect for this serious business. Actually it probably isn't their fault, poor dears. They really haven't gotten much chance to cook game, for most men after coming to shaving age are bright enough not to take wives, sweethearts, or other feminine attachments, on camp-hunts or into duck blinds.

Thus far in our life we have known just 3 decorative women who, when in the field, didn't scream at many little things; and who, when they got any firearms in their pretty hands, could hit the proverbial bovine in the pelvic structure with a mop. And women who can't shoot shouldn't be taken hunting. And women who don't get taken hunting aren't sympathetic or interested in cooking game, except to confuse the male who is eagerly trying to whip up some amateur masterpiece. Naive and eagerly willing friends of either sex, incidentally, are the poorest form of risk in a kitchen. Give them easy indoor games and let them go away and play until the dish is ready to serve. This last bit of advice will save time, temper and friendships.

LET'S NOT SNEER too QUICKLY at all THOUGHT of STUFFING WILD DUCKS

There's a welter of accusation and rebuttal on this question also, mainly instigated by haughty addicts to bloody duck. Just why anyone pays attention to them we have never understood, for invariably they are men who don't get to eat many duck. For instance, in 1934 when British Columbia had a 20 duck limit, and 6 guns shot, the opening 3 days saw around 360 birds—ducks, brant and Canada honkers—hung in the meat safe under the buttonwood trees on the Kootenai River bank; all to be put in cold storage for future delectation, and with photographs to prove it. We ate duck on our houseboat camp; plenty of duck. We ate plenty more duck back home. We can swear you can get mighty sick of roast duck. You can get so tired of roast duck you welcome corned beef, only you don't—you think up different ways of cooking duck. . . . Some honest amateur chefs think that we of the occasional-duck-stuffing school use such stuffing to flavour the birds, or cover up their own natural flavour. That is incorrect. We think up duck stuffings because duck stuffings are damned tasty, and most ducks are strong enough in their own right not to be overwhelmed by a few condiments and bread crumbs; in fact we would like to make one additional duck statement before we get accused of conceit and undue authority on the subject:

Many ducks have quite strong gamey tastes. Diving ducks all tend toward this, especially salt water divers. The tippers who feed on grasses, wild celery, seeds and like vegetable and cereal produce are more delicate and sweetly flavoured. Divers that breed in the far north are sweet until they get to cavorting down south in tidewaters and sounds, then the fishy taste comes. A widgeon that has spent 4 weeks in Palm Beach may need stuffing to get our mind off himself, if you get what we mean. Any duck is usually better than no duck at all, even if it means eating only the skinned breast marinated overnight in salted water and lime juice. The whole business is comparative. There can be no hard and fast rules. There certainly should not be sneers and loud speech from gold-trigger gentlemen who eat a brace of duck every twelvemonth. Let's be reasonable, logical and happy about the thing!

MEDITATION on WILD GEESE, & on the SIN of OVERCOOKING

Wild geese are roasted much the same as tame, but a big 15 lb Canada gander can be tough. We've seen some with sinews that would make the village blacksmith look like a chorus boy. Most chefs we know make the mistake of extra long roasting, which is a boomerang in that instead of tendering the beast it merely adds temper to the metal of his deceased earthly shell, and after 2 or 3 hours carving may require 40% dynamite and a jackhammer quarry drill. He is totally different than his hand-fattened domestic brother. Cook him until he is well done all through. Beyond that man cannot go.

HOW to CHOOSE & USE a GOOSE, when THERE IS a CHOICE

1. Choose youngest and fattest, preferably a 6 months' old of the summer's hatching. His bill will be flexible at tip; his plumage lighter, his throat markings vague, his legs smooth and less horny than last year's bird.
2. Pluck, singe, draw, and wipe out thoroughly with damp cloth. Reserve liver—minus gall sac—heart, and in young birds the gizzard, for giblets.
3. After proper hanging for a period of 4 to 6 days, rub him inside and out with plenty of salt and pepper. Either stuff with some highly seasoned dressing, or be a goose purist and tuck 2 stalks of coarse celery —cut into 4 pieces—into the yawning cavity; or an unpeeled, quartered

orange; or a cored, quartered apple. In the first case sew him up; in the latter two, don't sew up.

4. Truss legs in place with piece of string tied around drumstick ends, and passed under his back.
5. Sear in very hot oven from 450° to 500°, for about 15 minutes, cut down heat by opening oven door slightly, then cook in slow oven around 300° until done all through; either basting frequently, or better still in a covered roaster to gain all steaming benefits from gravy. For basting merely add ½ cup water and ½ cup orange juice to the natural fats in pan after searing. Goose must be well done.
6. Pan gravy will be too rich so discard all but 2 tbsp of the fat, and tune up with seasonings to suit taste.

GROUSE DONE in the SCOTTISH MOORS FASHION

All grouse are delicious, and only our own western blue grouse is a bit strong, due to his diet among the conifers. Although very easy to cook there are a few points to remember. . . . Go slow in plucking so as not to tear skin, which is tender. Never wash in water after drawing. He should be moderately done—neither rare as duck, nor well done as goose. Young birds require around 20 minutes; mature birds nearer half an hour. The oven should be fairly hot—around 375° or 400°. Young birds may be known by their tender, downy feathers under wings; more pin feathers, and short, blunt, undeveloped spurs in the cock bird.

Your Scotsman would cover the whole body with rashers of smoked bacon, pinned on. Cover him with a discreet kimono of brown paper tied shut fore and aft, or in a paper bag. Roast 2/3 of his time thus, then remove paper, brush with butter, dredge with flour, mount on Scottish Trenchers, given below, or on plain buttered trencher of bread, and finish brown. The curse of most grouse is that they are cooked too dry, and lose flavour thereby.

SCOTTISH TRENCHERS for GROUSE, & TRADITIONAL GARNISHES

Take grouse livers and heart, cut out green gall sac. Grind up in fine blade of meat chopper, or pound smooth in a mortar. Add 1 pinch of salt to each liver-heart, a dusting of cayenne, a little melted butter. Mix well and spread on 3/4" thick lengthwise slabs of bread cut long enough to bed down the whole bird.

Several tarts and sweets go well with grouse: cranberry jelly, currant jelly or jam, brandied peaches or apricots, or the plain gravy from the birds themselves, served separately in a sauce boat. In such event do not use trenchers to blot up these cooking juices when doing the final browning in oven, but supply them later.

A BRITISH EAST AFRICA BASTING SAUCE for GUINEA FOWLS

Guineas are splendid fast-flying game in Africa, and we have a friend who went out there recently on a shoot, and preferred eating them to any buck; kicked them up out of the cover, cut them down with a 20 gauge, while someone else backed him up with a .375 Winchester Model 70 magnum—just in case. The receipt given here is English.

In greased roasting pan add 1/3 cup Burgundy or claret, 2 tbsp chicken broth, 1 tbsp tomato paste, 1/4 tsp nutmeg, salt and cayenne to taste. Rub bird all over with pepper and salt, paint with lime juice, place in pan and brown nicely, basting frequently. Thicken with a trifle of flour worked smooth with same amount of melted butter, and add. Then at the last stir in 1 tbsp port wine, and serve in a gravy boat.

PARTRIDGE with an HUNGARIAN TOUCH, & which also Would Serve as Well for Grouse, Prairie Chicken, Sage Hens or Valley Quail

This is a happy receipt from friends who shot in Hungary in the merry days before Swastikas and things. It came from Esztergom in the Danube valley below Budapesth, and almost within biscuit toss of what then was Czechoslovakia.

First rub 2 birds inside and out with salt, brush with olive oil and a trace of crushed juniper berries or leaves—lacking this a drop of essence in a little wine. Make a basting sauce from 1/3 cup dry red wine, 1½ tsp onion pulp, salt and cayenne, a handful of chopped almonds and the same of halved malaga or muscat grapes—or plumped raisins if no grapes on hand. . . . Sear birds to nice colour in hot oven around 400°, then reduce heat a little, add basting fluid to pan and cook until done. Reduce this basting at the last, thicken with a trace of flour, and pour over the birds.

A WILY GRECIAN METHOD with PARTRIDGES ROASTED in CHEMISES MADE of FRESH GRAPE LEAVES, and NOTED DOWN in ATHENS in 1931

The Grande Bretagne Hotel, mentioned elsewhere in these volumes, once afforded a chef named Jean Kriticos and while the routine cookery at this hostelry, like most others in the Near East, was nothing to weave sonnets about, this chef could on occasion produce surpassingly fine dishes. Actually the employment of grape leaf chemises in meat and game cookery is quite typical in that section of the world; Turks, Armenians, Syrians, all admire this touch. The dish is equally good with quail, snipe, woodcock, or any relatively small birds.

Brush birds with olive oil, rub lightly with garlic, and then dust with salt and cayenne. Inside the cavity of each put 1 pinch of rosemary. Brassiere them neatly with 2 or more large green grape leaves, pinning in place with skewers or toothpicks. . . . Remove gall sac from livers and chop them up with other giblets, chop an equal quantity of tender mushrooms, and saute them until half done in plenty of butter—also seasoning to taste. Then stir in enough tart white wine to do for basting. Now grease a casserole and seal cover on with a strip of pastry, baking in a medium oven at 350° for 45 minutes. The wine-giblet basting goes in with the birds. If uncovered, we were assured and later discovered for ourself, the leaves would turn dark brown at once and impart an unnecessary taste to the game. Reduce gravy at the last and pour over birds.

AND NOW A REGAL STUFFED PHEASANT, *MAXIMILIAN,* which Is also Known as *à la BOHÉMIENNE,* & *à la CHASSEUR ROYALE,* Sufficient in Itself for any Reunion in Vienna

For generations fine chefs have named dishes after their royal patrons. It means nothing except confusion to the amateur, and whether the tragic Archduke who met death before the firing squad in Mexico ever knew the dish really does not matter now. It is the dish that matters, and there comes a time in the life of every man when a dinner gesture is in order—whether he has shot that brace of ringnecks himself, or bought them—they average little more than young chickens! —in New York's Washington Market from Joseph, or Tingaud's on rejuvenated upper Sixth Avenue. And also 4 or 5 snipe or plover, or 2 squabs—for reasons now disclosed. These are for the stuffing.

Broil the small birds for only 4 minutes, along with a slice of Virginia ham or a rasher of home smoked bacon. Mince the meat from the birds, dice ham or bacon, add ¼ cup of sliced truffles—or half-cooked mushrooms. Season highly with salt, pepper, add 1 pinch each of thyme, marjoram and sweet basil; also 1 tsp chopped parsley for each pheasant. Saute this stuffing for 5 minutes in hot butter, then draw aside. Bind with a little beaten egg, dredge with a tiny bit of flour, and stuff birds—being careful to sew up neatly. . . . Roast them in a buttered ovenware dish around 350° until tender, basting with plenty of melted butter mixed with a little white wine. A gravy may be made from the cooking juices, either reduced with a trifle of sherry added at the last, or with finely chopped giblets—already tendered in butter—stirred in just before serving. Heat 2 tbsp brandy, pour over pheasants and serve flaming. Garnish with sprigs of holly, grape leaves; anything decorative from the forest.

WORDS to the WISE No. XVIII, BEING TWO THOUGHTS on the TENDER SUBJECT of QUAILS

Never forget that quails are particularly "dry" birds; and relatively tasteless when thus dried out in cookery. Therefore lard with strips of bacon, or smother in lots of butter, when grilling or frying. . . . Also consider the strange and proven affinity of quails with raisins, and sometimes put a handful inside the cavity of each bird, plumping the raisins first in scalding water.

A PROPER ELIZABETHAN MARINADE for VENISON, & the More Tensile Large Game Meats

Venison, except when too young to be legal, is apt to be tough. Cooked in steaks it is certain to be dry, but may be bettered by handling like *Tom Davin's Steaks-in-Salt,* on Page 141. When roasted it is imperative that basting be unremitting, and this basting, together with cooking juices form basis for later sauces. This receipt dates back to the year 1592.

1 large mild chopped onion	2 large chopped carrots
2 tbsp chopped spring onions	½ tsp each of usual sweet herbs
3 or 4 whole cloves	5 tbsp olive oil or butter
1 cup tarragon vinegar	Lots of salt & pepper

Fry out vegetables in the oil, add herbs and seasonings, then put through a coarse sieve. Brush venison with oil, dust with lots of pepper and enough salt, and pour this marinade over the meat. Turn every 2 hrs of the 8 the venison is kept in soak. Sear in hot oven at first, then cook meat slowly until done—basting with the marinade every few minutes to keep moist and tasty.

A SELECT GROUP of GAME SAUCES

A FRIENDLY SAUCE of BRANDY & the Pulp of Apricots that Is Justly Famous in the Old World, & Equally Good on Wild Flesh or Tame; on Animals or Fowls

Put ½ cup of apricot pulp through a sieve. Add 1 cup water, ½ cup of sugar; then simmer. Thicken with a little cornstarch worked smooth with the syrup; simmer up again and add 1 tbsp cognac brandy or 1½ tbsp apricot brandy. Make tart with juice of ¼ lemon.

THE AUTHOR'S OWN DEEP SOUTH BARBECUE SAUCE, for all sorts of MISCELLANEOUS GAME such as 'COONS, 'POSSUMS, BIG FOX or CAT SQUIRRELS, MARSH RABBITS, WILD SHOTE & GOD KNOWS WHAT ELSE of DARK FLESH, or GAMEY FLAVOUR, or BOTH

We've been hungry plenty of times on camp hunts, and seem to have eaten just about everything that swims, flies or runs, through the Florida flatwoods, the pine islands in swamps and Everglades, or in the vast sawgrass marshes. We've nourished on alligator tail, sand hill crane, limpkin, crow, rattlesnake, 'possum, 'coon, wild razorback shote, pelican and—credit it or not!—whippoorwill. 'Coon, 'possum, and big brown marsh rabbits are good eating, but have to be smothered in a sauce hot and potent enough to disguise the gamey meat. This sauce is fine to add to the braising pot half an hour before meat is tendered, or to work up while game is being grilled, roasted, smothered, or what not. Make it plenty hot with peppers.

1 lb odd trimmings from the animal
1 big chopped onion
4 tbsp butter
1 to 1½ tbsp flour for thickening
Salt and lots of black pepper
1 big chopped carrot
½ tsp dry hot mustard
½ cup evaporated or fresh cream
2 to 3 tbsp lemon juice or vinegar
1 piece yellow lemon peel
1 tsp or more of worcestershire

Soak strong meats as long as possible, overnight is best, in strongly salted water, then use this sauce, made as follows: brown the chopped game trimmings, onion and carrot in 3 tbsp of the butter. Cream mustard with a little gravy, and add to trimmings pan. Take some roasting juices from the meat from time to time, and add—along with lemon juice and seasonings. Smother and simmer until rich; strain out bones and sinew, pound vegetables fine, thin out with more of the cooking gravy, reduce 1/3, and finally thicken with 1 tbsp flour and same of hot butter—worked smooth—adding the cream at the last.

MALAGA or MUSCAT GRAPE SAUCE for Duck, Partridges, Quails, Pheasants, Guineas, and other Game, from Paris

1 lb grapes, malaga or muscat	¼ cup Malaga or Madeira wine
2 or 3 tsp dried mushrooms	4 tbsp butter
1 or 2 pinches ground clove	1 scant tbsp lemon juice

Stem grapes and scald in enough water to cover, simmering gently until nicely plumped. Drain and put in a saucepan with butter, wine and spice. Cover tightly and simmer for 6 minutes, no longer. Stir in dried and finely chopped mushrooms—truffle is even better—and after simmering a minute more, serve in a sauce boat. We find a handful of finely chopped hazel nuts add a good touch.

AN OLD ENGLISH JELLY-WINE SAUCE from the Time of George III, Who May Have Been Fallible in Brain & Statesmanship, but Cared for Fine Food. . . . Excellent for Duck, Grouse, Partridge, Rabbit, Snipe & Dark Meated Game Generally, including Venison

Slowly melt 1 cup of black or red currant jelly in a saucepan, add 1 cup red wine; mix up well and simmer gently while we add 1 pinch powdered ginger and the same of clove, 1 tbsp lemon juice. Thicken with equal parts game gravy—strained—and flour, worked smooth. Just before serving add 1 tbsp cognac brandy. Serve in a boat.

A MATCHLESS BITTERSWEET ORANGE SAUCE from Shepheard's in Cairo, upon the Occasion of a Consummated Duck Hunt along the Nile with Certain Friends in the Blinds of Russell *PASHA,* British Commissioner of Egyptian Police

We needn't explain that Shepheard's, for all of its vast and gay nineties interior and equipment, is one of the world's greatest hotels. After we hung up sixteen ducks—mostly teal and mallards—the Swiss manager arranged with the fine chef to arrange a duck dinner intended, among other things, to impress our then fiancée into believing ourself to be not only a wing shot of parts, but a widely clever fellow through arranging such a repast—complete from gimlet cocktails to two precious bottles of *Romanée-Conti '19,* which we obtained through treason and stratagem, if not out-and-out bribery, from Shepheard's special reserved bins!

This platter of ducks was garnished with tiny Jaffa oranges cut into baskets, filled with pulp and honey, dusted with brown sugar and grilled alongside the 18 minute birds. The breasts were removed in two parts; bones and carcass were pressed and the juice brought to the buffet close by, and while the matchless array of duck breasts and candied grilled oranges sizzled under their gleaming silver dome, and we worked up our courage to proposing marriage as soon as we could inveigle the young lady into Shepheard's gardens, the master magician of the chafing dish wove his spell.

The whole secret of this sauce is the *bitter* tang which comes with equal gusto from Seville bitter oranges, the Cuban *bigarade,* the Florida wild sour orange, or the Florida bittersweet. Grapefruit peel is the next best substitute, and a good one too. Therefore to the gently simmering juices of 6 ducks the following is added.

4 tsp grated bitter orange or grapefruit peel; using yellow part only
3 tbsp sour juice of any kind, like limes
1 or 2 tiny dashes of worcestershire
1 tbsp Curaçao
6 big tbsp bitter orange marmalade
Salt and cayenne, to taste
2 tbsp brandy

Mix well, adding spirits at the last. Pour a little over duck breasts, put the rest in a gravy boat. The duck platter was swiftly bound with a ring of heated brandy, and served flambée. . . . There was a hush, exclamations of delight. Then later, much later, coffee on the terrace —sweet Turkish coffee in tiny cups; and thimbles of Drambuie. We found courage, we proposed, we were accepted. We have always had a warm spot in our hearts for bittersweet orange sauce with ducks—or with anything else, for that matter!

A DANISH ORANGE SAUCE for DUCK WILL BE FOUND under the CHAPTER DEVOTED to *POULTRY & the INNER DRESSINGS of FOWLS,* PAGE 106

A FINE OLD ENGLISH WALNUT SAUCE DATED 1761, but which Is PIQUANT & TASTY on MANY other MEATS & GAME, being FOUNDED on a BASIS of PICKLED WALNUTS, & a TRIFLE of BLOATER PASTE

To 1 cup of the juice from pickled black walnuts add 2 of the nuts themselves, 6 chopped capers, 2 or 3 tsp of bloater or anchovy paste, 2 tsp finely chopped chives or shallots, 1 tsp of brandy. Simmer up just once and rub through a sieve. Wonderful for all sorts of game, and especially baked fish.

AN OLD ENGLISH STUFFING for SMALL GAME of all KINDS, DATED 1829

Quite a few old stuffings ignore onions now and then in order to permit the flavour of the game in hand to permeate better. This receipt works well with almost any sort of stuffable game.

All the chopped tender giblets and 1/3 as much chopped lean smoked bacon
1 tsp chopped parsley per cup
1 pinch nutmeg per cup
Enough bread crumbs to bind, and moistened with lemon juice and beaten egg
1 pinch thyme per cup
Salt and cayenne, to taste

Shape into small forcemeat balls, which may either be placed inside the game, or ranged around it and browned at the same time. It is simple and quite delicate.

A STUFFING for GUINEAHEN, *à la KENSCOFF,* BROUGHT back from a TRIP to HAITI, in MARCH 1933

Back in that incredible time when Toussaint Louverture, Dessalines and Cristophe, were conniving, each in his own way, to rule black Haiti, and the cane fields ran red with the blood of French men and women until there were no more, and even Napoleon's brother-in-law Le Clerc, and Pauline, and the French fleet were beaten off, there lived a monster in a marble villa high up in the cool hills a mile or so above the sea on the trail to dread Morne la Selle who hides her dark and fearful head in a perpetual scarf of tradewind cloud—Monsieur le Compte de Kenscoff. Only he didn't stop with murdering *blancs;* while the *vaudou* drums beat out the wicked heart-tempo of Africa, he would get his peasants inflamed on *clairine*—raw white sugar cane rum—and watch them in the courtyard below his terrace turn from caricatures of men to naked Africa herself. And then when this palled, he would send them home and put an amusing postscript on an evening's jollity by pretending to let one of his lovely yellow captured mistresses escape through a secret door, and when she had reached the open garden, Monsieur le Compte would lift a finger, and the bloodhounds would be released to tear her to pieces while he watched and delicately plied himself from a jeweled snuffbox of raw yellow gold, with its self-appointed crest done in diamonds and emeralds.

It is a far cry from this to guineahens, but near the site of this marble palace, long fallen to ruin, a canny, jolly little Frenchman has an inn, and through the wit of France, the produce of the lush tropics, and the half-wild cookery of African chefs he discovers things now and then. We speak of him again in this work.

Enough coarse bread crumbs browned in deep fat to fill ½ bird cavity
Enough red bananas to fill ½ bird
Salt and cayenne, to taste
½ lemon, juice and grated rind
1 tsp brown sugar; ¼ tsp nutmeg
1 tbsp brown rum

Mix everything into a coarse paste, stuff the guinea and sew up. Heat a little white rum, and serve the roasted fowl flaming, garnished with preserved guava hulls, or 1" quivering ruby cubes of guava jelly. The bananas are first sliced, then made into a pulp with a large fork.

A STUFFING of SMALL WHOLE OYSTERS, CHOPPED PECANS or other NUTS, together with WILD RICE, which will SERVE to DRESS WILD or TAME DUCKS, TURKEYS or GUINEAS, with EQUAL DILIGENCE & DELIGHT

This amazing dressing came from a sportsman friend named Samuel Galland, out in the Pacific northwest, who shoots a great many things and knows how to cook them—*has* cooked them, in fact around the world, and from British Columbia to *Baja* California, where, fairly recently he had his schooner burn from under him, his sole salvage being one locker drawer with which he returned to his home, containing underwear and socks. The small Olympia oysters of the west coast are indicated, but barring these tiny chaps, command the smallest oysters your source can supply. They will do as well.

Simply boil enough well-washed wild rice as the birds may require, in lots of salted water. Drain, then dry the rice well in a *warm* oven; and for each cup of rice allow ¼ cup tiny oysters, 2 tbsp chopped hazelnuts, 1 pinch of thyme and sweet marjoram—both of which harmonize with duck. Donate finally 1 tsp scraped onion pulp; salt and cayenne, to taste.

A NORFOLK PEANUT STUFFING, ESPECIALLY GOOD for DUCK, but MARCHING HANDILY with TURKEY, GROUSE, PARTRIDGES or PRAIRIE CHICKENS

We always ducked out at the Virginia Capes when going north in *MARMION* in the spring of the year, and on each visit to Norfolk we collected something interesting on game, Virginia hams, or southern oyster dishes. The mixture is in this proportion: to 4 cups of dry bread crumbs add 3 cups of *re-roasted,* quite dark brown, and crisp, peanuts—first put through fine blade of the food chopper—together with 1 medium sized onion, ½ cup crumbled cornbread, salt and black pepper to taste. Stir in 2½ tbsp melted butter. Moisten with a little veal broth and Virginia Dare white sweet wine—equal quantities; bind with 1 beaten egg. Stuff the bird. . . . This stuffing should not be too wet; merely a stiff paste.

ROY LAMMERS' PEPPER STUFFING for TURKEY, which Is a CLASSIC in the PACIFIC NORTHWEST, & ESPECIALLY AMONG those WHO MAKE YEARLY PILGRIMAGE to the BEAUTIFUL KOOTENAI VALLEY, when the NIGHTS GET CRISP and the BIG DUCKS & HONKERS START PITCHING in from the FAR NORTH.

Remember the tempo of this stuffing is very hot and high. Keep adding pepper and sage until we have reached our limit in pungency. Then stuff bird and roast him. . . . Take enough stale bread almost to fill the turkey, reject crusts and tear into small pieces. Work in 3 big chopped mild onions, 2 tsp baking powder mixed well with the salt; lots and lots of sage; lots and lots of black pepper—preferably ground with a hand mill. Moisten with just enough milk to make stuffing mesh together without too much compression, bearing in mind that the contented version in tin will harmonize just as well as dairy fresh. This is a masculine stuffing for those who want warmed innards and hot seasoning. Better taste as we mix in herbs and pepper, not forgetting that sage under cooking heat is far stronger than sage uncooked and dried, in packages.

NOW as a FINALE WE OFFER A RED RIVER PECAN—*PUCK-awns,* as THEY ARE CALLED THERE—& MUSHROOM STUFFING, further EMBRACING WINE & VARYING HERBS & other HELPERS, FROM NACHITOCHES—PRONOUNCED NACK-A-TISH—LOUISIANA

There is some mighty fine quail and turkey shooting in that old Red River country, and a gangling turkey shooter, recently enamoured of a Ph.D. degree at Columbia, entered this in our index of stuffings not-to-be-ignored. Pecans also are, and have been for long, a serious part of the cookery technique of that part of the south. Known in New Orleans as *pralines* they marry well with game in many ways. For a big bird allow the following comestibles.

2 cups chopped fresh pecan meats
4 to 5 hardboiled eggs, chopped
1 big onion, chopped fine
2 tsp celery salt
1 tsp nutmeg
3 or 4 tbsp chopped parsley
Heart and liver, chopped up
10 to 12 slices dried bread
1½ cups chopped mushrooms
¼ lb butter
Salt and black pepper, to taste
1 tsp powdered thyme
¼ tsp ground mace
2/3 cup, or so, sherry wine

Parboil giblets in enough salted water to cover, and while this is under way roll the dried bread to a powder, sifting larger bits out by using a coarse sieve. Blend all herbs and seasonings well with the crumbs, adding the pecans and hard eggs. Drain giblets, put through a coarse sieve and fry out with the coarsely chopped mushrooms, using half the butter. Tender the onions in the other half of the butter, then mix everything together, finally seasoning to taste with salt and hand-ground black pepper. Moisten stuffing with enough sherry so it will hang together, but under no circumstances should it be wet or pasty. We want the sherry flavour to point up the whole procedure, but when bird is taken from oven this stuffing should be fairly dry and crumbly.

Incidentally there is a Spanish turkey stuffing from the heart of ancient Castile which is identical with this one from Nachitoches. Substitute coarsely chopped almonds for the pecans, add 1 clove of crushed garlic, let chopped green olives pinch hit for the mushrooms, and finally add ½ cup of tiny dried apricots stewed gently until tender, and the transformation is done.

> "We have some Good Families in England of the Name of *Cook*, or *Coke*, . . . but they may depend upon it, they All originally Sprang from Real and Professional Cooks; and They need not Be Ashamed of their Extraction, any more than the *Parkers, Butlers*, & c." (NOTE: Not to mention Smiths, Candlers, Wheelwrights, Hunters, Millers, Carpenters, Masons, Waggoners, Shipmans, Woolworths, Mercers, Boatwrights, Sadlers, Farmers—and Bakers! . . . *Author*)
>
> *Quotation from a British Volume on Cookery, not of this Generation.*

CHAPTER VIII

MEAT DISHES *BOTH* TEMPERATE & TROPICAL

Concerning Beefs, Lambs, Porks & Veals, in such varied substance as Cuban Grilled Beefsteak *Bigarade,* a Costa Rican Affair of Ground Beef and Red or Yellow Bananas entitled *Empanadan de Plantano Maduro;* the Timely Matter of Russian Suckling Pigs, Lamb *Shashlik* and a North Indian *Sikh Kabab*—which are the Same but Different; to Say Nothing of a Russian *Piroshki* of Chopped Veal Kidneys and Other Goods Re-Stuffed and Browned in Rolls, and a Mexican Tongue of Veals *Taxcueño*—which means from Taxco.

UNFORTUNATELY or fortunately man is still a carnivorous animal. True, there are religious sects like the East Indian Jains who not only don't eat flesh but won't take the life of a serpent about to strike their own firstborn. There are thousands of more or less vegetarian folk who live and have their being in wide ignorance of meat, either for health's sake or one fanatical preference or another. But, by and large, they are all lean and tweaky pieces; prone to colds and random nervous tone, second rate in athletics, baffled by sudden problems, irascible, over-serious if not downright pessimistic, and of inferior reproduction.

No army, Olympic team or explorer can long keep energy fires alight without meat. The severe tendency of the Japanese soldier toward nose and throat fallibility is traceable to unbalanced rice diet over centuries, and insular lack of meat. Commander Byrd did not attempt to baffle Little America on a diet of prunes, canned corn, beets, beans and spinach. Inasmuch as the human alimentary routine seems to require flesh to fire our furnaces toward lively energy and companionate nerves, we have set out to collect proven—and sometimes strangely toothsome—methods of meat preparation, each noted in its own land and not unshot with cunning and imagination.

If any of these serve to elevate the flesh of some deceased quadruped into appetizing, odd and tasty nourishment, then our task in collection and presentation here has been most pleasant.

TOUCHING on the IMPORTANT SUBJECT of BEEFS

CUBAN BEEFSTEAK, *BIGARADE,* from Our Twelfth Stay in Cuba, which Was in 1937

This pungent way of grilling steaks first came to us from a friend who has been some eighteen years on the Island, and was tried on our grill before tasting the native dish ourselves. It is easy, quick, and makes a nice surprise at a steak roast.

Bigarade is the name for the Seville bitter orange, the one they make all the good Scotch marmalade from!—which, as has already been cited, Columbus took to Cuba and which has gone wild in bush, both there and all over southern-central Florida, where it has turned into the mongrel "sour orange" with rough bitter rind. If these are not available use lemons, or limes, or better still small sour grapefruit.

Choose ½" thick steaks, not too large. Have the butcher pound quite thin, or do it in domestic privacy with one of those square small wood mauls with waffle-iron patterned face found in any household supply store. Next cut oranges in half and rub and squeeze well all over steaks to get maximum oil from the rind onto every part of the meat. Crush garlic cloves very fine and spread a trifle on steaks also. Salt lightly and place in bowl, squeezing juice on each layer. Let marinate 2 hours, brush lightly with olive oil and grill over fierce heat, or live coals; searing briefly first—one side then the other. Have salt and hand pepper mill at elbow, and season as served. A little butter helps now, and of course they should be served sizzling.

NOW a RATHER AMAZING AFFAIR of GROUND BEEF & *PLANTANOS,* or Large Cousins of Our Familiar Banana, which Costa Ricans Call *EMPANADAN de PLANTANO MADURO*

We once attended a boys' academy with a son of the current President of Costa Rica, and later on when on two occasions journeying down the Central American west coast from Acapulco, Mexico, to Panama we were able to gather many tropical and exotic dishes—Guatemala, Salvador, Costa Rica.

For those of us with no true plantains within plucking distance we recommend red bananas, or yellow; preferring those not too ripe, for once. In fact, their texture should be quite firm. Now much of the beef native to Costa Rica is well muscled from climbing the volcanic peaks of that region, and not always tender in original form, so a food chopper is everywhere necessary to save the teeth of the old ones!

To every ½ lb ground top round beef allow 1 average mild onion, red preferred, ¼ clove crushed garlic, 4 hard bananas; salt and black pepper to taste. Grind and regrind meat with onion, garlic and all seasonings. Parboil bananas, or steam *with skins on*. Crush to pulp, stiffen with a trifling amount of flour, and make a waffle shaped patty, put enough ground beef in center and fold over to seal in meat completely; pressing edges down with a fork. Fry in deep fat, olive oil preferred, at 370° Fahrenheit. A big deep skillet will do if no fat kettle and cage are at hand.

WORDS to the WISE No. XIX, on the NECESSITY of THAWING out ALL SORTS of MEATS, so that WE MAY NOT BE HOIST on the PETARD of RAW CENTERS

A great many folk, especially ladies, take meat directly from cold refrigerators and pop it into hot stoves. Under such a frigid barrier all time tables are off, as to how long to cook. A cut or joint will be well done on surface and raw within. Therefore let meat stand in kitchen for an hour at least before cooking.

BEEFSTEAK, *MOLOKAI,* which Last Is a Mighty Rugged Island in the Hawaiian Group, once Known for Father Damien's Leper Colony but Now for Its Cattle Ranches, Its Goat and Pheasant & Its Hospitality

Big thick juicy steaks come easily out there, and we have noted a trio of beefsteak dressings brought to us by the classmate of a big rancher gentleman; and which added zest and flavour to his outdoor grilling picnics set on stupendous cliffs pitching down a half mile or so into the sea, where waterfalls arc outward into pale white plumes, and die, and are whisked away by the urgent trade winds.

Sauce No. 1. Mix 4 tbsp roquefort cheese with 2 tbsp evaporated (or fresh) milk; add 1 tsp worcestershire, 1 tbsp scraped onion pulp, juice 1 lemon, a little salt and 1 dash tabasco. Spread on when steak is just done, top side only; pop back under broiler and count 10 slowly. Outdoors, spread both sides, put to fire for same time.

Sauce No. 2. Here is a fine background for a big 3″ juicy steak! . . . Melt ¼ lb butter, add 1 tbsp onion pulp, ½ clove crushed garlic and 1 can button mushrooms, sliced thin. Simmer 5 minutes, season, add ½ cup red wine and 1 tbsp soya sauce. Add pepper and a very little salt, to taste. Thicken with a very little flour if necessary, first working smooth in liquid. Simmer up again, and pour over steak when done.

Sauce No. 3. Mixed deviled Virginia ham with prepared mild mustard, half and half. Just before steak is done, spread on lower side and then broil up; spread on other side, and repeat briefly. This is really more of a cooking adjunct than a sauce.

Sauce No. 4. Simmer 3 tbsp chopped yellow orange peel in same of water for 5 minutes; strain liquid and reserve. Melt out 3 tbsp guava jelly and to it add the orange-water, 2 tsp orange juice, same of lemon juice, ½ tsp ground ginger, 1 tsp prepared mustard and 2 tbsp port wine; pinch of salt and 1 tsp paprika. Spread this on sizzling steaks just before serving. Modify to suit taste at any point.

A TRUE BEEFSTEAK & KIDNEY PIE from the FILES of OUR FRIEND the LATE C. H. B. QUENNELL, ESQ., of CRAB TREE LANE, BERKHAMPSTEAD, HERTS: a GENTLEMAN, SCHOLAR, ARCHITECT, & the ONE MODERN AUTHOR WHO HAS BROUGHT the *EVERYDAY HISTORY of ENGLAND* CLEARLY & PLEASANTLY to Us in HIS BOOKS under such TITLE

One very pleasant summer we spent in Boxmoor, Hertfordshire, wandering about the countryside in a negligible motor car, visiting friends, meeting others. Quennell's intellect, his intimate knowledge of England's past, meant a great deal to us. This beefsteak & kidney pie dates back well into the 17th Century.

Cut 2 lbs ½" thick rump steak into pieces 1" x 1½" square. Slice 1 lb veal kidneys thin, after trimming away useless addenda. Melt out 4 tbsp butter and toss in beef and kidneys, meantime seasoning with 2 tbsp minced chives or spring onions, ⅛ tsp powdered clove, 2 pinches each marjoram and summer savoury, rubbed fine, 1 broken bayleaf, pepper and salt. Saute 5 minutes, add ¼ cup sherry and a very little water. Simmer up and take off stove. . . . Beard ½ pint oysters; or leave as-is, depending on preference. Simmer these in their liquor, and simmer gently, while we count thirty, uncovered. Then take off. Pour off meat juices and reserve.

Take greased pie dish, put in layer beef and kidneys, then oysters. Repeat again, ending up with beef-kidney layer on top. Make roux of 2 tbsp each butter and flour, and thicken the reserved mixture juices and pour onto everything. Cover with ½" layer of any good puff paste, to be noted in any good routine cookery book. Moisten edges and press down very firmly. Prick holes in center for vents, protect edges with circle of greased paper. Brown 10 minutes at around 400°, then reduce to 300° for around 1¾ hours. A little cold milk, powdered milk, powdered egg, or butter brushed on will glaze the crust.

TOM DAVIN'S STEAK-in-SALT, Broiled & Couched on Lengthwise-Cut Trenchers of Bread

Tom Davin, a quick-minded gentleman of Irish extraction, is also an eating man of most interesting and random career, varying from editing the *Natural History Magazine* up at the American Museum in New York, to marching with quaint and disordered fellows in May Day parades in Union Square. . . . We use his own words.

"Buy a decent steak, and a bag of salt for a dime. Either semi-coarse salt of ice cream generating variety, or the ordinary non-pouring table variety.

. . . Mix a bowl of salt and water until it is the identical mixture of your five year old youngster's sand pies, then spread it evenly on one side of the steak until about ½" thick. Just to make it sound complicated, pat it with the hand to make firmly smooth on top. Pop under broiler not over 1" from heat. And salt side up, naturally.

Broil as long as you usually do, no longer. A guide will be when the salt is a bit browned. Draw forth, turn over, repeating the salt paste process on the other side. Broil again. Take out and break the tile-like carapace with any handy hard object. Butter and pepper to taste. . . . There will be no gravy yet, it's all in the steak. Nor will there be cooking bouquet. That is in the steak too. There are no burned, dried out areas whatsoever, and you can cut it with a badminton racquet."

This routine may be varied ad infinitum by brushing with any series of marinades desired, and here again the salt chemise insures that all flavours be sealed in until the juicy finale when they are yielded up in all their unshared fragrance under knife. Our own routine is to turn steak, adding 2d salt layer, when 1st layer is barely hard.

BUBBLE-and-SQUEAK, Being Fried Salt Beef & Cabbage, which Is One of England's Classic Dishes

Our first introduction to this was through a London resident whom we met "under the clock at Charing Cross," and accompanied to a nearby many-storied restaurant corresponding in a gay nineties sort of way with our own Childs; only, if possible, noisier. Taken with a pint of bitter ale it makes an easy and fairly indigestible one-dish meal. The cooking sounds inspire the title. Even if we do not love this dish that title is worth a trial, certainly!

First brown slices of somewhat underdone boiled corned, or salted, beef in plenty of butter. Cook sliced young cabbage in lightly salted briskly boiling water for 10 minutes, no more. Drain and after removing cooked beef, put pan to fire again and toss cabbage in the butter. A minute or so is enough. Finally heap cabbage in center of serving dish, stack beef in a ring around it. Season with pepper, and don't skimp on the butter. A little hot or mild mustard is the traditional garnish.

THE ORIGINAL *CALALOU*, from which the GREAT MISSISSIPPI DELTA COUNTRY INHERITED HER MODERN VERSION often CALLED by the SAME NAME, WAS a RIB-TICKLING & MIGHTY DISH

This vast catch-all stew dates back to the dark heart of West Africa, back beyond the cruel slave ships. It was conceived within earshot of the drums of Damballa, the snake god, crying out their sinister message of *vaudou*. It came down, varying with tribes and seasonal larder, until it finally reaches us through Afro-American tutelage from slave cooks to modern kitchen boys or mammies. Palm oil was largely used in its original cooking; sometimes a sort of lard; and, later on, peanut oil. Olive oil is near enough for our palates, and easily had.

Simply cut up chunks ½″ x 1″ x 2″ of any raw meat: beef, pork, chicken, lamb, mutton, game. To this add more chunks of West Indian or Florida crawfish, shrimp, northern lobster; a cut up rabbit, a jointed duck, pigeons, doves, coots, squirrels,—anything! Heat plenty of olive oil and brown everything slowly for 15 minutes. Save a little of the oil. This seals in flavour and parallels the jungle roasting over coals. Now put in a big heavy kettle with a little water, cover tightly.

Cut up an equal amount of mixed vegetables: okra, quartered tomatoes, cubes of cucumber, eggplant, onions, green corn off the cob, yams,—anything on hand. Although the Chief's wife didn't bother about herbs she knew salt, pepper substitutes, and an aromatic or two—therefore we urge addition of the following: bayleaf, 3 or 4 to each 2 quarts of solids, a small bunch of parsley, a handful of chopped peanuts, several pinches of marjoram, rosemary or savoury. Add enough beef broth or water to make a liquid stew-soup, simmering slowly until meat falls apart. There is literally no limit to the additional variations possible through using worcestershire, sherry or other wines, garlic, chopped up orange peel, chutney, capers, hard sliced bananas, in quantity and fineness to suit our mood of the moment. . . . It is like our own Brunswick Stew, the Spaniard's *Olla Podrida*—that dish of the oddly translatable name which further adds bacon, saffron, cinnamon, pork sausages, chick or black eyed peas, turnips, lean ham, corned beef, whole cloves and a pig's ear!

Calalou is the best big pot camp dish we know; serve with roasted potatoes and heaps of boiled rice—white or wild. A bottle of still Burgundy, Chianti or any not too tart red wine is companionate.

CORNED BEEF & CABBAGE FIT for an EMPEROR, from DINTY MOORE'S in SHANGHAI

Time before last, when we steamed slowly up the muddy Whangpoo River, past the ruined Chinese forts gaping from the high-explosives, past platoons of Japanese soldiers thumping out bursts of machine gun fire at indefinite targets for our American benefit, it was to find Chapei—the native Chinese business and residential quarter, a smoking shambles of crazy tottering walls, staring unglazed windows, and splintered trees. Under the scowling gaze of suspicious, stocky little Japanese sentries we went about with our f-2 Leica, then back to town again in the raw March wind, up a back street not far off Nanking Road, and there a sign *Dinty Moore's* cheered us mightily. . . . We'd give them back their oriental civilization and undeclared war, just becoming fashionable. There we'd find something we needed, something literally to sink our teeth into, something homely and lacking in evasions and racial arrogances; something to make us forget those limp dead Chinamen in faded denim lying unburied in the pools of water—and God knew if there is anything deader-looking than a denim-clad dead Chino boy, we'd yet to see it!

Then Dinty Moore's and the hearty sight of American gobs and marines, and corned beef and'! . . . The quality of the beef is what counts, and the brown sugar is the touch to point it up. *Kirin* beer washed it down in Shanghai; we suggest any good ale at home.

Command 5 lbs of good brisket, cut from butt end, and not overburdened with fat. Trim off ragged unsightly edges, for corned beef when properly done is a fine rose-petaled thing, not a drab frayed-out mass of fatty fibres! Put in plenty of cold water to cover, boil up *very* slowly and skim well. Let boil briskly for 5 minutes, skim again; add ½ cup brown sugar and then barely simmer for 3¼ hrs or so.

Draw off the fire and let cool somewhat in ½ the cooking water. Then put on platter, place plate on top with heavy weight on it to press firmly. Meanwhile have big pot of briskly boiling salted water containing ¼ tsp baking soda, and a chunk of smoked pork, or hambone. Cut cabbage in quarters. Cook uncovered for 15 to 18 minutes. Condiments needed: lots of butter, mild mustard; potatoes boiled in jackets, brushed with lard, and dried in oven.

A TONGUE of BEEF, Cooked with Butter-Fried Chopped Almonds, Herbs, Spices, and Swimming under a Delicious Mexican Sauce

Cuernavaca, summer colony out of Mexico City, lies in a raw red earth valley over the 12,000 foot range to the westward. Here in 1937, among other things, we found a civilized manner of living almost feudal in its self-sufficient exclusiveness. Each house has its own high-walled compound; its stout bolt-studded gates. Outside it is dry, almost barren; within we find green turf bordered with brilliant flowers. Purple bougainvillea flings its blazing fan across pale salmon pink walls, its vibration tone so high as almost to be physically felt through the eye. Birds in cages, running free; men and women in the smartest slack suits like Palm Beach or Juan les Pins. Conversation of merit; discreet flirtation, food, wine. It is a small jewel-perfect world sufficient unto itself. Then for the mid-day, the heavy, meal—this tongue *Mexicano.*

Take fresh beef tongue, soak an hour in salted water; drain, trim neatly, then set to boil in cold salted water skimming every 10 minutes or so. Simmer gently until tender. Meantime chop 1/3 cup blanched almonds, brown in 2 tbsp butter containing a 2″ piece of cinnamon bark and 6 whole cloves. Set aside. . . . Fry out ½ a large red onion, minced fine, and 1 clove garlic, in 1 tbsp lard. When gently tendered add 4 peeled, quartered tomatoes; then salt and pepper to taste. Add 1/3 cup sherry, 1 tbsp guava jelly, simmer up, rub through coarse sieve. Slice tongue, arrange on platter. Garnish with nasturtium blossoms and leaves. Pass sauce separately. . . . Chestnuts, piñon or pine nuts, and hazelnuts are also used at times.

A VARIED PARADE of LAMBS, & YOUNGER MUTTONS

LAMB BROCHETTE in the CAUCASIAN STYLE—or *KAVKASKI SHASHLIK*—which MAY NOT BE IGNORED

A *brochette* is French for a large skewer, of course; and that first time in Paris, in the spring, and living at little Hotel Daunou over Ciro's famous restaurant, our day began with the ordained pilgrimage across the narrow street to Harry's American Bar where we would meet the One Girl, and two New Orleans silver fizzes—treated elsewhere in this work—then a happy rambling about: to the Bois, to see Helen Wills at the Rolland Garros stadium; to Versaille, then like as not ending up at Kasbek, mentioned elsewhere, to hear the Tsar's guitarist, hear the superb chorus of big breasted Caucasian girls, the dagger dancers, and to consume *Shashlik* packed on bayonets, and brought into the small dark place flaming and spitting fire.

This receipt is not just the usual grilled lamb, but with things besides, such as Russian spiced vinegar for grilling.

Order 5 lbs of lamb with a little fat. Cut into 1½" squares about ½" or so thick, first pounding lightly to flatten well. Marinate 2 hrs in the Spiced Vinegar, noted below. Dry on a cloth, run onto skewers, alternating with squares of smoked bacon. First, brush with the spiced grilling vinegar, given below. Broil over coals or under broiler for about 10 minutes, turning now and then. Heat a little brandy, put on with spoon, serve flaming by candlelight—and there we have a smart bit of business.

RUSSIAN SPICED GRILLING VINEGAR

Take ½ cup red wine vinegar—tarragon-flavoured is best—and put in mixing bowl previously rubbed with a trifle of garlic and 1 tsp salt. To this add ¼ tsp black pepper, ¼ tsp clove, ¼ tsp nutmeg, ½ cup tart white wine and ¼ cup olive oil. Whip up well and pour over squares of lamb just before putting to fire.

WORDS to the WISE No. XX, how to DISPEL the TENDENCY of all LAMBS & MUTTONS toward STRONG TASTE

The answer is very simple: just remove all skin and the very tough fatty tissues, leaving the clear meat and pleasant fat.

A CHINESE METHOD of FRYING THINLY SLICED LAMB, together with PINEAPPLE, MUSHROOMS, SOYA SAUCE, & BAMBOO SHOOTS

In early spring of 1932 we were booked to see Mei Lan-Fang perform at the big Chinese theatre just off Chienmen Road, which fetched him in some five thousand dollars Mex each week, and our rickshaw boy Limo, a Manchu, took us to a native restaurant where, of all the typical Chinese dishes, this seemed easy enough to remember and record here. The Chinese cabbage looks like an overgrown stalk of celery and is in every decent market these days. Whereas sesame oil is correct for Chinese frying, in most cases, use butter or olive oil.

To 4 tbsp frying fat in a big pan, add 1 lb thinly sliced lamb in 2″ square pieces, brown very lightly. Then put in 1 cup thinly sliced bamboo shoots, 2 slices canned pineapple recut very thin into 1½″ squares; 1 cup thinly sliced fresh mushrooms, 4 cups sliced Chinese cabbage; 1 mild onion sliced thin also, 2 tbsp soya sauce, a speck of crushed garlic, a pinch or 2 of powdered ginger and 1 cup beef or veal stock. Season to taste. When meat is tender thicken with a little flour worked smooth with hot sauce, stir in 2 tbsp of any white wine, saki, or sherry. Serve on hot platter.

CURRIES & LIKE ADVENTURES, BEING MADE USUALLY out of CHICKENS, ARE DISCUSSED in the CHAPTER DEDICATED to *POULTRY & the INNER DRESSINGS of FOWLS*

Curries may also, and properly, be made out of lamb, sometimes of veal, but never of pork. Any right thinking Muslim would shudder at the very thought. Therefore, with curry in view and chickens scarce, our first suggestion would be curry of lamb—proceeding exactly as though curried chicken were in process, merely substituting one flesh for another. . . . Again let us emphasize that the usual error with western world curries is that we fail to cook the curry sauce into the meat over sufficient period of time, but tend to whip up a quick curry sauce or gravy, pouring this over meat that has been cooked with no curry powder in the pot. . . . For this reason the flavours do not really penetrate as they should, neither do they taste as they should, not having experienced enough, or continuous, cooking heat necessary to extract their best efforts.

LAMB, *HAWAII,* Being Something Very Different from a Ranch on the Northern Slope of Mauna Kea, on the "Big Island" of Hawaii

We have only seen the snow capped top of Mauna Kea, soaring nearly 14,000 feet into the blue Hawaiian sky, once. It was before the days of regular inter-island flying, and for reasons not so valid now we and another kindred soul chartered a small Sikorsky Amphibian, and took off from Honolulu to beat our steamer into Hilo, or to have more time that previous night in Honolulu, we forget now which. But there was a dusty head wind, and after quitting Maui, we weren't making 60 miles an hour over the water, and the gasoline gauges weren't too cheering, and finally our pilot said "There's Mauna Kea, you fellows, and somewhere in a nice sugar cane field on that slope is where we land."

Yes, he was right all right, and we saw Mauna Kea's dazzling white cone up there; only it wasn't a sugar cane field at all where he set that box kite down but a sort of pasture, and not nearly as smooth as it looked from upstairs, and the cactus plants were doing a Virginia reel under our landing gear as he pancaked her upwind. So there we were, nowhere in Hawaii, and when we looked up again—that quick—Mauna Kea snow peak was gone in a plateau of white cloud, and the mountain was so big the slope looked gentle on both sides of us, as though all the world were gently tilted—cactus and sugar cane and grazing cattle and all—toward some invisible top to everything. . . . Lamb, *Hawaii,* like many things to eat and drink in that charming fleet of islands, requires pineapple—either sun-ripe or canned.

Have the butcher bone a nice 6 lb leg of lamb; weighed after boning.

Crush ½ clove of garlic, mix it with 1 tbsp scraped onion pulp, turn into a pan with 2 tbsp melted butter, 2 tbsp finely chopped parsley, ½ tsp ginger, salt and pepper to taste, and finally 1 cup pineapple pulp. If canned add no sugar, if fresh add 1 tbsp brown sugar. Toss lightly for 5 minutes.

Meantime, or about 2 hrs before, brush outside of lamb with lemon juice, rubbing with cut rind. Stuff bone cavity with the spiced pineapple dressing after thoroughly mixing with 2 cups toasted bread crumbs. Sew up neatly. Dust outside with a pinch or so of ginger, salt, pepper, and flow on 2 more tbsp melted butter. Sear in hot oven, about 425°, then reduce oven to 350°, cover roast and baste with pineapple juice every ten minutes or so. When done make pan gravy by working a little flour smooth with hot basting juices; reduce to good thickness on top of stove, then put through coarse sieve and serve in sauce boat.

BOTH *JAMBALAYAS*—THOSE AFRO-AMERICAN ADAPTATIONS of FRENCH-SPANISH CREOLE DISHES, and the EAST INDIAN *PULAO*, SEEM to SUIT WESTERN PALATES BEST when CONSTRUCTED of CHICKENS, and ARE therefore LISTED under *POULTRY & the INNER DRESSINGS of FOWLS*, on PAGES 91 and 95

However, by substituting beef, veal, lamb, mutton, shrimp, lobster or any other miscellaneous flotsam and jetsam—and using the same receipt proportion given for chicken—will quickly readapt the dish to what is on the larder shelf, or in the amateur chef's cooking mind at the moment.

A SIKH *KABAB, KABOB* or *KEBOB*, a DISH from BRITISH INDIA'S NORTH COUNTRY BORDER not too FAR from KHYBER PASS, where THERE ARE MINGLED IDEAS & MINGLED PEOPLES from MANY OUTLANDS, such as AFGHANISTAN, THIBET, MONGOLIA & the RUSSIAS

Sheep used for food is traditional to Mohammedans, and through various conquests and interpenetrations this dish of the Sikhs is much like Russian *Shashlik* noted above. Oddly enough, too, it is quite similar to the way Cubans grill thin beefsteaks. As for the Sikhs themselves, we greatly admire them. They are the most loyal, most dependable soldiers Britain owns. Throughout the vast East—from the Church of the Nativity in Bethlehem where we met one with full side arms and pistol keeping watch to make sure the Armenian Christian priests and the Greek Orthodox priests didn't pull one another's hair due to the latter walking across a rug corner belonging to the former—they help police Britain's Empire. Being Muslim, Sikhs may eat lamb, mutton, veal or beef, but pork is forbidden—while neighbouring Hindus in India may eat pork, whereas consumption of veal or beef invites eternal damnation. This *Kabab* can be made of lamb, mutton, beef or veal; but lamb is best, and preferred out there.

Select 2 lbs of boned lamb with some fat, but have gristle and tough fibres removed. Pound lightly with back of a heavy chef's knife to firm, then cut into pieces 2" x 1½" x ½" or so thick, saving all juices. Make marinade either of vinegar base, or juice of 2 lemons—about ¼ cup total. Mix well with ¼ cup olive oil. To this add 2 pinches each of powdered mace, nutmeg and clove; ½ clove crushed garlic and 2 tbsp onion pulp. Heat is supplied with cayenne, dry mustard or black pepper—to taste. Salt fairly strongly. Brush pieces of lamb with this and let stand 1 hr. . . . Run on long skewers: a slice of lamb, a thin slice of onion, a slice of lamb—5 of latter total. Baste with marinade now and then. Grill over fierce fire and don't worry if meat is slightly burned on edges, as this is typical. . . . We recommend olive oil here as the semi-rancid fats so often used in the Orient will give an average westerner "a turn!"

Traditional accompaniment is a dish of *Chupattis,* which are unleavened cakes made of whole wheat flour mixed briskly with enough water to form a pancake batter consistency, lightly salted. Cook like pancakes, on a griddle. *Chupattis* are used with equal efficiency to blot up succulent juices on plate, and also to tidy up the face from eating our *Kabab* off skewers corn-on-the-cob fashion! . . . A trifle of curry powder is often added to the oil marinade.

A NOBLE QUINTET of PORKS, Ranging from a Wine Treatment for Our Own Immortal Virginia Hams to Spanish Haunch of Boar, to a Delightful Method by which Danish Gentlemen Deal with the Common—and too often Ignored—Item Known as the Spare Rib

VIRGINIA PEANUT FED HAM in a Fragrant Chemise of Brown Sugar, Honey & Spice, Garbed in a Pastry Jacket, and Baked in Native Scuppernong Wine, *à la JAVA HEAD*

We have spent some little time in Virginia, in school in Charlottesville where in one cellar there were still the oak pins for raising the slave beds during daytime hours; cruising the Chesapeake, and through the Sounds and Canals of the Inland Waterway. From our friend Pender, whose old-time grocery in Norfolk is a perfumed and aromatic cave of romance, we were taught what a peanut-fed Smithfield ham was, which other hams may not be. Taught how to boil and bake such hams; then from a friend in Keswick came news of the pastry jacket; from Paul Garrett—whose family has made Virginia Dare wines for a century, we learned about scuppernong wine. The rest was our own idea.

Scrub a 2 year old Virginia, or other plump country-smoked ham, and soak 3 or 4 days in cold water into which has been added ½ cup of vinegar. Change water twice daily. Simmer then, very slowly, in water to cover which also contains ¼ cup vinegar—or in ½ water and ½ cider. Change water after 3 hrs. Allow ½ hr per lb; when tender trim off skin neatly. . . . Now score lightly with sharp knife, cover with a not-too-moist brown sugar and honey paste to a good ¼" thickness, into which has been worked 1 small handful of cloves; then cover further with a ¼" chemise of good pastry dough—being sure to form a jug-like neck on top. Form a stopper, roll this in flour. Put in the neck lightly.

Put in slow oven around 325° Fahrenheit until dough sets hard. Take out again, remove stopper and *slowly* pour in all the Virginia Dare scuppernong wine that sugar-honey jacket will absorb. Cork up and brown in same slow oven for 1 to 1½ hrs, depending whether ham is medium or large. . . . Yes, men and women may come and go, revolutions wrack monarchies, wives and husbands deceive us, taxes mount, the mechanized age buffet our ringing heads, but one of these affairs will renew faith in the universe. Presidents, kings, premiers, dictators, head waiters, cinema stars and glamour maidens become merely animated organisms doing mad and aimless jigs, but such a ham is a gem pure, serene, comforting. To our wry and lawless mind such a ham is, during these chancey days, one of our few remaining importances.

ENGLISH BOILED HAM, from JOURDANS, BUCKINGHAMSHIRE, 1932, INVOLVING SUCH MATTERS as BLACK STRAP MOLASSES, DARK or LIGHT BEER, BROWN SUGAR, and OTHER AIDS to SUCCULENCE

Scuttling through the hedgerows we went to Jourdans to see the grave of William Penn, lying chaste and with nicely timed impartiality between his two wives, and to photograph the so-called "Mayflower Barn," framed throughout with oaken timbers taken from that worthy vessel after being broken up. Stopping for luncheon at the home of family friends we were delighted by thick cuts of boiled ham offering something entirely new in flavour. This is the answer, and if English hams are used, choose Buckinghamshire or Hampshire.

Scrub smoked ham and soak for 3 to 4 days in cold water; changed daily; the firmer the longer. Trim off dark portions, put in a kettle with 1 pint of beer, 2 cups black strap molasses, 1½ cups brown sugar, and 1 cup each of chopped onion, carrot and cabbage. Add just enough cold water to cover ham; simmer up slowly and cook well covered until tender. Then 20 minutes before taking off stir in a double cup of sherry. This is extra good served cold, with ale.

ROASTED FRESH RAZORBACK HAM, ADAPTED from the SPANIARD'S ROAST HAUNCH of WILD BOAR, or *PIERNA di JABALI*

In Spain, barring revolutions, roast boar's leg was a favourite delicacy. But to our mind boar of any nationality and diet is a bit strong fare. In fact, from our rather long experience in the Florida marshes, and, briefly, on India shoots, we really don't care for any part of boars, for several reasons not requisite to mention. While perhaps not so sporting, the rear end of a tender, discreetly wild and woods-ranging shote has far more stove-appeal, to our school of thought. Especially in the Fall when the acorns drop, are they succulent and worthy of turning this—or the other—cheek. And instead of putting them to fire in crude backwoods fashion let's treat them more kindly with the Spanish touch that their inherent gamey taste may be enhanced as much as possible.

After hanging in the refrigerator for 2 days, well rubbed with salt and lots of hand-ground black pepper, take out and put in a pan. Pour 2 bottles of tart white wine, ½ cup brandy—Bourbon whiskey here! —3 good pinches each of sage and thyme, 6 crushed bayleaves, into a vessel. Mix well. . . . Now rub ham with big cut clove of garlic, then cut several rough lemons, sour oranges of the wild southern variety, lemons or limes. First squeeze juice over ham, then rub hard with cut rinds to extract every drop of oil possible. Pour wine-brandy-herb marinade over the ham and hide in refrigerator for a day and a night.

Take out, save the marinade for basting. Let thaw for ½ hr. Paint ***well*** with olive oil, and first sear in hot oven at 450°, then open door to drop down to slow oven around 300° or just above. Roast thoroughly and slowly, figuring around ½ hr per lb. Baste every 15 minutes ***without fail,*** employing the Spaniard's marinade for this use.

WORDS to the WISE No. XXI, a WORD on the VIRTUES of BASTING PORK in any FRESH FORM, and of SLOW, THOROUGH COOKERY in EVERY CASE

The secret of pork cookery, that which is so marvellously understood by southern darky barbecue cooks, is cook ***very slowly until well done,*** and baste ceaselessly. Rare pork is a thing not to be served to any man; dry and juiceless pork is just as bad as dry and juiceless baked fish.

NOW in PASSING, in CASE YOU'VE EVER WONDERED, HERE'S ONE of the BEST TRADITIONAL OPEN-PIT BARBECUE BASTINGS from the REALLY DEEP SOUTH. . . . BASTE OFTEN, and THEN BASTE!

Heat 2 cups of vinegar, add 3 tbsp butter, 1½ tsp black pepper, 1 tsp cayenne, 2 tsp salt and the proceeds of 1 can tomatoes put through a coarse sieve to eliminate skin and seeds. Mix well.

POLISH PORK LOIN, POACHED *à la POTOCKA,* an EXOTIC from WARSAW, & OWNING a NOTABLE SAUCE MADE from a BLEND of MADEIRA WINE, HONEY, SPICES & TART FRUIT CONSERVES

In America boiled pork, like boiled turkey, is unknown and unbelievable. Sweet sauces also are ignored, the usual apple sauce being good enough. But here is a thought dating long before the day of Ignace Paderewski or the Polish Corridor.

Order a choice boned loin cut into 3" lengths. Boil slowly in salted water—starting cold and skimming well—with 3 or 4 bayleaves, the juice of a small lemon, 3 minced spring onions *and* their tops, a pinch of sage, and the same of rosemary if we have it on shelf. Done when tender. . . . The sauce amount depends on size of pork cut, but in any case it is made the same. Take a pint of veal or beef broth and when it boils add 2 tbsp bitter orange marmalade, the same of currant jelly or tart cherry jam, the same of quince or crabapple conserve. Stir well, add grated yellow rind of a lemon, ¼ tsp powdered clove, ½ tsp cinnamon, the juice of 1 lemon for tartness, ¼ cup sherry or Madeira. Mix well, stand aside.

Now blot the pork loin dry, cut into ½" thick slices, dip in egg yolk lightly beaten, fine crumbs, and brown lightly under broiler. Serve sauce in separate boat, or pour over on platter, as desired.

HOW OUR COPENHAGEN GOURMET WOULD TREAT the SERIOUS CHALLENGE of PORK SPARE RIBS

Outside of the deep south, pork spare ribs fetch steaming dreams of sauerkraut to most of our minds, but here's a variation from Denmark to try out on that outdoor grill with the sheet-iron roasting oven, we've just built!

Cut ribs into pairs, allowing 4 ribs per person. Brush with lemon juice, rub with salt and pepper, dust on a little ground mace. Let stand. . . . Soak large prunes overnight, allowing 1 per rib. Have 1 tart apple slice per rib; enough butter, melted, to brush well, and a little milk for basting. . . . Cut flesh between ribs, but not quite through. Put 2 stoned prunes and 2 apple slices in each slit between ribs. Skewer with toothpicks; put in buttered roasting pan and cook in hot oven around 400°. Sear uncovered for 5 minutes, then cover. Add milk to juices for basting. The cooking job takes around 40 minutes, or slightly less. . . . Just in case the name may be of use to us—and it probably won't—the official name for this dish is *Svinemorbrad*.

EXPLODED OLD WIVES' TALE No. V, on the FALLACY of AFFIXING a RED APPLE, or any other FRUIT for that MATTER, in the MOUTH of the SHY & TENDER PORKER, *before* ROASTING. ALSO ONE GARNISH ITEM

We had cooked our third suckling pig, under varied circumstances, before some wise ally informed us that the only possible method of serving him with a nice red apple in his open mouth was to introduce a small block of wood—apple size—between his teeth *before* roasting. When done, remove the wood block and substitute the shiny apple. . . . Red bird peppers of small size will replace the bleary eyes with a scarlet touch; likewise red maraschino cherries or fresh ripe cherries will do the job even better.

SUCKLING PIG DONE in the TRUE POLISH STYLE, and CONTRARY to USUAL AMERICAN CUSTOM, SERVED COLD & BOILED—not ROASTED & HOT

This dish was recommended to us by a random and unruly associate who distinguished himself by disembarking both himself and a motor car of parts at the northernmost tip of Norway and driving the blooming thing all over the Scandinavias, Finland, Poland and into Russia where, along with other more important things, it was impounded by some of Mr. Stalin's right bowers. His final instruction was to chill the meat *very* cold before serving.

Instead of cooking whole, have the animal jointed. Cover with cold water—no herbs or seasonings whatever, just water! Salt is added 10 minutes before taking off the fire,—just why, neither our friend nor his Polish informants could satisfactorily explain. This should be after from 1½ to 2 hrs, depending on size of piglet. . . . Chill cold as possible, serve sliced with chilled horseradish sauce made by grating *fresh* horseradish—under no condition employ the stale bottled type!—and mixing in the following proportion: ¼ cup horseradish, 1 tbsp tarragon vinegar and 1 cup sour cream. Cold tart white wine is in order, rather than the more conventional red. Receipt for sour cream is given elsewhere, Page 19.

THE LAND of FORMER PREMIER PADEREWSKI CONTRIBUTES, further, a DEVASTATING STUFFING for ROAST SUCKLING PIG, which WE COULD in NO CONDITION REFUSE ADMISSION

For an out-and-out man's party we have never found anything so satisfactory as a small porker weighing, say, 25 to 30 lbs, and roasted by an amateur; served brown and fragrantly sizzling with a bright red apple in his mouth; or perhaps covered with hot brandy and set alight. The usual stuffings of bread, onion, salt, pepper and sage, offer little variation; and as the stuffing is what men also admire almost as much as the piglet himself, we believe a bit more attention to the subject is likely to cause an amateur chef's name to be noted in the land.

Remove the green gall sac from 4 chicken livers and cut small. Chop 2 big mild onions quite fine. Put these in a wood mixing bowl and add 1 tbsp each of chopped fresh dill, marjoram, basil and tarragon, the last 3 rubbed between palms. Next add 2 tbsp chopped parsley, ½ lb melted butter, 3 or 4 cups of chopped mushrooms, 1 chopped tart apple, ½ cup coarsely chopped chestnuts, and 3 beaten eggs necessary to bind. . . . Now put in as many bread crumbs as may be needed to fill the cavity, first browning them lightly in a little very hot lard or olive oil. Mix thoroughly and add just enough rich brown gravy to moisten everything. Pack in well, and sew up with stout thread.

The distinction of this stuffing comes through lack of the eternal sage which in America always seems to walk hand in hand with any pork stuffing.

EXPLODED OLD WIVES' TALE No. VI, on the UNREASON of TRYING to CHOP FRESH PARSLEY in a BOWL after the MANNER of AUNT AMANITA

Ignore all antique advice toward bowl and vegetable choppers. Take parsley in left hand, or vice versa, and snip as fine as desired with a plain pair of scissors. It is vastly faster.

AND FINALLY WE INCLUDE a Brief but Intriguing List of Five Methods for Preparing Young Veals

FIRST of all ARE CUTLETS of VEAL, *á SEVILLANO;* Employing, as Is Now & Then the Case, a Small Amount of Bitter Chocolate in Connection with Meat Cookery

Brown 4 nice delicately salted cutlets, trimmed and lightly pounded, in 1/3 cup of quite hot olive oil. Brown ¼ cup chopped hazelnuts in a little hot oil also, while this is going on. . . . Take an oven dish, earthenware preferred, grease it and stack cutlets inside with several very thin slices of lightly grilled smoked ham in between each. Add 1½ cups of chopped fresh mushrooms, pour in ½ cup veal or chicken broth or stock, cover and start gently simmering. . . . Meanwhile gently tender 1 diced red onion in the oil used to cook the hazelnuts, add ½ cup tart white wine, 4 tbsp tomato paste, 2 pinches of saffron, and 1 pinch each of powdered mace, clove, and thyme. Heat in a saucepan, and into this put ½ square of bitter chocolate, cut into shavings. When thoroughly melted and mixed, put through a coarse sieve, reduce by about ¼; and along with the chopped nuts put into the cooking dish.

Simmer in a hot oven for 10 minutes longer; arrange meat on platter, surround with mushrooms in a ring, also the strips of ham; and cover with sauce.

VEAL CUTLETS or OLIVES, *alla ROSSINI,* DEDICATED to a COMPOSER WHO not only COULD COME out with SUCH MASTERPIECES as *WILLIAM TELL* & *STABAT MATER,* but also WAS a GOURMET as well

From Pesaro Italy we bring this to you. It is very simple indeed and utterly delicious. . . . Have choice cutlets of veal trimmed and cut thin; pounded lightly. Spread each on one side with a slight coating of anchovy paste, and a sprinkling of finely chopped capers. Roll tightly, secure with a toothpick. Dip first in lemon juice, then in milk, then in beaten egg, then in flour. Fry in deep hot olive oil at 370°.

A RUSSIAN *PIROSHKI* COMPRISING ROLLS STUFFED with a FORCEMEAT of VEAL KIDNEYS & other DESIRABLE THINGS, then BROWNED in OVEN

There probably weren't as many *Piroshki* variations in old Russia as there were *filets* of sole in Paris and curries in India, but the list certainly was limited only by the several imaginations of all the chefs in the land, and the food on the shelves. This one is especially attractive, and is easily done.

First poach or saute 2 veal kidneys in butter and a little white wine; then trim and chop fine. Next amputate the cap from one end of a hard French roll and set someone to work scooping out the soft interior, being sure they don't fracture the outer shell. . . . Now chop up 2 hardboiled eggs, mix with kidneys, and 1 cup of firmly cooked rice. Season with 3 tbsp finely chopped parsley, 2 tbsp chives or small spring onions, chopped fine, a finely broken bayleaf, ½ lb or less of melted butter, and a handful of sliced button mushrooms. Season delicately with salt and cayenne. Moisten with any saute juices and 1 tbsp sherry.

Stuff back into evacuated rolls, skewer lid in place with toothpicks, brush all over with plenty of melted butter and brown in hot oven around 400°. If kidneys are poached without using any butter, use a little sweet white wine rather than water. A lovely touch.

VEAL, *à la RUSSE,* Being Virtually Poached in Common White Wine, Concerned with Sweet Herbs, Spices, Lemon Rind, the Whole Being Smothered at the Last in a Delicious Sauce of Black Caviar, the Reduced Cooked Juices of Veal & a Touch of Sour Cream

This is the finest way of handling veal fillets that we have ever known. It is a *chef d'oeuvre* to keep secret until the dinner guest looms up who matters. Then, Ah then!

Have the butcher lard a fine 4 lb fillet with fat pork. Put in a large saucepan or average kettle. Put in a chopped pair of small spring onions, a pinch each of the usual sweet herbs: thyme, marjoram and savoury; 2 broken bayleaves, 12 whole cloves, 12 black peppercorns, the grated yellow rind of a lemon, and delicate seasoning of salt and cayenne. . . . Turn in 2 cups of dry white wine, and add enough veal stock or broth to cover the meat. Bring to a boil slowly and poach gently in this fragrant bath—skimming devotedly every 10 minutes, and 3 times during the first 5 minutes.

When veal is tender put it on a hot platter, slice it neatly, and keep hot. Reduce cooking sauce in saucepan by 1/3, strain through a coarse sieve, thicken with a little melted butter and flour, worked smooth, add 1 tbsp lemon or lime juice, additional salt or cayenne to taste, and finally 6 tbsp good black caviar. Simmer up once, serve hot, either out of a gravy boat or poured over the sliced veal. Garnish with green leaves, slices of hard egg, thin slices of lemon. A dry white wine, properly chilled, is complementary.

WORDS to the WISE No. XXII, concerning the RIGHT & PROPER MANNER in which to PREPARE SWEETBREADS before COOKERY

Many amateur chefs blush faintly when confronted with a veal sweetbread *au naturelle,* so to speak, hastily chop it up with averted gaze, assuming that in such dealing all the proprieties have been observed. Nothing could be farther from truth. . . . Face the sweetbread determinedly, eye to eye. Wash under the cold faucet and stand in slightly salted cold water for an hour or so. Blanch by dropping in a quart of boiling water containing 2 tbsp vinegar or 3 tbsp lemon juice—for from 10 to 15 minutes, depending upon age. Drain, pop in ice water, and put in refrigerator to keep attractively white. When needed for use, trim off any ragged portions, muscles or excess fat, split or cut into cubes. It only takes 5 minutes to broil or saute or poach, after this treatment. And remember, a sweetbread must never be rare; must be done *all* through. Therefore sample a small bit before serving.

SWEETBREADS, *alla BASILICA ULPIA,* as DISCOVERED by OURSELVES in ROME, in 1926, after a day SPENT at VILLA D'Este, at TIVOLI

Basilica Ulpia, that fascinating restaurant set in an ancient church cellar in Rome, is treated tenderly and at considerable length in the introduction or elsewhere in Volume II of this series, so through lack of space we must devote ourselves on this page solely to the dish in question.

Blanch, trim and firm as noted above in Words to the Wise, then poach gently in enough thin cream to cover, being very careful not to scorch, with lid tight on saucepan. When tender add 1 tbsp Marsala, Madeira or sherry wine for each cup of cream used. Season delicately with salt and cayenne. Thicken sauce slightly with a little white roux. . . . Now trim off bottoms of steamed artichokes, toss them gently in quite hot butter for 5 minutes or slightly less. Cut sweetbreads into fairly small pieces, mount on artichoke bottoms, and mask with sauce. Dust well with plenty of blanched almonds or pistachio nuts cut into thin slivers, surround with glazed halved apricots, well spiced. Pop in a very hot oven for just a moment. May be served flaming. Just pour a little heated brandy in a ring around the dish and set alight.

"As . . . Health & Spirits depend . . . upon Our Vivid Enjoyment of Our Meals, it seems to be a more Worthy Subject of Study than those . . . Occupations about which So Many busy Themselves in Vain."

The Art of Dining,
By the Honourable Thos. Walker,
England, 1825

CHAPTER IX

SALADS & SUPER-SALADS, *TOGETHER WITH* ODD VINEGARS & HERBINGS

Embracing an Elect Brotherhood from Famous & Humble Mixing Bowls around the World, such as Charles Nordhoff's *I'a Ota* from Faraway Tahiti; *Aguacate, Cubaño;* a Spine-Stiffening Matter of Bahama Conchs; a Vast Green Salad out of Damascus, & finally an Imperial Russian Affair of Crabmeats, Mushrooms, *Smetana,* & the Deity only Knows what Else, *à la Youssoupov.*

NO ONE yet has satisfactorily explained why America, which makes the best fancy salad in the world, can produce the most horrific green affairs to be found on this confounded globe of ours. To our uncomplex and wry mind it can be due only to two causes: either we decline to learn the few conventional principles of the green salad, or when we do learn we don't give a tinker's dam.

With wide variation in native climate, more refrigeration than all the rest of the world combined, and with shops bulging with salad materials from Canada to the Argentine, we still slice our iceberg lettuce paper-thin with knives, and spill horrid, sweet, characterless liquids over the discouraged leaves, which labels laughingly inform us is "French Dressing." Inasmuch as our simple green salad came directly from France it, even in simple form, is an exotic. Salads made from vegetables or fruits having solid pulps are even worse here in the land of the free, for we naively douse sliced tomato, cooked artichoke, beets, and avocado, with the same ruddy fluid on moment of service—whereas one hour is minimum for marinating such victuals in dressing, and 3 to 4 hours is better. This last permits the oils, vinegars and seasonings to penetrate into the tissues of the basic ingredients, and changes them into a consummated salad, not merely cut up garden produce shedding dressing off like water from the proverbial duck, and in flavour finding itself flatter than a stepmother's kiss.

WORDS to the WISE No. XXIII, being a RIGID WARNING AGAINST the EVER-PRESENT SEPTIC-SALAD-MIXER, or S. S. M., and a PLEA for HIS IMMEDIATE SCOTCHING

This warning is no light matter we can assure you, for no matter what odd and unlikely spot we may find ourself in, just rig up salad bowl and condiments and, Presto! from some termite hole in the woodwork, out pops the S. S. M. . . . By septic we don't refer to the salad, poor innocent, but the self-anointed Mixer—that human microbe who for reasons known only to his progenitors and baby nurse, feels himself to be the sole elect person present at any gathering with grace or judgment enough to produce salad. His manner is condescending, his gesture, his tones, are mainly for the eye of the reasonably attractive female guests happening around.

His eye gleams with a baleful light, a fanatical light. The host is elbowed aside as an adolescent fallacy. We solemnly swear that if we don't scotch him then and there—be his name Percy J. K. L. Ponsonby-Foulckes, Bart., or Henri Etienne Vidal Compte de la Pharamonde, or Herr Doktor Wolff Chlodvig Putzi von Schnurrband, or just plain John Smith—that formerly emerald pile of crisp endive, brittle romaines, and curly chicorys, lively cresses, those fresh basils and chives for which we beat the markets, will all be weary, wilted and drowned; suffocated in a white hot brown highly seasoned liquid that tastes like a blend of the Boston Tea Party, chop suey, and muriatic acid.

For years we suffered in fulminating silence, while the addlepated women who had been as near France as "that cute restaurant on lower 5th Avenue," Oh'd and Ah'd; thinking such nice homey solutions as cyanide, arsenic gravy, slow strangulation over long periods of time with his own salad tongs, and an hors d'oeuvre of rat biskit and Stilton cheese causing him to die outside the house, seeking water.

No, valued friend, if we want a pleasant salad mix it as planned, *with our own hand*. It is only too easy to divert the S. S. M. into verbal demonstrations about how he startled the chef at Foyot's, and that time he baffled the Frogs by drinking three bottles of claret after his coffee. Thus snow-blinded by the brilliance of his own self-mesmerism he is static for at least the 10 precious minutes we need to barricade ourself in the farthest pantry and see the thing through properly.

FIRST, then, the TRUE FRENCH GREEN SALAD, Rules for which Are Simple, & 9

1. Chill oil and vinegar until moment of use.
2. Chill greens. Discard old leaves. Trim brown stem ends.
3. If we are really a purist we'll store greens in the fragrant wood mixing bowl, in the refrigerator. Chilling both.
4. If really necessary for sand or sanitary reasons to wash, do so; if not, please do not. Blot off all trace of water or moisture with a cloth, or between cloths. As has been told, salad dressing simply will not cling to wet surfaces and the dressing does not stay put.
5. Break up the salad greens in the case of iceberg lettuce, with the fingers, don't cut into slices with a knife—just why we cannot explain. Neither can anyone explain why gentlemen should pay unpleasant ladies alimony. Just break up the greens willy-nilly.
6. Rub bowl with garlic clove, lightly or heavily as desired, *after* salt has been tossed into the wood. The abrasive action is perfect, and becoming attached to the solvent and soluble salt, the garlic promptly permeates the dressing.
7. Pour dressing over salad in the bowl. Toss briskly but never violently, *at once,* while leaves are crisp. Stop tossing when each individual leaf is coated. Soon we can proportion dressing so that when tossed the greens are coated and not one supernumerary drop remains in the bowl.
8. Serve on the instant, if crisp salad is desired.
9. If a moderately wilted salad is preferred, *fatiguer*—make tired—the lettuce by further tossing; or by letting stand for a few moments after the first tossing siege.

WORDS to the WISE No. XXIV, concerning the INEVITABILITY of GARLIC in GREEN SALADS

No salad mixer worthy of his bowl ever omits garlic from a green salad, and onion simply won't substitute. . . . The rules are simple, and 3.

1. Chopped garlic, *no matter how fine,* must never be used in an American salad.
2. Either toss salt in bowl before rubbing garlic around on the wood; or for more delicate palates, rub garlic on a bit of toast or hard stale bread called a *chapon,* for debatable reasons, and toss this instrument about and among the greens.
3. About ¼ clove of average size, rubbed off on the wood, will suit average tastes.

A FINAL FEW THOUGHTS on SALADS GENERALLY, GLEANED from all over the WORLD during OUR VARIOUS WANDERINGS

We have discovered that for the heavier Italian and Spanish salads it is wise to use olive oils from those countries, which are somewhat stouter in taste than the more delicate French oils—which last in their turn suit French salads to perfection.

Don't forget to get a couple of bottles of red wine vinegar for especial occasions, and that a cut up trio of garlic cloves kept perennially in the vinegar cruet will add a touch so delicate even dear Aunt Aspasia won't remark except how well the business tastes.

Any sweet herb goes well with salad, and in the case of chervil, basil, chives, tarragon and parsley, the fresh chopped herbs lend a more delicate and different taste than those dried. Salad is a chilled business, therefore use half again more herbs than in a like amount of food to be cooked. There are many sources for herbs among the bigger, more famous shops, but in all our experience there remains one source—a plant-wise Englishman come to these shores; an herb man and botanist of parts, who not only grows his own herbs, but picks them at dawn with the dew still fresh, and dries them as they should be dried—in shade, but in circulating air. There are no twigs or woody fibres, just tender leaves. He has a package of six: tarragon, summer savoury, basil, rosemary, and parsley in transparent celluloid jars with airtight screw caps that he will send with a booklet or leaflet on herbs for 1¾ dollars postage paid. Through no wish to employ commercialism, but for strict purity of product and merit we list his name: H. C. Pratt, Esq., Glen Tana Herb Gardens, Spokane, in the State of Washington. We have used his herbs for years. In cookery they will show more in a pinch than the usual in a teaspoonful.

When the salad requires onion pulp, simply cut the end off a large mild specimen, then scrape it with the concave side of a tablespoon. Pulp flavours evenly and inoffensively, which is not guaranteed with chopped onion, no matter how fine.

HERB VINEGARS to ADD that DELICATE TASTE & AROMA So DEAR to AMATEURS of the SALAD BOWL

Garlic vinegar has been described and tarragon vinegar is on the shelf of every grocery now, so we list 5 others worth knowing.

1. *Sweet Basil Vinegar:* Fill jar loosely with herb sprigs of dried basil. Fill with cider vinegar.
2. *Caper Vinegar:* Add 4 to 6 tbsp chopped capers to pint of cider vinegar.
3. *Elder Flower Vinegar:* Fill jar with washed flowers, no stems, leaves or entomological specimens. Fill with *boiling* cider vinegar.
4. *Sweet Herb Vinegar, Old English Style:* Take a wide mouth 1 qt jar and put in the following to the amount of 1½ oz each: summer savoury, shallots or chives, marjoram and tarragon; chopped fresh mint and balm, handful of each. Add cider vinegar enough to fill the jar.
5. *Dr. Kitchiner's Piquant Vinegar, probably the most Famous of All. Circa 1817, England:* Take 1 oz freshly ground or scraped horseradish, 1 tbsp salt, 1 tbsp hot made mustard, 1 tbsp minced shallots, ¼ tsp celery seed, ⅛ tsp cayenne (Or we suggest: to taste). Add 1 pt tarragon vinegar then handle as the others, noted below:

SALAD or HERB VINEGAR ROUTINE: Pound dried herbs fine, cover with vinegar, screw on top with a rubber ring, stand in the sun for 2 weeks. After this fermentation, strain, wring or press remaining juices from damp herbs. Let settle for 2 days, strain through cloth. It, or they, will add a delightful touch to any green salad, mayonnaise and so on.

EXPLODED OLD WIVES' TALE No. VII, on the FALLACY of USING MALT VINEGAR in SALADS

Forget the conventions of Aunt Mehitabelle, and keep malt vinegar for pickles, where it belongs! Also take guard from the storekeeper who will invariably thrust it at us when we ask for "vinegar." Use cider vinegar, and, if a purist, use red wine vinegar, which is far milder but Oh what a bouquet and taste!

NOW A DUTCH SALAD DRESSING from ANCIENT HAARLEM

Take 1 cup of thick sour cream, 2 tbsp tarragon vinegar, 1 tsp finely chopped chives, ½ tsp sugar, and salt and cayenne to taste. Mix just before using, and it is especially devoted to sliced cucumbers or mild onions. Be careful on the sugar.

A PROPER FRENCH DRESSING

There was only one Bernhardt, one Napoleon, one du Barry and there is only *ONE* basic French dressing which ethically may be varied by adding sweet herbs, and/or a trifle more vinegar. . . . 3 parts of the best French olive oil, 1 part wine vinegar (or a trifle less of cider), salt and hand-ground black pepper, to taste. Mix well; chill.

A SALAD DRESSING ITALIAN STYLE, from a VISIT to MILANO

This is especially valid with tomatoes alone, or tomatoes incorporated with mixed green salad. . . . ¼ cup Italian olive oil, 1½ tbsp red wine vinegar, ¼ tsp chopped fresh basil—or dried basil rubbed fine between palms; to this add ¼ tsp dry mustard, worked smooth with vinegar—or a trifle less, to taste. The final touch is 1 level tsp of anchovy paste, or a trifle less, to taste. Add no salt!

A SALAD DRESSING, *MEXICANO,* as PREPARED by the CHEF at the CASINO de la SILVA, which Is in CUERNAVACA, ANCIENT & MODERN SUMMER CAPITAL of MEXICO'S RULERS from CORTEZ to the PRESENT

This is a fairly torrid affair, and it has been toned down here to the tenderer *Americano* palate. Vary proportions of oil to vinegar, with vinegar strength.

3 tbsp red wine vinegar
1 small round red bird pepper
½ can scarlet pimentos
¾ tsp dry mustard, worked smooth
Add enough salt to suit taste
9 tbsp Spanish olive oil
1 medium sized onion, chopped
½ tsp sugar; brown is best
½ tsp worcestershire, to taste
½ clove crushed garlic

Pound up hot pepper, onion and garlic in a bowl, and rub it all through a coarse sieve—pouring vinegar through at the last to capture all the lily oils. Blend dry seasonings then work smooth with the olive oil. When well mixed turn into the rest. Stand 4 hours to marinate within itself, bearing in mind if no hot bird peppers use from ¼ to 1 tsp tabasco depending on the throat lining insulation against heat! Or 1 small red hot pod pepper will do.

WORDS to the WISE No. XXV, on LESS OIL INCORPORATION into DRESSINGS for AVOCADO, or ALLIGATOR, PEAR SALADS

From its first civilized use the avocado pear salad dressing has tended erroneously toward being dressed with liquids containing *more* olive oils than usual, when the *reverse* is required. Use at least 1 part vinegar to 2 or 2½ parts olive oil. Just remember these pears are the sort of rich stuff we pick nuts all day to get—oily beyond belief, so we must avoid over-richness in the dressing. Personally we prefer lime juice to vinegar in this case.

TO MAKE a PROPER AVOCADO SALAD

Please let's not slice up the pulp in every salad. Just pass a sharp knive lengthwise of fruit, continuing in to the seed along this line, all the way around. Lift off halves, lift out seed, and put dressing into the seed cavity; eat with a spoon. *Chill very cold always.*

ENSALADA de AGUACATE, FINCA el SITIO, a CONTRIBUTION from CUBA

As we mention elsewhere, there are dozens of small farms, or *fincas,* in and around Havana, which we can visit in order to see a little of Cuba's country life—can see enormous royal palms growing in forests, coffee, cacao, avocados, mangoes, papayas, pineapples, sugar-cane, bananas, and heaven only knows what else, growing in tropical profusion; there we can see cock fights, drink heady rum drinks, eat surprisingly lusty and excellent *Cubaño* dishes,—dishes with saffron rice, of pork and chicken, and seafood. The dressing we ran into in 1937, during our last stay in the Island:

Into the seed cavity pour the chilled blended total of: 1 tbsp strained lime juice to 2 of Spanish olive oil, 1 pinch raw brown sugar, salt and hand-ground black pepper, to taste, and about 1 tsp of rum—*Carta de Oro* Bacardi preferred. Chill *aguacates* also.

BAHAMA, & FLORIDA KEYS, RAW CONCH SALAD—sometimes CALLED "CONCH SOUSE"

This receipt for us dates back to a winter and summer spent in a tent on Upper Matecumbe Key, on the ocean side, precisely where the veteran's camp went out in the Labour Day hurricane of 1935, and which would have taken no lives at all due to risen waters if our father's advice had been heeded when he was engineer for the then-building railroad to Key West—he pleading for a viaduct, *not* a fill, at this point where the whole blooming Bay of Florida empties and floods with the tide every few hours.

We might tentatively mention in passing that throughout the West Indies the conch is endowed with certain mythical properties, and some not so mythical. Raw conchs are to clams what a diesel streamliner is to the de Witt Clinton. He is credited with the amazing birth rate of the Bahamas, with making confederate veterans behave like adagio troupes; he is guaranteed to insert a 1" structural steel reinforcing rod into the latex spine, and create sudden interest in the fair sex when such random inclinations had long thought to have joined outdated and betrayed considerations such as the League of Nations and the sanctity of national borders. Be all this as it may, we affirm to one thing, that a decent conch salad is the best picker-upper when withering on the vine from varying injudicious causes, than anything else on the face of the earth. We break out a dish whenever we start on a hard day's fishing, just as canny folk like Ernest Hemingway, Tommy Shevlin and Ray Guest employ its virtues in firing the energy furnace and sharpening the wits, when fishing big blue marlin or giant tuna.

6 conchs, pounded with mallet or knife
3 average sized tomatoes, in eighths
1 to 1½ tsp worcestershire
¼ cup lime juice; lemon will do
1 small bird pepper, or red hot pod type
3 large mild onions
2 green sweet peppers
¼ cup cider vinegar
4 to 6 tbsp olive oil
Salt, to taste; black pepper
Key West *Old Lime Sour,* 1 to 2 tsp

Cut conchs into small bits, and give same treatment to all the other ingredients. Mix everything well, marinate *on ice* for at least 3 hrs, and overnight is better. This allows the lime juice to "cook" the raw shellfish. If no hot pepper we can substitute hand-ground black pepper and tabasco. Vary with sweet herbs.

KEY WEST "OLD LIME SOUR," a RECEIPT which BEARS REPETITION

To 2 cups of strained fresh lime juice add 1 tsp salt, strain through a cloth and put in a pint bottle and let stand until it stops working—which will be in 1 ½ to 2 wks. Cork then, and it is ready to use any time. By adding 1/10 of 1% benzoate of soda to this fluid, it will keep indefinitely; otherwise it will tend to cloud after some days, especially in hot weather. It has an odd and weird flavour, used *sparingly* as-is, or mixed with other salad dressings and sauces it is a wonderful addition on seafoods, cold meats, green salads, avocado pears. Gourmet guests will exclaim with delight, wanting the secret!

A MAGNIFICENT DAMASCUS GREEN SALAD, in the STYLE EMPLOYED for a NEAR-EASTERN FEAST; a RECEIPT PICKED up from a FELLOW WAYFARER in TIBERIAS, as WE JOURNEYED to JERUSALEM around the CIRCLE by WAY of NAZARETH—NONE of which ARE in SYRIA

Personally we would not be caught dead eating this, or any other, green uncooked salad in Damascus; for in spite of all the Thousand and One Nights romance hanging about that French-administered city, we certainly would be caught dead if we did, which doubtless sounds involved, as typhus and cholera and certain unplayful amoebic disorders smite all white peoples haunch, paunch and jowl, who consume uncooked provender, icecreams, soft drinks, or unboiled milk and water, in those areas. However it is a salad among salads. Save it for a vast gathering, with appreciative guests invited. It is the finest we have ever known.

1 bunch each, romaine and dandelion; chicory and endive; 1 head lettuce
1 bunch small spring onions or leeks
2 tender centers of celery
1 bunch fresh green spearmint tips
2 sweet peppers; peeled; no seeds
4 average, and ripe, tomatoes
⅝ cup wine vinegar; or ½ cup of cider vinegar
Salt and hand ground pepper, to taste
Nasturtium blooms; marigold petals
2 cloves crushed garlic
1 average bunch fresh parsley
3 small cucumbers, sliced thin
2 bunches pink small radishes
1½ cups olive oil, any kind
1 tsp each, basil and thyme
2 cans scarlet pimentos
1 tsp cinnamon; ½ tsp ground mace

Routine from this point on resolves itself into 3 simple deeds: mixing the dressing, slicing and marination of the solids, tomato and the like, in a smaller wooden bowl for 3 hrs. Then finally the arrangement of the greens and garnish in the biggest wooden bowl in the township, in order to feast the guest's eye just before the *piece de resistance,* the sacred ceremony, of its mixing.

The Dressing: Toss salt and pepper into the small wooden bowl—about 1 tbsp of the former and not too much, at first, of the latter—then using these as abrasives, garlic cloves should be rubbed until nothing remains except discardable husks. Now mix in the vinegar and oil, the herbs and spice. Solids must be skinned, by scalding or with the knife, then cut very thin. Turn into dressing, and baste with a spoon; set to marinating, as above. . . . When fetching to table arrange greens as follows: with stems pointing inward and down, first the leaf greens, set in rings, each after its own kind. Have a partly opened head of iceberg lettuce in the center, this last garnished with chopped hard egg yolk to imitate flower pollen stamens, frame with a ring of white of egg slivers, and tiny dots of scarlet pimento. . . . The outer edge of greens can be ringed first with thin strips of pimento, then with nasturtium flowers, and all spaced with pairs of marigold petals—*all of which may be eaten with the greens, and each donating its own delicate tang to the whole!*

Now fetch both bowls to table with proper ceremony, and when guests have looked their fill, turn the marinated stuffs and the dressing into the bowl of greens; toss mightily but quickly, then serve.

TAHITI'S OWN FISH SALAD, called *I'A OTA,* which CAME to Us via CHARLES NORDHOFF, AUTHOR & GENTLEMAN, WHO DWELLS in PAPEETE, FRENCH OCEANIA

Nordhoff's co-authorship with his fellow Lafayette Escadrille flying mate of such volumes as *Mutiny on the Bounty, Pitcairn's Island, The Hurricane,* and so on, needs no mention here. When our sailing mate "Sherry" Fahnestock got there a while back headed for the Fijis in his old Maine pilot boat *DIRECTOR,* he set her much traveled and fan-tailed backside against the quay at Papeete for a couple of weeks, and she lay there 7 months! He visited Nordhoff now and again, and consumed his share of raw fish too. Let us use Nordhoff's own words:

"To make this you take a fish of not less than 5 lbs in weight and in the pink of condition, remove and bone the 2 fillets and cut them into pieces about 1" square and ½" thick. . . . You then put these pieces in a fairly deep dish and squeeze out enough fresh lime or lemon juice to cover, leaving the fish to "cook" in this citric acid for not less than 1 hour and ½. . . . At the end of that time you throw all the liquid away and serve the fish in 1 of 2 manners:

"With raw, very thinly sliced onions and a French dressing made of vinegar, olive oil, salt and hand-ground black pepper.

"In a sauce made by grating a coconut (kernel) into its milk, then squeezing through a cloth to extract the cream; adding salt, white pepper, thinly sliced raw onions, and a bit of garlic if you like it.

"The native name of the dish is 'I'a Ota.' The fish is anything but raw, for it is *completely cooked* in the acid of the lime juice. I think that you and your friends would pronounce this dish a most delicious variety of hors d'oeuvre; and it is widely known and appreciated in the South Seas as a specific for the man who has looked too long upon the flowing bowl the night before."

AUTHOR'S NOTE: We have tried this dish several times and find it everything Nordhoff has said. We used tarragon vinegar, and strained lime juice, not lemon. Enriched coconut milk is done as in *Chicken Tortola,* on Page 103, and the result is a bit more rich and satisfactory than by the usual manual squeeze.

NOW LET US INVESTIGATE, if WE WILL, a SALAD of PERSIAN ORIGIN, from TEHERAN, which, by the WAY, Is a THING of GAYETY just as TEHERAN Is a SMART & MODERN METROPOLIS SET upon ANCIENT FOUNDATIONS that ARE OLDER than TIME

Just slice plenty of ripe oranges and when we have enough for 4 people, halt. Stone 2 doz ripe olives, by this we mean peel in a spiral, then cut up, and add to 1 cup of mild onion cut thin-as-thin. Chop up 1 tbsp fresh green mint, the same of parsley, and sprinkle on as garnish after dressing oranges, onions and olives with a French dressing warmed well with cayenne, and containing ½ tsp basil leaves rubbed between the palms. Chill for 2 hrs before service. A very delicate event, to our way of thinking.

OFF ON OUR MAGIC CULINARY CARPET to OPORTO, which Is in PORTUGAL, & to a SPRIGHTLY AFFAIR CALLED *SALADA de PEPINO*—CONSISTING of SPANISH ONIONS, & VARIOUS IMPEDIMENTA, INCLUDING—of all THINGS!—CHESTNUTS

1 big red Spanish onion; ¼ clove garlic
2 big tart apples, not sweet
2 sweet green peppers
½ cup Spanish olive oil; or Italian
Salt and hand-ground pepper, to taste
2 average cucumbers
2 big ripe tomatoes
3 or 4 slices scarlet pimento
¼ cup lime or lemon juice
1 cup coarsely grated chestnuts

Take the sharpest knife possible and slice onions, cored pared apples, cucumbers and sweet peppers, as thin as can be. Take a chilled platter and arrange in a colourful design. Make the dressing by rubbing garlic on the bowl with salt; mix well and pour evenly over the salad. Marinate 1 hr. Boil chestnuts, the big kind, grate *while piping hot*—then when cold dust evenly over the salad. Garnish with hard chopped egg and strips of red pimento.

A SUPREME SPANISH SALAD of SALTED CODS, of ANCHOVIES, OLIVES & FINE RED ONIONS, not FORGETTING other NECESSARIES NEEDFUL to FABRICATE ENSALADA *á BILBAINITA*

We mentioned once before that it took a Spaniard and a Portuguese to show Boston what to do with their smoked or salted coat of arms! This is truly something different, *Messieurs.*

6 heaping tbsp, flaked (*not* shredded & dried!) smoked codfish
1/3 cup red wine vinegar
12 anchovies, rolled in oil
1 can red pimentos, sliced in strips
1 clove crushed garlic
2 doz olives *stuffed with almonds*
1 cup Spanish olive oil
3 chopped sweet peppers
6 hardboiled eggs, sliced
Black pepper and cayenne
3 heads crisp lettuce
1 head endive, or chicory

Have greens cold, crisp, dry. Break heads apart and arrange in the bowl like a big green flower, with anchovies circling the heaped codfish in the center, the sliced egg stamens, the scarlet pimento pistils. Mix up the usual dressing and pour over everything, and serve. . . . Prepare codfish by soaking overnight in milk, draining, and simmering until tender—this last in ½ milk and ½ water. Bone carefully, then flake.

AND FINALLY, now, WE REFER OURSELF back to the SPANISH *GAZPACHO* which IS ACTUALLY CLASSED as a SORT of SALAD, & which IS LISTED under HORS d'OEUVRE, & other FIRST COURSE IMPORTANCES, on PAGE 22

The Spaniards really do consider this a salad. It is much similar to the Marseilles Frenchman's *aioli.* We earnestly suggest that either of these be exploded on the American scene as gently as may be. Just choose a nice rainy Sunday evening, with only our closest friends about; and no possibility of going anywhere! He who munches this salad-appetizer in the bosom of his, or her, family and then departeth abroad among the publicans and sinners—unless he equippeth himself, and them, or both, with gas masks enough for all citizens surrounding him—shall straightway find himself shunned like the Bubonic Plague. In truth there's nothing modest or retiring about a *Gazpacho!*

> "The greatest Care should be taken by the Man of Fashion, that his cook's Health be Preserved: one hundredth part of the attention usually bestowed on his dog, or his horse, will suffice to regulate her animal system. . . . should watch over her Health with Tenderest Care, and especially be Sure her *Taste* does not suffer from her Stomach being Deranged by Bilious Attacks. . . ."
>
> *The Cook's Oracle,*
> *Dr. William Kitchiner,*
> *London, 1817*

CHAPTER X

PARTICULAR VEGETABLES *FROM* DIVERS STRANGE KITCHENS

Conniving with Various Specimens of Tuber, Seed & Bud; but with Emphasis on such Odd Events as *Moros y Cristianos*—"Moors & Christians"—from Cuba; our own traditional Hopping John; Egg-plants, *a Mallorquena;* Prickly Pear Leaves after Toreador Sidney Franklin; or Candied Yams, *Cap Hatien.*

IT HAS always been a source of mingled pain and amazement how the average American cook could take all those nice pretty vegetables, set his jaw, and with the grim devotion of a knight praying beside his armour, reduce them to the watery, careless bogs of iniquity that he does. Then we lived in England for a while!

But the fact that we can level a superior finger at England's fantastic sins among the vegetables is no more excuse than a chap who cabbages a locket from a sleeping babe is pardoned the act just because his neighbour is a bad fellow and robs an orphanage trust fund.

The intelligent amateur on these shores already knows how to cook vegetables as well or better than the next—boiling, baking, or what not. Heaven knows it is not our mission to speak about boiling asparagus with the lid off—started fiercely hot; and boiling carrots with the lid on, started cold. Every passing cookery book cries this sort of lesson. We cling to the hope that these dishes, found in varying places and under varying, but always happy, circumstances may suggest certain points of departure for the amateur. So be of good cheer, and furthermore be surprised at nothing!

ASPARAGUS after the ROMAN MANNER, ADVOCATED for the SUNDAY MORNING BREAKFAST

One memorable year found us again in Rome, and happily in funds, and crisply nested at *Grande Hotel de Russie,* in whose rather impressive halls was a room boy, or *valet de chambre,* or whatever we should call a fellow who replaces broken shoelaces, cracks ice for varying heathenish American liquids, prays for the lost soul of a guest who visibly has no rosary by our bedside, bargains for us at not more than ten per cent backsheesh for himself, and generally advises ourself on all of the more intimate human relationships—both extra, and intra, mural—named Luigi. . . . Now one morning, with our mortal visibility somewhat withered on the vine from doing as the Romans do, we wondered what things interesting might be kitchened for breakfast. And this gem Luigi suggested asparagus, first verbally, then at our evident poor Italian, not too clearly through a rough pencil sketch—more starkly phallic than anything vegetable—leaving much to be desired. This is it.

Asparagus, enough to satisfy
1 tbsp, or so, of grated Parma cheese
1 shirred egg, as noted
¼ cup olive oil
Salt and cayenne, to taste

Trim off all tough portions of the asparagus, parboil in briskly boiling water containing salt and a trifle of soda. Drain and reserve. Take a shirred egg dish, put in 2 tbsp olive oil and tiny sliver of garlic, 2 pinches of rosemary. When garlic browns, discard it. Let dish cool somewhat, stir in 1 tbsp sour cream, season highly, and break in 2 eggs. With a small spoon cover eggs with plenty of the basting, and bake until they set just hard enough to be lifted out with a spatula without breaking—*not* until rubbery and tough! . . . While this baking goes on, heat rest of the olive oil in a pan—quite hot. Brown asparagus carefully, so as not to break stalks. Arrange platter with the eggs nested in a hexagonal ring of asparagus. Sprinkle the latter with the freshly grated Parmesan, pop for a brief instant under broiler, and serve.

MOROS y CRISTIANOS—or "MOORS & CHRISTIANS"—being BLACK BEANS & RICE in the TRUE CUBAN STYLE

We've always loved certain kinds of Cuban cookery, and this is a favourite *Cubaño* dish; simple and satisfying; easy to make. . . . First requirement is the "Christians," a nice mound of dry, boiled rice. Next come the "Moors," the black beans which must be soaked overnight. To 1½ cups of black beans, boiled in salted water until tender, add 4 chopped rashers of lean bacon fried out with ¼ clove of crushed garlic, 1 diced onion. Season with 1 tsp chili powder, salt and cayenne. Add enough meat stock to cover the beans, 2 tbsp of good mango chutney, and simmer until beans fall apart a little and make a thick, rich sauce for the pale, warm Christians. Seasoning is typically quite hot.

BARBECUED CORN NAWTH CA'LINA STYLE

This is one memorable dish we found during a summer of 1936 which we spent high up in the cloud-masked mountain ranges out of Asheville. The fillip of peanut butter with fresh green corn is a touch of genius discovered by an amateur sportsman chef we know up in those hills who has much to do with various forms of American tobacco.

Choose tender ears of golden bantam or country gentleman corn. Without necessarily removing more than the outer layers of husk, plunge 10 minutes into fiercely boiling, salted water. Husk now, trim off stems flush and wrap each ear with 3 thin rashers of home-smoked lean baçon skewered with toothpicks. Impale the ear on a long peeled rustic wand, paint well with a basting made from ½ butter and ½ peanut butter, lusciously melted together; then broil over the coals—turning to brown on all sides. . . . When at home use the oven broiler, omitting the wands entirely. If corn is not parboiled first it takes a long time to cook, burns cheeks, hands and bacon; tends to make the corn too tough.

A PENNSYLVANIA DUTCH CUCUMBER FRY, WHITE-MARSH STYLE

Having Pennsylvania Dutch and Quaker branches on both sides of our family, we have always cherished memories of the brick Dutch oven one ancestor had built back of the main house down on a Florida plantation of all places!—which puzzled negroes would journey far to inspect—and of visits to Germantown and Whitemarsh where food was wonderfully ample and satisfying. The only cloud later to mar, materialistically and figuratively, all these pleasant Philadelphia recollections was later discovery that "Roxborough," our forebear's estate from a William Penn grant back in 1684 embraced some 1500 to 2000 acres, straddling the Wissahickon, and bordering the Schuylkill for a mile or more—and which went for one reason or another to outsiders. It would have been so nice to own Fairmount Park in this questionable year of Grace, with our very own bridle trails!

But back to our cucumber fry. . . . It is a simple dish, yet tasty; and it notifies us of one way of cooking a vegetable so often served raw, in salads. Just peel medium sized cucumbers and cut into ¼" thick slices. Marinate 1 hr in cold salt water, made slightly acid with vinegar. Dry in a cloth; dip first into milk then into beaten egg, then roll in fine crumbs and brown in deep fat at 370°.

A BLACK SEA CUCUMBER DISH, in the STYLE of ODESSA

All foreign races recognize the cucumber as food of importance. Turkish porters carry huge burdens, strengthened by a diet consisting of a fair proportion of this vegetable. The Hindu uses them in his curries often. Here our Russki stews them in sour cream and things.

Peel and slice 8 average cucumbers, and stand them in cold salted water 1 hr to firm them. Mince 1 big onion, donate ½ cup of chopped mushrooms, add a speck of crushed garlic, and brown lightly in 1 tbsp of butter. Now drain cucumbers and add them to the onion pan. Add 1½ cups of hot meat stock, thicken slightly with 1 tbsp each of butter and flour, worked into a smooth roux. Simmer until cucumbers are tender. Season with salt and cayenne, and finally add 1 cup of sour cream. Boil up gently once more and serve. A sprinkling of caraway seed is optional, but, to our experimenting palate, added nothing necessary.

A DISH of EGGPLANTS for the LOVELY LITTLE SEASIDE TOWN of SÖLLER, which Is in MALLORCA, where WE VISITED in 1932 and 1933

Spaniards, Italians, Turks, Greeks and Near-Easterners—all of them know things about an eggplant which we seem to ignore. This is a more or less peasant type of dish which will vary with larder and individual cooks; may be highly seasoned, or mild. Just peel and slice a couple of nice eggplants ½" thick, stand in strongly salted water for 10 minutes to extract bitterness, then drain. . . . Heat lots of olive oil very hot indeed, and brown slices lightly on both sides. Reserve, and brown a big finely minced onion with a trace of garlic pulp—much garlic is typical—then fill a greased oven dish as follows: a floor of fried onion, then a layer of eggplant, then one of scalded, peeled, and sliced tomatoes. Season each layer to taste, and if possible squeeze out as many seeds as possible from the tomatoes. . . . Dust this last stratum with 2 tbsp of freshly grated Parma cheese; and repeat the process—finally ending up with a goodly cheese donation which has been well dotted with butter. Brown in a medium oven around 350°, which takes about 45 minutes.

OLD SOUTHERN HOPPING JOHN, GULLA COUNTRY STYLE, which Is BASED on RICE, SMOKED "SIDE MEAT" and COW PEAS

We care for this name almost as much as England's Bubble and Squeak, for a dish title. For generations all true South Carolinians have been serving Hopping John. It is just as natural to the Gulla Country back of Charleston as balls of the sacred Boston codfish are to Beacon Hill, curry to India, chili pepper dishes to Mexico. Cow peas are the right and proper co-basis for this dish. Shelled fresh ones are by far the best, but dried are fine. Get in touch with any large grocery concern and fairly grant them a week to produce the dried items, and the most distant Maine Yankee can find them! Chick peas, pigeon peas and black eyed peas will do, but cow peas have a delicate and unusual taste all their own.

Cover 2 cups of the cow peas with 2 quarts of water, slightly salted, and toss in 4 rashers of smoked "side-meat," bacon—and home smoked country bacon is best—with rashers cut in half and ¼" thick. Simmer slowly until peas are not quite done. Pour off all but 3 cups of this cooking water, add 1 cup of brown or white uncooked rice. Put everything in top of a double boiler and draw off when rice is well-steamed and tender. . . . Pepper seasoning varies with each southern cook. There may be none, or she may put in a small red pepper pod, a red bird pepper, or lots of ground pepper. . . . If dried cow peas are used—and fresh are not obtainable in the north, be sure and soak overnight. The bacon usually is laid about the rice-bean blend. If no double boiler on hand, use very slow fire so as not to have rice stick to the pot. Rice may be boiled separately, using cooking water from the cow peas, but the method given is the one Susan Rainey our old "Geechee" negro cook used for many years in our own family.

A ROYAL STUFFED MUSHROOM, *à la MADAME SACHER,* in VIENNA—when VIENNA WAS ONE LONG HAPPY WALTZ, & KINGS WERE KINGS

Sacher's place is too famous to describe here, and there after the opera royalty would gather, and food and wine served that grew famous 'round the world. Alas it is no more, but the memory clings, and this receipt came to us from an Under-Secretary to the American Legation during the gay years.

We need 1 lb of large mushrooms. Amputate the stems and after discarding all tough parts of the stems, put both tops and reserved stems into plenty of boiling salted water. Simmer until tops can easily be punctured with a fork tine—which requires some 8 to 10 minutes, depending upon adolescence of the mushrooms. . . . Drain and choose the biggest for stuffing, chopping other tops and stems very fine indeed. Melt 2½ tbsp of butter in a pan, turn in chopped mushrooms, ¼ cup finely diced celery, 4 minced pickled walnuts, ½ to 1 tsp of worcestershire, 2 tbsp finely minced onion, 2 tsp chopped almonds. Toss in the hot butter for 5 minutes, stir in 1 tbsp sherry wine, and pack this mixture onto under side of the mushroom tops; dust with dry breadcrumbs, dot with a little butter and brown under a hot broiler. Serve sizzling. This is a nice midnight snack, at times.

EXPLODING OLD WIVES' TALES No. VIII, BEING an EARNEST PLEA for MAINTAINING the DELICATE FLAVOUR of MOST MUSHROOM DISHES

There has always been a tendency, as far back as we can remember, to try and fancy up mushrooms a bit too steeply, as to added high seasonings, flavours and what not. The main thing to bear in mind would appear to be, not what Aunt Williemette has always done toward disguising the mushroom taste, but that the mushroom's own delicate taste and aroma is essentially valuable. Like fine chilled oysters, caviar, or wild duck, it shouldn't be completely overwhelmed with other—commoner—tastes.

MUSTARD or COLLARD GREENS, with Hog Jowl or "Side Meat"

Fresh green mustard has been totally ignored by the north all these years, and is much better than turnip tops and all that sort of thing. Collards are a sort of loose cabbage gone wild in the bush, so to speak. It has a much stronger taste, and we strongly recommend mustard—which any garden can grow in 5 or 6 weeks from seed. . . . Hog jowl, the smoked kind, is something to take up with a place like Pender's in Norfolk; otherwise stick to hambone, or home smoked bacon cut in ¼" thick rashers. Boil the hog jowl or bacon in plenty of salted water until about tender, have pot really boiling when the greens go in—adding a pinch of soda. When the greens are tender, drain well to avoid the strong water; garnishing the sliced jowl or bacon rashers around the heap of green on the platter. Do not cut rashers less than ¼" thick, please.

TAMAS DAVIN'S IRISH *COLCANNON,* which Is a Fine Lusty for an Outdoor or Camping Dish

Citizen Davin, referred to elsewhere, fetched this to us after a recent visit to his own home village in Ireland. The words are his own.

"I can't give you many original Irish receipts. There is no great variety of cooking in the island; mostly bacon, cabbage and potatoes, ad infinitum. They just never think of varying it. Occasionally a bit of lamb, veal or beef, but usually only when there has been an accident on the farm! City cuisine is, of course, like any other—more or less international and nothing in particular.

"The only dish I know that is truly Irish, and one seldom duplicated elsewhere, is *Colcannon*—an old Gaelic name. . . . Just imagine it, will you!—One immense mound of mashed potatoes seasoned with pepper, salt, and so mashed and whipped with butter and cream until it is a fine light consistency. Leaning around the sides of this mound are strips of fried Irish bacon, cut in edible sized pieces.

"Sunken in the top of the foot-high mound, hollowed out like the crater of Vesuvius, is a half pound chunk of butter, which is put in while the spuds are steaming hot and allowed to melt. . . . *Colcannon is devoured by the whole family from the same dish, each member armed with fork or spoon.*

"Each grabs his piece of bacon, and while munching this scoops a gob of potato, dips it into the melted butter, and allows this amalgam to glide down the esophagus. . . . Much merriment is caused by the scrambling for the bits of bacon, and a free-for-all usually ensues near the end of the meal when the last dwindling remnants are scooped for—spoons and forks flying like hurley sticks—and it is then the true *Colcannon* artists begin to show their true mettle. This consists of slithering a portion of the stuff from a competitor's spoon before it reaches his mouth. Facial expressions of the losers add much to the atmosphere, humour and excitement.

"This dish is the real 'McCoy.' Dietitians have fainted at the amount of starch—about 94%, but huge and lusty families have been reared on it for centuries. Once in a rare while the variation of some cabbage may be added to the potato-maché heap, to provide vitamins."

ROSIN POTATOES in the Manner of J. Marquette Phillips & as Done at Black Caesar's Forge for Various Friends & Guests, at Various Times

Marquette Phillips, sometimes called "America's Cellini in Iron," forges all sorts of things out of metals up to and including birdcages of bronze, aluminum and valuable hardwares costing the interest on 100,000 dollars for a year. He also has dug himself a cave in the solid coral rock south of this author's hearthstone, honeycombed it with wine bins, rigged up grills and what not, and here gourmets go to broil things of their own devising. Here we find many Americans hibernating with their trenchers. The last occasion we were there we took Coe Glade, Chicago Opera's luscious contralto, and there was Hervey Allen, with a poet named Robert Frost; there was Grantland Rice, and some Senators, and Don Dickerman of the *Pirate's Dens,* and Errol Flynn and his lovely wife Lili Damita.

Suddenly beside the sizzling 4" steaks appear the Rosin Potatoes; and everyone laughs in superior fashion at them, and ignores them because they are wrapped in Walter Winchell's column, or pages from the *Commonweal,* or ancient *Atlantic Monthlies.* Then someone explains what in hell they are, and people cut them through with a sharp knife and plug them with gobs of butter and garlic salt or hickory salt, and Nepal pepper, then people start laughing and start asking pertinent questions on their later duplication back home. So here's the very simple secret.

Get enough common ordinary rosin to fill an iron cauldron or kettle ¾ full, and the bigger the better. Melt over a wood fire out in the open, and when that point is reached put in the potatoes. They immediately sink, and when done they demurely come bobbing to the surface. Take them out with a wrought iron fork or ladle but be careful and *do not puncture the skins.* Have 2 or 3 thicknesses of newspaper cut into squares big enough to roll potato in, and secure safely with a twist at both ends. The rosin sticks to the paper when it cools —which is at once. Cut straight across through the middle and break open—presto! there is the skin pulled away and a soft deliciously mealy affair that has literally been exploded in every inner cell from the high boiling point of the rosin, and which is better than any potato ever baked in mortal oven. . . . Besides all the virtue in the finished dish, the rosin pot makes a gesture of mystery about the thing. Also the aromatic yellow pine rosin smells so nice.

BOILED PRICKLY PEAR, or CACTUS, LEAVES, *à la SIDNEY FRANKLIN*

A while ago when Ernest Hemingway was headed back to Spain, he had Sidney Franklin, our American-bred bullfighter, stop off to see us. So as Pauline Hemingway had said once that we ought to get the matador to cook us some prickly pear leaves, we asked him to explain the dish between thimbles of Pellison Brandy, 1880, and Kirsch, and Drambuie, to Hervey Allen and ourself. Not believing much, either, beforehand.

You see we'd eaten prickly pear fruits of one shape or another, and cursed the whole cactus tribe hip and thigh when extracting their spines from our shins and the intimate rigging of Rip-Rap strain pointers we used to use on Florida quail shoots. We had seen dumb things like land turtles, asses and crabs, try to eat prickly pear leaves, but doubted their sense for human alimentation. But when Ernest said, "He fixed some down in Key West for Mommie and me, but watch out or they'll physic the hell out of you," we began to guess there might be truth in the thing—because both of them, and Mommie too, are gourmets, and like to think up new and eatable things.

Actually the business tastes like fine fresh okra; the supply is limitless throughout the far south and Gulf States. And cacti of the big, flat-leaved varieties grow the world around where nothing else *will* grow. Also we suddenly realized that lots of people in the tropics get fresh vegetables only about 6 months out of the year. And with cacti costing just nothing to grow why not see . . . ?

Choose the flat-leaved variety having leaf studded with little clumps of very fine spines, rather than the brutal single spine-to-a-spot type. Choose only the younger, tenderer leaves.

1. Trim off a strip 1" thick all around the flat leaf.
2. Place knife against the base of each spine tuft, and with a flip *toward the stem end of the leaf,* spines pop out roots and all.

3. Place leaf on flat surface and cut into lengthwise ¼″ strips; then crosswise, making ¼″ cubes.
4. Boil in three waters as follows: (1) Into briskly boiling salted water with a little soda, for 4 minutes. . . . (2) Repeat, only no soda. . . . (3) A brief stay in a third pot of boiling salted water will tender.

These three waters are needed to carry away excess mucilage. The native Mexicans have used cactus cooked in one water for centuries as a specific for indigent alimentary diligence, being a fine natural lubricant. Doctors consider it a specific of important rank, down there. For average table food three waters will cut it to normal. Serve with lots and lots of butter. The taste is like okra, the best okra, plus a strange exotic "something." It should make a wonderful basis for chicken gumbo, or crab gumbo soup. Arizona, New Mexico and Nevada, and of course inevitable California, actually have an inexhaustible free raw material supply.

CANDIED RED YAMS, *à la CAP-HAITIEN,* being a DELICIOUS AFFAIR from HAITI'S ANCIENT CAPITAL

Our ketch *MARMION* has dropped anchor in this port, surrounded with its wonderful mountains which pitch down to their eternal suicide in a sea bluer than man ever dreamed possible. Cap-Haitien it was that burned for 4 days when the blacks rose and put every Frenchman, woman and child to the machete, and took the richest island in the whole wide world for an African empire under Dessalines, then as kingdom under Black Cristophe, who built the fantastic Citadel on a mountaintop, and lovely Sans Souci at Milot —a ruined palace copied after part of Versailles which our friend Glenn Stewart almost acquired by certain devious yet legitimate tradings a few years back. . . . Yams are native to Haiti, and red yams are by far the best. These are obtainable in the States now, and don't buy the pale, rather tasteless sweet potatoes unless the others are impossible. . . . This particular receipt was fetched back to us by Christopher Clark on the Pan-American Clipper, after a six months' happy domicile on the island doing a series of paintings and immediately prior to a mural execution on our own dining room walls.

First parboil some well-scrubbed yams, and slice them. Take a casserole and butter it well, sprinkle the bottom with the grated yellow rind of 2 oranges, dust with 2 handfuls of brown sugar, flood with ¼ cup of dark rum and set alight. When the rum is half burned out, and the sugar well carameled, blow out the flame. . . . Now season this fragrant pediment with quite a bit more cinnamon than usually required, and plenty of powdered clove; then build up with alternate layers of yam and generous gifts of brown sugar. End up with a final layer of grated orange peel and the crown of sugar, also generously dusted with clove and cinnamon; and brown in a medium oven around 375°. Serve flaming, again using dark rum; and 2 tbsp are enough, heated first to insure good prompt combustion. Marshmallows and chopped peanuts are optional.

YAMS au MARRONS, FLAMBÉ à la FORT de FRANCE, which last Is CAPITAL CITY of LOVELY MARTINIQUE where WE VISITED

Many lovely things came from Martinique, including the Empress Josephine who was born on neighbouring Trois Isles. There the aristocratic French planters lived a life of luxury and ease seldom matched. There the school of creole cookery is toothsome, torrid and most original. The employment of candied chestnuts is a typically French gesture. . . . Choose round, fat yams. Scrub them and parboil until semi-tender. Slice lengthwise slices after peeling, and about ½" thick. Saute gently 5 minutes in hot butter, then arrange on a flat pottery or pyrex oven dish. Dust with sugar, the grated green peel of 3 limes; tee up 2 or 3 big candied marrons on each slice, ring each marron with raisins; and put under the broiler or into a hot oven around 400°. Arrange on a platter, garnish with small brilliant blossoms of any kind. Heat a ladle of cognac brandy and spill 1 tsp or so on each yam slice, serving with lights properly dimmed, *flambé*. . . . Personally we have found that any medium dark rum seems to marry with the tropical yam and the candied chestnuts, even better than the brandy. Martinique rum is procurable in all cities now. Incidentally this is one of the finest companion dishes to roast guineahen we have ever come upon; and it also suits wild duck, turkey, and all sorts of game. It is very rich and if served, cut the other vegetables down to perhaps a single partner such as broccoli *hollandaise,* wild rice, or artichokes.

WORDS to the WISE No. XXVI, DISCUSSING the EVIDENT COMPLEMENT of RAISINS & YAMS, ONE for ANOTHER

We have already mentioned how raisins and roasted quail were intended for each other, and we assure all gourmets that there is something in this mutual affection of raisins and red yams. Try them next time candied sweet potatoes are served. The result will be pleasant, especially if the orange peel isn't forgotten, and brown sugar is used instead of the entirely too usual white variety.

I pray & command you . . . *abstain from beans.*
Pythagorus, to his Disciples,
Athens, 541 B.C.

CHAPTER XI

DESSERTS, & FRUITS CONVERTED *FOR THE* FINAL COURSE

Encompassing Twenty-Nine or so Exotic Adventures such as Portuguese Pie of Crushed Almonds, Egg Whites, Spices & Wine; Bananas *en Casserole,* from Caracas, Venezuela; *Mousse au Miel,* or Honey Mousse, from Paris; Melons, *Glacé,* from Fabulous Rajputana in the Days of the Mughal Emperors; Stuffed Oranges, *à l'Indochine;* and Mrs. Joseph O'Dea's East Mayo Trifle.

ONE DELIGHT we have taken in assembling this book during all those years has been the splendid field, at long last, we had for turning our back on the miasma of bread puddings which through ministration of well-meaning female relatives constantly haunted our youth; to thumb a figurative proboscis at that whole septic tribe of tapiocas, floating islands, and sweet fancies generally.

Oddly enough when we resolved to collect a chapter of Desserts it never occurred to us that except for the French school of elaborate sweets, the finest possible desserts on earth were the countless fruits of tree, bush and vine, that so happily and generously bless mankind throughout the temperate and torrid zones. Another adequate and comforting discovery came with widening experience, and that was the inevitability of wines and liqueurs as being just about the only thing possible to take a ripe and perfect fruit, and elevate it to higher spheres—not merely confound its delicate natural flavours with lily gilding additions. In other words we discovered that heat benefits fruit in many cases, changing them entirely into new and adventurous taste poems, but treatment with delicately flavoured spirits carries the iambic pentameter of the oven to even more rarified heights.

So this, the final Chapter in this volume, we commend to you, and hope that from its files it may be possible to select some thing or other to leave a delicate and lingering fair taste in the mouth.

AND FIRST a FRAGILE and DELICATE ALMOND DESSERT MASTERPIECE KNOWN as ALMOND *SCHAUM TORTE*

Most Amateurs have been fearful of attempting this famous *Danska* delight. Chief cause of this fear and failure is that recommended cooking temperatures in receipts are far too high at start. Unless low first heat is used—actually it is a meringue-*drying* process as much as cooking—weird distortions follow. So here is a well-proven formula fetched to us by an American then high on the diplomatic staff in Copenhagen.

To well-beaten whites of 6 fresh eggs add 2 cups sugar; then beat stiff as stiff. Now donate 1 to 1½ tsps vanilla and 1 tbsp vinegar—Ah, there's a secret touch! Flavour with 6 or 8 drops (to taste) of almond essence. Turn into a buttered *and lightly floured* round baking tin. Start at no higher than 250° oven; then when *torte* has risen and set, turn up to 300° and lightly brown. . . . Serve with whipped cream between the two layers. It is especially delicious with your favourite ice cream on top. Cut into pie-shaped portions. The crisp fairy-light texture of this dessert literally defies description in cold print. Gourmets love it. . . . Also could be flavoured with spearmint or peppermint, or anything you especially admire. Will serve 6. Should be served with a nice and lightly-chilled sweet dessert wine.

BAKED ALASKA, *TROPICAL, et l'AUTEUR*

Our birthday, which occurs for better or worse on Christmas day, found us in Panama that winter of 1933. Theodore, matchless emperor of the Grill Room on *SS. RELIANCE*—recently and unhappily burned at her dock—was always a magician with cookery ideas. So this Baked Alaska was whipped up especially for us with enough tropical touches to make it worthy of notation; and here's a secret—we had it repeated in New York for our pre-wedding dinner!

One brick of rich tutti-frutti ice cream serves 4. . . . Now we need a plank or big cookie sheet. Next comes a sponge or angel's food cake layer 1" thick and same size or better still at least ¾" larger than the ice cream unit, in order to retain its subsequent jacket of meringue. . . . Beat 6 tbsp sugar, 4 to 5 egg whites, and 1 tsp of white rum, *kirschwasser,* or orange Curaçao, until very stiff. Mount sponge cake on plank, ice cream on cake, and spread on meringue in an even layer over everything. Now dust with 1 tbsp finely chopped cashew nuts mixed with the same of grated *fresh* coconut kernel. Have oven *already hot,* around 450°; brown meringue, and serve with utmost speed thereafter. . . . Please never attempt water ices in Baked Alaska; they simply won't stand the heat, and collapse with disastrous aquatic results!

CRÊPES SUZETTES, CUBAÑO, from the VEDADO CLUB, HAVANA, in the YEAR 1931

To Crêpes Suzettes addicts we submit the following variation: roll the French type pancake about a filling of guava paste, or jelly; dust with cinnamon and confectioner's sugar, moisten with hot, well-aged, brandy-like *Añejo* rum, and serve flaming.

VANILLA ICE CREAM, *PAULA,* BEING another FINE ORIGINATION of THEODORE on the *RELIANCE* ESPECIALLY for OUR (then) ONE YEAR BRIDE

We had just run into a dusty February no'theaster out of La Guayra, but it flattened out off the rocky coast of Dutch Curaçao, and to celebrate everyone's returned good humour there was a dinner given, with this fragrant dessert as a fitting period to it all. . . . Arrange 1 brick of vanilla or tutti frutti ice cream in a suitable dish with slightly over-capacity, and garnish the edges with glacé fruits. Brown 4 tbsp of finely chopped Brazil nuts in hot butter, and have these all drained and ready. Heap them on the ice cream in the form of a miniature volcano cone. First moisten this nut mountain with 1 tbsp orange Curaçao, then with 1 tbsp heated brandy; serve flaming.

MARRONS *PLOMBIÈRE,* another HIGH DISCOVERY from CAFE de PARIS in MONTE CARLO, in the YEAR 1932

We offer this as one of the finest desserts we have ever known. We don't know the name of the, then, chef at this fine restaurant in "Monte" because part of our original notes were destroyed; but he must have been a stark staring genius. . . . In few cases does a true French chef use what old coloured Susan Rainey called "store-bought" ice cream, but fabricates it himself very easily indeed.

Beat the yolks of 8 eggs with 1 cup of sugar. Stir this into 1 qt of rich milk flavoured with vanilla to taste. Heat slowly in a double boiler, stirring with a *wooden* spoon until it thickens. At this point step up the tempo with ½ cup finely chopped marrons lusciously soaked in a little dark rum, and 1 tbsp *kirschwasser.* Put into the ice cream freezer, freeze; then pack in individual moulds and press on a top layer of more rum-soaked marrons, broken into bits. Keep packed in ice and salt, or better still put into the freeze chamber of the refrigerator. Serve garnished with whipped cream, slightly sweetened, flavoured with vanilla and a tbsp more of *kirsch.* Dust a tiny bit of grated marron on top, and that's it! Incidentally a Gallic bit of wisdom: *kirschwasser,* pungently flavoured with an odd wild-cherry taste serves as a foil to amplify other flavours of a sweet dish such as this, and don't fear its evidently conflicting taste potency.

MOUSSE au MIEL, or HONEY MOUSSE, which Is a DELICATE and HAUNTING MEMORY—among OTHERS not PERTINENT to MENTION —of TIME-MELLOWED RESTAURANT LAPEROUSE

Laperouse has, easily for half a century, been considered one of Paris' fine restaurants; and for over a hundred years has been the old early 18th Century former domicile of Compte de Bruillevert. To romantically-minded patrons a slight emolument discreetly pressed into the hand of the proper gentleman will, unless already occupied, effect ingress to a tiny *cabinet particulier* off a minor stairway through a knobless door which when closed is totally unsuspected and invisible. With a charming companion at the time, we both were made to feel very stealthy, very wicked indeed—and imagined unannounced husbands, lovers or wives, storming in and vowing satisfaction of one species or another.

But regardless of the honeycomb of private dining rooms, Laperouse has a divine cuisine, an especially sound and sanely tariffed cellar. *Mousse au Miel* was our sweet, that day; and the amateur will find it easily created in his own kitchen. . . . Beat the yolks of 6 eggs so fresh they really should have been scheduled for laying tomorrow—for vintage eggs popping up in a honey mousse are just as bad as a vintage sweetheart popping up on a honeymoon!—together with 1½ cups of strained honey—the darker the more flavourful. . . . Put in a double boiler and stir diligently until it thickens. Chill well and fold in the whites of 3 eggs beaten stiff; then work in a pint of very heavy cream, also whipped. Now pack in mold, or molds, and store in the freezing chamber of the refrigerator exactly the same as *Plombière aux Marrons,* and do not agitate while freezing. Garnish with a dusting of finely chopped pistachio nuts, or better still do not garnish at all. There is something about the simplicity of this dessert so delicately perfumed and flavoured with the lovely gift of honey, that needs no additions whatsoever.

WORDS to the WISE No. XXVII, on the CHILLING of EGGS to be BEATEN STIFF

Please don't forget that if egg whites are easily to be beaten really stiff, eggs had better be well chilled first; especially in a naturally warm climate.

A SHERBET of VIOLETS, *alla FIESOLE*

There is no valid reason for dedicating this lovely ice to Fiesole, for it might have happened anywhere a chef drew breath with romance in his heart. But the fact is we were once, during a stay in Florence, impelled to call upon an American lady who for reasons of her own had taken up dilatory domicile in a jewel-like 17th Century villa near Fiesole. This sweet, served in a garden-close framed in century-old cedars, out of which peeped marble Daphnes and Satyrs and Fauns and what not, and the almond trees foamed with bloom, shall always remind us tenderly of Fiesole—and the lady. . . . To duplicate the dish is quite easy.

Put 2 cups of sugar in a saucepan and add just enough water to make a fairly heavy syrup; simmering gently for 10 minutes. Now add 1/4 cup *Crème de Violette* out of the clever shaped *Bols* bottle, and simmer 5 minutes longer to dissipate some of the alcohol which otherwise would hinder freezing. Draw off fire and cool, meanwhile adding 2 cups of grape juice and the strained juice of 1 small lemon or 2 limes. Now put in the ice cream freezer and when almost frozen, add the white of 1 egg and 2 tbsp of confectioner's sugar whipped together. Freeze well. . . . Serve in crystal sherbet glasses with under plate garnished with a green violet leaf, and 3 violet flowers mounted on top of the sherbet in glass.

MRS. JOSEPH O'DEA'S *EAST MAYO TRIFLE,* a DELIGHTFUL LUSTY from the FIELD NOTEBOOK of ONE TAMAS DAVIN, MENTIONED before, & GATHERED from HIS AUNT in IRELAND in the YEAR 1935

This Gaelic-descended Editor, for reasons not entirely clear, decided to go to Ireland that year, by way of Jamaica and Haiti, and came back fairly bursting with Irish village lore. This Trifle is evidently a mighty serious business, like *Colcannon* which it follows shortly, in a big Irish family. We quote:

"Line the bottom of a large bowl with fine sponge cake made about 1" thick. Spread with strawberry jam or your own favourite jelly. Cover this merry business with another layer of identical cake. Spread this, again, with jam; and continue the process until a few inches below the bowl top. Now pour in enough sherry thoroughly to saturate the cake and make it almost a solid mass—and don't worry, me *spalpeen,* it will saturate the eater shortly.

"Now pour over it a good boiled custard. Put in the coldest spot of the refrigerator for 1/2 an hour. Serve on very large dinner plates surrounded by sliced-up fruits—fresh, canned or glacé: but preferably very ripe and lightly sugared flesh of peaches, pears, apricots; or sliced oranges and seedless grapes. Be sure and allow huge portions for every guest at the start. They all sigh about the waist line, but invariably come back for more, and decide they'll start that diet tomorrow!

"And here is my Aunt O'Dea's Boiled Custard:

"Beat 4 egg yolks until pale yellow, work in 3 tbsp of sugar, and beat well again. Bring 3¼ cups of milk to the boil and pour over the yolks; and when well mixed, put in a double boiler and cook until custard thickens, stirring constantly from the bottom—paradoxical though this last may sound. Finally 1 tbsp of vanilla flavours it, and you won't need any sherry wine here—it's all in the Trifle already!"

SABAILLON, or *ZABAGLIONE,* or WHATEVER the DUTCH DO CALL IT in the EAST INDIES, *à la MELCHIOR TREUB*

The *Melchior Treub* in 1931 was one of those spotless little KPM—*Koninklijke Paketvaart Maatschappij* to us—circling the Dutch East Indies: Batavia, Soerabaja, Bali, Makassar, Singapore and Sumatra. We had flown ahead of our globe encircling steamer, to Soerabaja to board the *Treub,* and at 5 that afternoon, with chronometer promptness we met our old French and Italian friend with new flavours—and we found it a truly delightful lift compared to British tea or American Martinis. It, literally, is a drink pick-me-up eaten with a spoon. And so we sat in the Captain's wardroom with the sun plunging into oblivion back of the volcanic peaks over Tosari way, and the dark green velvet mystery of Madoera Island slipped past our port elbow, already shadowed with the imminent dusk.

The receipt: Must be done in a double boiler; or in a round bottom bowl—better still—standing in a pan of boiling water, like hollandaise sauce. . . . Whip the yolks of 6 fresh eggs, put in the bowl, then add 4½ to 5 tbsp of sugar—stirring and beating constantly with a wooden fork or spoon. When it gradually thickens to a very heavy cream, work in 6 drops of vanilla, and add a little at a time as much ½ cognac —½ orange Curaçao blend as the mixture will absorb and still remain fairly thick. It may be served hot or cold, depending on host whim. . . . This Curaçao flavour is typically Dutch, using liqueurs made mainly in Holland from peculiar oranges from the Dutch West Indian Island of that name.

Our Frenchman would use cognac alone, B & B, Cointreau, Grand Marnier; the Italian, Marsala wine and Italian brandy, half and half; the Spaniard, Sherry and brandy, *Anis del Mono.* A little white of egg is sometimes added in France and Italy. In Martinique or Haiti rum would naturally be used—using half light and half dark.

WINE JELLY, *à la TSARINA,* which Is another DELICATE REMEMBRANCE from the GRANDLY ROYAL DAYS of OLD RUSSIA

We include this as suggestion for a wine jelly dish to be sent to the bedside of a favourite hospital patient, or invalid, as a taste-change from usual wabbly desserts dietitians seem to delight in inflicting on helpless souls. . . . Put jelly moulds on ice where they will get really chilled. Fill with any good usual wine jelly flavoured with the fruit which is favourite with the subject, and sherry, being careful not to pass the half-way mark in the mould—retaining an equal amount of the jelly. . . . While this last is still liquid, add 1 jigger of *Gilka kummel,* and whip with an egg beater so diligently that it grows white and thick. Put enough of this into moulds to fill, and chill very cold indeed.

AND NOW for the EXOTIC FRUIT DESSERTS, from ORIENT & OCCIDENT; and ARABIAN NIGHTS BAKED APPLES, a BIT of a CEREMONY from MERRIE ENGLAND that WE FOUND ESPECIALLY COMFORTING on a CHILL FALL NIGHT

Take big red, tart apples; core them, and remove peeling 1/4 way down from the stem end. Stack them in a big kettle, but not touching each other. Add 3/4 cup of hot water and after filling cavities with sugar, dust sugar on top, toss in the peel of an orange, and colouring each apple with a drop or 2 of red liquid, the lid goes on tight and they are cooked *very slowly* until tender. . . . Now remove them to a greased baking dish, stuff tightly with the following mixture: Chopped dried figs and stoned dates—equal amounts; and this seasoned highly with clove, cinnamon, and 1 tsp Jamaica rum added to soak into the stuffing. Dust heavily with brown sugar and spices, and brown in a fairly hot oven around 375°—taking out immediately when sugar caramels. We inquired as to the Arabian Nights title, drawing a vague answer about figs and dates and other Mesopotamian things, and about it being a very old receipt. After all the title doesn't aid digestion, noticeably.

OLD ENGLISH TOFFEE APPLES, a RECEIPT from BANBURY, in 1932

We have seen children eating candy covered small apples up in Kalgan, that railway junction town above the Great Wall of China, not too far from the Mongolian border; in Korea, in Nikko, Japan, in England, and at our own old style county fairs. Ripe crab apples simmered a few moments in sugar syrup first, dried, then chilled, are favourites. We, however, recommend small sweet ripe table apples.

1. Make small wooden skewers the size used on lollypops.
2. Dig out bud end of apple. Put in skewer, and put near the stove so apples can thoroughly dry—but don't heat.
3. Make caramel, see any routine cook book, cooked long enough for it to crack in cold water.
4. Dip the apples in this hot caramel. Dry in warm oven, or near the stove. Repeat until well covered with several layers of sweet. . . . Caramel may be tinted with scarlet colouring for a more intriguing effect.

BANANAS en CASSEROLE, à la KENSCOFF

Six years ago we, and our better half, in Haiti, thought it would be a good idea to wander out of Port au Prince and up into the back-country hills through Petionville, and Kenscoff, for a look-see from the road-head at mysterious Morne la Selle which towers dark and aloof over the weird shadowed valleys where *vaudou* drums still throb of nights in spite of probation period administered by the U.S.

Marines, in spite of the professed and Paris-educated culture of the Haitian aristocracy. Yes, the *bambosh* dance is still danced until the dancers, wildly drunk on *clairine* vanish into the surrounding blackness to capture the partner of their choice. Yes, there are *mamaloi* and *papaloi* in those mountains, and goats and white cocks to be sacrificed before crude altars carved with the figure of Damballa, the Snake God, alongside clay figurines of the Virgin Herself. We have told already of Compte de Kenscoff, in the text of another receipt; so here is another, found after we had gone back there and seen Morne la Selle, after hiking seven miles up the mountainside beyond where the road was washed out—a stark, mournful peak soaring almost 2 miles into its neckerchief of trade wind cloud.

We got back to Kenscoff alright, and in our car which had all the audible virtues of an International Harvester, the soul of a wasp and springs of granite, we almost succeeded in officiating at the debut of our first daughter and heir on that rockiest road this side of Ethiopia. It really wasn't the bananas' fault!

Take six red bananas preferably, peel them, and split lengthwise—then cut once across. Brush with lime juice and brown delicately in hot butter, salting lightly. Make a syrup out of 1 cup sweet red *unfortified* wine, not port; 1 cup brown sugar, ½ tsp each of cinnamon and nutmeg; ¼ tsp powdered clove, 1½ tsp grated yellow orange peel. Put bananas in a small buttered casserole, turn in this spice syrup, and cover with a layer about ¼" thick made of equal quantities of crushed macaroons and very finely chopped almonds. Brown in a medium oven around 350°, and just before serving heat 1½ tbsp Haitian, or other dark, rum; fetch to table flaming.

NOW a CONSERVE of DRIED BANANAS, which WE HAVE ASSUMED as a DESSERT, MADE of DRIED BANANAS SPRINKLED with RAW BROWN SUGAR, a TRIFLE of DARK RUM, then PACKED in BAYLEAVES for MELLOWING & which the PARIS-EDUCATED HOSTESSES of PORT au PRINCE CALL *CONFITES des BANANES, SECHÉS*

In the true West Indian manner these fruits are split lengthwise and then across, and dried in the sun; but in the States it is saner to put them on a lightly buttered cooky sheet, and slowly dry at around 250° in oven. When they are thoroughly dry moisten them all over with rum, roll in brown sugar. Put a layer of rum-moistened bayleaves in a wooden box, then a layer of the sugared fruit, then another of bayleaves—and so on until a final layer of bay finishes things off, this being well sprinkled with rum. . . . Cover tightly and put in a cool place to absorb virtue and discretion from the varied aromatics in rum, herb and sugar. Inspect from time to time, during damp weather. These Haitian bananas make a sweetmeat, chopped up they garnish ice cream; with whipped cream or hard sauce they would make a dessert in their own right; or with a fine Philadelphia cream cheese, for instance.

FRUITS with DRY WHITE WINE, *á CHILEÑO y MENDOZA*

To a lucky few North Americans the very mention of Chile's Mendoza province brings to mind a sunny, happy land which is as near to Paradise as anything can be in this troubled world of ours today; a climate like California in many ways, a soil as finely suited to grape culture as any anywhere. Here the proprietor of vast *estancias* reigns almost as a benign feudal baron. He actually owns whole towns and villages, supplies church and padre; endows doctors, hospitals; tends to his workers like a father, nurses them when sick, marries them, delivers them and buries them. In a way he *is* their father, almost their God.

Our *caballero Chileño* doesn't sit on cool verandahs sipping mint juleps, he quaffs a mild and delicate drink emigrated there from Old Spain, of mingled wine and sun-ripe fruits. . . . Apricots, peaches; purple, red or green plums; ripe pineapple, anything on this order will do—but be sure they are really ripe. Simply peel, core, stone, and cut into fairly coarse pieces with a sharp knife—enough to fill a tall 16 oz glass 1/3 full. Chill both fruit and glass, then fill to the brim with iced dry white wine, like Chile's lovely *Undurraga Rhin* that we discovered back in 1933 on the Grace Line's *Santa Elena* en route from Seattle to Panama and Havana.

When drunk with a meal this blend is delightful. Glasses are refilled with cold wine as needed, and finally the well saturated fruits themselves are captured—making dainty tidbits of married wine and fragrant ripe pulp. *Undurraga* always comes in squat brown saddlebag type bottles, as much of Chile's wine goes into the Argentine where the *gauchos* pack them in saddlebags. We find a garnish of fresh green spearmint is a pleasant addition.

KILLARNEY CHERRIES

Next to negro mammies and levees and cotton fields, Killarney has probably had more songs dedicated to her lakes and dells than is credible, but, regardless of all this, her aristocracy was much quicker to appreciate fine Bordeaux claret than were their English step-brothers, if we are to believe the written histories of wines. This thoughtful dessert is original enough to satisfy the most critical gourmet.

Stem 1 lb of fine big black or red cheeked ox-heart cherries, being sure they are really ripe. Put them in a saucepan, cover with claret, and add sugar to make quite sweet; then toss in a stick of cinnamon bark, or 1 tsp of the ground spice; ¼ tsp ground cloves, or 12 whole cloves. When pot boils, reduce heat and simmer as gently as may be for 12 to 15 minutes, covered. Drain out the cherries carefully, reduce the sauce by about 1/3 through gentle simmering, add 2 tbsp of red currant jelly; let melt and let cool. . . . Put cherries in a deep silver serving dish. Chill everything very cold indeed. . . . Meantime make up some whipped cream, slightly sweetened, and flavoured with 1 scant tbsp *kirschwasser*—a cherry brandy—and serve as follows: first the cherries in silver, then wine sauce poured over, then whipped cream on top. Shaved or cracked ice in another silver dish, nesting the bowl into it for better chilling, is recommended. The taste fillip is the lovely cherry flavour pointed up with really chilled fruit and sauce. . . . These cherries served hot over any sort of ice cream except chocolate, are food for the gods—and this latter case, add hot cognac in chafing dish and serve in a sauce boat flaming.

RIPENED FRESH FIGS BAKED with VARIOUS LIQUEURS, *à la GRANDE CORNICHE*

Cooked ripe figs are almost totally ignored by Americans, although they grow well from the Carolinas southward and westward to California—both brown, purple and yellow varieties. . . . Now a whispered word of advice: ***never*** peel ripe figs to be cooked; merely wash them to remove travel stains and possible entomological companions. . . . In this receipt stand them in an oven casserole or baking dish, having a little water on the bottom; dust them well with brown sugar. Prick each fruit with a fork to permit egress of pent-up steam under heat, and bake very slowly at around 275° to 300°, basting frequently. When very tender, dust with cinnamon, a little powdered clove, and add ¼ cup of any fine liqueur like Curaçao, Cointreau, Chartreuse, Grande Marnier, *kirsch*. Chill them very cold indeed in the serving dish, being careful not to damage figs in removal from baking dish. Pour the sauce all over them. Make some whipped cream lightly flavoured with a little confectioner's sugar, and some of the cordial as is used in the sauce. This also is delicious as a crowning gesture to any delicately flavoured ice cream.

MUSKMELONS, *ORIENTALE*

Some years ago we were wandering alone across India, westward from Calcutta; Benares, Agra, Delhi and so on down to Bombay. In Jaipur in the State of Rajputana Agency, we were fortunate enough to meet the young Maharajah while inspecting his 300 or so polo ponies, a young gentleman of parts, who had awakened up one fine morning to find himself not only deprived of his august father, but wearer of the royal title and possesser of some 400 assorted wives and concubines of various ages, colours, dispositions and manners! We sat on a dais, or divan, under the General Electric *punkahs* in his lovely palace and compared notes on things western and things eastern—ethics, morals, liquors and foods. Some of his descriptions of the feasts and levees given for George V at the Durbar, beggared belief. He told us about Ambar, a few miles up toward Gulta Pass. We never think of the harem quarters of that deserted Ambar Palace outside of Jaipur—built in 1600 and abandoned in 1728—a lovely thing of fountains, cool water runnels, and marble fretwork jalousies, frescoed baths and cloistered gardens where they promenaded with attendant eunuchs—without thinking of those canny old bearded Rajput rascals taking their ease, as we might say, of a warm summer afternoon during the monsoon season, fanned with peacock feather fans, feasting the eye on their assorted ladies and feasting the lips on Muskmelons, *Orientale*. . . . Incidentally we might mention that when the young Maharajah's father, the Maharajah Madho Singh, went to England for Edward VII's coronation, he not only chartered his own steamship for the voyage but bunkered her up with enough wives, viziers, servants, food and water to last the trip there and back, and furthermore transported in addition to this modest equipment, a plot of Jaipur State soil whereupon to plant the royal *derrière,* when at meat or drink or what not, just so he would always feel at home. We challenge any adopted citizens of California to match that!

Choose only sun-ripened muskmelons or cantaloupes, and Persian or Spanish melons are the only type we recommend that are not entirely ripened on vine. First cut a slice off the bud end so melon will stand upright. Next, cut a 3" trap door out with stem in the center. Remove seeds carefully, scoop out flesh with a melon ball scoop—making small balls of the best part. Put in a bowl and add ½ as much of really ripe fresh pineapple. Add to each melon 6 halved scarlet maraschino cherries, sweeten well with powdered sugar, and replace in melon. Before closing again pour in 4 tbsp of arrack, or lacking this either *kirsch,* Cointreau, or other good liqueur. Chill cold as possible without actually freezing for exactly 24 hrs. Garnish with green leaves on the platter, bright blossoms, or scarlet cherries.

MUSKMELONS in the SPANISH MANNER, a ROYAL DISH from CASTILE that WE COLLECTED in SPAIN, in the YEAR 1931

This, amazingly enough, parallels the *Orientale* dish very closely. The fact is that the Mughal Emperors brought their luxurious ideas from Persia, and in turn many of those thoughts filtered back into Spain through the Mohammedan Moors after their conquest of the Iberian Peninsula. . . . Cut off a flat spot from blossom end, make the same trap door, take out seeds—only now instead of cutting flesh into small balls, merely turning in 1/3 to ¼ cup of *Anis del Mono,* or Anis of the Monkey-Head Label—substituting French or Dutch anisette if this is not available. Chill for the same length of time. This is a favourite dish around Badalona where much of the Spanish *anis* was then made, and thereabouts is called "Stuffed Melon of the Monkey."

BAKED STUFFED SWEET ORANGES, PACKED with CERTAIN TROPICAL LOOT such as DATES, FIGS, and COCONUT, not to MENTION CHOPPED CASHEWS or ALMONDS, *à l'INDOCHINE*

This is a classic from Saigon, overnight stop before journeying by motor car supplied by *Le Bureau Central du Tourisme Indochinois,* up into the amazing jungle country via Pnom Penh and Siemreap to Angkor Wat, in Cambodia; and donated to our volume by the chef of the Continental Palace Hotel as we sat in Cabaret Le Perroquet, in Saigon, studying human relationships.

For 6 oranges allow 9 pitted dates, and 8 small dried figs; also 6 marshmallows, 2 tbsp finely chopped fresh white coconut kernel, and 2 tbsp of finely chopped roasted cashews or unsalted almonds. Cut cap off stem end, remove pulp, and mix this last with the chopped dates, figs, and nuts. Dust well with brown sugar, after stuffing the orange shells, and bake for ½ hr in medium oven around 350°. Add 1 tsp cointreau to each orange, arrange on a silver platter and splash a little heated cognac over them. Serve flaming, and garnished with something appropriately tropical.

PECHES à la GRANDE BRETAGNE, which CONCERNS ITSELF with PEACHES in ATHENS, & CUNNINGLY DEALT with by AGENTS like CURAÇAO, CHOPPED PISTACHES & HAZELNUTS, and ALL of IT SERVED COLD as COLD

Peaches must be dead ripe, of course, for acid fruit spells defeat. First make a quart of sugar syrup, but not too thick. Add 1 scant tbsp vanilla and when it boils well, drop the peaches into this bath for exactly 2½ minutes. Remove them, slip off their skins without breaking the pulp, then pop back in syrup for 5 more minutes' simmering. Now add sugar, and let syrup thicken until it is fairly heavy. Arrange the peaches in a silver or china bowl being sure to leave a depression in the center which is filled with peach or apricot jam, or conserve. Take enough of the vanilla syrup to drench the peaches well, add ¼ cup or so of peach or apricot liqueur, and pour over everything. Now whip enough thick cream to mask well, adding 1 tbsp of the same liqueur to this also, for the characteristic flavour. Chill everything well, mask when served with whipped cream, and dust all over with finely chopped pistachio and hazelnuts. This is another stroke of genius by Chef Jean Kritikos in Athens.

ANOTHER DELICATE DISH, this TIME of SUN-RIPE PEACHES STUFFED with POUNDED ALMONDS, CHOPPED CITRONS, PEELS, and LIQUEURS, in the MAJESTIC ROMAN MANNER

We have already touched lightly on one stay in *Grande Hotel de Russie,* in Rome; and suffice it to say that this dish was observed on a festive occasion when certain expatriate Americans rendered a dinner on the Eve of our departure for Pisa and Paris. And for no reason at all it suddenly came over us that except eaten *in situ* under the bough, as peaches and cream, or in ice cream, America shrugs the peach off into unnecessary and undeserved oblivion. Consider, then, the following.

Choose ripe specimens, for as is the case with our modern virgins, many a blushing cheek may camouflage a hard and durable heart. Allow 2 whole peaches per guest. . . . Scald in boiling water for a moment, and slip off their skins. Halve lengthwise and remove stones. To stuff 12 peaches, pound 1 cup of chopped, unsalted, blanched almonds in a bowl or mortar—adding a few drops of cold water to prevent oiling—along with 1 tbsp of sugar. Now mix in 1 tbsp of finely chopped candied orange peel, the same of finely chopped citron, the crushed pulp of 1 ripe peach for a binder, and finally 6 lady fingers cut small. . . . Pack the cavities with this toothsome stuffing, rejoin the divorced halves, skewer with toothpicks, then put in a baking dish. Now wet them with white wine, dust with sugar, and pop in a medium oven around 375° until sugar caramels a little. These are delicious hot, with half peach brandy—half cognac, heated and poured over them, and set alight; or, better still, served cold with or without whipped cream, flavoured with peach liqueur or apricot.

PEARS in PORT, *ARMENONVILLE,* which ARE SUN RIPENED AFFAIRS TREATED FAIRLY, and FIRST POACHED MODESTLY in a BATH of WHITE WINE

Here at Armenonville in the Bois de Boulogne is a sort of chalet set beside a park lake, which at night changes itself to a fairyland. The glass enclosed lower part of the building makes it almost unreal—especially when viewed from the garden, where those both romantic and wise, choose to dine of a summer's evening. Perhaps the chef has forgotten that very especial dessert suggested to a certain two; perhaps not. Ah me—*tout casse, tout passe!*

Peel 2 big pears very carefully leaving the stem in, but do *not* core in this case. Poach, covered, in sweet white *unfortified* wine with a little sugar added, and when tender set in the refrigerator to cool. Now put 1 cup of ripe red raspberries or strawberries through a sieve, add 1 tbsp sugar and 2 tbsp of red port wine. Make a whipped cream using a little red port for flavouring. In service try and find a crystal bowl, or dessert dish, for the colours are pretty. First comes the pear, drowned in the port wine and berry sauce, then the rosy-hued whipped cream. Chill very very cold indeed.

PEARS, *à la CUILÈRE,* from MARVELOUS RESTAURANT JOSEPH, on RUE PIERRE CHARRON, in PARIS, RIGHT BANK

It hardly seems thirteen years ago since we were last in Joseph, and arranged our little dinner—calling at 10:30 in the morning to make sure of everything. And the pear was upon advice of the *maitre d'hotel,* and a wise one, that. . . . It is a mildly spectacular dessert, and one appreciated by those who know foods.

Take big ripe luscious pears, peel them with surgical nicety, and slice the bud end off ½" or so back, saving the slice. Remove core from this end, and pack the cavity with crimson bar le duc; or lacking this, with red or black currant jam—in either case mixed with 1 tsp *kirschwasser.* Now stand the pear stem end down in a big crystal goblet, chill as cold as possible without actually freezing, and serve with a liqueur glass filled with *kirsch,* this last to be added a drop per spoonful, as needed. In another place we found a little soft cream cheese put inside cavity in this manner: first 1 tbsp bar le duc, then 1 tsp cream cheese, ending with bar le duc at the last, *Magnifique!*

BAKED PINEAPPLE, *HAWAII*

Out Lanikai-way lived a friend of ours dating back to the first of our three voyages to that most charming fleet of islands, who considered this his pet dessert receipt. Much as we would like to shout the praises of our own ½ acre patch of Smooth Cayennes we really are forced to admit that Hawaii produces the finest "pines" on earth. . . . Choose a large sun-ripened pineapple, or one which has been stood in sun until beautifully coloured. With a keen blade, behead the top—cutting through 1½" down on the fruit; reserve this for future use. Now cut out the heart meat with a curved grapefruit knife, being careful not to dig through the shell. Discard pithy portions entirely, dice small, and toss with ½ cup or so of sugar until well coated. Now put diced meat back into shell, pour juices over, add 3 to 4 tbsp cognac, dust with 1 tsp cinnamon at the last. Put the cap back on, skewer in place with toothpicks, and bake in a medium oven around 350° until inner flesh is tender as can be. . . . Serve on silver platter, pour on 1 tbsp heated brandy and fetch to table blazing.

RIPE STRAWBERRIES, *à la TSARINA,* which ARE a FINAL THOUGHT on those INCREDIBLE DAYS in ST. PETERSBURG before the DEBACLE, when LIFE WAS LIVED, WOMEN WERE LOVELY, MEN GALLANT, and FIVE YEAR PLANS WERE NOT YET DREAMED of

Be sure berries are ripe. Stem 2 cups or so carefully an hour ahead of chilling time, tumble in a mound of powdered sugar, and put them in a crystal or silver bowl. Next we must blend 2 tbsp each of tawny port, orange Curaçao and cognac, and pour this over the sugared berries; or put immediately into the individual dessert dishes, portioning the sauce equitably. Make enough whipped cream flavoured with Curaçao to cover well. Serve with dishes in cracked ice—everything chilled as cold as possible.

> ". . . What does cookery mean? . . . It means knowledge of all herbs, & fruits, & balms, & spices, & of all that is healing & sweet in groves, & savoury in meat. It means carefulness, willingness, & readiness of appliance. It means the economy of your great grandmother, & the science of modern chemistry, & French art, & Arabian hospitality. . . ."
>
> *John Ruskin*

APPENDIX

WEIGHTS & MEASURES

Asparagus	20 stalks	1 lb
Bananas, skins on	3 big ones	1 lb
Beans, Green, fresh	1 qt approximately	¾ lb
Beans, Dried	1 cup	½ lb
Bread Crumbs	1 cup	2¾ oz
Butter	1 cup	½ lb
Corn Meal	3 cups	1 lb
Currants, Dried	2⅜ cups	1 lb
Dates, Dried, seeded	1 cup	5 oz
Flour, Bread	4 tbsp	1 oz
Flour, Bread	3 1/5 cups	1 lb
Flour, Whole Wheat & Pastry	1 cup	¼ lb
Lard	1 cup	½ lb
Lemon Rind, Grated	1 average size	3 tsp
Lemon Juice	1 average size	3 tbsp juice
Milk, Skim	1 cup scant	½ lb
Nut Meats	1 cup	5 1/3 oz
Raisins	1 cup	5 1/3 oz
Rice	1 cup	½ lb
Sugar, Brown	1 cup	5½ oz
Sugar, Confectioners	1 cup	4½ oz
Sugar, Ordinary Granulated	1 cup	5 oz
Tomatoes, average size	4 tomatoes	1 lb
Water	1 cup	½ lb

ALL MEASUREMENTS in THIS VOLUME, & VOLUME II, ARE LEVEL.

INDEX OF RECEIPTS

The Gentleman's Companion

VOLUME II

THE EXOTIC DRINKING BOOK OR, AROUND THE WORLD WITH JIGGER, BEAKER, AND FLASK

By *Charles H. Baker, Jr.*

INCLUDING:

A personally collected *Regiment of World-Famous Lively Liquid Masterpieces from Greater & Lesser Ports of Orient & Occident, & the South Seas.*

NOT FORGETTING:

The Proper & Civilized *Service of Beverages with Foods,* together with *Proven Formulae for Home Construction of Certain Bitters, Wines, Meads & Cordials;* a Meaty Kernel of Advice for *Those Departing for the Bars,* & in the Last a *Sextet of Temperance Delights,* & a Platoon *of Picker-Uppers of Proven Worth & Discretion.*

The Mint Julep is one of mankind's truly civilized inventions

DEDICATION

To all that Company of Friends, from Pine to Palm,
with whom we have So Happily Raised the Glass.

Drink no longer Water but use a little Wine for thy Stomach's sake and thine often Infirmities . . .

Saint Paul, the Apostle,
1 Timothy, V. 23

CONTENTS

CHAPTER I

A DESIGN *FOR* DRINKING

Being a Brief Dissertation on *This Pleasant Subject in General;* why *Too Many Cocktails Fail through Over-Sweetness & Plurality of Ingredient;* why *Hot Drinks must be Hot, & Cold Drinks Cold;* an *Ardent Plea for Accurate Calibration;* & finally a *Second Invitation to The Blender.*

As in the creation of *THE EXOTIC COOKERY BOOK,* this setting down in print of the first-fruits of fourteen years' liquid field work naturally credits all readers with fair fundamental knowledge on the subject of mixed potables. In any congregation of exotica there can hardly be room for formulae on such elementary subjects as the ever-present Dry Martini, the Manhattan or the Old Fashioned Cocktail. Our own native Mint Julep was included because it can, and does, stand proudly beside the world's best concoctions; a masterpiece in its own right, a true exotic of the Deep South which has been taken up and deliciously modified in other interesting places as far off as the Philippines.

It is also a physical impossibility to pretend that this volume is a complete treatise on beverages. There are some ninety-seven visible volumes on our own shelves dealing with wines, blended drinks, and tradition obtaining to this gentle art of imbibition—which is our coined word for the sport—and heaven alone knows how many more there must be in print that we've never heard of! Experts have spent whole lives covering one phase or type of wine—of which there are around sixteen hundred listed. We, therefore, will briefly mention which to chill; which not to chill; which types march best with certain foods and courses.

On the truly American matter of mixed drinks we feel we can speak from some slight experience, and with fair authority. Instead of listing a maze of receipts already listed in, and plagiarized from, professional bar lists and previous cocktail books, we will bring you famous liquid classics from odd spots of the world—classics which, through the test of time and social usage, have become institutions in the place of their birth. One volume in our possession naively lists seventeen hundred allegedly authentic cocktails, whereas there cannot possibly be that many *good* cocktails on earth—or a hundred and seventy, for that matter.

All those we list cannot please every reader, naturally. Certain normal friends of ours dislike Holland gin with a passion little short of fanatical. We've yet to meet the female who really likes Jamaica rum unmixed with lighter rums to modify the heavy molasses taste. Absinthe, for instance, can conquer the most desiccated puritan on occasion, but makes the heart of many agreeable folk shudder at the taste. Anisette, kümmel, tequila, Hawaiian *okolehao*—all have their enemies and champions. No, the best we can hope to do is thumb over our battered field book, our odd scrawled-upon bar chits, menus and scraps of notes from bygone days, and construct therefrom a sequence of drinks which for this reason or that, stand out in memory beyond their fellows.

The issue we take with current cocktail books is no reflection on their authors, but on their subject matter. It dates back to the year 1931 when we were headed around the world, and found ourself in the Free Port of Gibraltar. Well, the British pound sterling was down to $3.30 American—then—gold. Being a duty-free port American cigarettes were ninety cents the carton, Johnny Walker *Black Label,* eighteen the case. London Gordon around three dollars, eighty the case. With these few basic figures it proves the possible scope of our laboratory work.

We got back in the last tender out of "Gib," and if she wasn't down to her Plimsoll marks it wasn't through lack of brown paper covered packages destined for the vacant cabin on B Deck next to ours! That night we stowed our pelf—bottle on bottle of it. There was everything the wildest madcap mixer could demand for any known blended potation, fizzes, daisys, rickeys, cocktails, punches, and pick-me-ups.

We had bought the biggest cocktail book in print, and every evening thereafter we went to work. It was one of those thick volumes which sprouted on the damp soil of prohibition like wan, mad mushrooms. Along with two other stout hearts and chrome vanadium stomachs we attacked that plump book every evening for five solid months! We cut no corners; we didn't cheat. We measured accurately, chilled properly. We tasted and drank or promptly flung the abortive fluid out the nearest port hole.

To our naive mind, assuming that all drink receipts in print must have been put there through some sort of tested merit, the disillusionment was immediate and illuminating. By Suez we were groggy; we spent two days in Newara Eyliya, hill station back of Colombo, Ceylon, to get our breath. By Singapore we were cellars-dry, and bought again. We literally drank our way across Siam and Cambodia. We, along with our other fellow-scientists, popped corks and gulped our triple-threat through the Dutch East Indies, Java, Bali, Borneo, and Makassar to Zamboanga, to Manila, then to Hongkong in South China. On the Bund in Shanghai our heads were groggy but unbowed, and we bought again. By the time we quit Honolulu the bald-faced conclusions were plain as the nose on our face—much of that welter of mixed things with fancy names were the egotistically-titled, ill-advised conceptions of low-browed mixers who either had no access to sound spirits, or if they did have, had so annealed their taste buds with past noxious cups that they were forevermore incapable of judicious authority. It was no wonder that, like the originators of the latest parlour story, their originators would invariably hide incognito. We measured with laboratory accuracy, obeyed every law. Here's the verdict.

1. Out of all the thousands of cocktails listed in all books there are too many drinks calling for gin and vermouth. We admire vermouth in its place, but that simply isn't in 60% of our cocktails.
2. Entirely too many cocktails specified too much Italian vermouth and French vermouth with fruit juices. It is an evil combination, productive of evil enzymes and tastes.

3. Too many cocktails of delicate base specified too much of Italian vermouth, with result that the latter drowned out the basic and better flavour. Like absinthe, Italian vermouth is a dominant taste; and we must watch it.
4. Many cocktails seem to get into books more because of a trick or "cute" name—heaven only knows why!—than for the chemical soundness of its *raison d'être*. Calling a drink a *Widow's Kiss*, or a *Horned Toad*, really isn't any ticket to liquid immortality; for no inferior blend ever lasts out the night of its evil concoction.
5. Except for flavouring cocktails, and one or two rare Exotics like the Hongkong *Rosy Dawn*, immortal to our memory, no mixed drink having more than 3 main alcoholic ingredients but which becomes hoist on the petard of its own casual plurality. . . . In other words, barring Pousse Cafés and other feminine threats, no drink calling for 1 part gin, ½ of cherry brandy, ½ Curaçao, ½ apricot brandy, and ½ rye whisky, can ever prove out into anything but the taste melee it is. However it is possible to point up a drink with a *dash* of this and that upon a basically sound foundation.
6. Watch using liqueurs or cordials in cocktails. Most of these are very sweet and not only can make an otherwise good mix too sweet, but lose their own character through dilution.
7. Our thirty years of bending elbow above well-worn mahogany convinces us that far too many hosts mix too-small drinks in too-small glassware. Bigger drinks stay colder (or hotter) longer; and a fist-temperature Martini or a luke-warm Hot Buttered Rum are evil things, owning the same dispensability as luke-warm coffee or a luke-warm lover. All cocktails served at Java Head are big "doubles" put in pre-chilled 7-ouncer stemmed cocktail glasses, sometimes larger. . . . No ulterior motives here either: folk drink fewer and better to achieve like result, that's all.

HAVING come through this test by liquid, still sound in wind and limb, or as Fritz (*Alone in the Caribbean*) Fenger would say "unfrayed at either end," we are still heartily of the opinion that decent libation supports as many million souls as it threatens; donates pleasure and sparkle to more lives than it shadows; inspires more brilliance in the world of art, music, letters and common ordinary intelligent conversation, than it dims—as even a brief glance into the history of our finest lyric poets, musicians, artists, authors, and statesmen, will attest—

right from the day of Wull Shaksper to our own generation.

In the collection of this volume's data we gradually came to realize that the great drinks around the world, like the ethics of draw poker, the length of ladies' skirts and width of men's pantaloons—the *accepted,* the proven, thing is the right thing; the best thing, and all of these proven experiences march here.

Each one of them fetches joyous memory of some friend, place, or adventure; is flanked with happy memory of a frosted glass, a smile, the sip of something which is perfect. No, nothing shall ever pirate away those memories, or the recorded history of these two hundred and more drinks. We are faithful to them, Cynara, after our fashion!

AN EARNEST PLEA for THREE METICULOUS OBSERVANCES in the CONSTRUCTION of any MIXED DRINK—and ESPECIALLY that of the COCKTAIL

1. Measure accurately, and don't be betrayed by that insidious temptation to pour with a "heavy jigger." It is undeniable hospitality to wish guests to get their ample share of spirits, but don't force the amount. More drinks are spoiled through being too strong than being too weak.
2. Serve cold drinks *arctic cold.* Chill bottles and glasses, to speed up the process. . . . Serve hot drinks *steaming hot.* . . . Compromise in either of these events is merely bargaining with fault and disaster.
3. If there are guests present who appreciate decent cocktails, let's do the mixing ourself. The amateur will always take infinitely more pains than any houseboy or butler. Trust him for such usual fare as whisky-and-soda, the Tom Collins, and so on. They are easy. But the crisp pungency of a proven cocktail demands infinite care in observance of the simple mixing requirements. It is such a brief step from excellence to mediocrity.
4. Don't try and make decent cocktails out of cheap, briefly aged liquors. Stick to highballs, or else do the job up right. We can no more build a fine cocktail on dollar gin than Whistler could paint his mother's portrait with barn paint.

WORDS to the LIQUID WISE No. I, URGING all GOOD AMERICANS to LIFT a PROUD HEAD & MEET the WORLD EYE to EYE, when IT COMES to MAKING MIXED DRINKS

Your Britisher may scorn ice in his whisky-sodas, your Indian Colonial may insist on cellar-warm ale, your Frenchman may know all his wines by their maiden names—but remember that the American has invented, and always will invent, more of the world's good mixed drinks than all the rest of humanity lumped together. . . . Just read the pages of history. There they are: juleps, cocktails, cobblers, fizzes, daisys, sours, rickeys, coolers—these and more all originated in America, reached their highest technique here in America. . . . Whether the rest of the world cares to admit it or not, we started these drinks in circulation, just as we started the telephone, submarine, phonograph, incandescent light, electric refrigerator, and decent bath tubs. Oddly enough, outside the continental boundaries of the States the best drink mixers are American-trained Chinos, Cubans, Filipinos, Japanese, Swiss, and officers in His Britannic Majesty's army and navy!—not native English, French, or Italian citizens on their own soil.

A SECOND INVITATION to THE BLENDER

Just as in the volume on cookery, we again remind our readers that a decent electric mixer is just as necessary on any well-equipped bar these days as a horse in a stable. Of course most cold drinks may be mixed, or shaken, by hand. Of course underground tunnels may be dug by hand, but modern machinery saves hours of wasted time and effort. There are also several so-called Tropical drinks, notably the new style Daiquiri, which simply cannot be shaped up by hand at all. There is no wrist strong or deft enough to make any mix of liquid and cracked ice turned into frosted sherbet-like consistency so essential to these examples.

The Ramos Brothers used to have a battery of eight ebony black bartenders to shake their famous fizzes to perfection—each one working fiercely and passing the shaker to the next, when weary. The Waring Blender is not being revived again here in this drinking volume in any spirit of commercialism. As explained before, we do not even know Mr. Waring, but we like his music and his Blender. It is fairly expensive, but is assembled of as fine materials as man can make—to give hard professional service; to last. There will probably be imitative, cheaper electric mixers. There will also be violinists who imitate Messrs. Heifetz and Kreisler. For cooling Daiquiris, gin fizzes, making grenadine juice from pomegranates, for a dozen and one unexpected uses, we find this deft gadget indispensable. If this slight paean of appreciation and gratitude to Mr. Waring for his aid to the mixing profession should make even one person beat a trail toward him seeking his mousetrap, that result is amply deserved—just as correctly as the Frenchman who thought up the drip coffee biggin, the chap who fabricated the first double boiler, the first deep fat kettle for the preparation of food.

Future reference to this mechanical unit will refer to it plainly as The Blender.

AND NOW a COMPANY of 200 & 67 ASSORTED POTATIONS from AMATEUR & PROFESSIONAL HOSTS about the WORLD

AN ABSINTHE COCKTAIL, as MIXED for Us by an ITINERANT RUSSIAN PRINCE on the OCCASION of OUR USUAL MORNING PILGRIMAGE to HARRY'S AMERICAN BAR, which Is in PARIS

During several weeks domicile in Hotel Daunou over Ciro's across the Rue Daunou, we often groped to Harry when visibly withering on the vine—seeking aid and comfort. On this especial occasion a Russian gentleman spied our ambulant corpse, took pity, bowed Harry aside in his spotless white coat, and in a small frappe shaker compounded the following life saver. We advocate putting it in The Blender for a jiffy with finely cracked ice, straining the chilled result to avoid dilution.

Absinthe, 1½ jiggers
Anis or anisette, dash
Water, ½ jigger
Sugar or *gomme* syrup, ½ tsp or less
Orange & Angostura bitters, dash each
White of egg, 1 tsp
Twist of lime or lemon peel

This is an excellent appetizer and tonic. Twist bit of peel to insure getting oil on surface of the drink. Must be very cold.

JUST a WORD on the LARGELY MISUNDERSTOOD SUBJECT of ABSINTHE in GENERAL; & CONCERNING an ABSINTHE DRIP from LE PERROQUET, in SAIGON, FRENCH INDO CHINA, & an ABSINTHE FRAPPE from the HELIOPOLIS PALACE, in CAIRO

Technically absinthe is a highly toxic liqueur running between 70% and 80% alcohol, with an aromatic characteristic flavour of a kind of wormwood known as *Artemisia absinthium,* blended with little items like angelica root, sweet flag, dittany leaves, star anise fruits, hyssop and fennel. In other words it is a strange herb-alcohol brew acting potently on the nervous ganglia. Too much can cause hallucinations;—what we have lightly come to call D. T's. And other things not judicious to mention.

In mixed drinks absinthe has a flavouring value all its own. Usually a very small quantity should be used, as the taste is potent and will dull many other more delicate flavours. Due to French mishandling of the liquor, and the sorry plight of her addicts, its manufacture was banned in the republic. For years the old French Quarter in New Orleans turned out a good type, and now the Swiss seem to have an inside corner on the market. Pernod is the *capon* near-absinthe made in France now, with much of the taste but little of the lift—due to many simples being ruled out of the formula. Pernod is mighty good liquid though, but always use the 120-proof for crispest flavouring authority.

THE ABSINTHE DRIP as PROPERLY FABRICATED in SAIGON

One of the charms of so many far eastern colonies is that many of the old world laws, tabus, taxes and other civilized nuisances are tossed overboard at Suez. If there is any prohibition of absinthe in *Indo-Chine* we failed to see it, ever, and, barring corruption of natives and conspiring against France, there is little prohibition of any kind. In Saigon we found a diverse and international parade of people, none of whom apparently had anything urgent or immediate to do, except the coolies tugging their burdens. A Siamese aristocrat strolled by our lower window in the shade of a parasol held by a servant. He was wrapped in a smart white silk coat, pipe-clayed sun topee and a purple silk diaper twined between his sturdy brown thighs. A merchant from Rangoon in a blue and crimson skirt. Chic flexible Chinese girls with their exquisite figures poured into *shaams,* scabbard-like split dresses of pastel silk that so elegantly suit their type. A brace of snipe-legged little Japanese men with f. 2 Leicas swinging around their necks, half-inch thick eyeglasses, flat straw hats, muttering urgently at each other without the slightest trace of facial expression. A Javanese girl-mother with her naked brown babe swinging in a butterfly tinted sarong tied above her hips and tucked in with a cunning woman's twist. A Buddhist priest from far back in the wild hill country back of beyond, in his funny hat and worn robe dyed three centuries ago in a yellow hue which would be mellow and fair a century after its present owner was dust. Two short, plump, short-skirted French girls giggling, looking us squarely in the eye before continuing other inspection—totally without self-consciousness or inhibition as they audibly speculated on our origin, age, marital state and capitalistic solvency in a machine gun undertone of rapid French. This is just the briefest vignette of Saigon.

Before quitting this subject of absinthe perhaps we had better explain that taken in steady doses over a considerable period of time, it does nibble the keen edge off the brain until a man becomes a sorry sort of thing; aimless, listless, and generally—shockingly—lacking. This, and the habit it forms under constant usage, of course accounts for its ban in France. Actually, too, it happens to be one of the few liqueurs which more or less definitely stimulates the cavaliers riding herd about the altar of Aphrodite.

An Absinthe Drip isn't one of the black arts at all; nor something confined to Maupassant, and mystery, and low and devious dives all coagulated with *apaches,* and their *grisettes,* and sitting around all hours of the night with drooping cigarettes in the corners of their mouths, and long hair drooping in their eyes, and long knives up their sleeves. . . . The cute, almost doll-like Annamese bar-man took a small thin tumbler, nearly the size and shape of our Old Fashioned Cocktail glass. This he centered up with 2 cubes of sterilized ice, a lump of loaf sugar. Onto this he turned a jigger of absinthe. A tiny pitcher of cold water was supplied, this to be poured in 1 drop at a time, or at guest option, ladled in with a small teaspoon. . . . Under this routine the pearly, almost opalescent, sheen of the absinthe is even more apparent than in the Frappe; also its potency.

AN ABSINTHE FRAPPE from HELIOPOLIS PALACE, CAIRO, in 1931

Here is one of the most bizarre and startling hotels in all the world. We found it, and not doing so well, back in 1926; but later on, in funds, it drew the fashionable crowd out near the race track. . . . This drink was mixed in small silver cocktail shakers holding enough for 2 guests; fetched to table with chilled glasses of champagne saucer type. . . . Merely turn 2 glasses of finely cracked ice into a chilled small shaker, add two 2-oz jiggers of absinthe and 1 tsp *anis del mono,* or French anisette. Shake quickly and hard. Pour out, ice and all; and a short straw, bright green in hue, is the final touch. This again produces a pearly white fluid at odds with the greenish liquid in bottle.

Please don't ignore this small shaker, iced shaker, iced glasses business. When making drinks especially in small amount this is essential to chill cold enough—*but mainly to prevent much ice melting to dilute and injure the tone of the finished drink.*

WORDS to the LIQUID WISE No. II, STILL further INSISTING that SHAKER & GLASSES ALWAYS BE CHILLED—ESPECIALLY when MAKING COCKTAILS for a VERY FEW GUESTS

Mixing 2 cocktails in a huge, room-temperature shaker, and pouring them into room-temperature glasses, is careless business. The ice melts rapidly, dilutes the drink, and the whole mix warms so fast that instead of being really chilled the final outcome is also not far from room temperature. . . . A warm cocktail is like half-way objects in life—neither this nor that, and often a reflection on the judgment and discretion of those present.

ADIOS AMIGOS, ONE from the ARMY-NAVY CLUB in MANILA, & ONE to be WATCHED *SEÑORS!*

Bacardi, 2 ponies — Cognac, 1 pony
French Vermouth, 1 pony — Lemon, juice, ½; or lime, juice, 1
Dry gin, 1 pony

Shake well with lots of cracked ice, pour into a large flat champagne glass, and send for the Marines!

J. PIERPONT MORGAN'S *ALAMAGOOZLUM,* the PERSONAL MIX CREDITED to that FINANCIER, PHILANTHROPIST, & BANKER of a BYGONE ERA

This might conceivably be a punch, if handled like a Planter's Punch; just as it could be stirred in a pitcher. To tell the truth this is no exotic from a far land, but is such a tasteful and sound cocktail that we append it here, standing on its own legs and its own merit. To serve about 5 cocktails: take 1 jigger each of Jamaica rum, *gomme* syrup, and yellow or green Chartreuse; add ½ pony yellow Curaçao and ½ pony of Angostura bitters. Add 2 scant ponies of Holland gin, the same of water; donate ½ the white of an egg and shake hard with lots of cracked ice. Serve in a Manhattan glass.

THE AMER PICON "POUFFLE" FIZZ, from the BAR-LOG of an EDITOR FRIEND DOMICILED for a SUMMER & WINTER on the FRENCH RIVIERA, at ST. JACQUES CAP FERRAT, & in a VILLA & THINGS

This is a very odd and fascinating affair, we can assure everyone. Simply turn a jigger of Amer Picon into a shaker with plenty of cracked ice, donate the white of 1 recent egg, and a scant pony of grenadine. Shake well, put into a goblet containing a lump of ice and fill to taste with best club soda available. Add ¼ tsp Angostura; stir.

THE ANTRIM COCKTAIL, ONE WE FOUND in the QUAINT LITTLE OVERSEAS CLUB in ZAMBOANGA, on the ISLAND of MINDANAO in the YEAR of GRACE 1931

This classic, being invented by "Monk" Antrim in Manila 5 or 6 years before, had found its way down into Moro country, many hundreds of miles to the south. We will bring more news of "Monk" later, meanwhile this is his own special origination, later blended for us by his own Chino *barmeister* in Manila.

Use 1 pony each of good French cognac and port wine; toss in ½ tsp of sugar; shake with lots of cracked ice and serve in a Manhattan glass. This is a slow creeper-upper, so *prend garde!*

THE ASTOR HOTEL SPECIAL, from SHANGHAI, during a TRIP around the WORLD in the YEAR 1926, & on the OCCASION of OUR BECOMING MAROONED in that CITY, with OUR OWN SHIP & PERSONAL BELONGINGS GONE on to HONGKONG, & with a DELIGHTFUL YOUNG MAIDEN by WHOM WE WERE LATER REJECTED in MARRIAGE, & WHO LATER DISTINGUISHED HERSELF by ESPOUSING a VERY NICE GENTLEMAN WHOSE MAIN CLAIM to FAME Is that HE WAS once KIDNAPED by KARPIS prior to the LATTER'S ENTERING HIS SUITE in ALCATRAZ

That whole trip around the world was the fault of GRS stock because it went up over 200 points before we sold; and our epidemic of missing steamboats began in Shanghai and was the fault of this very blend—sitting in the charming old Astor, with fog setting in, and a big party given out at the Majestic if we'd stay. The formula is noted directly from the Astor's Number I Chino mixer.

Cognac, 1 jigger
Maraschino, 1 tsp
Egg white, 2 tsp
Absinthe, ½ jigger
Lemon juice, strained, ½ tsp
Club soda

Shake well with cracked ice, strain into a tall wine goblet, then top off with just a little chilled soda.

THREE VERSIONS of ATHOL BROSE, an ODD SCOTTISH INSTITUTION which, LIKE MANY THINGS SCOTTISH, IS FOUNDED on MIGHTY GOOD REASON, & IS GUARANTEED to PROFIT ITS USER

ATHOL BROSE No. I

This potation, like our favourite cordial, Drambuie, was coined far up in the misty Hieland country where two-fisted Scottish swordsmen swung two-handed claymores for Bonnie Prince Charlie, Mary o' Scotland, or their own feudal Laird. It is the traditional drink with that weird meat lusty, the Scotch Haggis. We personally prefer Athol Brose served hot on wintry nights, although this is not following custom. Please don't attempt to use any young Scotch whisky—use the best the shelf affords.

Really old Liqueur Scotch whisky, 1 part
Clear strained honey, 1 part
Cream, 1 part

Mix well, warm slightly to make smooth. Then cool and sample, or heat and sample while still hot, to insure a mix to taste. Drink cold. Never boil cream or milk in a Brose. "Milk boiled is milk spoiled," runs the Scottish proverb.

ATHOL BROSE No. II

Put a heaping tsp or so of strained honey into 4 jiggers of liqueur Scotch whisky, turning this into a tumbler. Fill tumbler with milk, heated beforehand. Cool before drinking.

ATHOL BROSE No. III

This is still another ancient blend: Use 1 part liqueur Scotch whisky, ½ part strained honey, 1 part thick cream. Heat carefully, as before. Serve cold.

WORDS to the WISE No. III, BEING an EARNEST PLEA NOT to SERVE an OVER SUPPLY of RICH CREAMY COCKTAILS before any DECENT MEAL

Being more or less of a meal in itself, this sort of rich creamy drink cannot whet or build appetite. For this reason it really should be served on other occasions than immediately preceding a notable dinner. This applies to Pink Ladies, Alexanders, and all their nourishing kin.

THE AUNT EMILY, a Creation of Sloppy Joe's, in Havana, Years before His Spot Got to Be a Sort of Half Way House for Every Itinerant American on the Island

Try and use good aged *Calvados*—fine French apple brandy—for best results in this creation,—not the usual, fairly new applejack. We have found under these improved conditions that it is a memorable cocktail well worthy of notation. . . . Mix ½ jigger each apple brandy, dry gin, dry apricot brandy, and orange juice. Add 1 dash grenadine for colour. Shake hard and serve in a tall cocktail glass with stem.

THE BAGUIO SKIN, being a VERY SIMPLE yet VERY UNUSUAL EXOTIC from OUR BEAUTIFUL HILL STATION away up in the IGOROTE COUNTRY among the HIGH MOUNTAINS of LUZON

Baguio happens to be the world's first and only *planned* hill station, beautifully laid out by Cameron Forbes. Beside it the Topsy-like British India hill stations at Mussoorie, Gulmarg, and Simla—that "jest growed"—are straggling, casual affairs with no organization or scenic plan other than that endowed by an ever-generous Almighty. Baguio is the summer, rainy season retreat of civil and military Manila. We found this drink there, 7000 feet up, sitting before an *open fire* at the Country Club, looking out through the windows while the cloud slowly came down and tucked the 18th fairway under its wing.

In a tall-stemmed wineglass put 1 tsp of sugar dissolved in a trifle of water; then 1 dash or so of orange bitters. On top of this place 2 thin slices of green lime—or lemon—3 ice cubes, and then add 2 ponies of *Carta de Oro* Bacardi. Stir briskly with a bar spoon and serve as-is, with a final dusting of grated nutmeg on top. We consider this one of the finest possible, and find that 1 pair of orange or jasmine blossoms starred in each glass lends the true tropical, the fragrant, touch that guests like.

BALAKLAVA SPECIAL No. I, as BREWED for Us by ONE CAPTAIN FERGUSON, ONCE A SHIPMATE OF OURS AROUND THE WORLD, & LATE OF HIS MAJESTY'S BENGAL LANCERS, ONE-TIME STATIONED in the PUNJAB, NORTHERN INDIA

This very unusual cocktail is dedicated to the spot made famous by the charge of the Light Brigade which was a spectacular, tragic, and rather unnecessary military gesture. . . . Fill a small-stemmed wine goblet brimming full with shaved ice—or very finely cracked ice. Into this pour 1 jigger each kümmel and cognac. A dash of any red syrup like grenadine is optional and pretty.

BALAKLAVA SPECIAL No. II, when LADIES ARE PRESENT

Just why handsome women prefer sweet and creamy cocktails has always troubled us, but they do; and anyway a lot of things about handsome ladies have troubled us, so why get tweaky about the business at this late date? . . . Put 1 jigger of kümmel, ½ jigger each of absinthe, cognac and *kirschwasser,* into a shaker. Add ½ tsp orgeat syrup and 1 to 1½ tsp of thick cream. Shake briskly and serve in a tall-stemmed cocktail glass. And for heaven's sweet sake don't think this snake-in-the-grass drink is a harmless and gentle lady's affair just because it has cream in it!

FIRPO'S BALLOON COCKTAIL, the CALCUTTA CLASSIC

Our college mate C. Byron Spofford, at the time American Commercial Attaché in Calcutta for all of India, Burma and Ceylon, once gave a dinner celebrating the farewell of a very opinionated pair of men wished on him from Russian Famine Relief Headquarters by Herbert Hoover. We seem to recall their names as being Sabine and Renshaw, but that doesn't matter—it didn't then, and it certainly doesn't now. The thing that does matter is that Firpo mixed us a special round of Balloons—named because the 5th one consumed is guaranteed to set us bobbing about up under the ceiling. Firpo's is Calcutta's one smart night spot. It was all very gay in spite of the Hoover sycophants. . . . To 1 jigger of really good rye whisky add the same of Italian vermouth and absinthe—substituting Pernod Veritas lacking the true wormwood spirit. Now donate 2 dashes of orange bitters, or Angostura if preferred, and 1½ to 2 tsp of egg white. Shake well. Serve in a big saucer type champagne glass. This is another one to watch cannily lest our pedal extremities fold up at some totally inappropriate moment.

THE BARRY COCKTAIL, from MANILA, and MET FIRST in 1926, then again LATER. As MIXED at the ARMY & NAVY CLUB

This is included through clinical mixing interest. It is exactly the same as a Martini, but using Italian vermouth instead of the dry French type; adding Angostura bitters rather than orange, and trimmed with ½ tsp creme de menthe, floated on at the last. Twist a curl of lemon peel for its oil. It is stirred in a bar glass and must be cold indeed.

BERTITA'S SPECIAL COCKTAIL, *con HABAÑERO,* BEING an EXOTIC WE HAVE PERSONALLY FETCHED BACK from TAXCO, which is BACK in the HIGH HILLS of MEXICO, where ARTISTS from AMERICA CONGREGATE for VARYING REASONS, & with VARYING SUCCESS

Bertita, diagonally across the southwest corner of the public square from de la Borda's matchless cathedral is a dingy but mildly celebrated place, noted twice in this volume. This is a potent drink poured with a heavy hand, as we found during a stay in Taxco in February 1937. . . . *Habañero* incidentally, means any of the light Cuban rums properly distilled from sugar cane by-product, and aged in the wood. Properly they should be called rum brandies, we imagine. Bacardi is the best known, but down there in Mexico the citizens blot up an amazing count of Cubaño rums we never even heard of, like *El Caney* in its slim Rhine wine style bottle. . . . To 4 jiggers of light Cuban rum add the strained juice of 2 limes, the strained juice of 1½ average sized oranges, 2 tsp of grenadine, or sugar or *gomme* syrup. Shake vigorously with lots of ice, serve in big champagne glasses—for 2 people. As we recall it Bertita served it with cracked ice still in the drink. It would pan out well in The Blender, incidentally. Personally we float on 1 tsp Jamaica, atop the finished drink.

WORDS to the WISE No. IV, on the WISDOM of ADDING a VERY LITTLE JAMAICA RUM to ALL COCKTAILS REQUIRING FRUIT JUICES of any KIND

This is our invariable rule now, as 1 tsp of Jamaica adds a definite something to all fruit juice drinks; and especially to those based on Bacardi or other light rums, which are so delicate that their virtues are cloaked in the more usual fruit juices themselves.

JERUSALEM'S BETWEEN the SHEETS, from the BAR BOOK of WEBER at the KING DAVID

Like the American Side Car, and other truly worthwhile cocktails this invention is totally sound, and is already quite famous throughout the Near East. We ran into it one dank day of sleet and rain in early January, just after the first Arab-Jewish riots which started with a murder of a poor old man stoned to death in a Haifa melon patch, between halves of a soccer match! and had just reached a climax beside the Dome of the Rock mosque—which has religious significance to both Arab and Jew, and unfortunately overhangs the famous Jewish Wailing Wall. We won't go into the politics of the thing, but it was a nasty mess, with British Tommies in the streets finally, and machine guns and barbed wire entanglements—all the modern civilized show. . . . We were disillusioned at all this wholesale murder in Christianity's own heart city, sad at the sight of a fifteen year old Arab girl—the daughter of a fine Arab friend—crushed under a heavy slab of masonry tossed from a rooftop as she returned from worship after the end of *Ramadan*—the Mohammedan Easter—and we were wearied at the thought of the drawn knives, the murder from ambush which would follow all this blood debt throughout Palestine. We had both sinuses pounding, were coming down with definitely *something,* as well—when in the weird, almost Egyptian-looking sanctum of the King David Weber took charge; first with a hot rum toddy, then—on evidence of renewed life—with the following origination.

Of cognac, cointreau, dry gin and lemon juice—strained—take equal parts. Shake briskly with lots of cracked ice and serve in a Manhattan glass. Cut down the cointreau to make "dry," to taste.

THE JAMAICAN BLACK STRAP, from the FORMULA of an AMERICAN FRIEND WHO INHERITED a MOUNTAIN PLANTATION on JAMAICA'S WINDWARD SIDE, not too FAR from PORT ANTONIO

This is a strange drink, and will arouse a lot of interest among strangers, only better be sure they admire Jamaica rum—many ladies don't, for instance! . . . Take 2 jiggers of old Jamaica rum, add 2 tbsp ice water, 2 tsp blackstrap molasses, and 1 dash Angostura, or 2 dashes of orange bitters. Shake with lots of cracked ice, and garnish with a thin stick of fresh pineapple.

THE JAMAICAN BLACK STRIPE, another HEARTENER from that TROPICAL PARADISE, that MAY BE SERVED either HOT or COLD

If served cold: work 2 tsp strained honey into 1 tbsp boiling water until well dissolved. Add 1 jigger Jamaica rum, shake with cracked ice, pour into stemmed cocktail glass and dust with nutmeg. Furnished us by Emerson Low, Esq., gentleman, student, Rhodes Scholar, author and delightful dilettant, who, for one strange not unromantic marital interlude, was denizened in Jamaica.

THE BAVARIAN "BRIDEGROOM'S CUP," a MEMORY from the GAY DAYS when THERE WAS TIME in which to LIVE a LIFE—& LAUGH, & LOVE, & SING, & DANCE, in MIDDLE EUROPE

We have a lovely friend, a girl, who married a Bavarian "von" who is our idea of what a "von" ought to be; and at their wedding in New York he introduced us to this delightful drink—which is doubly nice on a hot summer's day. . . . Take the biggest crystal goblet we can find, then chill it. Fill it 1/3 full of ice and turn in ½ bottle of good Rhine wine—well chilled—and 1 jigger of *kirsch*. Stir for a moment with a silver spoon, then garnish with a handful of crushed lightly sugared ripe strawberries—also chilled; only put them in with a spoon —3 tbsp total. Bedeck with a sprig of green mint, if in the mood. There we have it.

THE BROKEN SPUR, a CLASSIC FOUND in the PERGOLA of LEON ELLIS, 2d SECRETARY of the AMERICAN LEGATION in PEKING, in the YEAR 1932, and before a BUFFET DINNER of UTTER CHARM

Imagine Peking then, just before Japan had screwed up brass enough to defy Britain, and the rest of Europe's Legations, and ours too by the way!—and had quietly occupied most of Imperial North China while everyone sat back like a lot of spineless ostriches with head in sand, and another lot of spineless men who violated their own sacred signatures behaved like a lot of schoolboys playing grownup around the League of Nations table at Geneva throwing dice with an unfortunate and *colorado maduro* gentleman named Haile Selassie, whom no one much had ever heard of before. Imagine getting there on our third trip, and knowing people, and with a fiancée who had already agreed to the banns, and the plum blossoms frosting the Summer Palace gardens where Old Buddha once strolled, before we re-entered our motor cars and went to the foot of Western Hills where Ellis had sedan chairs and coolies waiting for the madcap, swaying, almost perpendicular climb to the very topmost ridge, past the American Minister's temple, and the other Buddhist temples the Europeans rent, through this connivance and that with the willing priests—to Ellis' Grotto of the Propitious Pearl. And there in back of his living quarters was a cave in the hills, where he has to let the pilgrims go day or night, and where the mummy of a famous saint sits lifelike, covered with some sort of plaster and tinted like real flesh. Imagine the view at sunset of the distant Tartar walls of Peking, just barely visible through the golden light, with everything powdered with Peking dust which is older than time itself. Picture an impossible grinning combination of Fu Manchu and Houdini who bowed and smiled and produced miraculous things from vast wicker hampers which had, through some other Oriental magic, transported themselves before us to this place. There between the 500 year old red lacquer columns of that Buddhist pavilion we sat and thought things about Jenghiz Khan, and fiancées, and sipped big 3 oz Broken Spurs served in hand engraved crystal champagne glasses.

To ½ a jigger of dry gin add the same of Italian vermouth; then 1 jigger of port wine, 1 tsp *anis del mono* or anisette, the yolk of 1 fresh egg. Shake briskly with big lumps of ice and when cold serve in a champagne saucer glass, dusting the top with a pinch of powdered ginger at the last.

THE BARBADOS BUCK, Being a Fine Refreshener We Ran into One Early January Afternoon upon Introduction to the British Club that Clings to the End of the Dock at Bridgetown like a Determined Spider

Tom Hartnett and Larry Stucky and I had been lying naked on a sugarwhite beach, talking about Gilbert & Sullivan, and about the days we used to play baseball against each other at Yale and Trinity, and then we went in to town for a quick one before all the West Indies cruise passengers had to be lightered off to the *RELIANCE* anchored out there, and a friendly British Lieutenant suggested this cooler, which is also a bracer. Put a large lump of ice in the biggest tumbler in sight —and 16 oz size is proper. Add 1 jigger Barbados rum (any medium dark rum will do) and the same of Bacardi, the juice of 1 small green lime, 1 tsp sugar; stir this friendly group to mix thoroughly, then fill the big glass with ginger beer, or some good ginger ale like imported Cantrell & Cochrane. Stone bottle ginger beer is best, buyable now in America.

WORDS to the WISE No. V, on the MODIFICATION of JAMAICA RUM when LADY GUESTS ARE PRESENT

Never forget. please, that only 1 lady in 12 really likes the Jamaica rum taste. Therefore dilute the rum this way: 3 parts light Cuban, Puerto Rican, or Virgin Island type to 1 of Jamaica. The aroma will be there and the full round Jamaica flavour too, but in a tempo inoffensive to the most rabid Jamaicaphobes.

THE CAFE de PARIS COCKTAIL from "MONTE," a PLACE WELL-MENTIONED ALREADY in OUR PREVIOUS VOLUME on FOODS; SAMPLED FIRST in 1931

To 1 jigger dry gin allow 1 tsp anis or anisette, ½ the white of an egg—very fresh please—and 1 tsp cream. Shake well and serve in the tall style cocktail glass with a stem. Ladies like it!

CASTLE HARBOUR SPECIAL, a MID-OCEAN COOLER from LOVELY BERMUDA

We've always loved the more outlying parts of this island since our first stay there of several weeks, back in 1928. In those days most of the islands in Castle Harbour were unsettled and we used to sail over there in a small boat, and swim the white and pink beaches in utter seclusion except for our companion, and the screaming nesting sea birds. Gosling Brothers brought out the liquid necessaries to our little hotel, and here are the proportions. Mix the following in a bar glass: 4 small dices of ripe pineapple, the juice of 1 small green lime, 1 tsp grenadine, 1 tsp of sweet pineapple soda fountain syrup, add 1½ jiggers Barbados, Demerara, or Martinique rum, ½ jigger white Bacardi. Stir with a lump of ice and either strain out as-is, or better still —as we found—turn into a small goblet half filled with cracked ice. The pineapple syrup gives the touch, and grenadine may be omitted, to taste. We find the pineapple much more important as a sweetening agent, and there is no conflict of delicate tastes.

FIVE DELICIOUS CHAMPAGNE OPPORTUNITIES, which Are not to be Ignored

CHAMPAGNE COCKTAIL No. I, Known as the Maharajah's *BURRA-PEG*

The word *Burra* in Hindustani means "big," "important," or "big-time," as the case might be; and "peg" throughout Britaindom means a "drink"—more often than not a Scotch-and-soda. This particular champagne affair was broken out on the eve of our departure alone across India, after a month with Spofford in his big Calcutta bungalow show in the fashionable Ballygunge section down Chowringhee, beyond Lower Circular Road. This Burra-Peg is to the ordinary Champagne Cocktail what Helen of Troy was to a local shepherd maiden. . . . We got aboard the Bombay Mail with our tail between our legs and lunged across Central India, and later on found ourself in Jaipur —already mentioned in Melon, *Orientale,* Volume I. And here in this amazing town in Rajputana, with its modern government and 120 ft. wide streets, where tigers are protected so the Maharajah may shoot without fatiguing travel much beyond city limits, where we found Ambar—India's most marvellous deserted city—and got mixed up in the yearly Festival of the Sun, starting from the Gulta Pass, and with more elephants, *fakirs* and jugglers than a three ringed circus; here we found probably the lonesomest Standard Oil man we'd ever seen.

So we joined forces, and of evenings we would sit on the rooftop of his bungalow, and while the sun set through the sherry-brown dust cloud that broods over Central India throughout the dry season, would listen to the vain male peacock's scream, and watched the Rikki-tikki-tavis—or mongooses, or mongeese, or whatever the hell they choose to call those trim little animals that would sooner fight snakes than live—scuttling about their mongoosing business among the bushes in the garden. And we would sip various tall things, including—on Washington's birthday of course—a quartet of Champagne Burra-Pegs, and he would recount to us certain toothsome bits of "under-the-punkah" tales about Maharajahs and people; and how, actually, the young new one we'd just met preferred one wife to the regiment of 400 or so his dad had thoughtfully left him!

Duplicating our experience we suggest: the largest chilled goblet in sight, at least 14 oz, and 16 oz is better. Into this turn 2 jiggers of good well-chilled cognac, drop in a lump of sugar doused with Angostura, fill up with chilled dry champagne and garnish with a spiral of green lime peel.

CHAMPAGNE COCKTAIL No. II, which with MODESTLY DOWNCAST LASH WE ADMIT IS an ORIGINATION of OUR OWN, & which WE CHRISTENED the "JIMMIE ROOSEVELT"

One spring we had the pleasure of turning our house into an oasis, between planes, for Colonel Jimmie Roosevelt and Grant Mason of the Civil Aeronautics Commission. No citizen—Republican, Democrat, Socialist, Townsendite, or any other political breed, can meet Jimmie and not at once be taken with his smile, his sense of humour and affable charm. It was warmish, and being a sort of Nephew-in-Law of Paul Garrett, dean of all American Vintners, and present "father" of Virginia Dare, we brought out 2 chilled bottles of Garrett Champagne, and created this one.

Fill a big 16 oz *thin* crystal goblet with finely cracked ice. In the diametrical center of this frosty mass went a lump of sugar well saturated with Angostura, then 2 jiggers of good French cognac, then fill the glass with chilled champagne, finally floating on very carefully 2 tbsp of genuine green Chartreuse—no pineapple, no mint sprig, no cherry garnish. It is cooling, refreshing, invigorating, a delight to eye and palate.

CHAMPAGNE COCKTAIL No. III, in the CHARMING STYLE of the JOCKY CLUB in RIO de JANEIRO

Choose a large tapering champagne cocktail glass; inside of this build a tower of 4 ice cubes, crown it with a lump of sugar saturated with 4 dashes of orange bitters. Against the sides of the glass lean 2 sticks of ripe fresh pineapple, encircle the ice tower with a spiral of green lime peel, and fill with well chilled champagne, medium dry, and not too acid in type. Now as the crowning gesture carefully float on 1 tbsp of cointreau.

CHAMPAGNE COCKTAIL No. IV, the CORRECT NAME of which Is the IMPERIAL COSSACK *CRUSTA,* and ONE of the MOST STARTLING & INTRIGUING DRINKS in the FAR EAST

We stumbled into this classic, as we did several other items of precious interest, in the French Concession of Shanghai long before the days of undeclared wars, and at the house of a friend whose name it is not seasonable to mention. It is an expensive cocktail as cocktails march, but now and again we find occasion to celebrate this thing or that, and no guest can fail to be favourably impressed by the appearance, size and taste of this formula—which came out of White Russia when Russia was Russia—and Kolchak wasn't retreating in Siberia ahead of that breaking tide of Reds; the prey of cowardice, politics and corruption.

Take a large champagne cocktail glass, and ice it well. Split a green lime, or lemon, lengthwise and rub its combined oils and juices over the whole inside of the crystal, and then on out and down a full ½" below the rim. First dip this lip into powdered sugar, then fill the whole glass with the sugar—emptying it out and permitting what sticks to remain. . . . Now add 2 dashes of orange bitters, 1 jigger of cognac and ½ that of kümmel, stirring for a moment in a bar glass with 3 ice cubes. Empty this into the goblet, fill with chilled dry champagne, toss in a scarlet rose petal and think of slender, pliable Russian Princesses and things!

ILE de FRANCE SPECIAL, BEING CHAMPAGNE COCKTAIL No. V

The bar *maitre,* one Reynauld, on this somewhat amazing craft has found that picker-uppers have to be even better than putter-downers the night before. Long devotion to his art has evolved this delicate appeal to the intellect, thus causing the numbed nerve centers to nod closer and closer together until they, at long last, touch—and the day is begun!

Into a large champagne glass put a half teaspoon fine sugar, a half pony of good cognac, fill with very cold dry champagne, and top off with a dash or two of yellow Chartreuse. The pungent herbs greet the nostrils, then the cool quenching of the viney bubbly. . . . This being passed along by an Ile de France habitual crosser, and not from the usual personal imbibition, naturally arouses our suggestion that two dashes of any good bitters would help tone the inner man—orange preferred—and not injure flavour or bouquet in any manner.

WORDS to the DRINKING WISE No. VI, EMPHASIZING the SPECIAL NEED for the CHILLING of GLASSES in MAKING any CHAMPAGNE COCKTAIL

One of the sharp charms of this drink is its icy coldness. The glass itself makes an efficient radiator, drawing much more heat against the liquid than the ordinary sized cocktail glasses. Therefore let's always chill our glasses. Warm champagne is a foetid thing, of brassy taste, astringent to the throat, an insult to the nostrils. Also never use tumblers for champagne cocktails, use stemmed goblets or champagne cocktail glasses. The heat of the hand soon warms a tumbler's contents.

CHAMPAGNE VELVET No. I, BEING the "MARIVELES" from the MANILA POLO CLUB

Mariveles is an extinct volcanic peak cooling its heels across Manila Bay to the westward, high above the rugged peninsula of Bataan, and when they set the tables out on the grass terrace just before sunset the gunsight notch in the dead crater frames the sun. It is a pleasant spot, this terrace, one of the loveliest, in fact, in all the tropics. For there is always a bit of breeze, the shaded lights lend an air of intimacy to each rendezvous of the moment—and, man, how they do rendezvous in those island tropics! There is even a mile-long plume of bats that exit from some distant mountain cave, and drift like a strand of smoke across the far off sky. The Polo Club not only produces crisp polo between service and civilian teams, but has always taken especial pride in the precision, the quality and service of its drinks. As Monk Antrim once said, "This Mariveles Velvet is an expensive sort of drink, but when you think everything over, it's worth it!" It will save life, nourish, encourage and induce sleep in insomniacs.

Chill dry champagne well, chill a bottle of Guinness Stout. Get a big goblet and pour these two liquids in 'arf-and-'arf. Stir gently, and there we have it.

CHAMPAGNE VELVET, *à la MARMION,* Invented One Memorable Cruise up Long Island Sound to the Cup Races off Newport in the Year 1934

Repeat this same process only use Bass Ale instead of the heavier, more bitter Guinness. Chill everything very cold.

THE PARISIAN CHERRY RIPE, One of the Very Few French Cocktail Inventions worth Its Measuring Time

This one we met eye to eye, and under circumstances not relevant to this work, on returning through the Bois de Boulogne from a view at the current vintage of Davis Cup tennis, not so long ago. It is potent, dependable, but one of the most foetid conceptions ever to come out of shaker when served improperly chilled—for then it is vilely sweet. Chill long and vigorously. . . . Take a jigger of dry gin, and half that both of *kirsch,* and cherry brandy of the French type. Better mix with shaved ice and put in The Blender. Float 1 tsp cherry brandy on top of the frozen product. Garnish with 1 green and 1 red maraschino cherry. Delicious and pretty, both at the same time.

THE COLONIAL COOLER, which We Met in Sandakan, British North Borneo, Some Fourteen Years Back

The water was so shoal there that the big steamer had to anchor fourteen miles out, and the two main motor lifeboats were lowered, and started towing the regular lifeboats. And after half an hour running both motors conked out, and a Borneo *prahu* with a sail like a striped butterfly and a gent in a G-string and a headdress that looked exactly like an American overseas cap, only made out of wine coloured velvet, was squatting right on top of the blunt, low mast supporting the big lateen sail, and the thing steering itself. Somehow we managed to convey the idea that we were not wallowing there on a glassy sea with a molten brass sun striking like a sword across our necks, because we wanted to. So he disappeared down wind and then two hours later a stuffy little British North Borneo Company tug came out and saved the day, and pretty soon we saw the raw, red cliffs back of Sandakan, and landed in a maze of godowns and Chinese "Loan Farms"—pawn shops to America—and fantan dives.

We first went out to the Sandakan Club—there'd be a British Club on Mount Everest if 2 Britishers could stand the cold there!—and had these Coolers, through courtesy of an American who was sentimental enough to fetch a mint root out with him. Then our last and most vivid memory, outside of the headstones in the little cemetery listing the violent causes of death—cobra bite, blow-pipe arrows tipped with gum from the deadly *ipoh* tree, fever, cholera—was the 12 foot hamadryad, or king cobra,—stuffed thank God!—in the museum. This thing had a head as big as a tennis racquet and with enough coil to strike there was still six feet of him off the floor—staring us coldly in the eye.

To 1 jigger of dry gin add the same of Italian vermouth. To this base donate 1 dash each of Angostura and Amer Picon, and 1 tsp of orange Curaçao. Stir with a goodly lump of ice in a small highball or sour glass, and top off with a squirt of soda, garnished with 2 sprigs of mint and a stick of ripe pineapple.

CREOLE CONTENTMENT, an Insidious Pleasantry from that Charming Hot-Bed of Intrigue & Culture which Is the Pulse of the Great Delta Country—New Orleans

This hazard and liability to consistent maidenhood came to our desk through office of a friend whose father once was Episcopal Bishop of Washington, and who writes books about pirates. Don't treat this one lightly, *mes amis*. . . .

Of cognac, Madeira wine and maraschino, take 1 pony each; turn this into a bar glass with ice; toss in 1 dash of orange bitters, stir well, pour into a big Manhattan glass or saucer type champagne, and garnish with 3 maraschino cherries: red, green and white. . . . Our personal experience is that it is better to cut the maraschino down by half, stepping up the cognac in that ratio. That business of the 3 cherries, while no doubt a pretty and chivalrous gesture to the feminine victim is, of course, sheerest swank. It is a good drink and needs little trimming.

THE *CUBA LIBRE*—or "Free Cuba"—Analyzed & Improved

This native Island concoction started by accident and has caught on everywhere throughout the south, has filtered through the north and west. Last summer, for instance, we ran into Kooba Lee-brays 5000 feet up in the North Carolina Mountains at High Hampton, the year before in Mexico City and Seattle. Last week in Palm Beach and Cat Cay. The only trouble with the drink is that it started by accident and without imagination, has been carried along by the ease of its supply. Under any condition it is too sweet.

What's to do? . . . After clinical experimenting for which our insurance carriers heartily dislike us, we tested several variations of the original, with this result: the Improved *Cuba Libre* consists of 1 big jigger of *Carta de Oro* Bacardi, the juice of 1 small green lime, and the lime peel after squeezing. Put in a Tom Collins glass, muddle well to get oil worked up over sides of the glass, add lots of ice lumps, and fill up with a bottle of chilled coca cola. Stir up once, and *salud y pesetas!*

THE BAKER *CUBA REFORMÉ*, an ORIGINATION with the AUTHOR, which WE HAVE TRANSMITTED WARILY to OUR FRIEND VESEY RAINWATER, WHO AMOUNTS to THINGS in COCA COLA, & which WAS PRONOUNCED GOOD

While not an exotic from Singapore, any drink originated after a Miami-Nassau Ocean Yacht Race that ended up with all sails blown out in a gale and lying stormbound for a week back of Cat Cay, is possessed of its own spurs in any company, we believe.

Fill a big goblet with very finely cracked ice, turn in 2 jiggers of good imported sloe gin, add the juice and spiral peel of 1 green lime—then stir vigorously to work the rind oil about, and fill with all the coca cola the glass will hold. A mild and delicious cooler, but is sweet enough that it *must be very cold indeed* to be good.

THE CUERNAVACA SPECIAL, from the FILES of ONE MANUEL who PRESIDES behind MAHOGANY at the HOTEL de la SILVA CASINO BAR

As we have indicated, Cuernavaca is Mexico City's summer resort for people who matter, a habit begun by Cortez himself after the conquest; and here small modern palaces rub elbows with 16th Century affairs built by the great Conquistador. Hotel de la Silva, until President Cardenas took the reins, was an unbelievable Mexican Monte Carlo—an incredible place of *moderne* cellophane drapes, exotic murals—*not* by Diego Rivera, praise be!—a vast pool of limpid mountain water outside for swimming, and roulette wheels, and every known device for acquisition of cash, inside. Manuel talks of the good old days now, but he has a twinkle in his eye, and originated this bit of genius as he expressed it—*por los señoras*. It is a nicer drink than the old favourite Pink Lady. Test it out next time.

Take 1 jigger each of cognac and dry French vermouth and put in a shaker with 2 tsp of *Crème de Cacao,* 1 or 2 tsp of grenadine to taste; the white of 1 fresh egg and 1 tsp of thick cream. Shake hard and pour into a big Manhattan glass letting a little of it foam prettily over lip of the glass. Garnish with sprigs of tender mint, hang a split red maraschino cherry over the glass edge too. Take 2 short scarlet cellophane straws, touch their lower ends onto the glass foot and press the top ends against the overflowed foam where they stick cleverly to the outside of the glass. A nice gesture with all fancy cream-egg cocktails, too, by the way.

WORDS to the WISE No. VII, OFFERING up an EARNEST PLEA for RECENTNESS in ALL EGGS to BE USED in COCKTAILS or DRINKS of any KIND, for that MATTER

A stale or storage egg in a decent mixed drink is like a stale or storage joke in critical and intelligent company. Eschew them rabidly. If really fresh eggs can't be had, mix other type drinks, for the result will reflect no merit round the hearth, no matter how hospitable it may be.

DAISY de SANTIAGO, a Lovely Thing Introduced to Us through the Gracious Offices of the Late Facuno Bacardi, of Lamented Memory

The Bacardi people were always mighty nice about taking visiting yachtsmen and other travelers through their factory, and the result was always amazingly gratifying in several ways. As many of us know they have erected a special small skyscraper in Havana, too, where visitors may go for free Bacardi drinks, and we must confess that our name appears in four places on pages of their guest book in a brilliant modern bar smart enough to make New York jealous. To our mind, along with the immortal Daiquiri, this is the best Bacardi drink on record.

Take a big thin goblet and fill to the brim with shaved ice. Take a bar glass and put in 1½ jiggers Bacardi, the strained juice of 1 green lime, 1 to 1½ tsp of bar syrup, optional. Stir well and pour onto the ice, stir up once, garnish with green mint and fresh fruit, and float on ½ jigger of *yellow* Chartreuse. Personally we find the Chartreuse brings all the sweetening we need, and a squirt of charged water adds a sparkle. A lovely thing indeed.

AND NOW, *MESSIEURS et MESDAMES,* the One & Only Tropical Daiquiri

We honestly believe that more people have boasted about the origin of this happy thought than any modern drink. We have had to smile quietly on at least 4 occasions; once overhearing 3 Cuban gentlemen who had never been out of Havana, 1 alleged German title on a West Indies Cruise, 1 Racquet Club Member on a fishing trip—why is it that so many German alleged titles and fancy club members seem to talk very loud and authoritatively?—and 2 female frequenters of the New York Colony Club. All of these assorted folk either had helped invent this drink or had been like *THAT* with the ones who had invented it!

The whole business is tommyrot, unless these persons knew a certain 2 officials of the Yankee-run Cuban mining firm taken over during the great war by Bethlehem Steel, and which operated in the mountains not too far out of Santiago de Cuba, where the firm of *Bacardi y Cia.*, had, and has, its being. The invention was simple, as so many good things in life are simple, and right smack after the Spanish-American war, too. In those days not 1 American in 10,000 had ever heard of *Ron Bacardi*, much less invented drinks with it.

There was fever. Doctors still thought that a lot of yellowjack malaria cases came from drinking water and swamp mists. They couldn't turn off the swamp mists but they knew that diluted alcohol was a disinfectant against germs. So they put a little rum in their boiled drinking water. This tasted pretty bad so some bright citizen squeezed a lime into the thing, and a little sugar to modify the acid. Ice made from distilled water took the tropical blood heat off the thing. The 2 originators were my friend Harry E. Stout, now domiciled in Englewood, New Jersey, and a mining engineer associate, Mr. Jennings Cox. TIME: summer of 1898. PLACE: Daiquiri, a village near Santiago and the Bacardi plant, Cuba. Hence the name.

Like the Martini, Manhattan, Side Car and other immortals, the Daiquiri marched straight around the world, and we have tried them in many places and circumstances—including the old Plaza, the Habana Yacht Club, Country Club, Hotel Nacional—between revolutionary bombings—Sloppy Joe's, La Florida, the Bacardi Building, and factory in Santiago; and other spots in Cuba. In spite of all the loud speeches on the subject we claim there is no "best" place for Daiquiris. The only thing that can go wrong, besides insufficient chilling, is that it is often made too sweet. Technique progressed from the days of drinking with 1 lump of ice in a tumbler, to the flute cocktail glass with the finely cracked ice left in; then came the electric vibrator mixer and the screen strainer to improve the thing further —and it became called the "Tropical" Daiquiri. Now that The Blender is available, it frosts beautifully, in a few seconds.

The original Harry Stout–Jennings Cox mixture for the Original Cuban Daiquiri was: 1 whiskey glass (1½ oz) level full of *Carta Blanca*, or *Carta de Oro* Bacardi rum, 2 tsp of sugar, the juice of 1½ *small* green limes—strained; and very finely cracked ice.

Either shake very hard with finely cracked ice and pour ice and all into a tall flute cocktail glass, or put the same things into The Blender, and let frost into the delicious sherbet consistency we so admire nowadays. . . . Never use lemon juice. And remember please, that a too-sweet Daiquiri is like a lovely lady with too much perfume. Sugar should be cut down to 1 tsp, to our belief, and a Manhattan glass is less likely to tip over, in steady service!

After some rather extensive carpenter work building Tropical Daiquiris Your Pastor has reached the following conclusions, betterments possibly, over the original Daiquiri mix. . . . About ½ to 1 average small green lime gives acid aplenty. We always allow 2 ounces of rum. Delicate crowning touch: Sprinkle 3 or 4 drops of Warrick Frères French Orange Flower Water over the finished drink.

ERNEST HEMINGWAY'S REVIVER * on Mornings after Anything, Made of Hollands & other Things, which We Called "Death in the Gulf Stream," but Found Most Valuable

Drinking Holland gin drinks is like the fanciful *cliché* about eating olives—when you like one you always like them. For many years

* During the six years since this stout receipt first saw light of day it may perhaps be of some interest to note that more masculine correspondence, more interest and praise, has come in to us treating with Ernest's so-called Death in the Gulf Stream than any other receipt—with possible exception of The Maharajah's Burra-Peg listed on Page 21 of this book: the latter being our own special feast-day drink here at Java Head. Author.

we had hated the stuff with a passion, holding its taste to be like fermented radishes mixed with spirits of turpentine. One January 2 years back we took *MARMION* in a howling no'theaster along with the, then, 4 year bride, a companion, and an insane steward, and pointed her down to Key West to get some receipts from Hemingway for the cookery book. We fished the Gulf Stream by day, and ate and drank and talked half the night. Even by the second day we were withering slightly on vine, and along with raw conch salad, or "souse," listed in *Volume I,* we got Hemingway's other picker-upper, and liked it.

Take a tall thin water tumbler and fill it with finely cracked ice. Lace this broken debris with 4 good purple splashes of Angostura, add the juice and crushed peel of 1 green lime, and fill glass almost full with Holland gin. . . . No sugar, no fancying. It's strong, it's bitter—but so is English ale strong and bitter, in many cases. We don't add sugar to ale, and we don't need sugar in a Death in the Gulf Stream—or at least not more than 1 tsp. Its tartness and its bitterness are its chief charm. It is reviving and refreshing; cools the blood and inspires renewed interest in food, companions and life.

FRITZ—FREDERICK ABILDGAARD & *ALONE-in-the-CARIBBEAN*—FENGER'S DOMINICA *TOPET*

When Fritz was sailing his sliver-size canoe *YACKABOO* and making his 50 and 60 mile open water ocean hops from Trinidad up to the Virgin Islands, he annexed this liquid threat to his log book; and double checked during the cruise of *DIABLESSE* several years later. "This drink," Fritz shouted with his fanatical look, which is a combination of a revivalist preacher and a cloven hoofed satyr, "is a drink for those of not too Scotch descent, and detailed instructions may be deciphered on Page 243 of *The Cruise of the Diablesse* (Adv.). So to fabricate 4 *Topets:*

"Take 5 ponies of any good medium dark rum, and in this soak the spiral of a sizeable green lime, muddling about to extract the essential oils. Now add an equal part of cold water, and the strained juice of the lime. Next put ½ tsp *gomme* syrup in each glass. Now carefully flow in the lime-rum mix, being careful to float it on so it doesn't blend with syrup. More carefully still flow on the Angostura bitters—at least a good ⅛" thick on top of everything. . . . It is a sort of Pousse Cafe in appearance, but far more artistic in results, and in the island of British Dominica it is served as an appetizer, before a good dinner, by the discriminating.

EAST INDIA COCKTAIL, which CAME to OUR DEVOTED ATTENTION also in FIRPO'S, in CALCUTTA

It is mild and appetite-inspiring in hot weather, and is now known everywhere, but we append it just the same. Into a bar glass turn 1 jigger each of dry French vermouth and really good *really dry* sherry —the usual sweet American sherry just won't serve. Add 2 dashes of orange bitters, plenty of big-lump ice, then stir with a bar spoon and turn into a Manhattan glass. Garnish with green cherry or not, to preference.

THE EAST INDIA HOUSE COCKTAIL, BEING ONE for ANY MAN'S BOOK, & GARNERED in THE ROYAL BOMBAY YACHT CLUB, INDIA, 1932, while the—then—FIANCÉE SIGHT-SAW across INDIA to DELHI, AGRA, BENARES & FATEHPUR SIKRI, & CALCUTTA

Take 1½ jiggers of cognac, 1 tsp pineapple syrup—the soda fountain kind—and put in a shaker. Add 2/3 tsp maraschino, 1 tsp orange Curaçao, 3 dashes of orange or Angostura bitters, according to preference. Shake with lots of fine ice and strain into a Manhattan glass, twisting a bit of lime peel on at the last.

THE CLAN McGREGOR EGG NOGG, BEING a LOVELY, FORCEFUL THING BASED on BRANDY, BACARDI, & FINE OLD SHERRY, from SCOTLAND

There are a hundred and one Egg Noggs about the world, and many of them already set between the covers of books, but this Scottish institution was rare enough to be the only one we include in this collection of exotica. It is a milder mix, which we consider a blessing.

Also, having no cream, it is more refreshing and not so likely to be gastrically disastrous as the over-rich customary formulae we have consumed on certain festive occasions.

This mixture needs simply to be multiplied for any company, and serve in thin 12 oz goblets, not the usual thick punch cups. . . . ½ pony of good cognac, 2 ponies of good Spanish *dry* sherry, ¼ pony of *Carta de Oro* Bacardi; 1 tsp or so of sugar, to taste, the yolk of an egg and 1 cup or so of chilled milk. . . . First put egg and sugar into the bar glass and beat well, then add spirits and 4 lumps of ice. Stir or shake briskly, strain into goblet, add cold milk and dust both nutmeg and cinnamon on top.

A FAREWELL to HEMINGWAY, Being a Sort of *KIRSCH* Collins We Invented on the Night We Saw Hemingway & Bull-fighter Sidney Franklin off on the Plane for New York, & Loyalist Spain

There is no reason to this drink. It just happened because Ernest prefers *kirschwasser,* and it was a muggy, half-breathless sort of night. The cherry syrup sweet, of course, can be varied to taste. . . . Take 1½ jiggers of *kirsch,* ¼ pony of cherry syrup—again the drug store kind—and the juice of 1 big green lime. Shake this mixture with 4 ice cubes, turn ice and all into a collins glass of at least 14 oz capacity, drop in a spiral peel of green lime, and fill glass not quite full with good chilled club soda. . . . We've later found that raspberry syrup is very decent, also.

MEXICAN "FIRING SQUAD" SPECIAL, which Is a Creation We Almost Became Wrecked upon in—of All Spots—*LA CUCURACHA* Bar, in Mexico City, in 1937

Now and again we found ourselves just a little fed up with rather casual Mexican mixes, and the guidance of 2 young Mexican *caballeros* whose parents mattered in official circles in that city of Mexico. We were herded into fancy, rather dull places, served too warm drinks. And finally on 1 occasion we broke off by ourself, sought out this bar,

—where an aristocrat native oughtn't to be seen!—ordered things in our own way.

This drink is based on *tequila,* top-flight distillation of the *Maguey* plant. Use a tall collins glass and snap fingers at the consequences. . . . Take 2 jiggers of *tequila,* being sure to purchase a good brand, for there are many raw distillations. Add the juice of 2 small limes, 1½ to 2 tsp of grenadine, or plain *gomme* syrup. Add 2 dashes of Angostura bitters. Chill the glass, pack with finely cracked ice, turn in the mixture and garnish with slice of orange, 1 of pineapple and a red cherry.

THE COLOMBO "FLYING FISH" which WAS TAKEN into the FOLD on a MEMORABLE NIGHT in CEYLON, under CIRCUMSTANCES PARTLY RELEVANT to MENTION, & already FRACTIONALLY DESCRIBED in the FOREWORD to this VOLUME

Take 1 jigger of dry gin, put in 1 dash of peach bitters, ½ pony of yellow Curaçao, ½ tsp of maraschino; then shake with plenty of cracked ice and serve with proper flourish in a Manhattan glass, garnished with a slice of orange. We have found that when peach bitters are not too readily available that a parallel, and most delicious alternative is to ignore the Curaçao and bitters idea entirely, substituting ½ pony of Cordial Médoc—a lovely French liqueur based on peach pits and other delicate Gallic interpretations. It is readily procurable at any spirits shop, and Americans should make its acquaintance—not merely stopping with benedictine and cointreau.

THE SPANISH ORANGE FLOWER COOLER, or *REFRESCO,* CALLED *FLOR de NARANJA, SEVILLAÑO*

From lovely Seville.

Oranges aren't absolutely essential, as fresh grapefruit juice will do —provided we carefully add what nature lacks in sweetening. Actually it is a modern Sevillian origination along the American cocktail route, and isn't bad at that. Use a 2 oz jigger, not one of those scant

1½ oz affairs which squeezes four or five extra drinks out of every bottle for our up-to-date barkeeps!

Chill glasses, dampen edge and dip in powdered sugar	2 jiggers dry gin
Put a small spiral of orange peel in each	2 tsp orange flower water
	Sugar to taste
	Juice of 2 oranges

Use pretty large glasses, as the ice must do a bit of diluting for us. Fill large shaker with lots of ice; frappe vigorously. Pour out and twist a bit of peel over each to add the fragrance of flavour of the essential oils to the ensemble.

THE FOURTH REGIMENT COCKTAIL, Brought to Our Amazed Attention by One Commander Livesey, in Command of One of His Majesty's Dapper Little Sloops of War, out in Bombay, A.D. 1931

This, we discovered finally, was merely a Manhattan Cocktail made in 4 oz size, spiced with 1 dash each of celery, Angostura and orange bitters—but why the last was included we never have understood as the Angostura dominates. Chill very cold and garnish with a twist of green lime peel squeezed so as to deposit oil upon the waters after the drink is poured.

LA FRAISE d'AMOUR, another Tentative Adventurous Offering from One of those Quiet Spots in the Bois de Boulogne, Referred to before, from Time to Time

Another spring, it was in 1926, we sat out under the trees and dined and danced and discussed matters that were old when Marie Antoinette rode to the guillotine in her tragic tumbril, or when du Barry passed in her royal carriage. This *Fraise d'Amour,* my dear friends, is not a woman's drink in the usual concept of the word; but, on occasion, can be very apt to a charming lady. It is a deceiver; mild-tasting, insidious, slow to act, but thorough at the last!

Into a bar glass put 1 pony of fresh ripe strawberry juice after being strained. Add 2 dashes of maraschino, 1 dash of orange bitters, then 1½ jiggers of good cognac. Stir and pour into a thin crystal goblet—not too large—filled with shaved ice, stir once and garnish with 1 dead-ripe strawberry teed up in the precise center.

GABY des LYS COCKTAIL, One from Old New York Pre-Prohibition Days when Diamond Jim Brady Was Alive, & the Winter Garden Was New York's only Smoking Theatre, and the Immortal Gaby Was Playing with Al Jolson & Harry Pilcer

Gaby the lovely, Gaby the delightfully mad, Gaby the free soul—who died too young and gave a fortune in pearls to the Paris poor! Gaby is gone, and Bustanoby's old Beaux Arts is gone, and the first Rector's is a memory, but her memory marches on—and this cocktail named in her honour.

It is very simple, crisp. To 1 jigger of good dry gin add ½ pony of orgeat syrup and 1 tsp of absinthe, or a trifle less. Frappe very cold indeed or it will tend to over-sweetness, and serve in a Manhattan glass.

THE FAR EASTERN GIMLET, Classic Now All over the Orient—from Bombay to Hongkong, & Further

Why on earth this stroke of genius stands unheralded and unsung in this fair and allegedly free land of ours shall, to us, always be a mystery like who it is that designs expensive radio cabinets, why all cinema stars long to ruin themselves playing highbrow roles, and why good prize fighters want to write fiction. . . . Throughout the whole swing of the Far East, starting with Bombay—down the Malabar Coast to Colombo; to Penang, Singapore, Hongkong and Shanghai, the Gimlet is just as well known as our Martini here.

The main thing in its favour is that, unlike most cocktails, it is not "warming" in hot weather, and in fact is a good cooler. It is simple, without fancy fizzings, and is one to experiment with until the precise amount of lime cordial is found, to taste. . . . This last is a British invention based on a similar essence to Rose's Lime Juice—which comes in the slender decorative bottle we see back of most good soda fountains—but is not quite so pungent. Soda fountain lime syrup also would do in a pinch. We have approximated it with fine results by diluting it with equal amounts of water. . . . Take a big saucer champagne glass, put in 1 jigger either of dry or old Tom gin, 1 tsp *gomme* syrup or sugar, ½ tsp—to taste—of lime syrup or lime cordial. Fill up with chilled plain water, add 1 ice cube and thin slice of big green lime. Don't use soda water, please.

GIN & BITTERS, THE GIN *PAHIT*—PRONOUNCED *PIE-EET*—OF JAVA, THE "PINK GIN" OF INDIA & POINTS EAST OF SUEZ

This of course has long since gone round the world, but it forms such an important part of men's drinking life in the colonies that we append it here. Either dry or old Tom gin is proper, and the latter appeals most to us. Take a thin, stemmed cocktail glass. Shake in 4 or 5 dashes of Angostura, tip the glass like the tower of Pisa and twirl it between thumb and fingers. Whatever Angostura sticks to the glass through capillary attraction is precisely the right amount, although a lot of old India hands whose stomachs are lax find that a lot more Angostura than that is in order to stimulate appetite. Gently pour off the extra bitters that do not cling. Fill glass with gin. That's all. Superfluous bitters go back in the bottle, on the floor, or out the port hole or window—depending upon who, where and what we are.

We personally drop a chip of ice into our Gin *Pahit* glass; and also twist a curl of lime or lemon peel atop, for its aromatics. One of the world's greatest, simplest drinks.

COMMANDER LIVESEY'S *GIN-BLIND*

We shall never forget the courteous open-hearted wardroom hospitality of the British navy in Indian waters, and Commander Livesey—together with his charming Australian wife—least of all. Along with another very mentionable discovery Livesey's head-bearer—a High-Caste high-binder in the Mohammedan priesthood on feast days, was a wizard with the shaker. . . . Livesey's words were: "We don't prescribe this just before target practice, gentlemen."

Gin, 6
Good cognac, 2
Curaçao, 3
Orange bitters, dash

Mix with lots of ice, shake vigorously and serve in a Manhattan glass. A twist of yellow orange peel is optional, to add oil.

GIN & QUININE WATER, or "GIN & TONIC"—ORIGINATED to COMBAT FEVERS, REAL or ALLEGED, & which LATER BECAME an ESTABLISHED DRINK in INDIA & the TROPICAL BRITISH EAST, & STILL LATER BECAME ACCEPTED over HERE by AMERICAN HOSTS WHO WANTED to IMPRESS FOLK with HAVING COMBED the ORIENT

This is merely a gin highball, using dry or old Tom gin—either 1 or 1½ jiggers—and filled up with chilled quinine tonic water. All Americans, and some Britishers not so hidebound as to insist on brassy, half-warm drinks, added 2 lumps of ice, and a twist of lime peel. We like the latter style better, but must warn all those who embrace this drink to remember it is a medicine and not primarily a stimulant only. On more than one occasion we have temporarily showed aberration on this subject, with the result that our ears rang unmercifully and next day we felt like Rameses II, *réchauffé*. We suggest from 2 to 4 drinks of gin and tonic as being plenty for any one sitting.

GIN FIZZES, to the NUMBER OF ELEVEN, which SHALL BE REMEMBERED LONG after THEIR SPONSORS ARE DEAD & GONE, & WHOSE GENIUS WE RANK alongside that of the INVENTORS of the MINT JULEP, & other TRULY IMMORTAL DISCOVERIES

FIRST of ALL the AZIZ SPECIAL, BEING the IMPECCABLE GIN FIZZ of AZIZ EFFENDI, MONITOR of the ONE & ONLY WINTER PALACE HOTEL, which IS in LOUCQSOR, in EGYPT, up the NILE FOUR HUNDRED EIGHTEEN ENGLISH MILES by RAIL, & FOUR HUNDRED FIFTY by DAHABEAH

Those of us who have journeyed up the East Bank of the Nile by train, Imperial Airways flying boat, or *dahabeah*—one of those odd, romantic looking and amazingly luxurious river sailing craft with their pointed lateen sails curving half moon style against the cloudless sky—to Loucqsor know the Winter Palace and Aziz Effendi; know his superb gin fizz. It is a wonderful thing to sit on the terrace of a wine-clear evening, pleasantly wearied from a day of marveling in incredible Karnak, and after our drive in a carriage down the Avenue of the Sphinxes, with a 14 oz example of Aziz' art in our hands. Actually what he has done is to take the original New Orleans Silver Fizz, and through meticulous chilling and the use of fine Schweppes club soda instead of carbonated city-main water, has immortalized the thing like a graceful imported, expatriated, work of art, and set it up again in the Valley of the Nile. It may be commanded with London dry gin or old Tom—to your wishes. The orange flower water is stepped up probably because the whole amazing East adapts perfume to many more uses than the American office of making lovely ladies smell like bowers of roses. . . . Using a big glass the call is for more gin than usual.

Put 1 to 1½ tsp of sugar into the shaker, add 2 jiggers of dry or old Tom gin—to preference—the juice of 1 small lemon, 1 pony of thick cream and 1 tbsp of fresh egg white. Put in lots of finely cracked ice, *shake hard and long,* turn into a big goblet leaving a few ice lumps floating. Add 2 or 3 good dashes of orange flower water. Now fill up with chilled Number 1 grade club soda. Stir once. Serve immediately and drink soon thereafter, since no gin fizz gains virtue even from brief neglect.

THE BIRD of PARADISE, a COLOURFUL, EYE-FILLING EXPERIENCE WE FOUND in SIGNING OUR NAMES to the BOOK at the *STRANGERS CLUB,* COLON, PANAMA

This strange little club has many famous names in its logbook, Robinson of the *SVAAP,* Alain Gerbault, poor Dick Halliburton whom we first met in Singapore before he flew to Sarawak in 1932, sitting at table with Ruth Elder and Walter Camp. We always have found a welcome there during the 10 or 1 doz times we have been in the "Zone" going west to east or vice versa. . . . Actually this Bird of Paradise Fizz is Aziz' Special to which 2 to 3 tsp of raspberry syrup have been added instead of the sugar, and juice of 1½ limes instead of the lemon. Float on a red rose petal, or any scarlet small tropical blossom, like bougainvillea, as a final garnish. *Shake hard and long.* Better sweetening still, is the same 2 or 3 tsps of blackberry liqueur.

THE CREOLE FIZZ, Being a Latter Day Hot Weather & Milder Variation of the Original New Orleans Silver Fizz, & Employing Sloe Gin to Lend Its Shy Blush to the Colour Scheme

Lyle Saxon gave us this one away back in 1930 during a visit to New York, telling us about his acquisition of the old French Creole house on Royal Street. . . . Take either the Aziz Special or New Orleans Fizz and substitute an equal amount of good imported sloe gin, and cutting cream down a trifle. Garnish with a sprig of fresh green mint and that's all.

THE GIN FIZZ *TROPICAL,* Being One More Sound Bit of Liquid Nourishment from where, to Our Routine Mind, Exists the Best & Most Consistent Group of Mixed Drinks—& Mixed Drinks Mixers—on Earth: Manila, P.I.

This again is an affair based on the New Orleans Fizz background but using pineapple syrup up to 3 tsp instead of sugar, and juice from 1½ green limes instead of lemon. Jim Steele introduced us to this one—he's Tourist Association head for the Islands—on our trip to the Pagsanjan—pronounced "pack-san-han"—River for the dugout canoe trip down the rapids through a stupendous wild mill-race flung through a rocky gorge of towering walls hung with weird tropical growths, peopled with gibbering monkeys and vivid unnameable birds; a feat for which we now possess a fine illuminated parchment diploma. Thermos carafes, ice cubes, hampers of civilized fodder both liquid and solid, made odd contrast to all of this primeval setting, to the native boatmen—2 to a canoe. Fresh green mint is the garnish, a few tender leaves, recently broken off and stuck in a round and fragrant rosette there right under the drinker's nose. Don't use a straw; the closer the mint comes the nicer.

THE MID-OCEAN HIGHBALL, which CONTRARY to NATIVE TITLE Is a LEGITIMATE FIZZ, BEING an EXOTIC from BERMUDA

Not so long ago we went to this charming island with St. Georges as a base camp. We pedalled, sailed, fished and golfed. Swam naked as Adam off small isolated islands with beaches like faintly rose-tinted granulated sugar. The Mid-Ocean Country Club had a gentleman back of mahogany who, then at least, took his art seriously. Actually he called it a "cocktail." Burt MacBride—Associate Editor of *Cosmopolitan*—who flew down on the first Bermuda Clipper with Pan-American Airways and first told us about the drink, called it a "highball," but in spite of this odds-on risk we call it a "fizz" still.

Take 1 jigger of old Tom gin, and ½ jigger each of cognac and French dry vermouth. Donate 2 dashes of orange bitters. Shake well with cracked ice, strain into a highball glass and add chilled club soda to taste. Twist on a bit of green lime peel.

THE NEW ORLEANS ORIGINAL GOLDEN FIZZ

This is simply the usual New Orleans Silver Fizz, only instead of using egg white the yolk of 1 egg is used; or a whole, quite small, egg. Fresh eggs are imperative, let us repeat.

NEW ORLEANS FIZZ No. I, with DRY GIN & a TOUCH of *KIRSCHWASSER*

This, to our mind, is the best New Orleans Fizz of the original type. It also may be used with old Tom gin, of course. . . . Take 1½ jiggers of gin, 1 pony of thick cream, the white of an egg, juice of ½ lemon, 1 to 1½ tsp sugar and 1 tsp *kirsch*. Shake hard in lots of cracked ice, strain into goblet and top off with chilled club soda, or seltzer, to taste. Orange flower water of course is optional. We feel that where *kirsch* is used that the two bouquets will neutralize each other. *So omit the orange flower water if kirsch is mixed with the drink, use it when not.*

THE AMER PICON "POUFFLE" FIZZ, SOMETHING NATIVE ORIGINALLY to PARIS, & ENCOUNTERED at the CAFE du DOME, where in SPITE of the AMERICAN INUNDATION of PSEUDO-BOHEMIANS IS STILL a MODERATELY CONSISTENT RENDEZVOUS for other AMERICANS over THERE WHO DO THINGS with THEIR BRAINS & HANDS

Simply turn 1 to 1½ jiggers of Amer Picon into a shaker, add lots of cracked ice, the white of 1 fresh egg, ½ jigger of grenadine, shake, then turn everything into a big thin goblet and fill up with club soda to suit taste. This is a fine stomachic, and inspires interest in foods.

THE ORIGINAL GIN FIZZ which WAS LONG a SECRET of the BROTHERS RAMOS, and which WAS GIVEN out by THEM, in a FIT of GENEROUS ABERRATION during OUR ALLEGED & RIDICULOUS DROUTH of the PROHIBITION ERA

The Ramos Fizz has long been synonymous with the finest in all the New Orleans art. Thinking that the formula, like any history dealing with the dead arts, should be engraved on the tablets of history, it was given to the world after the now rejuvenated Ramos bar closed for the "dry" era. The main secret of excellence was the platoon of 8 or 1 doz blackamoors who passed the shaker over shoulders to the next, after each had literally shaken his heart out chilling the drink. . . . Iced glasses, and iced soda, also were vital factors of excellence.

To 1 jigger of old Tom gin add 1 tsp sugar, 3 to 4 drops of orange flower water, white of 1 fresh egg, 2 tbsp cream, and the juice—strained—of ½ lime and ½ lemon.

The shaker is first iced with a tumbler of finely cracked ice, then ingredients go in, then the shake—which when done by hand should last at least 1 full minute. Serve strained in a thin goblet and top off with chilled club soda of best grade, to taste. . . . Here again we earnestly recommend The Blender, only using about ¼ goblet of fine ice. This Blender reduces ice to powder, changes consistency of main drink to a sherbet; then the soda, added and stirred, reduces this first frozen consistency to a creamy, slick, chill loveliness. We always use this method to save overheat from physical exertion. It changes the tempo of the drink slightly, due to a trifle of ice still remaining in it after final soda goes in; but like the present "Tropical" Daiquiri thus frozen in The Blender, it is an improvement over the old manual shaking method.

FIZZ, *à la VIOLETTE,* a CAIRENE INNOVATION SERVED Us in the HOME of AHMED SOLIMAN, whose FAMILY for 400 YEARS HAS MADE & MARKETED PERFUMES & PERFUME ESSENCES in the SAME SPOT in the KHAN el KALILI BAZAAR, CAIRO

Ahmed we consider one of our best friends in the Near East. He it was who arranged a duck shoot for us up in the Oasis Lakes in 1932, at Fayyoum; who sent us Ambar cigarettes on the occasion of our marriage, and other kindly gestures too numerous to mention. Long may his shadow extend—this man who numbers every crowned head among his clients—and thanks for this lovely Fizz, incidentally.

Omit the orange flower water from the Ramos Fizz, adding instead 1 pony of imported French or Bols *Crème de Violette* liqueur, or *Crème Yvette.* Mix everything else in exactly the same way, touch the outside of the crystal glass' lip with the glass rod in the flacon stopper of a bottle of *violette* perfume or essence. Serve with garnish of 1 or 2 violet blossoms floated on top. It is a pretty thing to look at, to taste, to smell. It has caused more than one bachelor to become heralded, with cause, as a stoutly clever fellow perennially capable of the right, the judicious, thing! . . . In our own practice—not trusting the value of taking perfumes internally, we supply 2 short purple cellophane straws, and touch the perfume to their upper one-third just beyond lip reach, yet close to the nose tip for fragrance.

THE JAMAICA "GINGER" COCKTAIL, from the GUEST BOOK RECORD of a FRIEND WISE ENOUGH to WINTER on the SHORES of LOVELY MONTEGO BAY; & DISCOVERED, A.D. 1930, under CIRCUMSTANCES UNIMPORTANT to this WORK

Take 1 jigger of dry gin, ½ jigger of claret or Burgundy, ½ jigger of strained orange juice, and 3 good dashes of Jamaica ginger extract.

Shake with cracked ice and pour into a Manhattan glass. . . . We find this a good picker-upper, a stomachic *par excellence,* a carminative of prompt efficiency, for ladies or gentlemen troubled with any of the various ailments from lack of appetite to plain old pre-war stomach ache or collywobbles.

THE IMMORTAL SINGAPORE RAFFLES GIN SLING, Met in 1926, & thereafter Never Forgotten

There are other good Gin Slings in the East. Spence's Hotel, a small one in Calcutta, frequented rather than the Grand or the Great Eastern, by business gentlemen who like good food, well mixed drinks, has the best in India—outside of those blended by amateurs at home. But the Singapore name clings to this famous drink, and along with the famous Shepheard's in Cairo, Hotel Raffles is probably the best known of any in the Orient. The Brothers Sarkies are canny managers with whom we have had some moderately large booking accounts on 2 occasions. Singapore stands at the cross roads of the East, and whoever has been to Singapore knows the Raffles. Here we can sit and watch steamers, warships, *prahus,* sampans, yachts, and God knows what else riding in the Roadstead off Collyer Quay. Just looking around the terrace porch we've seen Frank Buck, the Sultan of Johore, Aimee Semple McPherson, Somerset Maugham, Dick Halliburton, Doug Fairbanks, Bob Ripley, Ruth Elder and Walter Camp—not that this is any wonder.

We've had many Gin Slings out at Seaview, the summer seaside resort of the F.M.S., and where we found the quite delightful atmosphere marred with a quietly grim touch due to the whole bathing area being surrounded with tough wire netting to dampen ardour and appetite of the sharks infesting those warm seas. But we still concede the palm to the Raffles for the best Gin Sling. Hotel Nederlander, the Harmonie and Concordia Clubs in Batavia, Java, also make good Gin Slings—the Harmonie Club—where we are eating and drinking at table in a lovely courtyard one minute, feel a breath of cool night air, and see one of the most startling sights in the world: a couple of hundred men and women suddenly getting up and sprinting for the quadrangle of verandahs before the torrential rains put 4" of water where they were sitting 5 minutes before! But the Raffles drink is best, why we don't know, except that the best Planter's Punch on earth is at the Myrtlebank in Kingston. When our soft-footed Malay boy brings the 4th Sling and finds us peering over the window sill at the cobra-handling snake charmers tootling their confounded flutes below he murmurs *"jaga baik-baik Tuan"*—"jaga bye-bye, too-wan," as it sounds in English—or "take care master" as it means in English. The Singapore Gin Sling is a delicious, slow-acting, insidious thing.

The original formula is 1/3 each of dry gin, cherry brandy and Benedictine; shake it for a moment, or stir it in a bar glass, with 2 fairly large lumps of ice to chill. Turn into a small 10 oz highball glass with one lump of ice left in and fill up to individual taste with chilled club soda. Garnish with the spiral peel of 1 green lime. In other ports in the Orient drinkers often use C & C ginger ale instead of soda, or even stone bottle ginger beer.

Our own final improved formula calls for 2 parts dry or Tom gin, to 1 part cherry brandy and 1 part Benedictine. This is dryer, not too sweet. We also use a trifle more ice in the glass than the Raffles technique. One lump melts too quickly where we live among the coconut palms!

THE SAHARA GLOWING HEART COCKTAIL, from the Hands of one Abdullah an Arab Muslim Wizard back of Mahogany at the Mena House Bar, near the Pyramids of Ghizeh, which Are Just South of Cairo, Egypt

Watch this one when out under the moon in a desert overnight camp, riding camels out across the vast dunes, or strolling in the moonlight around the Sphinx with some congenial young woman companion. Full many a mere man has gone and committed himself for life under that desert moon after a brace of Glowing Hearts, as we have seen with these failing and rheumy eyes. The effect on us was that, along with another American ne'er-do-well, we untethered all the camels while the Arab boys haggled over some eternal native unimportance, tied them in a line, and mounted most insecurely on a pair of dromedaries of antique perfume, doubtful morals, and the manners of a horned toad, we led them to the Sphinx and tethered them to the claim-stakes of some random excavating party then in operation during daylight hours, between the Sphinx's feet. It didn't make sense then, and it doesn't now, but the row those Arabs and dragomen tossed up when they found the whole mess of camels vanished was something to take down on a sound track.

Take of dry gin, 1 pony, absinthe, 1 pony, dry imported apricot brandy, 1 pony; donate ½ pony of bright rose coloured grenadine. Shake with lots and lots of ice and strain into a large saucer champagne glass, and pray Allah for forgiveness of all imminent and future sins of the flesh. . . . To us this drink tastes a bit sweet; also a bit dominated by absinthe or Pernod Veritas. So why not experiment to taste along these lines? . . . Ignore the grenadine, step up the gin to a jigger, whittle the absinthe to a dash or two inside the empty glass just before pouring the chilled drink.

THE GRANDE BRETAGNE COCKTAIL No. I, Being to Our Ungoverned Mind One of the Five or Six Chief Cocktails of the Whole Wide World

One dank, chilly, and snow-carpeted day in January of 1931 we wore out shoe leather, shins, and temper in the name of "history" and "art," hiking all over the Acropolis in Athens; skidding from the Temple of Diana, around the Parthenon, and back down past the Erectheum and its divine caryatids, and to our motor car and to Athens proper. Here we met Eddie Hastings, now cruise director for the M.S. *BREMEN* with Raymond-Whitcomb, and he told me about the little Greek barkeep in his tiny bar and his miraculous inventions. . . . This Grecian male had been abarring for over 40 years, man and boy. During that time he had devoted ½ hr daily to the pardonable indoor pastime of testing new and radical mixes all his own. The Grande Bretagne Nos. I and II, were the final result—the pinnacle. Using lime juice we found later is far better than lemon, although lemon is plenty good enough. Use *dry* imported apricot brandy, never the sweet syrupy American copy. . . . No. I: 1 jigger of the best dry gin possible, ½ pony apricot brandy, ½ pony or so of strained lime or lemon juice, 1 tsp of very fresh egg white, 1 dash of orange bitters. Shake with lots of ice and turn into a chilled Manhattan glass. . . . No. II: substitute *kirschwasser* for apricot brandy, omit orange bitters—using 1 dash of peach bitters if available, or 1 tsp *Cordial Médoc.*

The domestic Bridge Table cocktail, the 3-to-One, both copy this Grande Bretagne, but the apricot brandy content is too heavy, and no mention is ever made that unless fine *dry* apricot brandy is used, the result is sweet, abortive, disillusioning in the extreme. . . . It is amazing, though, how such a small amount of *apricot* or *kirsch* comes zipping through to lend bouquet to this brisk drink.

THE BARRANQUILLA GREEN JADE, from a STAY in COLOMBIA in the YEAR 1933, and again in 1934

This amazing jumping-off town for emeralds, oil and gold in Colombian hinterlands, has already been described; how the ancient Spanish town rubs elbows with the most modern American practice. We have fond recollections of one charming hostess in Barranquilla who served us whole shrimps boiled in deep olive oil, bits of popcorn tossed in garlic butter, little fritters of *plantano,* and many strange tropical, chilled, fruits—mangoes, carissas, mangosteens, Surinam cherries, rose apples, mawmees, heaven only knows what else with long Latin names! . . . The Green Jade is a crisp thing, too, fine for hot weather like the Grande Bretagne, the Gimlet. . . . 1 jigger of dry gin, ½ jigger of green crème de menthe, ½ jigger cream and 1 tsp or so of egg white. Shake with ice, strain into a saucer champagne glass, and garnish with 1 green cherry and a sprig of fresh mint. Serve with a green straw affixed with same technique as in the Cuernavaca Special already listed.

THE HALLELUJAH COCKTAIL, a PALATE-TWISTER from the ISTHMUS of PANAMA

This was originated by our good friend Max Bilgray, of Colon,

Panama, somewhere around 1929, and dedicated to Aimee Semple McPherson as a result of an alleged visit to his Bilgray's Tropic Bar and Cabaret, long a gay spot on the Isthmus. Now whether Aimee ever went to Bilgray's under the alias of Betty Adams; and if she went there, whether or not she found anything she wanted, are matters beyond our deductive powers. All we know is that we arrived one night just after this alleged inspection, and that Bilgray was mailing out post-cards, postage *gratis*—as many as we wanted—listing the Hallelujah ingredients. . . . Of course many thousands went out, and a million dollar lawsuit was instituted, and Aimee's mother forgot her squabble with daughter, and rallied to her defense. Even remote, pure and austere sheets like the New York *Times* had special cables, and we thought the whole business hugely amusing—and strangely enough, the drink is good. Quote:

Babylonian Grape Brandy (Cognac) .... 1 pony
Ice from the Crest of Mount Sinai .... Lots, finely cracked
Lemon from the Desert of Sin .... Lime juice, 4 drops
Gomorrah and Sodom vermouth .... Italian, 1 jigger
Rum aged in Noah's Ark ....½ jigger; rye also used
Add Cain's syrup from the Garden of Eden .... ½ tsp Grenadine
You then give it the Hebrew shake and—pop a cherry on top
Say Hallelujah after drinking!

Not that it makes any great difference, but the initial letters of each line spell Bilgray's. Any drink known probably to a hundred thousand people in the last eight or nine years in Panama alone must have had something besides postcard appeal. . . . It should be served in a large saucer type champagne glass.

THE HONEYMOON COCKTAIL, or *LUNE de MIEL,* One of Many Strange Memories from a Place in Paris Known as *CHEZ MA BELLE SOEUR,* under Circumstances not Relevant to Mention

If the place still exists it can be found, if not we can assure those adventurous enough to be curious that the French *Sûreté* closed its doors upon those precious things of the long evening gowns, the slave bracelets about wrist and ankle; the pendant earrings; rouge, jeweled slipper and tiny fans. . . . It is a strange drink, and for all we know it may have its purposes and its moments. Take a sherry glass and build up as follows: *crème de cacao, parfait amour,* the yolk of 1 egg carefully unbroken, and finally *kümmel doré*—all chilled beforehand. Use about 1 pony each of the liqueurs, or slightly less.

THE MANILA "HOOP PUNCH," another MASTERPIECE from the HANDS of "MONK" ANTRIM'S NO. I CHINO, FIRST DISCOVERED in 1931

Take 1 pony each of cognac and orange Curaçao, add 2 ponies of port wine, donate 1 tsp of lemon or lime juice. Fill a goblet with finely cracked ice, turn in the mix, stir and serve with short straws—garnished to suit taste. . . . This can also be made not quite so sweet by changing the strained lime juice up to ½ pony and cutting down the Curaçao to ½ pony.

AND NOW SEVENTEEN or so "HOT HELPERS" CALCULATED to KEEP CHILL SWAMP MISTS at BAY, BANISH the MEGRIMS & WARM BODY, HEART & SOUL into a FINE & AMIABLE DISPOSITION

Of all the retinue of drinks listed in this volume, it is certain that Hot Helpers really will be of most grateful use to readers. For when a man is wet and chilled through, blue with cold and long exposure in such voluntary tortures as November duck blinds, the wheel of an ocean-going sailing craft in a winter chance, or in any chilly and depleted situation, a Hot Helper will in 5 short minutes recall him from being a sorry and useless thing into restoration as a warm-hearted homebody, kind to dogs, children, wives and even landlords—as we can surely attest! Out of the endless blends in glass and silver bowl we have listed these as the best and unusual from all over the civilized world.

FIRST MARCH FOUR BASED upon a MATTER of ALES

AULD MAN'S MILK, a Revivifier from the Heather Bound Slopes of Bonnie Scotland; and Fetched Back to these Shores after Residence in the British Isles in 1932

Take a bottle of Scotch ale, heat it gently in a saucepan and while it is gaining temperature dust with 1/4 tsp of powdered cinnamon, the same of nutmeg and ginger. Take the yolks of 2 fresh eggs, add 1 scant tsp of brown sugar; then beat them well. When ale is hot but not quite boiling, pour this egg-sugar mixture slowly in—stirring diligently. When thoroughly blended, turn in 1 to 2 jiggers of good Scotch whisky. A fine stout and nourishing drink, this.

YE OLDE GOSSIPE'S BOWLE, Based on Mulled Ale, and Dated, England, 1622

We, as a matter of principle, despise all titles with "Ye" in it—Ye Little Giftee Shoppee, and such ilk, but when we ran on the near-Elizabethan dating of this receipt we forgave all, for it is a grand title and one of England's oldest drinks—sometimes called *Lamb's Wool*.

Strong ale, two 12 oz bottles, 1 qt; Bass preferred
Good white wine, 1 pint
Nutmeg, 1 tsp
Brown sugar, to taste
Roasted crab, or other small, apples; sugared and spiced

Mix ale and wine, add sugar and spice, heat slowly. When piping hot add the roasted apples, serving in wide mugs if you have 'em. Not too much sugar on the apples, please. Crabs are best.

LORD RUTHVEN'S "GOSSIP'S CUP," or *TEWAHDIDDLE,* a Charming Mix of Ale, Brandy, Spices & Sugar, & Dated London, 1654

We imagine that this is an older drink even than the Olde Gossipe's Bowle, given above. And of *Tewahdiddle*—what a name, what a name!—the immortal Dr. Kitchiner says:

"Before our Readers make any remarks on this Composition, we beg of them to taste it: if the materials are good and their Palate vibrates in unison with our own, they will find it one of the pleasantest beverages they ever put to their lips. . . ."

Lord Ruthven says in his volume *Experiments in Cookery,* London, 1654:

"This is a right Gossip's Cup that far exceeds all the Ale that Mother Bunch made in her lifetime."

Ale, one 12 oz bottle or pint
Brandy, 1 tbsp or a trifle more
Brown sugar, 1 tsp
Lemon peel, 1 curl, yellow part only
Ginger, 1 pinch
Nutmeg, sprinkling

Mix all these and heat on the fire, but do not boil. . . . This drink is a warmer of the heart, and would be a neat one to produce some cold fall or winter's afternoon or evening, before a snapping wood fire.

NOW, finally, DR. WILLIAM KITCHINER'S "YARD of FLANNEL," which IS SOMETIMES CALLED an "ALE FLIP," *CIRCA* 1817

This is another hot helper based on ale, and calculated to cheer up any long winter evening while the wind whistles about the eaves.

Ale, 1 qt; or 2½ to 3 12 oz bottles
Eggs, 3 beaten
Brown sugar, ½ cup
Ginger, 1/3 tsp
Nutmeg, 2/3 tsp
Good cognac, or rum, ½ cup
Lemon, yellow peel, ½

Take the yellow peel of ½ lemon, put into the ale and bring to heat; meanwhile beating up eggs with spices, sugar and rum. When the ale steams—but still isn't boiling—pour into a pitcher; then turn the egg-spice blend into another. Now pour back and forth briskly until everything is creamy and smooth.

WORDS to the LIQUID WISE No. VIII, on the SPECIES of ALE for MULLING

In all receipts calling for heated, mulled, or otherwise spiced ale, again we recommend English Bass, or any English Musty Ale, most heartily in preference to our present list of domestic products, and in spite of the cost made necessary by our ridiculously high tariff duties on products which we never have made here, and probably couldn't make as well if we did try.

ONE, now, BASED on APPLEJACK—which IS AMERICA'S TERM for APPLE BRANDY, & CALLED the JERSEY LIGHTHOUSE

It is rather unfortunate that our prohibition era through its raw applejack and Jersey Lightning, managed completely to deflect American taste against this fine spirit. Decently aged-in-wood applejack is a fine thing, just as French *Calvados*—a superfine apple brandy from Normandy and the orchards of Ausse and Bessin—is a lovely stuff, as fine in its way as any cognac, especially the brand marketed in the flask bearing an apple, on a leafy branch in bas relief.

We met the Jersey Lighthouse sitting in the back room of a small New Jersey inn one horrid winter night, with William Faulkner, Tony Sarg's puppet maker Bil Baird, and Eric—*Midget Magellans* and *Blow the Man Down*—Devine, our sailing mate on *MARMION*. . . . Into a tumbler place 2 lumps of sugar, a dash or 2 of Angostura, 3 or 4 cloves, a spiral of lemon peel. Onto this pour 2 jiggers of ancient applejack, fill with boiling water, float on 1 tbsp applejack at the last and serve blazing merrily. Those of us who read Bill Faulkner's *Light in August* renamed the drink *Light in February*.

A HOT HELPER FOUNDED upon BEER from DENMARK & CALLED the COPENHAGEN—PRONOUNCED as NEAR as WE CAN DO IT, "KERN-HABEN"—BEER TODDY

It is a fine one to use after winter sports, in an Alpine ski-camp, anywhere like that. Take 1 average bottle of good Danish or Bavarian dark beer, beat 1 to 2 egg yolks well with 1 tbsp of brown sugar; and after heating beer in a saucepan put beaten eggs into the mug, turn in the hot beer, stirring diligently the while. A dusting of nutmeg is optional.

FOUR HOT ONES BASED on BRANDY, or BRANDY-RUM BLENDINGS, the FIRST of which Is the APRICOT, or PEACH, *FLAMBÉ*

This is a delicious and totally different touch from all the others, from the usual hot drink. Take 3 dried apricots or 2 dried peaches—plumped in hot water beforehand; put in a silver cup and add 2 tsp of brown sugar. Pour ½ jigger of cognac, heated, onto this foundation and set alight, blowing out when sugar starts to melt well. Now turn in 1 jigger or so of cognac, stir well, and add very hot water to taste. A pinch of powdered clove, or 3 or 4 whole cloves, form optional touches.

THE SO-CALLED "ENGLISH BISHOP"—CONSIDERED by the AUTHOR to be ONE of the MOST ATTRACTIVE HOT CUPS ever INVENTED for the AID & COMFORT of CIVILIZED MAN, DISCOVERED in the SUMMER of 1932 in BOXMOOR, HERTFORDSHIRE

Take an orange, stud it thickly all over with whole cloves, dip it in cognac and dust with brown sugar. Now brown well until sugar caramels, either spitted upon a skewer or stick before the fire or under the broiler. Cut it into quarters; now take a saucepan or other vessel, turn in 1 qt of red port wine, simmer tightly covered for 20 minutes, add 2 jiggers of cognac just before pouring. Can be served *flambé* with a little brandy floated on top.

CAFÉ DIABLE, which Is neither ALTOGETHER BRANDY nor ALTOGETHER COFFEE, nor MERELY A HOT DRINK—but a MELLOWED & DRAMATIC INSTITUTION from the CREOLE DELTA CAPITAL of NEW ORLEANS

This is always an impressive bit of business when dining with a handsome young lady, *chez nous* and *à deux*. Be sure to turn out all the lights before trying it, however, or the effect will be spoiled. The successful brewing of a *Café Diable* somehow instills a bit of admiration for the imminent male in the stoniest feminine breast. It causes her to think that here in truth is a monstrous clever fellow, a man above other men. Don't disillusion her. . . . For this routine have two cups and a fire extinguisher handy.

> Really strong black coffee, 2 cups
> Brandy, (Elaborate but worth it!) 1½ cups or so
> Peel of orange and lemon, both pared off very thin
> Sugar, 8 lumps (Some use four to six)
> Whole cloves, 4; or more, to taste

First warm your silver bowl—for china may crack. Put in peel, spice, and pour in brandy. Light candle and cut lights. Heat ladle by holding beside candle flame—not over it because of soot. Dip up a couple tablespoons of brandy, and put in two of sugar. Set alight and lower ladle into bowl—being sure that neither your Perfect One nor your own eyebrows are too close when it puffs into a blaze. . . . Now dip up a ladle full and let it fall back, then after the proper applause start putting in coffee gradually, ladling busily all the time. Finally the flame will flicker and die, and before our audience's interest flickers and dies, ladle into demitasse cups.

The SHANGHAI COSSACK PUNCH, Come upon at a Most Vulnerable & Romantic Moment, which Shall Never Be Forgotten; and a Fabrication which We Have always Held to Be the Finest Hot Drink Extant

Those of us who knew Shanghai before the red Russians were chased out and the white Russians were dissipated and scattered to the four corners of the globe, remember what we remember. We recall one drizzly afternoon after the races, a house in the French Concession whose host again it is not necessary to mention, and among other interesting selvages of that afternoon—the following, fetched by him from Siberia during those incredible days when Kolchak's army was dispersed. . . . This day it was served hot, in tall Russian coffee glasses.

Good brandy, 1 pint	Dark rum, ½ pint
Curaçao, yellow, ½ pint	Lemon, strained juice, 4
Lemon peel, yellow part, 2	Orgeat syrup, 1½ tsp
Hot tea, 1 quart	Orange flower water

This was simmered up once over a spirit lamp, and poured off steaming to each guest, who sweetened to taste—most adding a dash or two of orange flower water.

HOT HELPERS BASED upon BURGUNDY or CLARET or PORT WINES

THE ENGLISH BISHOP IS FIRST, & MENTIONED under BRANDY DRINKS just above this JUNCTURE & in the SAME CATEGORY, PAGE 54

NOW WE COME UPON a MATTER of MULLED CLARET & PORT, together with COGNAC, SPICES, PEELS & other MATTERS; from a RECEIPT in the TIME of GOOD QUEEN BESS, *CIRCA* 1578

Mix 3 cups of claret and 1 of red port; add ½ cup of cognac, the spiral yellow peel of a lemon, and 2 good pinches each of cinnamon and nutmeg. Toss in ½ doz whole cloves, cover well and heat hot—but do not boil. Take off immediately it is hot enough to suit taste and not a moment longer, an' it please you! Boiling ruins port instanter, evaporates all alcohol and leaves a bitter lees calculated to spoil the best ingredients.

MULLED BURGUNDY *à la* GULMARG, FROM THE SHOOTING LOG OF a BRITISH COLONIAL CAVALRY OFFICER upon the OCCASION of a SHOOT of *CHIKOR* or MOUNTAIN GROUSE, & WILD DUCK—the FIRST in the FIR CLAD SHEER SLOPES and VALLEYS around GULMARG, & the LAST on WULAR LAKE, which Is in the FABULOUSLY LOVELY VALE of the KASHMIR some TWENTY MILES to the NORTHEAST

This must have been something in a Kashmiri mountain hut in late September, nearly 2 miles above the sea, with the perfume of ½ doz plump grouse sizzling before the coals on a rock slab hearth, the air outside clear as wine, and the summit of the nearer Himalayas walking up to the white, deathly still, roof of the world—where only the wind and the snow and the cold could dwell. . . . Then in 3 days back to the heat and confusion of teeming Bengal, to Calcutta 2d largest city in the British *Raj* after London itself; to orchids, and jasmines and Paris frocks and intrigue.

It requires 2 bottles of still red Burgundy, 2 limes or 1 lemon, cut into thin slices and seeded, ½ banana cut into slices. Tie the fruit together with 2 sticks of cinnamon, 1 doz whole cloves and 6 allspice, in a bit of cheesecloth. Put along with the wine into a covered pot, simmering for not over 10 minutes. Discard cheesecloth bag and contents, turn in 1 cup of dark rum, ½ cup of brown sugar to taste, and 1 cup of club soda or seltzer. Stir and *serve foaming,* garnished with curl of lemon peel.

THE TIMKE LOCOMOTIVE from FAR AWAY LUZON, which Is a SMOOTH, DELICATE, GENTLE, HOT REVIVER, DISCREET ENOUGH for the TENDEREST MAID, the MOST CAREFUL SPINSTER

Monk Antrim's spirituous spirit leans over our shoulder again, for he it was who told us about this drink. As we have said Baguio, the Philippine hill station, is cool o' nights even though it is right smack in the hottest tropical belt. The formula noted on the back of a Baguio Country Club score card, with a gross not creditable to mention, reads as follows: take a small saucepan or chafing dish, and before putting to fire turn in 1½ wine glasses of good Burgundy or claret, ½ pony of orange Curaçao, and 1 pony of honey mixed with 1½ tsp of sugar. Stir well until honey is entirely dissolved, stir in 1 lightly beaten egg, then put over the flame. . . . When it first simmers up pour into a mug or silver julep glass, and with another in the opposite hand pour briskly from one to the other for a final mix. Add 1 thin slice of green lime or lemon, dust with a little cinnamon and that's it. A most unusual blend of flavours; all delicate, and affording total distinctly low in alcoholic strength. A beautiful drink for any invalid or convalescent wearied of usual routine liquids.

AND NOW, FINALLY MARCH CERTAIN HOT AIDS FOUNDED ON RUMS

THE JAMAICA BLACK STRIPE, BEING SERVED as OFTEN HOT as COLD, MAY BE FOUND by TURNING to PAGE 18

NEXT MARCHES THE BAKER "HORSE COLLAR," * ORIGINATED by the AUTHOR, A.D. 1935, upon RUNNING into STONINGTON, RHODE ISLAND, ahead of a HOWLING NOR'EASTER when HEADING SOUTH from LAWLEY'S YARD to FLORIDA in *MARMION*

This hotter toddy was invented by these sere and palsied hands, quite through luck and by accident. Our 56 foot ketch *MARMION* having just been discharged with a new and costly main trys'l re-rig from Lawley's Yard, the split-sprit necessary to spreading that fancy triangular bit of canvas became known as the "Horse Collar." On the run from Cape Cod to New York, we stuck our noses into a snoring nor'easter, which added up so quickly that we dropped the hook at Stonington, Rhode Island, rather than be shaken up any more than necessary. It was nearly November and cold as hades. Well that night all hands screamed for hot rum, and we found no lemons in the lazarette—and to many otherwise cultured folk a hot rum without a dash of lemon is like the Democratic Party without the ghost of Jefferson, Tom without Jerry, a Cuban without his mistress. But we had oranges!—and thereby hangs a tale. For suddenly we thought of orange peel—and orange peel roasted with wild duck and how superbly fragrant it can become. Scarcely daring to hope for anything virtuous coming out of the effort we proceeded as follows.

Tin cups for mariners, silver julep cups for fancies
Carta de Oro Bacardi, Jamaica, Barbados, or Haitian rum, 2 jiggers
Orange peel, 1 to each cup, cut in unbroken spiral
Brown sugar, 1 tsp per cup
Whole cloves, 6; or powdered clove, 1/4 tsp per cup
Boiling water, enough to fill
Butter, 1/2 tsp, optional

* We here confess (with modest blush) that this Baker Horse Collar has attracted more attention than any other hot one listed between these boards: letters from everywhere: from a placer gold outfit the hell and gone above the Arctic Circle in Alaska to Newara Eyliya, situate high up in mountains in Ceylon; to Quito in Ecuador, New Zealand and the Argentine. Author.

Line cups with spirals of orange peel, first dipping them in rum to moisten. Dust sugar on peel, then cloves the same. Put a jigger of rum in each cup, put cups on hot stove, and after a moment set aflame. Let burn until edges of peel start to brown and sugar to caramel. Blow out. Take off stove, add other jigger of rum, fill up with hot water, give a brief stir and serve—either with or without a lump of butter on top the size of a hazelnut. . . . This sounds complicated, but the whole thing takes only a couple of minutes. Cups and rum must be heated or when set alight the moisture in the peel will come out and smother the flame. . . . The *Horse Collar* thus has four delicious aromatic scents and savours: first the rum itself, then the nut-like perfume of burned oil of orange, then the brown sugar, slightly carameled by the flame, then the toasted spice.

THE OXFORD UNIVERSITY HOT RUM PUNCH, a CLASSIC that Is SIMPLE & SOOTHING & SATISFACTORY, and DATING back into the DIM, DISTANT PAST

Take 1½ bottles of Barbados, or lighter Jamaica, or 1 bottle of Demerara 160 proof; add 1 bottle of cognac, 3 quarts of boiling water, 2 cups of lemon juice. Add brown sugar, to taste, and a handful of whole cloves. Put a spiral of yellow lemon peel in each cup, and there it is. Most excellent for anyone coming down with anything, due to the lemon juice.

EXPLODED OLD ALEWIVES' TALE No. I, BEING a WARNING against OVER-INTRODUCTION of CITRIC JUICES into HOT ALCOHOLIC DRINKS

No matter what dear old Aunt Florina-May Fittich may grumble about how she used to cure Grandpop's cold with hot lemon juice and spirits, let's lend at least ½ an ear to certain master rum drinkers who claim—probably with justice—that alcohol and sugar and lemon juice, *under heat,* work toward an acid condition of the gastric machinery most conducive to spleen and vapours. It is just a thought anyway, and we really don't expect anyone to heed the warning after all.

HAROLD PETER'S HOT BUTTERED RUM

Anyone who has sailed with Pete—whether around the world on *PILGRIM,* to EUROPE on the schooner *LLOYD BERRY,* or south to Florida from Cape Cod on some ship like our own *MARMION,* as we did, remembers his magnificent tattooed masterpieces, haunch, paunch, back and chest, and his Hot Buttered Rums at the end of a cold, wet, Fall chance. Our first introduction to them was running from Woods Hole to New York, one late October day, with the wind whipping up a dry nor'easter, and our new main trys'l pushing us along close to nine knots.

Into each average sized glass put a teaspoon of brown sugar, a twist of lemon peel, a teaspoon lemon juice, four to six whole cloves, and a spoon. Take a "futt" dish and heat water on the galley stove—and in case we don't remember Pete's definition of that time-honoured bit of New England addenda, a futt dish is the flat tin handleless sort of pan we see on top of bullet heating stoves down east, to keep the air humid. Actually any pot does as well.

To each glass donate two ponies of Barbados, or any stout rum—two full ounces—add boiling water to taste, stir, and with the spoon which has kept the glass from cracking, slide in one teaspoon of butter on top. Drink as butter becomes wholly melted. . . . When getting really fancy for Harbour Furl Company, Pete may float a spoon of rum on top, and set aflame, but not for anyone less than a full Commodore!

WORDS to the LIQUID WISE No. IX, on the EXCELLENCE of ALLSPICE in HOT RUM DRINKS

To vary the usual clove and nutmeg add half a teaspoon of allspice to the next hot toddy. The result is quite aromatically happy.

RETURNING to our RETINUE of COLD DRINKS again WE PRESENT the JAMAICA BUCK, BEING a SHANGHAI BUCK—already NOTED—only USING JAMAICA, or other DARK RUM instead of BACARDI, & ADDING HALF a LIME for FLAVOUR

We found this years ago in Kingston, on a jaunt through the West

Indies, during our editorial days with Doubleday, Doran & Company magazines. Take 1½ jiggers dark rum, turn into a collins glass with large lumps of ice, squeeze ½ lime in and add the crushed lime itself; now comes 1 tsp sugar, and fill up with ginger ale of some decent sort, or better still with stone bottle ginger beer. It is a satisfying cooler. By using ½ dark rum and ½ *Carta de Oro* Bacardi the drink will suit feminine Jamaicaphobes.

NOW, GENTLEMEN, at LONG LAST ARE EIGHT or so MINT JULEP CEREMONIES—BEING VARIOUS ADAPTATIONS of this PEERLESS AMERICAN CONCEPTION from ALL PARTS of the WORLD where IT IS PROPERLY REVERED

Right from the meaning of the word Juleps have been a spill-and-pelt of contradiction and disagreement. . . . The very name itself never was midwifed on any honeysuckle-bowered southern balcony, but comes from the Persian *gulab,* or Arab *julab,* meaning rose water. . . . No sane Kentucky planter, in full possession of his faculties will yield an inch to any Marylander when it comes to admitting rye is superior to bourbon in a Julep, when actually, a Julep is international and has been international for years—just as the matters of radio and flying are international. It is a drink composed of whiskey or brandy —and, of late—rum; sweetened, iced, and flavoured with aromatic leaves of the *mentha* family.

So before the shooting starts let's explain right here and now that there's no more chance of getting the various Julep schools to agree on fabrication of this most delectable of drinks, than we have of getting a proud Atlanta great-grandmother to concede General Sherman a nice, gentle, well-meaning, big boy.

First of all there is the silver cup versus the glass school; the chilled glass versus room-temperature school; the slightly bruised mint versus the all-bruised school; the rye versus the bourbon school; the fruit garnish versus the plain school.

Feuds have begun because someone breathed the possibility that city water would make a Julep as well as water dipped from a fern-draped Blue Grass Country spring. Men have been shot at for heaping fruit juices, slices of citrus, and maraschino cherries on a Julep completed. Families have faced divorcement about the slight-appearing concern of red-stemmed mint.

A gentleman who discards the slightly bruised mint from his drink views another who permits the bruised leaves to remain in glass as one who did not have quite the proper forbearance on the distaff side. . . . And so tell they the tale—

Getting right down to cases, there is no more need for argument of violent nature along such lines than there is that a flashing-eyed Spanish girl is any less functional in life than a lovely honey-haired Scandinavian, than a titian English maid, or a jet-haired and urgent daughter of the Killarney Country.

On this matter of Juleps we can boast to a thorough Julep research, without pride or prejudice, for we have put in some years of mighty clinical home-work on the matter!

We've sipped Juleps on a shaded upper gallery brewed by a genuine Colonel, from Versailles, Kentucky. We've tried Juleps in Charleston, Cape Cod, Toronto, Kelly's in Panama City, and the Royal Hawaiian in Honolulu; we've sipped other Juleps in Nassau, Cumberland Island, Georgia, Seattle, Los Angeles, and that little Overseas Club—or whatever the right name is—that sits up on stilts by the pier-end in Zamboanga; we've tried—of all places—a Julep in Sandakan, British North Borneo. . . . We've buried this inquisitive proboscis in green, spicy-cool mint foliage under king coconut trees, looking out over the coffee and cacao plantations of central Guatemala, in shadow of the Shwe Dagon Pagoda in Rangoon, Burma, on the start of the road to Mandalay—which last is hundreds of miles inland and a mountainous table-land without flying fish, and China isn't across the bay either.

But the best Julep of all, up to date—an' Ah mean that Suh!—was mixed by Monk Antrim's Number One Chino boy at the Manila Hotel, Luzon, P.I., and A.D. 1926. . . . Just *good* bourbon—yes, Manila never was dried up by our experiment and much of the finest bourbon found its way out there—really tender, fresh, red-stemmed mint;

a big glass, plenty of fine ice, a little sugar, a teaspoon of Demerara rum floated between the two ripe sticks of fresh ripe Pasig River valley pineapple, in a big sloping-sided glass holding a full English pint of sixteen ounces. And *lots* of mint, for it takes a real clutch of the herb for fragrance.

But let us inject a word of caution to seekers after this miracle of frosted perfection. No man can rough and tumble his Julep-making and expect that luck must always be on his side, that a lovely arctic frosted thing shall always reward his careless ignorance.

Especially on yachts or boats, for instance, no Julep glass can frost when stood in any considerable wind. Frosting depends solely upon condensed moisture being converted to minor ice through the excessive chill of melting cracked ice and liquids within that glass. Therefore if the breeze whisks it away there can be nothing left to frost. Paradoxically, when the outside of any Julep glass is moist from careless rinsing, handling, or standing about only partially iced in humid weather, frost will be in total lack due to *excess* moisture.

Likewise no Julep can ever frost when caressed by the warm, *bare* palm of an impatient host or guest—not any more than decent frosting can ever result from wet, half-melted cracked ice that is more liquid than solid. Just obey the rules, few but important, and success will crown every amateur effort.

Actually if we would forget all the eternal nonsense about Juleps and obey the few common sense rules, everyone could save their strength for enjoyment of this institution.

1. Chill glasses, whether silver cups or otherwise.
2. Use glasses of sixteen ounce capacity.
3. Use two and a half jiggers of likker for sixteen ounce glass, two for fourteen ounce.
4. Use red-stemmed mint, simply because red-stemmed mint is more pleasantly aromatic. Use fresh mint, and cut stems short just before putting in as final garnish—to make them bleed.
5. Don't bruise that first installment of tender mint leaves more than very slightly. The inner leaf juices are bitter and cannot have profitable

flavour. Bruise one between the teeth, then chew it up to find out.

6. Don't expect to get a whacking good Julep out of six months old "bourbon" or "rye." We can't.
7. Don't use coarse ice, use finely cracked ice—very fine.
8. Don't over-garnish with sliced orange and random fruits. With Juleps, and in fact any drink of delicate quality in its own right, don't add anything with a different strong scent—and orange, lemon, and certain other fruits have a very potent aroma. . . . The aroma of a bourbon Julep should be bourbon and mint—not bourbon, mint, and a fruit store. Garnish simply without trying to gild the lily. A julep is more than a mere chilled liquid; it is a tradition which is to be respected. The mint itself is a delight to eye, just as we admire parsley against a fine red snapper, or permit feminine associates the use of red nail polish, or grace a mother's table with flowers. So let the Julep feast the eye and nostril properly—not supply unending, edible diversions from the main theme. We don't need to eat all the trimmings, after all—but *we* always do! . . . That is why ripe pineapple is so beneficial—and eaten after the Julep is gone, the marinated fruit is delicious.
9. Take care that all sugar is worked into syrup before ice and liquor are put in. Reason: If sugar is left in granular form, when chilled the dissolving process is radically slowed down. Especially when sipping through a straw you will suddenly find yourself inhaling a furiously saccharine slug which will ruin the memory of the lovely drink just preceding this disastrous end. . . . This is why we personally use *gomme,* or bar, syrup for all juleps. (See Page 154.) Mint leaves muddle as well in it as they do on sugar; the muddled bits of mint stick to the glass' inner walls even better than with the sugar-water mix. One final stir before garnish goes in distributes this quickly dissolved syrup evenly through the entire drink. Ergo. . . .

MONK ANTRIM'S MANILA HOTEL MINT JULEP No. I, with BOURBON or RYE

Sugar, ½ tbsp; water 2 tbsp
Fresh mint, tender sprigs, 6
Ripe pineapple, 2 sticks or fingers
Good old bourbon, 2½ jiggers; or rye
Fresh mint, 1 bunch
Cherries, 4, scarlet
Demerara or Barbados rum, 1 or 2 tsp, to smell
Finely crushed ice

Ice glasses, and without wasting any time do the following: toss in sugar, then water, then the 6 mint tips. Muddle *slightly,* being sure that the volatile oils are smeared all over inside of glass. Discard this slightly bruised mint entirely. . . . Pack glass with ice, pour on bourbon—and do not stir, letting wise nature take its course. . . . Then distribute rum slowly in drops. Cut mint stems off *quite short* up to the leaves, and make glass look like a green bouquet, with two pineapple sticks peeping out on opposite sides, and the hot red of the cherries nestling in the mint. . . . Serve with two very short straws, but let stand until thoroughly frosted before handling, and always escort it with a small napkin, to handle the melting frost on outside of glass. Omit the rum if a Marylander or Kentuckian is present.

MINT JULEP No. II, with Bourbon or Rye

This is another variation, and also good. . . . Simply proceed just as in the Monk Antrim version, only leave the slightly bruised mint in the glass. Half fill with ice, and add a few more sprigs of slightly bruised mint. Fill with ice, and finish exactly as above, only omit the touch of rum. . . . Handle bourbon and rye exactly alike.

MINT JULEP No. III

This would be the same as No. II, only use the tenderest sprigs of mint and don't bruise at all—leaving the herb to be its own delicate prophet. . . . Having tried all ways we find this has least mint aroma of all, and as mint saturating the whole affair is so gratifying to our personal preference, No. III does not include when we are at work.

MINT JULEP No. IV, from Santiago de Cuba, Employing, Naturally, Bacardi

This is not the usual Julep, and we don't want any sleep lost over the idea. A Cuban gentleman of parts got it up, likes it still, gave us four and we liked all of them. . . . It isn't a Julep as we know it, but after all who are we?

Carta de Oro Bacardi, 2½ jiggers
Pineapple juice, fresh if possible, 2 tbsp
Lime, juice, 1 fairly large
Grenadine, 2 tsp
Fresh mint and garnish

Using a fourteen ounce tall glass or goblet, bruise six sprigs of tender fresh mint very lightly, rubbing over inside glass. Pack full of very finely crushed ice. Pour on lemon juice, pineapple juice then Bacardi, and finally the grenadine. Do not stir. . . . Garnish with bunch of fresh mint cut off close up to leaves just before putting in, and add pineapple stick, slice orange, and what not, to taste. . . . Let frost before serving.

LAMARR PEACH BRANDY MINT JULEP No. V

Down Macon way there are more and better peaches than probably any other spot on this testy globe of ours, and one family named Lamarr—of whom we know one of the daughters—seems to part-own three whole counties or something, and has probably gazed on larger numbers of acres in peaches than any young lady of our acquaintance. In fact she claimed to have an uncle who was written up in *Fortune* because he developed a machine for taking the fuzz from peaches—a fact the late Mr. Mack, of Moran & Mack, would have been pleased to know. . . . It is therefore we give credit to a Southern lady who told us about this good jollifier and all good men take note. 'Struth and 'tis no drink for weaklings!

Cognac, 1½ jiggers
Bar sugar, 1 tsp
1 doz or so sprigs of fresh mint
Georgia peach brandy, 1 jigger
Long thin slice ripe peach
Spring, or well, or rain, water

Put sugar in large silver or glass Julep glass, and add just enough water to make it an oily syrup. When smoothly dissolved break off a couple of the tenderest mint sprigs, and muddle very, very slightly—leaving them there in aromatic harmony. Take six other sprigs and gently crush up and about, that no spot may be overlooked of that glass's inside.

Fill with very finely cracked ice, pack down slightly, and pour in the blended brandies. Garnish with sprigs of mint, and on the straw drinking side, insert a single stick of sliced ripe peach. . . . Do not stir. That prime liquor will percolate through the ice to the very bottom without any trouble. Just sit by quietly and watch the whole lovely process of frosting. . . . Then, and then only, drink!

PEACH THUNDERBOLT, BEING No. VI, a Long-Hoarded Julep Treasure from Old-Time Georgia

This Thunderbolt business is no quip about the effect, but simply the name of the place just south of Savannah, where we first stumbled onto this nectar of the gods, this eyefilling, mild, pleasant debauch of three senses.

Carta de Oro Bacardi, 3 jiggers—yes, we said 3!	Sun-ripe, fresh Georgia peach, 1
Fresh mint, dozen sprigs	Lime, juice, ½ large; 1 average
	Sugar, 1 tsp

Take a large goblet and pack it half full with finely shaved ice, put in half the sugar, a trifle of water, and six tender mint heads. Muddle gently for a moment, rubbing mint all over interior of goblet. The flavour thus penetrates better. In the center put in a peeled and stoned peach, cut in halves and stood on edges. Mix rum, lime and rest of sugar. Pack glass full and pour in liquids. . . . Garnish well with the remaining mint sprigs, and serve with two *short* straws so the nose can browse in it. . . . Don't make the mistake of garnishing with a lot of other fruit, or using cherries. It is the ripe peach which is picked up by the rum. . . . We have, however, discovered that a teaspoon or two of good peach brandy floated on before frosting, helps amplify the basic flavour of the unit.

PENDENNIS CLUB MINT JULEP, BEING No. VII, & Severely Ungarnished

Martin Cuneo has for many years manufactured his own conception of a proper mint Julep to members of Louisville's famous Pendennis Club—mentioned elsewhere in this volume. There are several minor variations in the gentle art of Juleping, and his is enough off the usual track for inscription here—as he does not bruise mint, even slightly.

Take a sixteen ounce silver Julep cup, or the same in glass. Into the bottom put a lump of sugar and dissolve it in a little spring or well water. Choose the tenderest mint sprigs and toss in three—arranging them in the bottom, and don't crush or bruise at all. Fill the chalice with finely cracked ice.

Turn in two jiggers of the best old bourbon the cellar can afford, and stir once to settle. Add enough more ice to fill; a complete small bundle of tender mint comes next, trimming the stalks fairly short, so as to give out their aromatic juices into the Julep. Place in the ice, and stand aside for a few minutes to frost and acquire general merit.

MANILA POLO CLUB BRANDY JULEP, LISTED as JULEP No. VIII, for ALPHABETICAL *not* QUALITY REASONS

Met out in the Philippines in 1926, in '31 and '32—and never forgotten.

Sugar, 1 tsp
Cognac, 2½ jiggers
Fresh fruit, *du jour*
Water, 1 pony
Mint, 1 doz sprigs
Any medium dark rum, 2 tbsp
Powdered sugar, 1 tsp for garnish

Use sixteen ounce glass. . . . Dissolve sugar and water, and toss in six tender sprigs of mint. Muddle lightly, pack glass with finely shaved ice, stir once, then turn in the cognac. Decorate with two sticks fresh ripe pineapple, cherries, a slice of ripe peach, or what not. Now float on the Jamaica; dust with the final powdered sugar, and spot in the other sprigs of mint, stems down. . . . Serve with two short straws. Drink when well frosted. We first saw this Julep in a huge tumbler with wide mouth and sloping sides, holding around 16 ounces.

ADDITIONAL JULEPS, of RUM and BRANDY

Since neither Scotch nor Irish take kindly to julepry, the variations —when those same Marylanders and Kentuckians are absent—can be any sort of rum, and any sort of brandy. . . . In the latter case remember that most fancy brandies like apricot, cherry and peach are very sweet, so mix with cognac half and half. In the former, try and avoid a 100% Jamaica base, as this is a trifle heavy for the average palate. Either dilute Jamaica with white rum like Bacardi, or some medium rum like Barbados. Don't forget that Demerara can be as high as 160 proof!

WORDS to the LIQUID WISE No. X, on the ABBREVIATION of MINT JULEP STRAWS

The final garnish of emerald mint is not merely to look at. If we must have, or prefer, straws—make them short straws. Just a couple of inches peeping out is correct. Thus the olfactory proboscis must be buried in the fragrant herbage, something not the case with the crude long affairs through which certain folk drink ice cream sodas.

THE KINGSTON *CRUSTA,* Being a Parallel Thought to the Martinique *CRUSTA,* on Page 74, only from Jamaica

Hardy Jamaican planters turn this same Martinique drink into something vastly different by the startling addition of ¼ tsp of Jamaica Ginger, or the equivalent of Hell-Fire Bitters, see Page 153. . . . Still hardier Jamaicans even wind this business up further by dusting some cayenne pepper on top.

KIRSCH au CAFÉ—or the Famous Black & White Cocktail

This revivifier was found in the home of a Cairene resident before going out on the Nile of a moonlight night, and on his *dahabeah*—a luxurious and incredible sailing craft originated and maintained in his case, for no good purpose. . . . Take *kirschwasser* and black very strong coffee, 1 pony each. To this add ½ pony of good cognac, the white of 1 small egg. Shake hard with cracked ice and serve in a tall flute cocktail glass with a stem. *Allah, il Allah!*

THE KNICKERBOCKER "PUNCH," a Memory of the Good Days of 1915

How many of us remember the Maxfield Parrish *Old King Cole* when it formerly hung—not at the St. Regis at all—in the old Hotel Knickerbocker bar on the southeast corner of Broadway at 42d Street? . . . It smiled benignly down upon all sorts and conditions of men, over a free lunch buffet too rich to be credible—and which saved more than 1 hungry college boy in the days when the Dolly Sisters, the Castles, Gaby des Lys, Bert Williams and Hazel Dawn were stars behind the footlights, on the dance floor; when the late Pauline Frederick was so starkly beautiful in *Joseph and his Brethren;* when deliciously tiny Emma Trentini was imported by our round the world cruising fellow-passenger Rudolph Friml to sing in his operettas; when the old Rectors, Delmonico and Louis Martin weren't just names out of the rosy past. In our college freshman—and financially always debted—days we recall the good old Knickerbocker and the snacks there; and here is one of their specials. . . . Into a goblet strain the juice of ½ a lemon or 1 small lime, add ½ tsp of sugar, a fat jigger of St. Croix or other medium dark rum, 1 pony of water and 2 dashes of orange bitters. Ice with lots of finely cracked ice, stir to chill, decorate with fresh fruit galore, then finally float on 1 pony of still red Burgundy. A sprig of mint and short straws are in order also.

THE LALLA ROOKH COCKTAIL, a Receipt Given Us on a Trip Home from Yokohama in 1931, by Clymer Brooke

Clymer Brooke and 2 or 3 other Yale men set off from New London to circle the globe in their 65 foot schooner *CHANCE,* and Brooke liked it so well in Tahiti he jumped ship and got himself a vanilla plantation on the loveliest island possible: Moorea, across the bay. We met him the day out of Yoko, our ship first bound for Honolulu, when he was headed back to Long Island to marry him a bride, and being "in vanilla" as we might say, through having a South Sea plantation of that orchid vine, the drink was typical. Peerless Theodore, mentioned so often in Volume I, had it specially mixed for us in the *SS RESOLUTE* Grill.

Just why it was called Lalla Rookh is something neither Brooke nor logic could explain. . . . Take 1 jigger of good cognac and mix with ½ jigger of brown rum and ½ pony of vanilla extract. Now add 1 tbsp thick cream. Chill well in a shaker with cracked ice, strain into a flute cocktail glass. Vanilla may be cut down or added to, to taste.

Some people admire ½ tsp of sugar or *gomme*. It makes an insidious drink that ladies prefer, often to their eventual risk, joy, and sorrow.

THE MANILA "LEAP FROG" COCKTAIL, another MEMORY of the CRISP DAYS & COOL NIGHTS up in BAGUIO, back in the IGOROTE COUNTRY of LUZON

Take 1 pony of Bacardi, the same of dry apricot brandy, add the strained juice of 1 small lime or ¼ lemon, colour with 1 tsp of grenadine. Shake with lots of cracked ice and strain into a saucer type champagne glass. . . . After home fabrication of this fine drink we have found very definitely that the original Manila formula may be improved by using 1½ ponies of Bacardi and ½ pony of *apricot,* everything else remaining the same. We must not forget that *apricot* is an insistent and penetrating flavour. We only need a small amount to point up a single cocktail—never 1 pony! Gold Seal Bacardi is best, again; the white lacks flavour.

THE BACARDI "LEAVE IT to ME," from the BAR BOOK of an INFANTRY MAJOR STATIONED at FORT WILLIAM MCKINLEY, near MANILA

Fill the shaker ½ way with cracked ice, then put in 1 jigger of *Carta de Oro* Bacardi, 1 tsp maraschino, the juice of 1 small green lime, 1 tsp raspberry syrup. Turn into a saucer champagne glass with 3 or 4 small bits of ice, and hit with a spot of chilled club soda. A pretty, flavourful and refreshing cocktail.

MONK ANTRIM'S *LINTIK* COCKTAIL, which REALLY ISN'T any SPECIES of COCKTAIL at ALL, but a SORT of LIQUID TRIPLE THREAT ORIGINATED for REASONS STRICTLY DISHONOURABLE, but ELECTRIFYING; & in ADDITION a BRIEF SORT of BIOGRAPHY of the GENTLEMAN HIMSELF

We appear to refer to Monk fairly often in this volume, and there is a reason besides his being a careful, almost clinical, student of potable liquids. He happens to be one of the most interesting chaps who ever hit the Islands. When we first knew him Monk lived vividly, to say the least. He had a drink memo book, contents of which had been religiously donated by a series of gentlemen who, at the time of our first trip to the Islands, were either in various sanatoria for alcoholic treatment, had been invalided back to the states as incurable dipsomaniacs, or were dead from probably spirituous causes.

A few years back a chap named Walter E. Antrim showed up from somewhere down in the South Seas, came to the Manila Hotel and got him a job as dishwasher—so sing they, speak they, tell they, the tale—it being Uncle Sam's largest and finest hostelry, and the pride of the Philippines, naturally.

So, as the old silent movies used to say, time passed, but didn't pass Monk by. When we got there first in 1926, he greeted our Cruise Staff at the end of a mile or so of new concrete pier, and we met him then —the *Manager* of the Manila Hotel.

Now Monk knew how to live life in his own way, and he lived it: high, wide, and handsome, making friends as he went along. Monk would roll you, flip you, cut cards with you, for anything from a steam yacht to a thousand dollars gold and never turn a hair. . . . The last we heard he had espoused himself to a handsome titian-haired creature, and vanished from Manila. Why or where? *—we just don't know. . . . Anyway we have Monk's letter before us dated March 4th, 1927, passing along several Manila liquids, and calling attention especially to the *Lintik* Cocktail. Quote:

". . . the *Lintik* is the smoothest drink which I've run into lately. . . . *Lintik*, as you may know, being Tagalog for 'Lightning' (Tagalog being the language of a tribe of that name down in eastern Mindanao, the big island below Manila).

"The main drawback to this concoction is that it must be aged for two weeks, then chilled in an ice bucket without ever coming in contact with ice. . . . But the final result is well worth that little bother. . . . Will be seeing you next trip out, and we'll test a few in my laboratory, with Wong to do the mixing!"

* A sad dual immediate answer came in to us regarding Antrim's whereabouts. He'd married and suddenly quit Manila and the Philippines (we were advised by a friend of his), had ended up in Mexico, where he (from undisclosed reasons) became virtually blind, and died quite suddenly at Hotel Reforma. . . . His own mother wrote us that she had clipped all of our frequent references to her son, appearing from time to time in the magazines; was keeping a scrapbook of his fabulous adventures. after his death. Author.

Good dry gin, 3 bottles | Lemons, juice 15; peel 10
Water, 2½ cups | Angostura, 2 full tbsp
Sugar, 1¼ lbs

Strain lemon juice carefully through 2 cloths. Boil sugar and water for 2 minutes, strain and cool. Add gin and bitters. Bottle, placing the peel of 2 lemons in each bottle. Store in a cool spot, not too cold, to age. Serve chilled and under no condition add any ice. This will make around 4 to 5 bottles of *Lintik* Cocktails.

ALFRED BARTON'S SURF CLUB *MANGAREVA* COCKTAIL

If there is an exotic spot on our whole Atlantic Seaboard it is the Miami Beach Surf Club, and Alfred Barton is its guiding genius. His gala nights, incredible affairs, make Hollywood fetes look like modest Quaker meetings. He imports whole circuses, ferris wheels, elephants, clowns and God alone knows what else if he wants a circus; a midway, sideshows, appropriate murals. This *Mangareva* is Barton's *chef d'oeuvre,* along with his staff brain trust, when recently seeking a really unusual drink. Honey has long been a French admiration in certain intimate drinks. *Calvados*—or Normandy apple brandy—and honey would be best, but if not possible use the corresponding applejack and honey available in the open market.

First the container: this being a coconut shell sawed off at the top to a 2½" opening, and the kernel taken out. Clean up the outside with sandpaper or steel wool. Mount this in a ring of fresh pineapple and garnish with galax leaves, and serve with brightly coloured cellophane straws. . . . Now the mix: turn 1 part *triple sec,* 2 parts strained lime or lemon juice, and 5 parts Hildick's Apple and Honey into a bar glass. Mix well and allow 3 oz to each coconut shell. Now fill with finely cracked ice, stir once, close the opening with Pineapple Paradise, *et voilà!* Even the cleverest guests cannot guess its formula; furthermore it speaks softly but packs a Big Stick.

WORDS to the LIQUID WISE No. XI, on the EXCELLENCE & DIVERSION of PACKING a COCKTAIL GLASS with SHAVED ICE, ADDING HALF a TEASPOON of STRAINED LIME JUICE, then FILLING with OUR FAVOURITE LIQUEUR

Just try this some day when the taste flags, when ideas run dry or bar shelf is bare of the usual high proof spirits. . . . Try it with Cointreau, Benedictine, Grand Marnier, Chartreuse, Cordial Medoc, Drambuie, Certosa, or any of the myriad French coloured liqueurs coined for devious Gallic purposes, but each notable for this or that fragrance or flavour. . . . Such drinks are lovely to look at, dry enough through the lime juice, and each one radically different from its neighbour!

THE MARTINIQUE *CRUSTA,* which We Found Waiting for Us in Fort de France on the Occasion of Our First Trip through the West Indies, in 1929

This effective and eventful drink uses no man-made cup, but the reversed skin of a small orange or lemon, first moistened inside and on the lip with lemon juice or rum, then dipped in lots of fine white sugar, until encrusted evenly on inner yellow side of the whole *reversed* skin. . . . Now stand this in any stemmed glass that will fit it.

The other method is to peel off a small orange, or lemon, in a single unbroken spiral. Take a small goblet, moisten inside with lemon juice or rum, then line with the spiral peel, and the whole dipped in fine sugar, leaving what clings, clinging.

Now chill either type of container for a good hour in the refrigerator, and into it strain the following, after shaking well with cracked ice.

St. Croix or other Martinique rum, 1½ jiggers
Lime, juice, 1 average size
Maraschino, 1 tsp, scant
Angostura, 3 dashes
Gomme syrup, 1 tsp, to taste

Garnish with a stick of fresh pineapple, a slice of orange, or anything that suits.

MI AMANTE, which Means "My Beloved," and Was Given to Us by Two Young Gentlemen from the Argentine, from B. A., & Who Own Polo Ponies, Ranches & Things

Our young Argentine knows how to live life we can assure you, and does. He is smart, modern, full of fun, often as not a superior athlete. He knows American cocktails, and originates quite a few on his own account. . . . We tried this during a recent local heat wave with results entirely at odds with the first reaction to its written formula.

Take of the best gin possible, 1½ jiggers, of coffee ice cream, 1 cup. Put into a chilled shaker and shake well, or better still, in The Blender. Some people add a few lumps of ice to help the chill—straining the latter out in serving. Pour into large saucer type champagne glasses.

TWO ACCEPTED VERSIONS of the WORLD FAMOUS ONE-&-ONLY MILLION DOLLAR COCKTAIL, which IS ESPECIALLY FAMOUS throughout JAPAN & the PHILIPPINE ISLANDS

MILLION DOLLAR COCKTAIL No. I, as MIXED by SHIDEAKI SAITO, No. I BAR BOY at the IMPERIAL HOTEL, TOKYO, JAPAN, 1926, 1931 & 1932

First fill shaker 2/3 full of cracked ice then put in 1½ jiggers old Tom gin, ½ pony of Italian vermouth, 2 tsp pineapple syrup, 1 tsp of grenadine for colour, 2 tsp strained lemon juice, 2 tsp of thick cream and ½ the white of a fresh egg. Shake hard, strain into a big opulent-looking saucer champagne glass, and that's that. . . . Vermouth content is immediately varied by Saito to suit the palates of his various Million Dollar clients in Tokyo—running from 1 pony down to ½ pony. Some prefer French dry vermouth, but the standard blend calls for Martini & Rossi.

MILLION DOLLAR COCKTAIL No. II, as MIXED by NOMURA, the No. I BAR BOY at TOR HOTEL, KOBE, DATING from 1926, to 1931 & 1932

His formula was exactly the same as Saito's masterpiece except the vermouth was stepped up to 1 pony, and the lemon juice to 1 tbsp, strained of course; then 1 tsp grenadine.

THE MIYAKO HOTEL SPECIAL

From Kyoto, Japan, during the Cherry Blossom Festival, April 20th, 1932.

Japan is heart-breakingly beautiful enough by itself, and Kyoto was its ancient Capital. Being there for a third time was romantic enough surely, but being there for the great festival was something else still—especially with a fiancée by our side. . . . Well, we were all of these, and our bland friend Mr. S. Suda, bar baron at the Miyako Hotel, concocted this after considerable thought, and added his blessing on our whole picture. . . . The results were benignly immediate.

Dry gin, 1 jigger	Cointreau, 1 jigger
Fresh pineapple juice, 1 pony	Lemon or lime, juice, ½ pony

Shake with finely cracked ice, and pour into a tall four ounce cocktail glass with stem. It is fairly sweet, so step up lemon a trifle and cut down pineapple, if preferred.

SLOPPY JOE'S *MOJITO,* which Is a BACARDI COLLINS, PLUS

Cubans and snobbish *Americanos* can sneer all they please at Sloppy Joe's, the fact still remains that there are as good, and better, and more varied cocktails suitable to our somewhat exacting taste than any other spot in Cuba. Granted that the Vedado Club, the Country Club, the *Nacional, La Florida*—all have their known specialties, still Sloppy Joe's assortment is not with them.

This is a greatly improved rum collins, and is best made with *Carta de Oro* Bacardi, or any good medium light Santa Cruz, Haiti, or Barbados rum. If Jamaica is used, don't use it straight, mix with white rum, one part to four of latter.

Put several lumps of ice into a 16 oz collins glass, toss in 1 tsp sugar or *gomme,* insinuate a spiral green lime peel about the ice, turn in 1½ jiggers of Bacardi; white, or Gold Seal, and the strained juice of 1 small green lime—not a lemon. Stir once, fill with really good club soda and garnish with a bunch of fresh mint. . . . If for a lady, use grenadine instead of sugar.

WORDS to the LIQUID WISE No. XII, on the PRETTY SENSE of USING VARIOUS COLOURED FRUIT SYRUPS for SWEETENING ALL SORTS of COLLINS DRINKS

Mix the usual Tom or John Collins, only instead of using sugar use raspberry, strawberry, mint, cherry, or other soda fountain syrups. They add a slight bouquet and taste, make a pretty looking drink. Vary by using stone bottle ginger beer for soda.

THE MOOD INDIGO, Being another One from another Year's Cruising, Found at Gould's Casino, in Nice, France, in 1932

Once again we happened into the *Palais de la Mediterranée,* accompanied by a young and fluent maiden, to look about, to risk our top limit of 20 dollars—then—gold on roulette. That Gould's Palace really is something—and to our mind a modernistic dream conceivable only by a hybrid of Nero, Alice Foote MacDougall, and our friend Donald Desky. As the French maitre d'hotel told us—quoting from the book —*"Tous les Galas de la Saisôn attirent-ils une assistance d'elite dont l'elegance et la chic eclipsent les plus eccalantantes societes mondaines."*

Be that as it may Gould's made the over-publicized and faintly funereal Casino at Monte Carlo look like a shabby country cousin—they are reviving its sinking fortune with Keeno now, imagine it!—and someone suggested a Mood Indigo, and we wondered if it were a liquid compliment to Duke Ellington's music, and ordered 2—one of which we introduced to the young maiden, who then introduced herself to us. . . . Take 1 jigger of dry gin, ½ pony of cognac and anywhere from ½ to 1 pony of *crème de violette,* or *parfait amour.* Adding 1 tsp of egg white is optional, and usual. Shake viciously with lots of cracked ice, serve promptly, and drink vis-à-vis. *"Et quel dommage, M'sieu et Ma'mselle?"* . . . A violet blossom is the prettiest garnish.

EL MOROCCO, which Is a Cocktail from North Africa, not any Product of New York Restaurants of Similar Name

This is from the field notebook of a trusted friend on a Mediterranean cruise in 1938, and dated from Tangier, North Africa. Take 1 pony each of cognac, red port wine and ripe pineapple juice, putting it in a shaker with lots of cracked ice. Flavour further with 1 tsp each of grenadine and orange Curaçao; and make tart with 2 tsp of lime juice, strained. Shake and strain into a tall flute cocktail glass with a stem. . . . Personally we have come to omit all grenadine. The port gives it all the sweetness needed, also pretty colour.

WIL P. TAYLOR'S *HOTEL NACIONAL* SPECIAL, which, along with the TROPICAL DAIQUIRI & the SANTIAGO de CUBA MINT JULEP IS ONE of the THREE FINEST BACARDI DRINKS KNOWN to SCIENCE

Who, who knows his Havana, does not know, or has not heard of, Wil Taylor. We met him back in 1931 when in charge of World Cruise Publicity for Hamburg-American Line, and got into Havana one time in 1933 just after they had mighty near blasted a marvellous hotel off the map, to get at those Machado-phile officers hiding there. And Taylor kept right on managing just as if it had been old times! . . . But that time with pineapples sounding off all night along the Prado, we elected to stick to the old downtown Plaza, what with wife and child, but that did not prevent our remembering with great pleasure Taylor's own Bacardi concoction. . . . It is "mighty lak" a Mary Pickford, but still not, as the latter omits her limes.

Carta de Oro Bacardi, 1 jigger
Lime, juice ½
Fresh pineapple juice, 1 jigger
Dry apricot brandy, 1 tsp

Shake with cracked ice, strain, serve in a tall cocktail glass with a stem. . . . We indicate Gold Label Bacardi for the simple reason that *Carta Blanca* is so delicate in flavour it barely comes through any rich drink.

THE *OKOLEHAO* COCKTAIL, KNOWN out in the ISLANDS as the "OKE"

Having made three visits to these enchanted isles, both during and after prohibition, we have seen, smelled and tasted some pretty strange beverages out yonder. Actually *okolehao* is a spirit made from a certain root, fermented and distilled. During her very strict prohibition administered by a lady who apparently got as much joy out of life as a newt or an eft—see Webster—Hawaii's "oke" was made from fermented pineapple juice, from the bud sap of coconut palm, from taro, from sweet potatoes, sugar cane, and heaven alone knows what else. Now the original native liquor is legal once again, here's the accepted island cocktail for them as likes it. . . . Take 1 jigger each of *okolehao* and fresh ripe pineapple juice, add ½ jigger of lime juice, properly strained, and shake with lots of ice. Garnish with any sort of bright, small, tropical-appearing blossom.

THE PARISIAN COCKTAIL, Being a Fine Appetizer & Tummy Toner

We got to like this rather odd tasting beverage after a stay in Paris. It is simple and worth noting. Take 1 jigger of Byrrh wine, add the juice of 1 small green lime, strained. Shake with lots of cracked ice briskly and serve in a Manhattan glass with no further trimmings at all.

SHELBY LANGSTON'S PALMETTO PUNCH, which Is an Exotic Invented on a Florida Camp Hunt

Perhaps our readers have noted a fairly persistent mention of sour oranges in *Volume I.* It seems high time that Americans lucky enough to live in the Deep South should realize what a truly wonderful flavouring agent they are—this wild descendant of the original bitter rind Seville oranges brought to Florida and West Indies by Columbus himself, has flavour both in juice and peel so delicious, so exotic, so superior to other sour citrus fruits, that it should be much more appreciated. The Cubans know it, and their Steak *Bigarade* is listed in *Volume I,* on Page 138. . . . Our good friend Shelby Langston, like ourselves, has shot quail, wild turkey and deer along the great headwater hammocks and marshes of the St. Johns River, in Florida, and squirrels in Nawth Ca'lina. Sour oranges can be found in many old deserted clearings, and his discovery in camp of this mixture should rank in Florida with our friend's invention of the world-famous Daiquiri, noted on Page 30.

The proportion of sour orange juice to that of sweet depends on the sweetness of the sweet oranges. It will only take a few trials to learn what suits personal taste—and here's to you lucky Floridians. No one sells sour oranges, they give them away, for not one person in a thousand thinks they are worth picking off trees.

Old Tom gin, 1 part; (Dry gin will do)
Sour orange juice, 1 part
Sweet orange juice, 2 parts

Shake quickly and hard with lots of ice, pour through strainer, and twist a small piece of sour or sweet orange peel over each glass to get the oil of orange aroma and flavour.

PAN AMERICAN CLIPPER, from the NOTEBOOK of ONE of OUR PILOT FRIENDS WHO—when OFF DUTY—MAY SEEK ONE

Applejack, 1 jigger; *Calvados* apple brandy is better still
Absinthe, 1 dash
Lime, juice, 1 scant pony
Grenadine, 1 tsp

Shake with cracked ice and serve in Manhattan glass.

PANCHO VILLA COCKTAIL, another CLASSIC from the PHILIPPINES that WE ABSORBED in 1926, for the FIRST TIME

The late Filipino gentleman of this name was probably the greatest man for his inches that ever drew on a pair of fighting gloves. In Manila he is still a national hero, his monument is impressive, and when Monk Antrim's Chino Number One whipped this one up in his honour, it proved more than good enough for us to insert here.

Carta de Oro Bacardi, 1 pony
Dry apricot brandy, 1 pony
Pineapple juice, 1 tsp
Dry gin, 1 pony
Cherry brandy, 1 tsp
Stuffed olive

This is a sweet one and must be very cold. Fill shaker with fine ice and pour into a big champagne glass. It is one of the very few cocktails calling for several conflicting ingredients that is worth its own weight in bicarbonate of soda.

THE PENANG COOLER, a New Tropical Exotic We First Met in Penang, Prince of Wales Island, F.M.S., Following a Swim in the Milk-Warm Waters of the Straits of Malacca

After a swim at the Aquatic Club, we came back to town and ran into this, unexpectedly proposed by a semi-Chino barkeep at the Eastern and Occidental Hotel. The mint gives it coolness, bite, and character.

Dry gin, 1 jigger
Fresh pineapple juice, 2 jiggers
Green crème de menthe, 1 pony

Shake with shaved ice and serve with it in a tall cocktail glass with stem. A flat glass was used out there, and ice was strained out—but the more modern technique is best, using an electric mixer and leaving ice in.

THE PENDENNIS CLUB'S FAMOUS SPECIAL

To 1 jigger of dry gin add ½ jigger of the best dry apricot brandy procurable. Squeeze in the juice of 1 lime or ½ a small lemon, strained of course, and trim with 2 dashes of Peychaud's bitters which has been made for generations in New Orleans. . . . Split a ripe kumquat, now available during the winter in most big grocery or fruit stores; take out the seeds and put the 2 halves in a Manhattan glass. Stir the drink like a Martini with lots of cracked ice and strain onto the golden fruit. This is a sweeter Grande Bretagne, see Page 47.

TWENTY and SEVEN PICKER-UPPERS for the Nineteenth Hole, which Can not only Enable Us to Greet the New Day Undismayed but May—on Occasion—Save a Life

There are times in every man's life when, through one reason or both, a man feels precisely like Death warmed up. In such sorry plight there is but one thing to do if we do not wish to sit and suffer through a whole day waiting for the cool hand of normalcy to stroke our dry and fevered brow—a Picker-Upper.

This little list of variegated hairs of the dog, has been hand-culled from quite a few joustings of our own with this sort of human withering on the vine. We have, from sad example set by several friends, come to distrust all revivers smacking of drugdom. It is a small, tightly vicious circle to get into, and a bit of well-aged spirits with this or that, seems much safer and more pleasant than corroding our innards with chemicals of violent proclivities, and possible habit-forming ways.

For years before our ignoble experiment, civilized man had been trying to civilize his drinking, and when we think back just yesterday—as world's time is measured—man's one drink was a crudely fermented affair: juice, seeds, saps, and the like.

Now take an eye filling look at any well-stocked oasis, and consider progress in colour, taste, bouquet, and result. This early civilization in America—except in the main centers like Charleston, New Orleans, Philadelphia, and New York—with the possible exception of the matchless julep, commanded hard likker with a chaser, if any. Now since the insanity of the nineteen-twenties man is studying his spirits sanely and with revived artistic interest in their possibilities.

The field of the great gray Morning After is one which this same civilized mankind is trying to graduate from undiluted hair of the dog that bit him, to something less regurgitative, and shocking to the whole mental and nervous network. With this thought in view we quietly suggest any of the following.

WORDS to the WISE No. XIII, on the NECESSITY for GOOD SPIRITS for MAKING PICKER-UPPERS

Just as we don't serve mediocre acid red wine to the delicate sensibilities of a prize gourmet friend, neither do we give the timid and demure morning-after tummy a turn with raw, new, bilious atrocities. Here, if ever, the smart host will have a special cache of a few prize jewels—for his very own sake. The vile odours arising from improperly aged spirits are just about all a chap needs to set him to withering on the vine permanently. . . . Use only the best ingredients, for after all we don't do these things very often, and it's better to be safe than sunk.

FIRST on the LIST MARCHES CHAMPAGNE, although IT HAS already BEEN DEALT with SYMPATHETICALLY under CHAMPAGNE COCKTAILS, PAGE 21, *et sequitur*

A plain chilled pint of champagne per person with two or three simple biscuits is probably the finest picker-upper known to civilized man. The champagne must be *very* cold, and can either have bitters, a little added brandy, or both.

The Maharajah's *Burra-Peg,* and the Imperial Cossack *Crusta,* are the most magnificent examples of this we have ever known.

Champagne in this role is somewhat more expensive than any of the other remedies collected, but when we think back there is stark realization that the time comes to every man when relative expense means little; and rather than risk a "turn" from sight of raw egg, or taste of sweet ingredients, the refreshing, chill tartness of the bubbly is a dispensation straight from heaven.

ABSINTHE FRAPPÉ and ABSINTHE DRIP

These two picker-uppers are already given on Page 8, *et sequitur*.

ABSINTHE PHOSPHATE

There is no doubt about this one working. . . . Simply put two dashes of lemon phosphate in a bar glass, add a jigger absinthe and a pony of Italian vermouth. Stir for a moment and pour into a claret glass filled with finely cracked or shaved ice. Vermouth can easily be cut down slightly to taste.

BARRANQUILLA PICK-ME-UP

Barranquilla, as has already been pointed out, is the residential center of near-coast Colombia for many of those Americans who do things in oil and emeralds. And here, we found, a man can need a picker-upper just as well as anywhere else.

Cognac, 3 jiggers
Dubonnet, 2 jiggers
Angostura, 2 dashes
Egg, white 1

Shake well with cracked ice and serve in a tall glass with stem.

CAROLINA PLANTATION BRACER

After dancing the night through, or possibly a gentleman's game of draw poker—nothing wild—until the wee sma' hours, our tide-water blade knifing his way about the selvages of Charleston's society was wise in his pick-me-ups. This suggestion from Bill Heyward, schoolmate of years back, given between boats one winter afternoon is something to note, lest we forget.

Cognac, 1½ jiggers
Egg, 1
Port, 1½ jiggers
Gomme syrup, 1 tsp; optional
Jamaica or Barbados rum, ¼ tsp

Shake with cracked ice until busily frothing, and pour into a tall cocktail glass with stem. . . . Other neat flavour touches can double for the Jamaica: Curaçao, Cointreau, Cordial Médoc, Drambuie, Benedictine, Chartreuse, Grand Marnier.

PARISIAN "GOOD-MORNING"

Absinthe, 1 jigger
French vermouth, ½ tsp
Bar sugar or *gomme* syrup, 1 tsp
Yellow chartreuse, ½ tsp
Lime or lemon, strained juice, 1, or ½
Anis or anisette, 1 tsp

Frappe with cracked ice, strain into old fashioned glass, add small bit of ice, and a little soda or seltzer, stir and pote.

HARVARD CLUB PICK-ME-UP

This, as Frederick A. R. Thompson, the then Managing Editor of *THE COMMONWEAL* informs us, is the brain-child of former British naval officer now, for this reason or that, Head Factotum behind mahogany in the New York Harvard Club. The request is to serve them three ounces at a time, and as cold as may be with chilled glasses. . . . Three of these have been known to change a blue, murky,

Monday morning into a nascent glowing thing, all rose and mother of pearl.

Good rye, Pernod Veritas, Italian Vermouth, 1/3 each
Two dashes Lemon Phosphate, per drink

Frappe well, and strain.

HOLLAND RAZOR BLADE

This rather rugged bit of canine fur was introduced to us by a Hollander who brought body and soul within hailing range on the occasion of certain dawn flight from Batavia, via Semarang and Soerabaja, to Bali, in the year of Grace 1931. . . . It is for those who can stomach Hollands and is one of the promptest.

Holland gin, 1½ jiggers
Lemon, juice, ½, or juice whole lime
Dust with cayenne just before drinking

This may be shaken with broken ice, or not. We would say yes.

THE ISLE de FRANCE SPECIAL, Being in First Analysis a Champagne Cocktail, as well as One of the Finest Picker-Uppers Known to Frail Flesh, Is Consequently Listed on Page 24

KILROY'S BRACER, Long an Accredited Morning-after Rejuvenator Everywhere

Cognac, 1½ jiggers
Lime or lemon juice, 2 tsp
Egg, 1
Angostura, 3 dashes
Anis or anisette, ½ tsp
Shaved ice

Shake well, turn into a goblet with some of the ice, and fill to taste with well chilled seltzer or club soda.

LEFT BANK SPINE STIFFENER

Dated Paris, 5:10 A.M. May 6th, 1926, and well remembered, too!

Cinzano, or good Italian vermouth, 2 jiggers
Absinthe, or Pernod Veritas, 1 jigger

Shake with fine ice until well chilled, turn into a whisky glass and top off with a trace of seltzer, leaving in three teaspoons of the fine ice to keep the chill edge on.

BIARRITZ "MONK-BUCK"

Something to cause nerves to join and coordinate for that morning-after—and rather chill (we've found) swim which characterizes the Mediterranean when we got there too soon, one spring.

Simply throw two and a half jiggers of cognac in a sixteen ounce collins glass already lined with a long spiral peel *à la* horse's neck. Pack half full of fine ice, fill with the best ginger ale or ginger beer the place affords, float on a couple of tablespoons yellow chartreuse, and let it settle to the bottom. . . . Don't plan on more than one, for a little while.

MORNING GLORY No. I

Dry gin, 1 jigger
Lime, juice, ½
Egg, 1
Green crème de menthe, 2 tsp, or so

Shake with cracked ice, serve in a tall cocktail glass with stem.

MORNING GLORY No. II

Good rye, or bourbon, 1 jigger
Gomme syrup, 1 tsp
Curaçao, 1 tsp
Cognac, 1 jigger
Orange bitters or Angostura, 3 dashes
Absinthe, 1 tsp

Mixing technique seems torn between stirring in a bar glass with ice, straining into a whisky glass, and adding a little seltzer topped off with a twisted lemon peel—or stirring in the same bar glass, and turning into an old fashioned glass with a lump of ice, a squirt of club soda, and a twist of peel. . . . Some sane folk merely shake with ice and a jigger of soda or seltzer. The latter works more suddenly than the more diluted drink. . . . Absinthe is difficult to recommend to suit others—increase or decrease to taste. Pernod Veritas will do.

MORNING "DOCTOR"

Take 1½ to 2½ jiggers of good brandy, a trifle over a cup of very fresh milk, and a teaspoon of sugar, and beat the whole business with an egg-beater.

OLD PEPPER

This is nothing for children to toy with, but for action and plenty of it we report that little is lacking on that score.

Good rye, 1 jigger	Good bourbon, 1 jigger
Lemon, juice 2/3	Worcestershire, ½ tsp
Tabasco, 3 drops	Chili sauce, ½ tsp

Frappe hard, and serve in any sort of fireproof glass.

PORT ANTONIO PUNCH, from JAMAICA

This is a mild and delicious tropical invention which is very easy to make, and which—unlike so many Jamaica drinks—doesn't insist on one hundred per cent rum in its spiritual makeup.

Squeeze and strain through a sieve juice of two lemons, one orange
Donate a pony of old Jamaica rum, 4 jiggers of cognac
Stir in two level tablespoons of brown sugar
Two bottles Rhine, or one quart chablis
One bottle of iced club soda
Sliced fresh fruit *du jour*

Simply ice, shake, and garnish. This is utterly delicious, but be sure and use fresh pineapple slices, not canned—and ripe pineapple at that!

PORTO FLIP

From the Army & Navy Club, Manila, P.I., 1931

Port wine, 2 jiggers	Sugar, 2 scant tsp
Egg, fresh essentially, 1 whole	Chartreuse, 1 tsp
Thick cream, 1 pony	Grated nutmeg
Cognac, 1 pony	

Send this up on the breakfast tray of the tweakiest and most jangled week-end guest on the casualty list, and watch the smiles wreathe—and be sure it goes down on an empty tummy for best and most soothing effect.

Simply mix everything with a lot of cracked ice, shake hard and serve in a small goblet, floating chartreuse on top with spoon, and adding a good dusting of grated nutmeg.

THE SO-CALLED PRAIRIE OYSTER

We once had a shipmate who insisted on a morning dip in Long Island Sound even in November; just so we have other hardy friends who eat enormous cream oyster stews for mornings after, or toss off prairie oysters, which seen eye to eye would simply mean one gyration of our adam's apple and a free ticket to a marble slab in the morgue. . . . However, for such hardy souls, we might as well set down its precise preparation.

Egg yolk, in its unbroken state, 1
Salt, good pinch
Lemon juice, 1 tsp
Worcestershire, 1 tsp
Ketchup, 1 tsp
Vinegar, ½ tsp
Tabasco, 1 drop
Cayenne, pinch on top

Shut eyes, open mouth, murmur prayers for the soul, pop in and swallow whole. . . . This *has* been administered for the evening before, but its benefits have proven to be base canard, a sorry snare and delusion.

RANGOON STAR-RUBY, a Picker-Upper from Burmah, on the Road to Mandalay

This affair is properly listed among the exotics from Far Ports, on Page 126.

SAINT MARK'S MIRACLE, Annotated One November Day in Seattle, after a Washington-Stanford Football Game, at the Advertising Club

This name is of doubtful origin, and all we know is that the receipt found its way to England across Europe, from the Venetian canals, where it has an enviable record of revivition after the unwise cup on a night before.

Champagne *fine,* which of course is liqueur brandy of great age, 2 jiggers
Angostura, ½ tsp
Yellow Curaçao, 1 pony
Lemon, juice, ½
Orange bitters, ½ pony

Shake briskly and strain into any sort of glass best calculated not to fall from our numb and listless clutch.

SWISS YODELER, which WE EMPLOYED ONCE at VILLA d'ESTE, which Is on LAKE COMO

We always wondered what made those Swiss alpenstock wielders such staunch and hardy fellows, so consider this for a warmer-up of waning flesh. The egg white is heavier than most absinthe cocktails.

Absinthe, 1 jigger
Anis, or anisette, 1 tsp
Egg, white 1

Shake well with cracked ice and pour frothing in tall cocktail glass with stem.

WHITFIELD SMITH'S *SUNDAY MORNING COCKTAIL,* No. I, & this ONE's a DARB!

This is another contribution from Fritz Abildgaard Fenger, and should be served in a 4 oz glass, same as a proper West Indian Swizzle. This makes four drinks.

Put 2 fresh egg yolks in 4 oz glass, and fill with ice water. Add one and a half more glasses water, and add a teaspoon of sugar or *gomme* to taste. To this contribute 4 teaspoons Angostura, swizzle—or shake in shaker to break yolks—and add four ponies of rye or bourbon whisky. . . . In go 2 oz—½ a cocktail glass—of cream, and a little Crème de Cacao or Benedictine, to taste. Swizzle again and grate nutmeg on top. . . . If no cream handy, use water.

NOTE: Our suggestion would be to omit sugar if any sweet liqueur is used, or it may be too sweet.

SUNDAY MORNING COCKTAIL No. II

Cognac, 1½ jiggers	Egg, 1 whole
Port wine, ½ jigger	Sugar, ½ tsp, to taste
Black coffee, 2/3 pony	

Shake and pour in tall cocktail glass with stem.

THE PEKING TIGER'S MILK No. I, from the PRIVATE FILES of M. GERBER, the *WAGON-LITS,* LEGATION STREET, PEKING

This we consider the most amazing milk drink we ever tasted. Its formula—not known to many—and its history are noted on Page 130.

TIGER'S MILK No. II

This variation was accumulated by us from the Siamese Head Bar-Boy at the Phya-Thai Palace in Bangkok, Siam, in the year 1932, after a trip up-country from the Siamese port of Pak-Nam. Turn to Page 131.

TIGER'S MILK No. III

This is a West Indian picker-upper from the Windward side of Jamaica, and dedicated to our friend, gentleman and Rhodes Scholar, Emerson Low, who lived there. Use Jamaica rum & No. II.

WORDS to the LIQUID WISE No. XIV, on the EARNEST PLEA for a BIT of OUTDOOR EXERCISE to those HUMAN VICTIMS of the "MORNING-AFTERS"

Science has just recognized that with the tummy linings well saturated with last night's ethyls or methyls, it is best remedied by increased natural circulation removing much of this condition. Therefore, after any Picker-Upper, let's not lie supine and bewail hard and unjust fate, but take a walk, play pingpong—any physical activity not inducing actual death, and no matter how slight or brief, cannot but help; and is urgently recommended!

"PINEAPPLE MILK" or *LECHE PREPARADA PIÑA*, Collected in the Lovely City of San Salvador, Capital of the Central American Republic Bearing the Same Name

This is a truly delicious beverage first brought to my attention by a lucky friend who stumbled upon it on a trip we made down the central American coast, in 1934 in the quite amazingly modern capital of San Salvador. All the ingredients are easily found.

Pineapple, sun-ripened until good and soft, juice and pulp, 1
Vanilla bean, 2 inch long piece; or 1 tsp extract
Good sound liqueur brandy, ½ cup or so; or white Bacardi
Milk, 3 cups
Sugar, brown, to taste; white will do

Pineapple is topped, pared and sliced off core. Then either chopped into small pieces or crushed in a mortar until almost a pulp—saving all the rich juices. Blend everything together, let be for two hours, and serve well chilled and garnished, if in the mood, with incidental slices of orange, pineapple, sprigs of mint, or maraschino cherries. It is a grand hot weather potation, and has been known to cause chronic invalids to take up their—and other—beds and walk.

PINK LADY No. I, from Miramar Club, out by Old Panama City, Panama

We've sat and swum from Miramar Club seven or eight times on different trips across the Isthmus. The Pink Lady there is enough different from the usual to make it well listable here.

Old Tom gin, 1 jigger
Lemon, juice ½ small; or 1 lime
Orange bitters, 3 to 4 dashes
Beaten egg white, 1 tbsp
Sloe gin, 1 jigger
Absinthe, 2/3 tsp
French vermouth, ½ jigger
Grenadine, 1 tsp, to taste

Half fill shaker with cracked ice, add egg, then the rest. Shake well and serve in goblet. This is a drink of considerable shocking power, and after consumption keep out of the sun, and in touch with friends.

CURAÇAO "PONTOON BRIDGE"

We snupped this during the spring of 1933 when circling the Caribbean for reasons not pertinent to drink-mixing. After a few hours in the perfume and other bazaars, we sat on the antique upper balcony of a little sort of Stranger's Club overlooking the odd steam-donkey-engine-driven pontoon bridge connecting Willemstadt with our part of the city, and a traffic policeman sitting in a high chair under a huge umbrella advising us of the fact that the only honest shop in the place was this or that. . . . Having sampled all colours of Curaçao liqueur until it was virtually oozing from our pores, we still stuck to our guns, and were treated to the following—which having no name, we called the Pontoon Bridge.

Fill a large glass with shaved ice, then mix two ponies cognac with one pony Curaçao, juice half a lime, and a dash of orange bitters. Pour over ice, and garnish with a stick of really ripe pineapple. Cherry is optional. We found no cherries in Curaçao.

A RAKISH FAMILY of SIXTEEN *POUSSE CAFÉS,* Including a Squad of Angels Who Never Had Wings, Being Various & Sundry Pretty Liqueurs Combined in this Fashion or that—for a Purpose

A liqueur, technically, is any alcoholic beverage sweetened and variously flavoured with aromatic substances: oils, herbs, and so on. . . . A *pousse café* is an arrangement of one or more liqueurs originally designed by Gallic progenitors as a "coffee-pusher"—hence the name —to be drunk with the after dinner cup, but like many other French ideas started out for one purpose, it has been diverted into other, and rosier, fields where dalliance may be made more pleasant and profitable through quiet absorption of these pretty rainbow-hued drinks.

Now we are great believers in the Up-and-Doing, Derring-Do, and Go West, Young Man. There's no nonsense back of our inclusion of this seductive list of jewel coloured drinks here. We include them for their original purpose of pushing coffee down, and leave criticisms to the judgment of Jurgen's discreet Tumble-bug.

Actually we do think *pousse cafés* have been slightly diverted from their original coffee-pushing intent, for if anyone can imagine following a good demitasse of strong black Mocha with half a dozen sweet cordials roosting on the yolk of an egg, we pass! . . . Some of these affairs may seem to have rather strange names but, like many other things which have gained recognition through the usage of years, we feel it only the stout thing to do to write them as they are called, and not drop the modest lash to hide our possible blushes.

WORDS to the LIQUID WISE No. XV, on the NUMBER of RINGS in a *POUSSE CAFÉ*

For reasons known only to barkeeps and their ancient patrons, a proper *pousse café* should contain seven, five, or three, contrasting rings of different coloured liqueurs. Just why these numerals are sacred we have never quite learned—any more than why seven and eleven count profitably on the first roll of dice, or why folk like Haile Selassie had three-decker parasols.

The liqueurs are poured in ever so carefully with a spoon, and sit each on top of the next, unmixed, brilliant each in its own right. The successive sips give varying taste thrills.

ONE CAUTIONING TALE about the Gentle but Unsafe Amateur Art of Breeding *POUSSE CAFÉS*

We first got this idea in Spofford's big bungalow out in Ballygunge, Calcutta, one pre-monsoon evening in 1926. A tremendous Bengali curry, then coffee on the terrace under the low, hot stars, talking over college days, friends here and there, impending marriage, birth, death, while big bats the size of kittens shuttled back and forth over the level green of the tennis court. . . . Then the idea, we would get every cordial and liqueur in the place, and brew bigger and better *pousse cafés*—and each time one went bad—mixed up hopelessly instead of remaining in distinct jewel-sharp layers, the culprit responsible had to toss it off bottoms up. When a successful one was brewed with five layers or more, the result was shared.

To be exact this whole affair is a matter of precise specific gravities as we tried it then, for instead of flowing each layer on carefully out of a teaspoon, we poured direct from bottle—so that any heavier liquid sank at once into the lighter, and mixed results were usual.

All memories of that especial evening faded into a tropical afterglow by about eleven o'clock, when Chidsey the Dodge agent tells us he came over hoping for a spot of stud poker, and found the two of us, heads bloody and almost bowed, still muttering and mixing with exaggerated care more and bigger *pousse cafés,* while a brace of Mohammedan bearers peered at us through doorways, and marvelled at the madness and triviality of certain white Sahibs who would thus procure child's size glasses into which they continued to pour the same pretty coloured liquids.

Recalling this in Havana last month, we made it a point to collect types from the best *cantinas* and fancy tourist bars, to see if there might be anything new in the routine. We found a couple of fancies, which appear below, each in its proper place, and now turn the whole business over to readers, depending on their judgment and decorum to the last.

FIRST A BRIEF COMPANY of SIX ANGELS

Aunt Belladonna Fittich may blink a bit at this short list, but when things have been going on as long as this "angel" business it belongs to history, whether or no. We have our own personal idea, not convenient to mention, of just why angels were born; but be that as it may, full many a lusty swain has screwed up his courage to the sticking point and proposed honourable marriage to the maid of his choice while either—or both—were being swayed by the gentle caress of an "angel." . . . They are too sweet for serious consumption, and all end up with a nominal amount of thick cream—whipped, or from the bottle. Ladies and gentlemen we give you: The Angels.

ANGEL'S BLUSH

Pour in ¼ each of the following: Maraschino, *Crème Yvette,* Benedictine, thick cream.

ANGEL'S CHERRY, a NOMINAL RISK WE MET SUCCESSFULLY in MENTONE, near the ITALIAN BORDER, on a SPRING DAY in 1932

This addition, whose title meaning is debatable, is a newcomer to the fold. Those of us who take the trouble can find Damiana in any decent wine merchant's shop, and a perusal of the label illustration alone should be worth the price of admission. . . . *Pour la Patrie!* . . . Needless to say Damiana is alleged to possess certain properties which wise men have sought for many centuries, with greater or less result—mostly less. . . . Benedictine, Damiana, and cognac, 1/3 each. Top off with a tablespoon of thick cream, center with the largest and reddest cherry the neighbourhood affords, and be about our business.

ANGEL'S DREAM

Omit the Benedictine, and use 1/3 each Damiana, *Crème Yvette,* cognac and heavy cream.

ANGEL'S KISS

This heavenly, and hypothetical osculation has scant value as an historical beverage here or abroad, but as long as we are going in for items of more or less serious nonsense, it shall not pass.

Float in, and on, 1/5 each of the following: Damiana, *Parfaite Amour,* yellow chartreuse, Benedictine, cognac, and beaten egg white. On this is superimposed a layer of thick cream, and on it ginger, clove, or nutmeg—a slight pinch—depending on the perquisites of the occasion.

ANGEL'S TIT, No. I, BEING the ORIGINAL FORMULA

First encountered on one of those Canadian week-ends at Niagara on the Lake when many nice people seemed to forsake these United States seeking oasis for reasons of their own, during prohibition.

Maraschino, ¾ Whipped cream, ¼

Garnish with scarlet cherry in location diametrically exact.

ANGEL'S TIT, No. II

A Parisian indication of chancey origin, but of definite value.

Damiana, or *Parfaite Amour,* ¾
Cognac, ¼
Whipped cream about ¼″ on top

A similar cherry, accurately teed up in traditional style.

TEN MORE which ARE NOT CALLED ANGELS

PARIS' *ARC-en-CIEL*—the WORLD-FAMOUS RAINBOW

This is probably the most famous *pousse café* ever conceived, and is not only beautiful but logical—as it takes the whole seven colours of the spectrum and places them before you in all their jewel colours to be sipped pensively out of a glass, one layer at a time, and experiencing the gamut of seven delicious tastes. Simply spoon in one-seventh each of the following: *Crème de violette, crème de cassis,* maraschino, green *crème de menthe,* yellow chartreuse, Curaçao, cherry or other red coloured brandy.

EVE'S GARDEN, from a *FOLIES BERGÈRE* ENTR'ACTE, in a not-too-DISTANT SPRING, in PARIS

One third each Damiana, *Crème Yvette,* and dry apricot brandy—all finished off with a spoonful of thick cream and a *green* cherry in center. . . . Cognac is also indicated for the apricot, and to our thought is much better, as the drink is sweet enough anyway. . . . This sort of thing only goes to show what grown men will do to keep from devoting their time to something constructive in life.

FRENCH TRI-COLOUR

One third each of: Grenadine, maraschino, *Crème Yvette.*

THE JERSEY LILY, which INCIDENTALLY, CAME from FRANCE

Into the usual cordial or *pousse café* glass pour in half a jigger green chartreuse, then with a spoon float half jigger cognac, finally ten drops of angostura or other, preferred, bitters. First the bitter, then the strong, then the pungently sweet—that is the order of drinking tastes. Something like the *Dominica Topet,* already noted in proper order.

L'AMOUR TOUJOURS, BEING NOT PRECISELY a *POUSSE CAFÉ,* but rather a *POUSSE l'AMOUR*

Build layers as follows, and very carefully: 1/3 maraschino, egg yolk, 1/3 Benedictine, 1/3 cognac. Build this one in the conventional sherry glass. *Et bon chance, mes garçons!*

LIQUID SYMPHONY

Into a wine glass of shaved ice add the following in order mentioned: *Crème de rose,* yellow chartreuse, *crème de menthe,* and finally some well-aged brandy. Garnish with two red cherries on top.

LOUIS MARTIN'S FAMOUS POUSSE CAFÉ No. I

Take a large cordial glass, with stem, and mix in order given the following amounts and types:

Yellow curaçao, about ¼ full
Kirsch, same thickness layer
Green chartreuse, a little thinner than the others
Yellow curaçao, enough to fill glass

In the old days Louis Martin's was New York's premier night spot. As we recall it Vernon and Irene Castle started there, as well as being the rendezvous for important folk of all sorts.

LUNE de MIEL, which of COURSE MEANS "HONEYMOON," HAS already BEEN NOTED on PAGE 49

POLSKI POUSSE CAFÉ, STRAIGHT from the POLISH CORRIDOR, and the SUPPOSEDLY FREE CITY of DANZIG at ITS END

Into a sherry glass put a quarter of chartreuse, the yolk of a smallish egg, and fill to the brim with *Dantziger Goldwasser,* that amazing liqueur in which tiny bits of pure gold leaf arise and sail gracefully about each time the bottle is agitated. . . . This drink is to be held up, studied, and taken in one or three gulps—the latter preferred, so the curaçao can seal with its sweet and citric kiss all hint of egg.

HAVANA RAINBOW *PLUS*

Another of Sloppy Joe's specialties, and although the colour sequence isn't too scientific, the reaction upon guests is guaranteed true to form.

One-seventh each of: Grenadine, anisette, *Parfaite Amour,* green *crème de menthe,* yellow curaçao, yellow chartreuse, Jamaica rum. . . . Serve with rum flaming, and make peace with thy neighbour!

LA ZARAGOZANA'S *NE PLUS ULTRA,* Noted in Havana, February 24th, 1937

This restaurant, frequented mostly by wiser Cubans is one of Havana's leading places for seafood, and especially Morro Crab, see Pages 67 and 68, *Volume I.* It hasn't the atmosphere of some of the older spots, but *amigos,* what red snapper, what *langostas,* what *saumon*—the Habañero name for the rare, delicious, mackerel-like ocean runner, "salmon."

Apricot brandy, benedictine, chartreuse, cointreau, cognac, and *crème de cacao*—1/6 each. . . . Then a dash of *anis del mono,* or any good anisette. Frappe quickly and serve promptly. . . . A really delicious blend. *Anis del Mono,* or "anis of the monkey's head" is a specially good and dry Spanish anis, their favourite morning eye-opener.

THE POMPIER HIGHBALL, a French Concession Sometimes Called Vermouth *CASSIS*—the Latter Being the Juice of Currants

Sitting under awning at any Parisian sidewalk cafe we can see all sorts and conditions of men seated at small round metal tables, and drinking various things for all sorts of reasons. The average Frenchman is a funny chap who confines his plain and fancy drinking to 3 grooves, 2 of which are the eternal wine with meals, and to stimulate hunger. . . . This Pompier Highball falls into the latter class, and besides all this it is very cooling and refreshing, has a sharp tangy taste due to the herbs and simples in the vermouth. Take ½ jigger French dry vermouth and the same of *crème de cassis*. Put in a couple of lumps of ice and fill the glass with club soda or seltzer. Serve in a tall thin glass and only fill ¾ full, please.

THE HABANA *PRESIDENTE,* now Known to Many, but Sound Enough in Its Own Right for Listing in any Spiritual Volume

This has long been one of Cuba's favourite drinks and every visiting Americano should go to La Florida and get one from headquarters. The mix is simple and satisfying. . . . Just put 1 pony each of Bacardi Gold Seal, and dry French vermouth, into a bar glass with cracked ice. Donate 1 tsp grenadine and the same of curaçao. Stir and serve in a Manhattan glass with a scarlet cherry for garnish. Finally twist a curl of yellow orange peel over the top so that the oil strikes the surface of the drink, then drop the peel in. . . . Sloppy Joe's own Special is merely the *Presidente* with the juice of a small lime added, and the twist of lime peel handled as above.

RITUAL of the PUNCH BOWL

This inheritance from the Orient and Europe—and especially from old England—is probably interwoven with more tradition than any other form of drinking. From those grand days when landlords really did fill the flowing bowl, before and after riding to hounds, on feast and saints' days, or holy days; at weddings, births, yes and even death —the cheering and soothing bowl was all part of the affair.

Oddly the word itself is another Oriental derivation like "toddy," and comes from the Hindustani *panch,* meaning five, and indicating the number of ingredients employed by the wily Hindu: Toddy or arrack, lemon or lime, tea, sugar and water.

Anglicized, it is literally any drink made of rum, whisky, brandy, wine or other liquor, in combination with water, fruit juice, and sugar —or of fruit juices and the rest without any spirits at all—and properly served, either very hot or well iced, from a larger or smaller bowl, into cups or glasses.

For centuries this sort of thing has been concocted in the Far East of varying materials to suit head, stomach, temperature, and heart. In England it soon trickled its way into fine society, possibly in the effort of the British East India Company to attract notice of the world to tea and other Oriental importations of the Empire.

Besides all of this tradition which came to us few things in life are more kind to man's eye than the sight of a gracefully conceived punch bowl on a table proudly surrounded by gleaming cohorts of cups made of crystal or white metals, enmeshing every beam of light, and tossing it back into a thousand shattered spectra to remind us of the willing cheer within. . . . The colours too are delightful—the purple of the grape against silver or crystal, the scarlet and gold and green of fruits, the tawny ambers of other wines, the fragrant scent of sugar cane, sun-ripe grapes, apricots, grain, peaches, what not—all are a challenge to eye, nose and lip; all blended into a perfect and harmonious whole.

The very amplitude of the bowl itself suggests hospitality, and an invitation to quench thirst, which no service of single small glasses can ever effect.

In place of the eternal afternoon tea, a really unusual punch not only delights guests, but saves the hostess the usual maze of questions about who takes lemon, or cream, or sugar. There is no conceivable occasion which cannot be served with a good punch—whether we prefer it with or without the spirits.

It takes a little imagination and ingenuity to make a visibly attractive punch, but we have tried to confine ourselves to punches which not only taste well, but look well also.

RULES for a DECENT PUNCH ARE FEW—but INFLEXIBLE

1. Use fresh fruits, for although canned fruits will do, as a general rule they lack the pungency, the aroma, of fresh.
2. If sparkling water, wine, ginger beer, or ginger ale is to be added—wait until the very moment of service. The whole object of a sparkling punch is to have it sparkle—and as bubbles soon escape into the atmosphere after pouring in bowl, save that pouring until the last second.
3. Don't use small ice, except in emergencies requiring quick cooling—or

in Planter's Punches and West Indian Swizzles, treated on Page 109. . . . Fine ice melts rapidly, dilutes the punch. Dilution beyond a certain point courts sure disaster through loss of flavour, weakness and anaemia of otherwise prime ingredients. . . . Use a single fairly large block of ice.

4. Chill all ingredients at least an hour or two before putting in the bowl, if a punch is to be served cold. Pouring room-temperature liquids on any sort of ice is a withering shock to the ice itself, requires a great deal of refrigeration in a very short period of time, and can only succeed in too-rapid ice melting. . . . A big block of ice in pre-chilled punch will last a long time and melt slowly.

WORDS to the LIQUID WISE No. XVI, BEING THREE ORIGINAL TOUCHES in GARNISHING or FLAVOURING the PUNCH BOWL

Those of us who have a large freezing drawer under the ice cube section of a mechanical refrigerator can add a colourful and dainty touch by adding a little harmonious colouring matter to the water before freezing into cubes. . . . We can also add fruits like cherries, strawberries, and the like, to the water, thus freezing them visibly in the ice. . . . Instead of ice we can use water ice or sherbet flavouring with the basic taste of the punch like pineapple, grape, orange, and so on. This should be put in a little bit in each cup when serving, and makes things very cold. . . . Grate a little fresh coconut kernel, have it in a gravy boat, and dust a teaspoon on each cup when served. This adds a delicate, nut-like flavour which brings out the other tastes, only don't use the ordinary shredded coconut. It simply won't do as well.

A HAND-PICKED LIST of TWENTY & SIX PUNCHES from MANY GAY LANDS, & INCLUDING SOME ELEVEN WEST INDIAN PLANTER'S PUNCHES & SWIZZLES BASED on FIVE CRUISES through that FASCINATING CHAIN, & NOTES from YACHTSMEN FRIENDS on CRUISING to the OUT ISLANDS

FOR THOSE WHO ADMIRE HOT PUNCHES, a BRIEF SELECTED LIST MAY further BE FOUND under *HOT HELPERS,* STARTING on PAGE 50, onward

FOR THOSE WHO WISH to MIX NON-ALCOHOLIC PUNCHES

We have carefully selected several very original, fragrant, and flavourful punches as a relief from the eternal orange-lemon-fruit scramble which has hog-ridden us for generations. These are listed in a separate group under *TEMPERANCE DELIGHTS,* on Page 139.

BENGAL LANCERS' PUNCH

Captain Ferguson, late of His Majesty's Cavalry in upper India, gave us this one back in 1926, and it was a specialty of his Colonel on quite special occasions.

Champagne, 1 qt
Orange juice, ½ cup
Fresh pineapple juice, ½ cup
Jamaica or Barbados rum, 3 ponies
Claret, 2 pint bottles
Lime juice, ½ cup
Cointreau or curaçao, 3 ponies
Charged water, 1 pint
A little sugar, to taste; and keep it dry and not too sweet

Ice as above, and garnish with very thin slices of green lime. This is a particularly delicate punch, and Barbados rum is less likely to overpower the delicate wine flavours than Jamaica.

PUNCH *à la DUC de BOURGOGNE*

Red burgundy, 2 qts
Red port, 1 pint
Lemon, juice, 2
Cherry brandy, 1 cup
Fine sugar, ¼ lb, or so
Orange, juice, 2
Charged water, about 1 qt, or a trifle more

Ice as above and garnish with pitted red cherries.

FISH HOUSE PUNCH, DATING from 1732, the STATE in SCHUYLKILL CLASSIC

This is America's most famous punch receipt; at least it is known by reputation to more people than any other. The mix has come from 1732 right to this date—practically 200 years, unchanged and unimproved for the simple reason that it could not be improved upon!

Jamaica Rum, 2 qts; or for ladies: equal portions of Jamaica and Bacardi, 2 qts
Cognac brandy, 1 qt
Loaf sugar, ¾ lb
Water, 2 qts; spring water is indicated
Lemon juice, 1 qt; lime would be even more delicate
Peach brandy, 1 wine glass

Put sugar in bowl, put on enough water to dissolve completely, then contribute the various spirits and liquids—stirring diligently. Center as big a lump of ice as may be in the bowl, permitting the brew to stand unmolested for a couple of hours. . . . Our alternate suggestions are in no way intended as heresy, but simply indicate what substitutions, if any, are possible. Many entirely worthy folk both on the Schuylkill River and the Mississippi, don't happen to care for Jamaica rum. All our male parentage having come from Philadelphia or Germantown or the Chester Valley out the "Main Line," and at least two of our kin were remembered members of the famous State in Schuylkill, oldest club in America, where Fish House Punch was born; therefore we know a bit of how Philadelphia tradition, good or poor, carries on serenely in the midst of an otherwise crude and bustling world. . . . Also bear in mind that while many Jamaica rums come in full quarts, both Bacardi and Cognac invariably seem to come encased in fifths, so calibrate accordingly. . . . Warning: there are a horde of so-called "Fish House Punch" receipts that include benedictine, curaçao, bourbon, and God knows what else. Eschew them. There is but one receipt, unwavering, invariable. This is it.

KIRSCHWASSER PUNCH, *à la ARLÉSIENNE*

Kirsch, as we keep emphasizing so often, has the peculiar faculty of enhancing other delicate flavours—both in drink and food. Its ratio here with maraschino is suggested as being the best balance, although sometimes the amount of the latter is cut down slightly, and the kirsch stepped up to the point where there is a ratio of three to one of maraschino, and in some cases the maraschino is left out entirely.

Kirschwasser, 1½ cups
Rhine or sauterne, 2 pint bottles
Fresh pineapple juice, 4 cups
Sparkling water, 1 pint
Maraschino, ½ cup
If Rhine is used, add 1 extra tbsp sugar
Sugar, fine, ½ lb

Ice ingredients first, then mix in bowl with large lump of ice, and garnish with bits of really ripe pineapple, and grapefruit pulp. . . . A sprig of mint in each cup is a nice touch.

LATIN AMERICA PUNCH, from a MOUNTAIN PLANTATION HOUSE out of SAN JUAN, PORTO RICO

Carta de Oro Bacardi rum, 1½ cups
Rhine wine, 2 pint bottles
Lemon juice, 1 cup
Thin small slices fresh pineapple
Orange curaçao, ½ cup
Champagne, 1 qt
Orange juice, 1 cup
Sparkling water, 1 pint

Ice for two hours beforehand, pour in bowl with large lump ice, have a gravy boat filled with fresh grated coconut kernel, and sprinkle a level teaspoon on each glass as served. *Don't* use shredded coconut—that is only for cakes and so on.

FRITZ FENGER'S PINEAPPLE "BOLA," which Is a PUNCH of PARTS

Fenger's dossier has already been given at some length, and we will merely state here that both the wording of this receipt and spelling of the word "Bola" are his—this last presumably an anglicized version of the old German word *Bowle,* or *Wein-Bowle.* The change from "It" to "Her" is also interesting.

"For evening use: Right after breakfast stalk a ripe but unblemished pineapple, and when agreeable, snatch it off its perch and take it home where—in the intimacy of the butler's pantry—we remove first her head, toes, hard heart, and finally her spiny corset.

"Dice her up very fine indeed and heap pieces and juices in a large punch bowl and cover with powdered sugar. Pour on a bottle of good bourbon or rye—not Scotch—and leave her lay *all day,* covered and safely beyond reach or range of the great dane. Meanwhile you can go back to your legitimate work, if any.

"After dinner sculp a piece of ice, at least 8" on a side, place it in the center of the bowl and over this pour slowly, bottle by bottle, scads, shoals and lashings of chilled dry champagne to the number of 3 or 4 at least—when a bit hard up use ½ champagne and ½ charged water, or 2/3 Rhine or Moselle and 1/3 charged water—only don't tell any Nazi I recommended this last!

"Now with a judicious ladle stir gently, just a trifle, to mix with the whisky-sugar-pineapple foundation. Dip in and drink. But when serving best put her smack in the middle of the table with chairs noosed all around; break out tobacco, musical instruments and yarns; for although this Bola does not make one intoxicated as we know the word [Note: We resent this! *Author.*] it does take your legs away, very thriftily."

Author's Note: Having tried this business out once our only suggestion would be to ignore all thought of ice and replace it as a cooling agent by 2 or 3 quarts of fresh pineapple sherbet or water ice. The unusual thing about this punch is that it requires no rum of any sort, for strength or flavouring.

PINEAPPLE MILK, or *LECHE PREPARADA PIÑA,* from SAN SALVADOR, C.A.

This mild, and almost startlingly delicious pineapple-milk-brandy-and-other-things punch is inscribed on Page 91.

TIGER'S MILK, Nos. I, II, & III

These successive formulae from Peking, Bangkok, and finally the windward coast of Jamaica, and which we consider the most amazing milk drinks extant, are listed on Pages 129, 130, 131, & 90.

NAPOLEON II PUNCH, sometimes CALLED PUNCH *à la l'AIGLON*

Time this so it will be made when wild cherries are ripe, barring that use sour red "pie" cherries.

Claret, or Burgundy, 2 pint bottles
Any sour cherry juice, 1 cup
Fine sugar, to taste; keep fairly acid
Vanilla extract, 2 tsp or so
St. Croix, Martinique, or Haitian rum, 1 cup
Pitted cherries, ½ cup
Charged water, 1 pint
Garnish with violets

Ice as above, and add a few bits of chopped violet petals to each cup as served.

THE *PFIRSCHBOWLE,* or PEACH PUNCH, for OUR REUNION in VIENNA, or ANYWHERE

This requires ripe peaches, *not* green ones a little coloured by standing in a shop. Scald, take off skins, slice, and dredge with plenty of confectioner's sugar, and let them marinate in their own sweet juices for two hours. First pour in a bottle of Rhine or Moselle wine, then a bottle of good Burgundy or claret. Put in the ice box, and just before serving uncork a bottle of iced champagne. Put an 8" cube of ice in the bowl, and pour over. . . . To our way of thinking a couple of ounces of drier type apricot or peach brandy couldn't hurt this thought a mite.

CHARLESTON'S ST. CECELIA SOCIETY PUNCH

Speaking of social niceties, for a good many generations no one in Tidewater South Carolina really mattered unless his name appeared on the annual ball list of St. Cecelia. Consequently it gradually became a fixed matter of family and the bluest of blood lines. Bank balances did not count as they did in New York's 400. Although the membership list has been expanded now and then along more sanely liberal lines, here is a Society started two hundred years ago, forty years before our Declaration of Independence was conceived, and whose prestige and power was so great that when the welkin rang in ancient Hibernian Hall, not one single newspaper ever mentioned a bit of what took place. . . . Gentlemen were gentlemen in those days, and the over-famed "freedom of the press" didn't pry into their social affairs, as they do nowadays with certain visible folk like, say, Ex-King Edward VIII. Furthermore the music plays behind a lace curtain, and ladies don't go to *la salle des dames* unchaperoned!

Peach or apricot brandy, 1 fifth; peach is traditional
Jamaica rum, 1 pint; and get good old rum
Dry champagne, 4 quarts
Cognac brandy, 1 bottle
Sugar, 3 cups
Fresh pineapple, 1 ripe one, sliced fine and cored
Lemons or limes, 6 lemons or 10 limes, sliced thin
Green tea, 1 quart
Club soda, or other good sparkling water, 2 quarts total

Slice lemon and pineapple and marinate, tightly covered, overnight with brandy. At noon of the evening when we plan to serve it add rum, tea, sugar and peach brandy. Blend well. Just before serving put in champagne first, then club soda. Chill cups for best results, and remember that good club soda, although costing a few cents more than the average local "charged water" or seltzer siphon, actually adds not a hint of antique brass to ruin the other worthy company of liquids! . . . Either Schweppes or Perrier are in order.

SIR FLEETWOOD'S *SHEPHERD'S SACK POSSET,* from the RECORDS of DR. WILLIAM KITCHINER, LONDON, 1817.

Centuries back it was quite the fashion to toss a bit of verse, blank, or blankety-blank, whether it were regarding a new or old sweetheart, a new horse, or a new drink. . . . Now this is a very old drink indeed, and Sir Fleetwood was a stout one with the wassail bowl. Of all the *Sacks* beloved by England, this was his favoured one. We quote it literally from the immortal Kitchiner.

"From fam'd Barbadoes on the western Main
Fetch Sugar, ounces four—fetch Sack from Spain,
A pint,—and from the Eastern Indian Coast
Nutmeg, the glory of our northern Toast;
O'er flaming Coals let them together heat
Till the all-conquering Sack dissolve the sweet;
O'er such another Fire put Eggs, just ten,
New-Born from Tread of Cock and Rump of Hen:
Stir them with steady hand and conscience Pricking
To see the untimely end of ten fine Chicken;
From shining shelf take down the brazen skillet,—
A quart of milk from gentle cow will fill it.
When boiled and cold, put milk and Sack to Egg;
Unite them firmly like the Triple League,
And on the fire let them together dwell
Till Miss sing twice—'You must not kiss and Tell,—'
Each Lad and Lass take up a silver spoon,
And fall on fiercely like a Starved Dragoon."

Don't judge the drink by the poetry, and just travel along cozily with this kitchen model Ogden Nash of a bygone century. . . . Sack, by the way, is any one of several light fairly strong wines imported into England from Spain and the Canary Islands. If you will substitute sherry, and perhaps a dash of good brandy there will be no complaints from the twice-singing Maid!

THE ANCIENT WASSAIL BOWL from an Ancient Elizabethan Formula, Circa 1602, & Truly Notable for Its Exceeding Mildness

In Saxon times this custom of the Wassail Bowl at feast days was an important ceremony, and later it became an accepted custom at Christmas Eve, when minstrels or choirs, or village singers went about singing carols where there was a candle lit in the window.

In the Feudal castles, and manor houses, the Wassail Bowl was borne into the banqueting Hall with songs and carols, and crowned with garlands.

Nutmeg, ½ grated; or 2 tsp powdered
Powdered or grated ginger, 1 tsp
Cloves, 6 whole
Cinnamon, 1 inch of stick
Sugar, 1 cup
Eggs, yolks 6; whites 3
Apples, 6 cored, but not pared
Mace, ¼ tsp
Water
Sherry or Madeira, 2 qts

Take spices and cover with a cup of cold water. Fetch to a boil; adding wine and sugar. Let heat up. . . . Meanwhile in the Wassail Bowl (Punchbowl) previously warmed:

Break in six yolks and three whites. Beat up. When wine is warm—not boiling—mix a teacupful with the egg. When a little warmer, add another cupful, and repeat until five cups have been used. . . . Now let the rest of the wine boil up well, and pour it into the bowl also, stirring well all the time, until it froths in attractive fashion. . . . Fill cored apples with sugar, sprinkle on a little of the spice and roast until nearly done. Time these to suit the end of the wine-pouring process. Throw them into the bowl, and serve the whole thing very hot. . . . Some stout hearts add a tumbler full of good cognac brandy to the whole—and we, after testing the business, heartily agree with them; since sherry of itself isn't potent enough to make any Saxon defend his native land, much less a 20th Century wassailer, with all we have been through during the one and a half decades that Saxons never even considered as drinkable fluid!

TEN WEST INDIAN PLANTER'S PUNCHES, Swizzles, and like Ceremonies of a Pleasant Nature

Any set rules for these tropical institutions would last about as long as a set rule for a mint julep to please Louisville and Baltimore. There are as many Planter's Punches as there are—or were—planters; as many Swizzles as swizzlers.

After stays in Nassau, Cuba, Jamaica, Haiti, Curaçao, Venezuela, and both ends of the Canal Zone, we have found most of this drink family extremely good, especially those made of special aged Jamaica rum we've imbibed in the Myrtlebank Gardens, Kingston. Those listed here have, for one reason or another, stood out in our memories. . . . If there is any one thing which is hard and fast everywhere it is this: Get decent well-aged rum, and brandy or cognac, for all punches and West Indian drinks. Just because they are a bit disguised with tropical fruit juice is no sign that thirty seconds swizzling, shaking, or stirring will make up for eight years the raw spirit should have lain in wood casks.

The charm of all these exotics is their mellowness, their smoothness, and the gentleness with which they come, see and conquer.

One other thing: Don't try to use canned fruit juices of any kind and expect notability. In other words, fresh fruit lacking, call it a rum-canned-grapefruit-juice-ade, not a Planter's Punch.

Extreme chilliness is the brand of excellence, over and above these thoughts, and for this reason the soundest mixers *chill glasses, or in-*

gredients, or both—and in swizzles this includes the pitcher too; if we really want to show off, a good ⅛" of white frost on the outside!

ADMIRAL SCHLEY PUNCH

This is supposed to have been named after the American admiral, and we shouldn't mind such a pleasant piece of business being called after us.

St. Croix or Barbados rum, ½ jigger
Bourbon, ½ jigger
Sugar, 1 tsp
Lime, peel and juice, 1

Shake with fine ice, and turn into goblet—ice and all. Garnish with sprigs of mint, a stick of ripe pineapple, and so on.

THE STANDARD ONE, TWO, THREE, FOUR, WEST INDIAN PLANTER'S PUNCH, No. I

This is the original receipt from the very first discovery of the drink.

1 of Sour (lime juice); 2 of Sweet (sugar or *gomme* syrup); 3 of Strong (Jamaica rum); 4 of Weak (water and ice combined)—and use shaved or quite fine cracked ice, please. . . . Doctor this with the usual dash of Angostura, shake hard and serve—with ice left in the glass.

America, when not having time to dally with its drink as a correct West Indian planter is supposed to do, sometimes transposes the quantities of "strong" and "weak"—making the rum four parts and the water three, instead of as given above.

Barbados, Demerara, Martinique, Haitian, or Cuban Rum, can always replace Jamaica; and if using Bacardi mix *Carta de Oro,* for fuller flavour, not *Carta Blanca*. Again we advise aged *Añejo* Bacardi, or liqueur Cuban Methusalem Rum. Also this classic, somewhat corn-y verse actually tends for a too-sweet "Planter's." Cut down sugar by half; then adjust one way or another, to suit taste.

SANTIAGO de CUBA, *CARTA de ORO* BACARDI PLANTER'S PUNCH

Bacardi Carta de Oro, 1½ jiggers
Sugar or grenadine, 1 tsp
Lime, strained juice, 1½
Mint and fresh fruit

Fill a large goblet with shaved ice well packed down, mix the liquids and pour over ice, then garnish with sliced orange, cherries, and a stick of fresh ripe pineapple, and plenty of fresh mint.

SAVANNAH PLANTER'S PUNCH

Cotton, lumber and naval stores, rosin, turpentine spirits, that was —and still is, Savannah. The whole world sailed to Savannah's door up Tybee River, and many a West Indian Colonial found it—with Charleston—a first mainland step before reaching England. . . . This Planter's Punch varies quite a bit from those punches and swizzles we've inspected and brewed along the great circle of islands from Haiti to Trinidad and Curaçao. But it's a sound one; and as all sound potables should be—it's simple. Also it's tall. For one:

First chill the glasses—whether silver or crystal
Good Jamaica rum, wine glass; or 2 ponies, to taste
Cognac brandy, 2 jiggers
Lime, juice, 1; or juice ½ lemon
Fresh pineapple juice, ½ jigger

Pack the glasses tightly with *finely* shaved ice, pour in the liquids previously mixed, stir briskly for a moment with long spoon or swizzle stick. Garnish with a finger of ripe pineapple, a cherry, or a bit of orange. Serve when glass frosts. There's no dodging the fact that we must expect to use decent rum. This recently born swarm of new, strange rums can no more replace even a fair Jamaica, Barbados or Haitian rum, than Mr. Kreisler can play the *E Flat Nocturne* on a turnip crate. . . . The cognac lends the original touch here.

FIVE WEST INDIAN SWIZZLES of a COMFORTING DISPOSITION, & EMBRACING ONE of JAMAICA RUM, and FOUR of AUTHENTIC ORIGIN and other BASES, from the ROUGH LOG of FREDERICK ABILDGAARD FENGER

A JAMAICA RUM SWIZZLE from a PLANTATION OVERLOOKING the NORTHERN, or WINDWARD, PORT ANTONIO SECTION

Jamaica rum, 1 full pint; or 2 measuring cups full
Lime, juice 8 small; 6 large; or 6 average lemons
Gomme syrup or sugar, 4 tsp
Fresh mint, 1 doz sprigs

Mix liquids and sugar in pitcher with ice, frost with swizzle stick, pour out into commodious glasses, and garnish with sprig mint, and stick of fresh ripe pineapple, if some is handy.

WORDS to the LIQUID WISE No. XVII, NOTING that PRACTICALLY any PLANTER'S PUNCH, if MULTIPLIED SLIGHTLY into QUANTITY & SWIZZLED in a BOWL or PITCHER, BECOMES a "SWIZZLE"

Don't be misled by the contradictory terms. A swizzle foundation could be any of the Planter's Punches given here—the usual technique for which parallels that of the Mint Julep, insofar as cooling goes.

THE FOUR so-CALLED "MALLINGHOLM SWIZZLES"—ALL of AUTHENTIC PROPORTION and CORRECT GEOGRAPHICAL ORIGIN, & furthermore MADE NOTABLE through the LOG of FREDERICK ABILDGAARD FENGER, OWNER & MASTER of the SCHOONER *DIABLESSE*

We seem to refer to Fritz Fenger quite a bit in this volume and if we do it is because he has covered the West Indies as thoroughly and intimately as anyone we know, and besides this is a gourmet and a compounder of spirituous liquids both potent and astonishing to the average landsman. Further than this he is a Danish-American yacht architect dwelling—to the public shock of the Board of Selectmen of whom he is a member—in the remote and pure town of Cohasset, in Massachusetts.

Back in the great sweep of Leeward and Windward Islands he is still known as "de mon on de boat," dating clean back twenty years or so when he sailed a canoe the size of an ample delicatessen dill pickle—as we have already mentioned—from Trinidad slap to the

Virgins. Now for the benefit of those who haven't sailed those waters we would like to remark that although this necklace of islands looks on the map to be within cruller toss of each other, they are actually separated by wide and rough cross-chop passages where the Caribbean and the Atlantic have a peas-porridge-hot game every six hours, pouring tides back and forth. The natives, who sail things out of sight of land we wouldn't use to cross an irrigation ditch, took one look at that canoe with its 4″ or so of freeboard and no rudder, and promptly began recollecting ancient prayers to sea gods. News of his progress went ahead of him via some sort of weird mackerel telegraph. And no matter where he would beach the *YAKABOO,* or at what hour, reverent dark men and women waited upon him, fearful of some sorcery, yet eager as children to touch him or any of his things. They fetched him food and drink, cured sea urchin festers, and stood and watched his tiny butterfly winged sails fade and vanish into a cockatoo-crest yellow dawn. At St. Thomas, capital of the Virgins, due to press of time, *YAKABOO* was hoisted aboard steamer and went thus to Boston.

Several years later *DIABLESSE,* a good husky down-east fisherman schooner retraced the course of the little *YAKABOO,* with greater leisure, plenty of seaworthiness, and with wife and young son as Mate and Bo'sun.

The first 4 swizzles garnered from Fenger are out of the files of a Dane he met in St. Thomas named Mallingholm, and who has since gone "where the angels (as Fenger says) live innocuously, so I've been instructed—dang it!"

He further informs us, with scant foundation of veracity—that these are mild and caponed affairs which "may be taken—in moderate abandon—without irremediable fraying out at either end."

These 4 excellent swizzles have been given in accurate scale drawings, so that the mixer may measure by eye by "placing a clean thumb nail at each level before pouring."

By adding 1 tumbler of ice water and ice enough, and 1/3 to ½ tsp of sugar, we get swizzles for 4 guests.

CALIBRATION CHART for FREDERICK ABILDGAARD FENGER'S *MALLINGHOLM* SWIZZLES, ABILDGAARD—CREDIT IT or not—BEING HIS GENUINE MIDDLE NAME & the ONE under which HE WROTE as *CAPTAIN ABILDGAARD* for SOME YEARS in *YACHTING* MAGAZINE

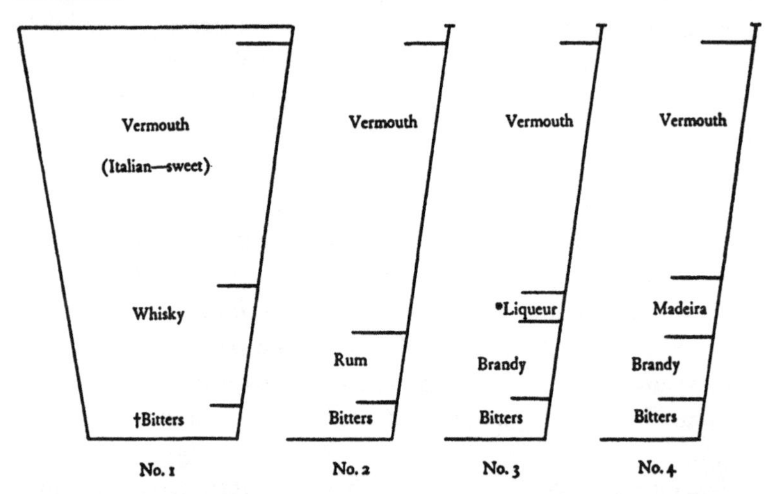

ADDENDA:

† Orange bitters lends a smooth change from Angostura in every case, when so desired.

* Indicates benedictine or *Crème de Cacao.*

The bar glass shown is the conventional 5 to 6 oz size called a Star or Sour glass.

The amount of vermouth may be lessened in No. 2, and rum increased. In general, after a bit of practice, both vermouth and bitters should be regulated, to individual taste.

AFTER ICING WE SHAKE in a SHAKER or SWIZZLE with a SWIZZLE STICK, but DO NOT STRAIN. . . . THERE SHOULD BE a BEAD on EACH GLASS

THE WEST INDIAN SWIZZLE STICK, what IT IS

There is a wide cloud of misinformation on this subject. The authentic swizzle sticks are the peeled stem of a plant owning, at base, a fan-like branching of roots—the latter cut some 3" long—and looking like small gnarled fingers. This branched end is sunk into the pitcher with ice and drink ingredients, the stem is held vertically between palms, and rotated smartly by sliding the palms back and forth. They are procurable in all British West Indian possessions, for obvious reasons, and are a romantic touch; actually however a swizzle made out of this routine is no better than one chilled with a modern chromium plated metal swizzle stick. Like airplane propellers made of wood, and metal, the main question is do they stir up the air?

THE WORLD FAMOUS QUARANTINE COCKTAIL, No. I

Favourite in Manila, where It even Outstrips the Perennial Dry Martini

This drink is quite rich, and one is enough before a dinner. The *anis del mono*—or "*anis* of the monkey head"—is the highly alcoholic type Spaniards use as a pre-breakfast eye opener all over the globe. If French anisette liqueur is used we had better increase the quantity to ½ tsp or so. . . . Take 1 jigger of Bacardi, 1 tsp each of gin and dry French vermouth, ½ jigger of orange juice, 2 tsp lemon juice, sugar to taste, and 1 tbsp of egg white. Add 1 or 2 drops of *anis,* shake with lots of cracked ice and turn into a Manhattan glass. Monk Antrim's receipt sent especially for this volume calls for 1 tbsp of combined gin and vermouth, and orange and lemon juice in equal amounts, about 1 tsp each. Egg white is more than the standard blend, being ½ a whole white.

THE QUEEN CHARLOTTE COCKTAIL; Named, so Tell They the Tale, for Queen Charlotte Amalia—or Amalie—now also the Name for St. Georges in the American Virgin Islands

This is a lovely warm weather affair of a mildness which even a Quaker miss could not shy at! It was donated by the charming wife of a Pan-American Airways pilot on the big *Brazilian Clipper* for them as likes their likker weak.

Fill a tom collins glass half way up with finely cracked ice, turn in a scant pony of raspberry syrup, 2 to 3 jiggers of claret or Burgundy, the juice of 1 green lime or ½ lemon. Fill up with lemon soda and garnish with a sprig of mint.

NOW a REFRESHING COOLER from BARCELONA CALLED "RED SNOW," a LUSCIOUS & PLEASANT THING for SUMMER, & MILD ENOUGH to SUIT the MOST SEDATE of MEN

The summer before several nations besides the Spanish undertook to alter the map of Spain to suit their own ideas, we had a very old and dependable friend who thought it a good idea at the time to cycle over Spain with a rucksack and paint box over her back. Spanish red wine is not vital, and we suggest Burgundy be substituted; or claret.

Strain the juice of ½ lemon or 1 small green lime, retain the spiral peel of the fruit, about 1 tsp sugar or grenadine syrup, 1 dash of orange flower water. Turn into this 1 cup of Burgundy, of Valdepeñas from Spanish La Mancha, or any good Spanish *vino tinto;* any good claret. Pack a big goblet with shaved ice and pour everything into it, or better still pour the blend into The Blender with a cupful of finely cracked ice, and make it into a sherbet-like rosy tinted condition which, when it is poured into a goblet, speedily melts enough to drink but remains cold far longer than the usual claret lemonade that has merely been iced in the refrigerator. Finally dust a little nutmeg on top; the Spanish touch.

REMEMBER the MAINE, a HAZY MEMORY of a NIGHT in HAVANA during the UNPLEASANTNESSES of 1933, when EACH SWALLOW WAS PUNCTUATED with BOMBS GOING off on the PRADO, or the SOUND of 3" SHELLS BEING FIRED at the HOTEL *NACIONAL,* then HAVEN for CERTAIN ANTI-REVOLUTIONARY OFFICERS

Treat this one with the respect it deserves, gentlemen. Take a tall bar glass and toss in 3 lumps of ice. Onto this foundation donate the following in order given: 1 jigger of good rye whisky, ½ jigger Italian vermouth, 1 to 2 tsp of cherry brandy, ½ tsp absinthe or *Pernod Veritas.* Stir briskly in clock-wise fashion—this makes it sea-going, presumably!—turn into a big chilled saucer champagne glass, twisting a curl of green lime or lemon peel over the top.

LEXINGTON, KENTUCKY, RIDING CLUB COCKTAIL

This is a fine whet to the negligent stomach, besides being an excellent cocktail seldom served in the north these Martini days. We are acquainted with a genuine Kentucky Colonel who serves this as his 1 concession to the cocktail era besides a Bourbon Old Fashioned. . . . Take of calisaya, 1 jigger, add a dash of Angostura and the same of acid phosphate. Stir with ice like a Martini and strain into a Manhattan glass. No garnish, please.

THE YOKOHAMA ROMANCE COCKTAIL, Being a Yellow Peril Concocted by One Toyama, No. I Bar-Boy at a Yoko Night Spot Called "Romance" Cabaret

We don't include this merely in an effort to be "foreign" for truth was that the "Romance" Cabaret was a sorry place of blaring music and taxi-dancing small Japanese men with lovely fluid doll-like Japanese girls with bobbed hair and bangs. But upon being urged by Toyama to sample his masterpiece and we declined with thanks, he frosted one for us on the house, with his compliments. It is, to put it commonly, an accidental "natural" and in it went. That evening was painfully punctuated later when, after having chartered a fleet of bicycles from some coolies, we attempted to navigate cross lots toward the main godowns and docks where our ship was tied up, we ran blindly into a mass of earthquake rubble still unremoved after the disaster of 1923—fetching up all standing in an inverted position and semi-conscious, and from which we were finally extricated by the combined and random efforts of a gentleman from North Carolina who made cigarettes and a gentleman from Kalamazoo who made stoves and shipped them, for increment, direct to you. The cycle was reported a total loss.

The cocktail: 2 jiggers of old cognac, 1 jigger of cherry brandy, 1/4 to 1/2 tsp of Rose's lime juice or lime syrup—the kind we see in soda fountains in the slender bumpy-surfaced bottle, and the juice of ½ a small green lime. Shake very hard with very fine ice and serve with some of this left in. Frozen in The Blender, tropical style, is still better. Serve in a big saucer champagne glass.

THE ROSY DAWN COCKTAIL, a BELOVED EVENT from OUR LAST VISIT to HONGKONG, from which WE REAPPEARED with a BRIDE without KNOWING IT, & WE SHOULD HAVE TOLD this ONE to BOB RIPLEY WHO WAS in TOWN at the TIME—SECRETARY & ALL

For sentimental reasons this probably outranks all other cocktails in our past and present life, for it was through its rosy-inspired courage we got ourselves a wife, only we didn't know it until long afterward, and after we were married back here in the States.

We have the ingredients all noted on the calling card of F. P. Franklin, who then—and we hope now—is editor of the Hongkong *Telegraph*. It was first introduced to us by J. Handley Pegg, Esquire, Chief Engineer of His Majesty's Colonial Highway Department there. It involved a routine cocktail party aboard the *RESOLUTE* on one April evening, then dinner at a West End Chinese Club, and later on still—after many Rosy Dawns, Mrs. Franklin got so sentimental about our recent fiancée that she said as long as she couldn't attend the wedding in person she would like to see us married somehow. So Handley Pegg went out of the room with her and came back with his collar and coat on backwards, and Franklin gave the bride away, and the gramophone played Mendelssohn, and there were flower girls and maids of honour, and God knows what else.

Then Mrs. Franklin started to cry and took off her own wedding ring, and said we had to use it. So we did, and Pegg married us out of the Anglican book of Common Prayer, and everything was very fine, and we capped the Rosy Dawns with vintage *Krug 1923*. Then just before sunrise Mrs. Franklin gave us a big cloisonné tub of freesia, and then we were sent down in Franklin's own chartered limousine, and our Bride started to cry in the motor launch as we got half way over to Kowloon-side, and said it was because she was so happy but also because she had lost one of her pet jewel jade earrings she'd bargained half a day to get up in Canton or somewhere. We never found the earring, and had to make the other into a necklace pendant too—and as for the tub of freesias, we toted the whole seventy pounds of them along the Bund at Kowloon—and the sight of your humble servant, thus burdened, was too much for the coolie roustabouts just scratching themselves awake for the day's labour, and they howled and giggled at the mad white man who would thus lose face aping the porter's trade when he could hire it done. And as we came finally up the spidery forward gangway the first fingers of a Rosy Dawn searched up and over the stark mountains surrounding Hongkong's superb harbour, and painted the hull of the *MARIPOSA* a maiden blush tint where she lay just to the eastward of our own berth. Here is the original receipt.

Take 1 liqueur glass *each* of the following: dry gin, orange curaçao, and cherry brandy. Add 1 tsp Rose's lime juice, or soda fountain lime syrup. Put in a big champagne glass filled with cracked ice, stir, and fill with a touch of seltzer. . . . We later have found that by cutting down the cherry brandy and curaçao to 1 liqueur glass total for both, and tossing in 1 pony of cognac, we have a drier mix, and not quite so sweet, yet still maintaining authority enough for any man.

THE SO-CALLED RUSSIAN COCKTAIL, a Memory of Peking, in 1926

In that year, which seems so very long ago now, Peking was a place of sheer delight. Trade was better after the war, the memory of the Revolution and massacre of White Russians was a vague and tragic business to Russians who were young enough to forget what had been. There was a lovely girl who maintained a shop selling jades and Imperial tribute silks, carved ivories and kingfisher feather screens, at the *Grande Hotel de Pekin*. And after a while we came to go about to odd parts of the vast city together, and one evening at the small jewel-like house on Pa-Pao Hutung where we had gone for some decent *sukiyaki*—the only place in Peking where we could *see* what made up the things we ate!—she commanded ingredients, and after a pause, had them brought to the small room with the sliding screens that gave out on a small garden close where the magnolias drifted the rose-snow of their petals against the high gray wall; and so she sat there in the bamboo print kimono they gave her to wear, and mixed a trio of these for old times' sake, to Russia as she had quit it ahead of bayonets in 1917, a pale gold haired child of 11 or 12.

Into a crystal goblet put 1 cup of finely cracked ice, and onto this pour 1½ jiggers of good cognac and the same of the best Gilka *kümmel,* stir for a moment and fill the goblet with chilled extra dry champagne. Garnish with a single flower petal, or bloom. It is not a drink to be taken lightly, but advisedly, reverently.

CAP HAITIEN RUM & HONEY, or *CLAIRENE au MIEL,* a Wary Exotic Contributed by Glenn "Stiff" Stewart of Easton, Maryland, & Miami Beach, Who Spent Much Time in Haiti as American Minister

We have mentioned Glenn Stewart briefly in *Volume I,* and we can assure all readers that he is a gentleman of parts, who knows many dishes, many drinks, and probably more about pre-Columbian history than any layman alive. . . . *Clairene,* in Haiti, is merely raw white rum, but we have found that when ½ Bacardi and ½ Haitian or any good aged dark rum is substituted, the drink acquires character, discretion and merit. . . . Dissolve 1 tsp or 2 of strained honey with 1½ jiggers of this rum blend into an old fashioned cocktail glass. Stir well, turn into this fluid ½ the glass full of finely cracked ice and stir like a Martini to chill well. No bitters, no garnish.

SABAILLON, or *ZABAGLIONE,* Food-Drink, Dutch East Indies, Already Mentioned on Page 195, Volume I

THE SAIGON SPECIAL, another Odd Drink from the Capital City of French Indo-China & Dating from the Year 1925

This dates back to 1925 when the good old *SS RESOLUTE* stopped in French Indo-China, and some of our friends undertook to fly upriver as near to the marvellous Cambodian ruins of Angkor, as might be sane, then to motor back via Pnom Penh—imagine a place called

Pnom Penh—to Bangkok to meet ship again at Pak Nam. . . . The plane reminded us of a celery crate decorated, respectively, with an electric fan and an evinrude motor. It sputtered and died finally coming to rest on the Saigon River, with no chance to walk home. . . . This addition to any anthology of dampness was one remembered aftermath when back in Saigon, and muttering about the contrariness of fate generally. On checking we find that it is a slightly sweeter Jerusalem Between-the-Sheets, plus a nip of egg white.

Cognac, 1 pony
Dry gin, ½ pony
Cointreau, ½ pony
Lemon juice, ½ tsp
Egg white, 2 tsp or so

Shake with cracked ice and serve in tall cocktail glass with stem. Garnish with cherry. Use no sugar, the cointreau lends sweetness.

SANTIAGO NIGHTCAP, from a STAY in SANTIAGO de CUBA, in the EARLY SPRING of 1930

This is another favour passed along to this field representative and wine tester by the late Señor Facuno Bacardi, it being his primary thought to donate something to woo sleep and restore the slightly frayed physical assembly. It is a simple drink, and would also make a fine picker-upper. . . . Take 1½ jiggers of Gold Seal Bacardi rum, add 1 pony of orange curaçao and the yolk of 1 egg. Shake hard with cracked ice and strain into a large saucer champagne glass.

THE IMMORTAL SAZARAC COCKTAIL, ONE OF THE WORLD'S TRULY GREAT MIXTURES; & ALL BOUND ROUND WITH LOVELY MEMORIES OF NEW ORLEANS

It is a sad and shocking fact that more people who should know more know less about this truly remarkable drink than is reasonable —heaven alone knows why. The Sazarac Bar-Chief, who has been building 'em for 40 years, showed us his way. As did the mixers at several Clubs, the old St. Charles; to say nothing about places like our friend Roy Aciatore's Antoine's Restaurant, Arnaud's, Gabriel

Galatoire's, Broussard, and others. The best drinks produced in New Orleans stick to the ancient, simple formula—and please, please, never try to vary it; for if you do you'll not be drinking a true Sazarac—just some liquid abortion fit only to pour down drains.

First thing is to get a Sazarac glass: a great big thick-bottomed thing which is nothing more nor less than an Old Fashioned glass blown up to twice normal size! Reason: thick bottom and thick walls keep the strong mixed liquor cold; and *warm* strong mixed liquor is like a chemical in the nostrils and throat, of course. These big crystal affairs are buyable at first-class glass stores; but may take time to order in. If none at hand use your brandy sniffers as substitute. . . . Routine is simple and inviolate: Frappe (pre-chill) glass and liquor. For each drink pour 2 ounces of the best rye whiskey you can find in a shaker, lash it with 3 or 4 good squirts of Peychaud's bitters. Shake hard and long with big ice. Then strain into your glass, which must be previously coated inside with 3 or 4 good squirts (use a bar-man's quill top bottle stopper for this) of absinthe or 120-proof Pernod; and turned or spun between the palms to make this said coating even and thorough. Strain drink in glass, and twist a long curl of thin-cut yellow lemon peel on top, for oil and aroma. Hold under nose, inhale the fragrant blend of scents, sip and relax. . . . This, then, my dear children, is just how little Sazaracs are born! Mark well. . . .

THE SEPTEMBER MORN, FIRST DISCOVERED at the *INGLETERRE* BAR in HAVANA, CUBA, in the MONTH of JANUARY 1926

This is simply the famous Clover Club, as mixed originally at the Belleview Stratford in pre-prohibition times, only instead of being based on dry gin, it employs the rounder, less pungent foundation of Bacardi rum. At the Polo Club, in Manila, the September Morn has in addition, ½ pony of dry French vermouth. . . . Therefore: take 1½ jiggers of Gold Seal Bacardi, ½ tsp sugar, 2 tsp of egg white, ½ pony of raspberry syrup. Grenadine may substitute, but raspberry syrup is conventional. Now add the juice of 1 small green lime, or ½ a small lemon, carefully strained, of course. Shake well and serve in a flute cocktail glass with a stem. No garnish, and straws may be stuck to the lip of the glass—scarlet straws, please.

KELLY'S SHAMROCK SPECIAL, from the BAR at the OLD KELLY'S RITZ, which WAS a FAMOUS CABARET at the WESTERN, or PACIFIC ENTRANCE of the BIG DITCH, & which USED to GROW MORE & MORE INTERESTING with EVERY FLOOR DATING from GRADE!

One of the eight or ten times we've prowled the Zone, it became prudent to spring two American friends from the local native city *Cuartel*—jail in Americano—where they were incarcerated for slight offenses not necessary to mention. The celebration, on St. Patrick's day, resulted in the following brain-child, in co-operation with the then head barkeep of Kelly's Ritz. . . . Barring this, shake with finely cracked ice.

Dry gin, 1 jigger
Lime, juice 1 small, ½ large
Green crème de menthe, 2 tsp
Bar sugar or syrup, ½ tsp
Egg, white 1

Mix with shaved ice, and frappe diligently—preferably with an electric machine like The Blender; shake through a sieve into a tall cocktail glass with stem, garnish with a clover leaf or shamrock—we used a sprig of mint. This sieve business builds the drink into a conical mound.

THE FAMOUS SHANGHAI BUCK, a CLASSIC in this VAST PORT which CONSUMES—or DID CONSUME, at LEAST, before the JAPANESE ISSUE—MORE BACARDI RUM than any other CITY on EARTH

The British Shanghai Club Bar, on the Bund at Shanghai, for years boasted the longest mahogany strip in the known world, but has of course long since been surpassed here, after America shrugged off the arid yoke of prohibition. The fact remains that it has more atmosphere right now to the square inch than most chromium plated night spots have per square acre. Years before the man on the street over here had ever heard of a Daiquiri, sane British colonials out in Shanghai's International Settlement knew and valued Bacardi rum for what it was—a *rum brandy,* mellowed and redistilled and aged.

. . . Now at 11 A.M. those who can spare the time foregather for Shanghai Bucks or whisky pegs—a habit very disastrous to productive activity during the remainder of any business day, we learned. . . . Take a big 16 oz collins glass, put in 3 cubes of ice, 1 tsp or 2 of sugar, pour in 2 jiggers of Bacardi—White Seal or Gold Seal—and fill up with good ginger ale. The improved Shanghai Buck adds the juice of 1 green lime or ½ lemon, and uses grenadine instead of sugar, to get the handsome colour. Personally we prefer stone bottle ginger beer to ginger ale. It is a Jamaica Buck, or Barbados Buck, only using Bacardi instead of dark rum, or blended rums.

WORDS to the LIQUID WISE No. XVIII, on the UNDENIABLE EXCELLENCE of a FINE DRY SHERRY, or SHERRY & BITTERS, instead of the PERPETUAL BARRAGE of COCKTAILS

Here's 1 case where old Colonel E. Sifton Ponsonby-Fittich is perfectly right—for the English appreciated sherry long before our war of independence, recognizing it as one of the truly civilized drinks enjoyed by mankind. But a word of caution: don't get a jug of local, sweet, last-month's sherry and expect any cultured results. Sherry should be properly aged, of the dry or drier type. Bitters are optional. . . . We now offer a kernel of heresy which probably will cause many English to wish us harm: chill the sherry decanter if sherry and bitters are used. The sherry taste is just as fine, the whole thing more crisp and pungent. We even do it with sherry alone when using the drink for a pre-dinner appetizer, in warmer weather. . . . We feel, strictly, that sherry *and* bitters changes old sherry tradition.

THE WEST INDIAN SHRUB, from the BERMUDA FILES of ONE WILKINSON, ESQUIRE, UNFORTUNATELY DECEASED, but WHO OWNED CRYSTAL CAVE, & THINGS DOWN THERE in BERMUDA, & WHO WAS VERY COURTEOUS & KIND to US on OUR FIRST TRIP to that ENCHANTED SMALL ISLAND

This mild and cooling summer beverage may be made in the more northern climates out of wild cherries, tame cherries—all except the acid red pie cherry type—strawberries, blackberries, raspberries; almost any flavourful, fairly tart fruit will do. And the same goes for the tropics, of course. Mixed with ice and cool sweet water in a tall thin glass this Shrub recalls the days of bronze-faced planters seated on their galleries overlooking green seas of sugar cane; rice, indigo, or tobacco. It is an especial relief to the man who is wearied of the constant small hammer blows of more insistent, highly proofed, beverages. Incidentally we list a "Temperance" Shrub in some detail on Page 149.

We need a big double boiler, or better still, an earthenware pot big enough to hold all the fruit; and another pot big enough to hold pot Number I. . . . Extract the juice by putting the fruit in the upper container, which stands in the boiling water of the lower vessel. Dredge with sugar and add a stick or 2 of cinnamon. Simmer until juices are pretty well extracted from fruit, then strain through a jelly cloth. Add enough *gomme* syrup to suit taste, and make fairly sweet. Stand in a chilled place until sediment settles out, rack off through another filtering process and add 4 oz—½ cup—of cognac for each 1 qt bottle of the clear juice. Cork well, seal with rosin or paraffin, or wax—then store in a cool place of even temperature. Good to use at any time now. . . . This fruit juice may be clarified or "fined" by the ancient and proper Portuguese method on Page 159.

SOUTH AMERICAN *ANEJO CANDIDO,* A Lovely Unadulterated Thing Conceived by a Gentleman Who has Found Oil in Tropical Venezuela

From first meeting we recognized this instantly as a truly great drink: Great not only in flavour and aroma, but—like the immortal Dry Martini, the Daiquiri and Sazarac—also great in its fine simplicity. In Spanish, *cándido* means "guileless," "unspoiled." The formula came direct to us from Latin America through intermediary offices of a mutual friend who, for reasons not profitable to mention in this work, was (and is) connected with matters pertaining to Naval Intelligence in the Caribbean area. . . . And he, in turn, had had it at hands of a distinguished gentleman who'd long been a resident of Venezuela, involved in oil, and decent things to eat and drink. From hundreds of "fancy" mixture attempts this worthy drink was born.

Take a big green lime, stand it vertically on end; and with a keen knife slice 3 long lengthwise slices from it—taking just enough pulp with outer peel to give you approximately 1½ tsp of resultant juice.

Take an Old Fashioned Cocktail glass, and squeeze juice into it, bending and twisting the peel as well, to work out all possible aromatic oil against the sides and lip of glass. On this sprinkle about ½ oz sugar; fill half way up with fine-cracked ice, add from 1 to 4 dashes of Angostura—to taste—and then turn in all the *Añejo* Bacardi, or ancient Cuban Methusalem Rum, the thing will hold. Stir gently like a Martini; and when perfectly chilled, there you have it. . . . Warning: Do not attempt this drink using any of those pallid horrific commercial rums now being designed solely to trade bad cane alcohol for too much cash; for it will prove an unprofitable thing, compared to one made from these musty, mellow, liqueur rums: both rums so fine that they can be drunk as Cognac with coffee!

WILSON'S SOUTH CAMP ROAD COCKTAIL, from JAMAICA, B.W.I. via TOM DAVIN

As usual with Davin, his words are worth a quote.

"If you include drinks with your eats here is my donation—which I captured in Jamaica enroute to Haiti, last winter. If you have no friend who drinks any good lawyer can prove it to be a fruit cocktail, even to the eyes of your very own Aunt Silica Fittich! Even your friend Hemingway, with his Anis del Mono-besotted tonsils will not be able to taste the ingredients. Try it yourself, but not more than two—and I mean that. . . . It was invented by a retired British army man—and how can England have any army when all her princely chaps are 'retired'—who lives in, or rather outside of, Kingston, named Wilson. His main vocation seems to be concocting odd beverages, and if this is any sample he's a wizard. Somehow this escaped his secret archives because he turned the formula over to the head barman at the South Camp Road Hostelry when dining some friends there.

Dry gin, 2 jiggers
Grand marnier, ½ pony
Juice of large lime
Dash angostura, dash orange bitters
French vermouth, 2 jiggers
Absinthe, or Pernod Veritas, ½ pony
Egg, white, 1, fresh as can be
Grenadine, to taste; about ½ tsp
Sugar or *gomme* syrup, about 2 tsp, to taste

"Shake with lots of cracked ice and pour into a large saucer champagne glass capable of holding some six ounces of T.N.T.

"Now," continues Editor Davin, "report me this when ye can. Maybe I had a touch o' sun when I tried it last!"

P.S. Orange curaçao can substitute for grand marnier; *anis del mono* could pinch hit for the absinthe, or *ojen*—the Spanish absinthe—would also work, lacking the real Swiss product.

THE RANGOON STAR RUBY, a WONDERFUL & STIMULATING COCKTAIL from LOWER-BURMAH

In 1926 we disembarked in Burmah from a round-the-world ship, and spent several days there before hopping off to Calcutta in a little "Bibby" boat carrying a mess of Mohammedan pilgrims headed for Mecca as deck passengers, and who did all their own cooking right down there in plain sight. In Rangoon we joined up with several folk in the Strand bar of evenings to chin about the romantic Mandalay country far up the Irrawaddy River, and to talk over gems with Hamid and his brother from Colombo and Bombay, and to acquire a really fine zircon for someone else and a set of star sapphire dress studs for ourself. One American headed out on leave from certain ruby mining operations up-country told us he had invented himself a drink that everyone up at headquarters liked so well he was going to shout it to the world so that no man might be denied its virtues. He popped behind the bar before we could say "knife" and whipped up the following mixture which, due to its colour, he had christened the Star Ruby.

Take 1 jigger of good cognac, ½ pony of cherry brandy, ½ pony of French vermouth, 2 dashes each of orange bitters and lemon phosphate, then for added flavour 1 tsp of *kirsch,* or ½ tsp of maraschino. Shake with finely cracked ice, pour into a wine glass leaving a little ice floating, and let fall 6 drops of grenadine in the center of this chilly expanse for the ruby colour touch.

SUNDAY VESPERS, from the REPERTOIRE of an AMERICAN OFFICIAL with PARAMOUNT FILMS WHO DWELLS near QUEEN ANNE'S GATE LONDON

Here's a gentle thought for that long quiet, house-bound afternoon, just prior to evening services, when both the spiritual and bodily reservoirs need aiding and abetting. It should be served, in summer, very cold, frappéed briefly with not-too-fine ice. *Pax vobiscum,* my good fellow. We met this aid to mankind in 1932.

Cognac, 1 jigger	Egg, 1
Black coffee, 1 pony	Sugar, barspoon
Heavy cream, 2 jiggers	Clove and nutmeg, dash each, on top
Port, 1 pony	

It should be served in some tall, stemmed glass.

NOTES on DRINKS with a TEQUILA BASE, & NATIVE to MEXICO

Tequila, along with Pulque and Mescal, make up the three national beverages. Pulque is the universal drink, mainly for the average person of average position. It is the fermented sap of the *Maguey* plant—which we call a century plant—and made by chopping out the central bud, or flower stalk so that the sap can collect in the scooped out heart of the plant itself. . . . Pulque is about as strong as beer, tastes like a combination of sour cider and whatever fermented fruit juice happens to be around, and smells—as has been told—faintly like a mildewed donkey. Needless to say it is not universally consumed by others than the hardy race in the land of its conception.

Mescal is the *distilled* fermented juice of the *Agave* or *Maguey* plant. The plant is dug up, leaves amputated and roasted. The juice is then extracted in a press, fermented and distilled. It is the same colour as our corn likker, has the same kick, plus an odd flavour which cannot be described.

Tequila is the finest of these three, being the distilled fermented juice of the *Zotol Maguey* plant, which grows almost entirely in the State of Jalisco. Properly aged it is a spirit of definite merit. It is very potent, colourless also, and has a strange exotic flavour which—like Holland gin—is an acquired taste.

The upstanding Mexican takes his tequila like our prohibition "Swiss Itch": First a suck of a quartered lemon, then the pinch of salt, then the tossed off jigger or pony of spirit. This process not only being a definite menace to the gullet and possible fire risk through lighted matches, we began going on a still hunt for some way to mix tequila. We were greeted with raised eyebrows, expressions of commiseration for waning sanity, open distrust. It was about the same situation which would parallel snooping about Paris for ways to dilute *champagne fine,* or aged brandy. It took several hundred miles of wandering about the surrounding towns and mountains before we struck our first evidence of cooperation—at the little corner place of one eminent lady known affectionately as Bertita, on the Cathedral Square of utterly lovely Taxco—pronounced "toss-ko."

What Bertita had done after long experimentation was to put in more lime juice and less sweet than we. As we said, tequila is an acquired taste, try it sometime. . . . Remember small ice makes the drink very cold, which improves the taste by taking some of the accent off tequila. Bertita's Special is listed 2d receipt below.

OUR OWN TEQUILA COCKTAIL, *ARMILLITA CHICO*

Armillita is the idol of Mexico, their foremost, most finished, most graceful, most dramatic bullfighter. His work with the cape, banderillas, and sword rank him with the Spanish immortals of all time. He gets fifteen hundred dollars for a Sunday afternoon's performance, Hollywood please notice. Mexicans are beginning to rank him with Spain's Juan Belmonte.

In dallying with tequila in the bosom of our own bar we finally set upon this formula as being worthwhile, and promptly dedicated it, a standing toast with Sydney Franklin by our side, to Armillita Chico.

Tequila, 3 jiggers
Limes, strained juice, 2
Orange flower water, 2 dashes
Grenadine, dash, for colour

Fill electric shaker with all the finely shaved ice this amount will cover, frappe well, serve through a sieve, shaking to make the frappe stand up in a brief rosy, temporary cone. When this subsides drink to Armillita Chico, the idol of Mexico.

TEQUILA SPECIAL, *à la BERTITA,* GARNERED, among other THINGS, in LOVELY TAXCO, in FEBRUARY of 1937

This is a shocker from the place of Bertita, across from the cathedral steps in Taxco, already mentioned. It is a cooler as well and Americans will find it very unusual. Take 2 ponies of good tequila, the juice of 1 lime, 1 tsp sugar and 2 dashes of orange bitters. Stir in a collins glass with lots of small ice, then fill with club soda. No garnish except crushed halves of the lime.

TEQUILA *por MI AMANTE,* or TEQUILA for MY BELOVED; MEXICO CITY, 1937

This is a prepared beverage requiring patience and from three to four weeks.

Tequila, 1 pint — Ripe strawberries, 1 qt, cut in halves

Wash and stem the berries, put into an airtight jar or bottle, pour on enough tequila to cover. Shut tightly and stand for at least twenty-one days. Strain. . . . This berry process extracts some of the raw taste, adds a rosy dawn touch. Our Mexican drinks it straight always. We opine that handled in the same way as sloe gin, discoveries would be made. . . . Other fruit like wild cherries, blackberries, and so on could be tried.

TIGER'S MILK, what IT IS, & WHY; DATED from PEKING, APRIL 1931

We honestly consider this one of the most amazing and delicious building-up drinks we've ever known. That year we didn't go from Fusan to Seoul, Korea, to Mukden and then down to Peking, because the Japanese puppet makers had just started slamming the door, but we did get there on the crack blue train via Tientsin, from Chingwangtao. Yes, we coasted in through the break in the huge breath-taking battlements of the Tartar Wall, to the station by the Water Gate—so vital to the Allies during the Boxer Siege of the Legations in 1900.

We got that strange lift under the heart all men get when they step from the world we know straight back into the heart of a city dating for thousands of years. . . . Then, later, we met Gerber, manager of the Wagons-Lits on Legation Street, and next afternoon we went out and watched him exercise his "griffin" polo ponies—those short, stocky, hairy, half-wild little horses brought down from the northern plains by Larsen of Mongolia. Ponies, Gerber told us, were bought at auction, unclipped and untried, so that everyone—millionaire and lowly civilian alike—might play polo without needing a fortune to finance his string. Actually regulation polo ponies are banned from the sport in Peking. Then we found it quite chill after sunset, and we went back to Gerber's snug bar at the Wagons-Lits, and he ordered his Chino to mix a brace of Tiger's Milks—directly from the receipt left with him by a chap named Seaholm some time before, and who was related to the King of Sweden allegedly; and the receipt itself unchanged one iota. They called it Tiger's Milk, as Seaholm had, and it has since gone forth and become gradually recognized all over the world—either in original form or slightly changed to suit local preferences.

The main thing in No. I: Never use anything but really good aged brandy, *champagne fine,* not the usual cognac. The latter doesn't do the job properly.

TIGER'S MILK No. I, from the GERBER-SEAHOLM FORMULA, PEKING, 1931

Command 2½ jiggers old liqueur brandy, or *champagne fine,* and put this in a shaker. Add 1 to 2 tsp of sugar or grenadine, to taste, ½ cup of heavy cream and ½ cup of milk—nothing else; no trimmings. Shake with several big pieces of ice and strain into a goblet. A dash of cinnamon or nutmeg is optional, but not originally authentic. We came, we saw, we drank. And later we imported a certain black eyed Russian peril, managed 1 for her; and we recall her first remark in syllables slightly husky, wholly charming, the slightly accented English slick as cream. "And do you now, mah frrrrahn, thees dreenk eet iss—how shall I say eet?—'food, dreenk, and lodging,' all at zee same tam!" . . . True, *ma soeur,* true!

TIGER'S MILK No. II, from the BAR BOOK of a TINY SMILING ANNAMESE BAR-BOY at the PHYA-THAI PALACE, BANGKOK, SIAM, in the YEAR 1932 . . . TIGER'S MILK No. III is on PAGE 90

We had come in from a day around town—looking at a sleeping

Buddha 90 feet or so long, at temples and *wats* searching upward to the sun; at *Wat Arun,* gleaming with porcelain insets, brilliant butterfly-hued tiles, at the temple of the Emerald Buddha, the Wat Phra-Keo, with the sacred Gautama himself carved from a single emerald so runneth the tale—but green jasper to us—some 60 centimeters high, and with 3 changes of jewel and gold cloth clothing, to keep him comfortable during the rainy, the cold and the hot seasons. We were wearied of Buddha and Yagas, or guardian demons; we were tired of sightseeing altogether and wanted to rest and relax before going to the Royal Dancers in the—of all ideas!—*Roman* Garden of the Phya-Thai Palace that gala night. We wanted something to forget our weary insteps, or sun-toasted eyeballs, before freshening up and changing for evening. We asked, through an interpreter of sorts, if the bar-boy might have anything possible to make a Tiger's Milk. The answer was that, evidently, the Gerber-Seaholm idea had penetrated there too, authorized by some hardy and careless soul like ourself with medical knowledge enough to realize that enough alcohol will strangle the microbes even in Siamese milk and cream—which is a chancey statement we might say. The Bacardi lends a typical British modification, a twist. . . . Old brandy 1½ jiggers, Bacardi Gold Seal the same; ½ cup each of thick cream and milk, then sweeten to taste. Shake vigorously for at least ½ minute with big lumps of ice and serve in a goblet. Dust with nutmeg, or ground mace, or cinnamon.

THE IMPROVED TURF COCKTAIL No. I, a MODIFICATION of OUR OWN from DIRTY DICK'S, NASSAU, B.I., 1937

We first sampled this drink in Nassau quite some time back, having flown over Pan-American Airways, after the official tourist season was finished, with a 6-year bride and 4 friends, to do a bit of sailing and swimming and basking on undiscovered white sand beaches by vitriol blue coral water that is clearer than anywhere else in the whole universe. A gentleman of colour suggested this as a dry, appetizing taste-thrill at Dirty Dick's, and found it to be merely Holland gin and vermouth—nothing else except Angostura—in a 2 to 1 ratio. . . . After a bit of later experimentation on self and friends we discovered that addition of ½ a green lime—strained juice—and ½ tsp of grenadine or bar sugar works miracles with this drink.

TURF COCKTAIL No. II, from the TAJ MAHAL HOTEL, on APOLLO BUNDER, in BOMBAY, SATURDAY, FEBRUARY 14th, 1931, to BE EXACT; SERVED after the RUNNING of the MAHARAJAH of RAJPIPLA GOLD CUP at the WESTERN INDIA TURF CLUB, LTD.

We had won all of sixty-seven rupees on this gold-cup, 23,000-rupees race, and were feeling very horsy and turfy, and tired of the eternal *chotapegs*—just plain Scotch and not-too-cold soda, without ice, of the last few days—and were open for suggestions. G. J. Mack, local Manager for General Motors Export, suggested a Turf Cocktail, of a recognized mix, and after a barrage of Hindustani this resulted, much to everyone's amazement: 1 jigger of dry gin, 1 pony of French vermouth, 1 tsp of absinthe, or *Pernod Veritas;* donate 1 tsp of maraschino and a dash of orange or Abbots bitters. Stir in a bar glass like a Martini and serve in a Manhattan glass, ungarnished.

TURF COCKTAIL No. III, from the HAVANA COUNTRY CLUB, WINTER of 1930

This is virtually the same as No. II, only using old Tom gin for a base, orange bitters, and everything else the same.

THE VIRGIN'S PRAYER, a MEMORY from VERSAILLES, in the SUMMER of 1926

That summer when we were living in Paris, we met many people across the street from our own domicile, in Harry's American Bar—already a happy memory to countless Americans. And one night we were there with a person not apt to mention, listening to Tommy Lyman sing *Montmartre Rose,* and wondering what we were going to do next day, when a stalwart young chap barged up and invited himself to our table—a practice which we are not likely to view with any great amount of enthusiasm in Paris, Paraguay or Patagonia.

But this time it was all right. His name was O'Malley and he had a Cadillac 8, and after the war he had married him a French wife who got lonesome when he took her to Union City, New Jersey—and we don't have to be French to be that!—and so he had brought her back to France, Cadillac and all. And why the hell did I spend 12 dollars a day to Franco-Belgique tours for a motor car when I could hire his for 9 or less. Certainly, why? . . . Well, O'Malley not only had a Cadillac 8 and a French wife, but he knew all 16 of the current crop of Tiller girls living in their dormitory with a matron and chaperones and all, over in Montmartre. But unless they had been misbehaving and were under censure, they were all allowed nights out until 12 midnight, so we started at the end of the line and went along, counting off from right to left; and what dancing partners; what grand fun they were! Well, one afternoon we and O'Malley and our current assignment of Tiller were out at Versailles absorbing French history, then toward evening we stopped at a big sort of a chateau turned into a restaurant-hotel not too far from the great Palace, for a little liquid nourishment. And while we were waiting they brought us a bowl of big red ripe cherries in cracked ice, and O'Malley had an idea. "I know," he said, holding up a cherry pit, "I'll *invent* a drink."

Now a gentleman from Union City, New Jersey, who had a French wife and a Cadillac 8, in Paris, and who hired out to Franco-Belgique tours yet also hired out for less to us, was shock enough for any one stay in Paris; but one who further invented drinks, made us slightly dizzy. "Of course. Sure. *Invent* one," we added with all the conviction we feel when we see cinemas of Senators kissing babies.

"Celeste's old man works at the Florida. Her old man invents drinks too. We invent drinks together," he explained. Celeste was O'Malley's wife, of course. "We invent swell drinks."

So O'Malley asked for a nutcracker in his Union City, New Jersey, French, and bottles of things, and a shaker and a bowl of ice, and the maitre-d'hotel had it fetched with a suspicious but he'll-pay-beaucoup-for-his-fun gleam in his agate eyes, and O'Malley mixed. He first cracked 4 cherry pits with that darned nutcracker and dropped them in a cocktail glass. Then he put 1½ jiggers of *kirsch,* 1 pony of cherry brandy, 1 tsp of maraschino, into the shaker, and shook it with the ice. Then he poured it onto the broken pits, stirred it for a second to let the aromatic bitter odour and taste penetrate the drink, then handed it to me. And it was good.

"That, Pal,"—O'Malley was the soul of companionship for a chauffeur-companion, we might state—"is a swell drink, see? That drink has what it takes—imagination, see? That's it, imagination. No drink is worth a damn without imagination. It doesn't take any imagination to just say 'Scotchansoda,' now does it? It's good enough to give Celeste's old man, and if it's good enough for that it's plenty good enough for a name. It must be garnished with 2 red cherries, Eh? 2; sure! . . . Let's name it the Virgin's Prayer. Eh? What do you think, Esle?" Esle was our Miss Tiller *du jour*. Esle was just eighteen, with curly brown hair and brown eyes, and breakfast ankles. She was very English, very sane, very passionate. She looked at him calmly. She sipped the drink.

"I don't trust the Irish, O'Malley," she said evenly; "or their names." . . . *"Garçon,* scotchansoda," she said to the hovering waiter.

Now of course we don't expect that when our most dutiful readers are faced with a bowl of cherries they will all have nutcrackers within ordering distance. Or Tiller girls. But if they have, and the spirit of adventure is not dead, they may try this pungent drink. Try an O'Malley Virgin's Prayer. It really is a sound cocktail, and worthy to be known among all men.

VANILLA PUNCH, another RECEIPT from the PLANTATION FILES of ONE CLYMER BROOKE, MENTIONED ELSEWHERE in this WORK

Brooke was the one who fell in love with Tahiti, and left the round-the-world cruise of the schooner *CHANCE,* along with Dodd and the rest of their Yale outfit, and whose adventures are neatly told in *From Great Dipper to Southern Cross.* Well, Brooke ended up hob-nobbing with princesses on Moorea, owning some sort of a vanilla plantation. We met him out of Yoko, bound for Hawaii in 1931 when he was bound back to the states like a sea-going Lochinvar to marry him a bride. . . . *Salut* Clymer.

Take a bar glass and fill it with shaved or very finely cracked ice, add 2 tsp of fresh strained lime juice, the same of yellow curaçao, and 1 tbsp of grenadine. Now turn in 2 jiggers of cognac, and either a scant ½ pony of vanilla extract, or 1 full pony of *Crème de Vanille.* Stir, turn ice and all into a tall thin glass or goblet, garnish with sticks of fresh ripe pineapple, a cherry or 2, and a sprig of something to brighten up attractively. This is fairly sweet, so be sure and step up the lime juice if a drier drink is wanted.

THE HARVARD *VERITAS,* Contributed by Frederick A. R. Thompson, at the Time Managing Editor of *COMMONWEAL,* a Catholic International Weekly

This drink is famous enough along the Charles River, and especially at the Harvard Club in New York, and good enough in its own right to be listed here. It is a sort of emancipated Between the Sheets, only with currant flavouring. Take 1 pony each of dry gin, cointreau and strained lemon—or lime, better—juice. Shake well with finely cracked ice, strain into a flute cocktail glass with a stem, and pour in 2 tbsp of *crème de cassis* for trimming.

COCKTAIL *au VICOMTE de MAUDUIT,* Being a Lovely Thing Made of Rose Brandy

Vicomte de Mauduit is one of Europe's most exacting gourmets and his volume *The Vicomte in the Kitchen* is one of the most charming volumes on food and wine ever printed in the English language. His knowledge of wines is thoroughgoing, but even though tartly French, his mental processes are still agile and cosmopolitan enough to grant brief space to decent cocktails. We have taken pains to test out this, his own especial origination, and can attest it to be one of the most delicate and palate tickling amateur originations we have ever met. In this one case we have taken the liberty of reprinting another's own formula, in the spirit of pleasant drinking and gentle living; and with a bow of thanks to Monsieur le Vicomte.

Take 1 pony each of dry gin, French dry vermouth and rose brandy—another original formula of the Vicomte's and which we also note with grateful acknowledgment on Page 155—and put in a bar glass. Stir with several fairly large lumps of ice and strain into a

Manhattan glass. Garnish with a candied pink rose petal carefully floated on top. A delicate, original cocktail indeed.

THE OLD WALDORF'S LAST, Invented—so Runneth the Tale —as the Last Original Cocktail to Come from the Mellow Old Waldorf Bar at Fifth Avenue & 34th Street

This is not, strictly, an exotic. It is a good ladies' drink under any condition, and any spirituous combination to put the period to those grand old days when titanic, two-fisted Wall Streeters and important folk from all over the world used to stand 6 or 8 deep before mahogany during the 5 to 8 P.M. cocktail "hour," is well worthy of inclusion on any list of international receipts. . . . Take 1 pony each of dry gin, orange curaçao and heavy cream. Shake and strain into a Manhattan glass. That is all.

THE VLADIVOSTOK VIRGIN, Being a Risky Little Heart-warmer from out Frozen Siberia, Disclosed by a Late Friend once Stationed there (only our Creator knows why!) with United States Troops, after what We Have Quaintly Come to Term as "World War I."

This is an odd, unlikely-sounding but valid cocktail, and (if our own ungaudy recollection doesn't play us false) was probably one of the few virgins of any type, above toddling age, in that somewhat dreary and otherwise frigid town which sprawls along the chilly waters of Amur Bay, west side of the slightly miscalled "Golden Horn." . . . This slightly alcoholic virgin's birth occurred as by-product of the arrival in this port of what must have been just about the first recorded batch of grapefruit juice ever to know export out of Florida—combined with a sort of bored sub-zero desperation to find some, any, new way of injecting fiery Vodka into the human frame.

Now don't, please, try to make this thing out of the fresh juices of polemoes. For just as cooked bananas have a widely differing taste from the raw, just so with all pasteurized juice of citric character.

Strangely enough, it is the odd, almost chemical-acid taste of the stuff which donates an unexpected crisp character to the drink. And incidentally we find that unsweetened, canned grapefruit juice gives a nice variation to mixes of the Planter's Punch family.

Drink is simple, strikes with high-voltage authority: 1 jigger each of Vodka and dry gin; add 1 pony, or slightly more, of chilled, canned, *unsweetened* grapefruit juice. A dash of Angostura bitters is optional; and, we think, good. Shake with big ice and serve in a large saucer champagne glass with a paper-thin slice of cucumber floating on top. This Vladivostok Virgin must be Arctic cold; warm, it's a brassy-tasting mess. . . . Now, then, *Tovaritch!*

Le *RAT BLANC*, or WHITE RAT, a Left Bank Touch, Sampled in Paris at the Urging of a Friend

This is a stout and pungent thing, so be wary of absorbing it in too ambitious quantity or we cannot be responsible for any subsequent inclination or action! . . . To 1 jigger of absinthe add ½ pony of *anis del mono*, or lacking this, anisette. Shake with very fine ice like a frappe, and serve in a Manhattan glass, leaving a trifle of the ice still in the finished drink. No garnish, please.

ZABAGLIONE, or *SABAILLON*, Food-Drink, Dutch East Indies, Already Mentioned on Page 195, Volume I

THE ZAMBOANGA "ZEINIE" COCKTAIL, another Palate-Twister from the Land where the Monkeys Have No Tails

This drink found its way down through the Islands to Mindanao from Manila, and we found it in the little Overseas Club standing high above the milk-warm waters of the Sulu Sea, on the suggestion of a new friend, just met; and while perusing the first edition of that Norm Anthony-George Delacorte opus *Ballyhoo*, which after having passed from hand to hand through most of the U.S. Army in the Islands from Colonels down was slightly tattered, but still placed in a rack of honour.

Cognac, 1 jigger
Maraschino, 1 tsp
Lime, juice, ½
Fresh pineapple syrup, 3 dashes
Angostura, 3 dashes
Twist lime peel

Shake well with shaved ice, letting some of ice go into glass; twist some of the peel on top to extract oil, and add one olive. Use a Manhattan glass. . . . Pineapple syrup same as used at soda fountains.

AN EXOTIC COCONUT-COGNAC COCKTAIL from *CAP HAITIEN, REPUBLIC de HAITI*, and which Is CALLED the *ZOMBIE* *

Any one who knows his Haiti and his *Vaudou* knows what a *Zombie* is; and for those who don't, a Zombie is merely a departed brother who, for reasons not generally attractive, has been called back from the Spirit World, labours without pay, without food, without complaint, in a weird sort of spirit bondage. . . . We have just helped "spring" an artist friend, Christopher Clark, from a five months' stay in Cap Haitien, where he had been soaking up material and madly painting the unbelievable scenery and even more unbelievable people of Haiti, as a follow-up to the wave of acclaim which greeted his *The Crapshooters,* in last year's American Art Exhibit at Rockefeller Center, and we fetched him via Pan American to do a mural for us.

Chris brought back a long list of amazing cookery receipts, too late for this volume, but we are squeezing in this *Zombie* Cocktail, he claiming that it will put the spirits to work for you, but whether they or ourselves, are in bondage, is something for each man to decide according to occasion and the needs thereof.

Enriched coconut milk, see below, 1 ½ cups or so
Cognac, 3 jiggers
Maraschino, 2 ponies
Angostura, 2 or 3 dashes
Very finely cracked or shaved ice

* It may be of some mild interest to our Lodge of Amiable Amateur Mixers that the Zombie formula set on this page was put to paper in the fall of '35; whereas the high-proof so-called Zombie known to most bar men did not raise its dizzy head until two years, or better, later. Author.

Put in shaker with lots of very finely cracked ice, shake hard and turn ice and all—*à la Daiquiri*—into small, chilled goblets. . . . Another variation, and a much better flavoured one we find, is found by using only two jiggers cognac, and one jigger old Haitian—or other medium dark—rum.

Enriched coconut milk: Get a ripe coconut anywhere. Bore two holes in eyes and drain out water into saucepan—being careful to strain out fibres or bits of shell. . . . Crack open nut, peel off brown outer skin from kernel, and either grate, grind, or cut up fine and add to water. . . . Fetch to a simmer for five minutes. Put through a fine cloth, squeezing out the final rich cream by hand. Ripe fresh coconuts can be had in most good grocery stores these days. . . . Those possessing The Blender will save an incredible amount of time by cutting up kernel, with brown part unremoved, into the top container of The Blender; turn in the coconut juice. Reduce to a pulp at high speed for 1 minute, then rub through a very fine sieve, or strain through several thicknesses of cloth. . . . *Clinical Note:* Quite recently not a few coconut cream drink-aids have come to light. Merely mix up any required amount to richness approaching that of honest Grade A milk.

AN EVEN ONE DOZEN TEMPERANCE DELIGHTS, which after ALL Is nearly TWO WEEKS' SUPPLY

NOT ALL intelligent folk approve or militantly disapprove of spirituous beverage. There simply happen to be quite a few rational souls who don't care for anything containing alcohol. Being half of Quaker stock we have noted such phenomena right in our own family. Also there are beverages for the extremely young.

This being the case, and refreshments are indicated, what to serve besides tea, coffee, milk or water? To our own rough and unpredictable mind there is nothing under heaven more discouraging than weak lemonade, once past the age of 10—except pink, and at circuses. How often in our own history have we seen guests gaze skyward and pray for a sign so that dear old Aunt Trilby Fittich wouldn't serve them cookies and lemonade! Therefore, sharply aware of this problem from our own case, we have gone to considerable effort in snupping these selected Temperance Delights. We now feel that we can face a P.T.A. meeting unafraid, look a strawberry social in the teeth without bowing our head in abject and citric shame.

Beside our own palm-shrouded cornerstone there is nothing under heaven's sweet canopy so baffling as suddenly being confronted with test of producing some non-alcoholic beverage claiming credit for anything but the usual bellywash of lemon, orange, sugar and ice. This is no laughing matter, either. This sort of zero hour may pop up to haunt us at any unexpected moment; and usually when brains are bled white, scraping an all-time low, and showing all the originality of stuffing for a kapok windowseat pad. Yes, it may easily be a neighbouring daughter's 6th birthday, or Aunt Deleria Fittich descending from Clebbett City in the worst hot spell since '83. And to our way of thinking there still never has been an excusable lemonade except pink, and at circuses!

These mild-mannered coolers come from here and there around the world, and the bare fact of presenting them in a drinking volume of our own conception makes us feel very fine, and remote and pure and worth while, for a change.

THE ANGOSTURA FIZZ, sometimes CALLED the TRINIDAD FIZZ, BEING a RECEIPT GLEANED from ONE of OUR FRIENDS PILOTING the BIG BRAZILIAN CLIPPER from HERE to TRINIDAD & RIO & on SOUTH to "B. A."

This mild fizz is again like initial olive sampling; either it suits or it doesn't, and subsequent trials often show sudden shift to appreciation. It is a well-known stomachic along the humid shores of Trinidad, in British Guiana; wherever the climate is hot and the humidity high, and stomachs stage sit-down strikes and view all thought of food—present or future—with entire lack of enthusiasm. Further than this, the cinchona bark elixir in the Angostura, the other herbs and valuable simples, are a definite first line defense against malaria and other amoebic fevers—especially in warding off their after effect in later months when all actual peril is past.

Take 1 pony of Angostura bitters, add 1 tsp of sugar or grenadine, the juice of ½ lemon or 1 lime, the white of 1 egg and 1 tbsp of thick cream—or slightly less. Shake with cracked ice like a cocktail, turn into a goblet and fill to suit individual taste with club soda, seltzer, vichy, or whatever lures the mind. Vary the sweet also, to suit taste. It is a very original, cooling drink as well as a valuable tonic to those dwelling in hot countries. Garnish with sticks of ripe fresh pineapple, always.

CASSIS & SODA, the OLD CLASSIC from anyWHERE in FRANCE

This is well known to all traveling Americans nowadays but is important enough to list for those who are merely contemplating a trip abroad. As we have already explained, cassis is the syrup and juice made from black French currants. . . . Take from 1 to 2 jiggers of cassis, chill as above, turn into a tumbler or goblet with ice and fill to taste with soda; or merely mix like an ordinary highball, directly in the glass without shaking first. Angostura is optional. It is very refreshing in hot weather, also.

THE PANAMA "MOCK DAISY" *CRUSTA,* from CRISTOBAL at the ATLANTIC END of the PANAMA CANAL ZONE, which ODDLY ENOUGH IS ACTUALLY *WEST* of the PACIFIC END at BALBOA

Take the juice of 2 limes and put into a tumbler or goblet with fine ice, the crystal having been rubbed first with the lime shells and the lip dipped in powdered sugar, allowing all possible to cling for about ½" down the side. Now add 1 pony of raspberry syrup, fill glass with enough club soda to suit taste, and float on ½ to 1 tsp of grenadine. Garnish with stick of ripe pineapple, 2 or 3 ripe raspberries frozen in ice cubes; a sprig of green mint.

EXPLODED old ALEWIVES' TALES No. II, PLEADING that JUST BECAUSE PAST TEMPERANCE DRINKS HAVE usually BEEN UNATTRACTIVE & UNGARNISHED, this SIN SHOULD NOT PREVAIL in MODERN TIMES

Again we urge readers to consider that any drink that intrigues the eye has already half conquered. Ice cubes may be tinted in a second to afford any desired shade; sprigs of green mint, cherries, strawberries, raspberries, and other fresh or candied fruits; rose and violet petals—*au naturelle* or candied, anything pretty the heart desires may quickly be frozen into each cube. The variety is limited solely by the imagination. . . . To suspend fruits in center of cube—freeze first with tray half full; then center up fruits, add water to fill tray full, and freeze again. If garnish is desired on top of cubes, fill tray almost full, freeze; tee up fruit and freeze again after adding a tiny bit of water.

To our mind a sweet temperance drink has to look mighty, mighty pretty to be intriguing. This may also apply to other citizens confronted with spirituous aridity at any current function!

GENERAL J. K. L. HARKRIDER'S FAMOUS STONE BOTTLE GINGER BEER No. I, a FINE TIME-TESTED RECEIPT for this AROMATIC BEVERAGE so ESSENTIAL in JAMAICA & SHANGHAI BUCKS, in SINGAPORE RAFFLES GIN SLINGS, as WELL as a TASTY COOLER in ITS OWN TEMPERATE RIGHT, FOUND in LONDON SUMMER of 1932

This is one of the oldest temperance beverage receipts we own, and dates well back into Georgian days in rural England, *Circa* 1766. To our way of thinking a rich ginger beer is to average ginger ale as Napoleon brandy is to Nawth Ca'lina white mule. Stone bottles may be ordered in for us by the country grocer, on a few days' notice, and in big towns we may find "empties" in any good delicatessen or provision store. Of course this ginger beer may be bottled in glass, but that too is like modernizing any mellowed and ancient custom, or like a charming girl in sport slacks who wears high heels; for then certain of the charm flies out the window, through needless inconsistency.

Brief comparison of these two formulae shows that No. II, that of the famous Dr. Pereira, employs honey and no yeast since . . . *"The Honey gives the Beverage a Peculiar Softness, and from not being Fermented with Yeast, it is Less Violent when Opened, but requires to be kept a Somewhat Longer Time before Use."*

General Harkrider's receipt calls for:

2½ lbs of sugar
½ oz cream of tartar
4 lemons, juice and rind
2 oz of ginger root
2½ gallons of boiling water
2 tbsp fresh brewer's yeast

Peel the lemons thin and put the cut up rind and strained juice in an earthenware crock, together with the bruised ginger root, the sugar and cream of tartar. Add the boiling water and when lukewarm stir in the brewer's yeast. Cover with a cloth and let ferment until next day. Now skim the yeast foam from the top, pour carefully through several thicknesses of cheesecloth, being careful also not to agitate the sediment in the crock. Put in stone bottles, thoroughly sterilized in boiling water. Ready to use in 2 weeks or so. If no ginger root is available add 1 tbsp of ground ginger to the hot water brew, or better still 2 tbsp of tincture of Jamaica ginger; stir well, and taste. Then add more ginger—ground or essence—1 tsp at a time until it suits the taste.

The lemon juice and rind are what point up this receipt. Sugar also may be stepped up slightly, to taste. This brew is enough to fill 3 doz average stone bottles.

STONE BOTTLE GINGER BEER No. II, without YEAST, from the FAMOUS RECEIPT of DR. PEREIRA on DISCUSSING DIET, and DATING BACK WELL over HALF a CENTURY; & DISCOVERED by US in LONDON, SUMMER of 1932

To our knowledge this receipt dates back more than 60 years in England, and has always been a favourite with home-brewers of their own stone bottle ginger beer. It is very simple, and once again we suggest using Jamaica ginger tincture or essence, if no ginger root is available; and ground ginger if no liquid essence—gradually increasing the dose and stirring into the boiling hot water until it is pungent enough to suit us.

5 lbs of sugar
¼ lb, about ½ cup, of strained honey
4½ gallons of water
1 scant tsp of lemon extract
½ cup of strained lemon juice
5 oz of bruised ginger root
¼ white of 1 egg
Cut up peel of the lemons

Boil the bruised ginger root in 3 qts of water for ½ hr; now add the sugar, lemon juice, honey and peel. Turn in the rest of the water—15 qts to be exact, or 3¾ gals, and briskly boiling at the time, too. Let cool gradually and when cold strain through several thicknesses of cloth, then stir in the egg white to clarify; also the lemon extract. . . . Let stand in a crock for 4 days, then bottle in sterilized stone bottles. This receipt will keep for many months, and is enough for slightly over 8 doz bottles.

Personally we prefer receipt No. I, as it has more sparkle and life—something essential to the drinks mentioned in this volume. We also suggest adding 3 cups of honey to No. II, deducting that much sugar.

CARDINAL PUNCH, from the FILES of the LATE C. H. B. QUENNELL, MENTIONED ELSEWHERE in these VOLUMES, and GRACIOUSLY CONTRIBUTED as a TYPICAL OLD-TIME ENGLISH RECEIPT from the COUNTRY in & around BERKHAMSTEAD, HERTFORDSHIRE

Take 2 qts of uncooked cranberries, and simmer them in just enough water to cover until soft, together with the yellow peel of 2 lemons. When berries are very tender crush them up and strain through a jelly cloth. Let cool and then add the juice of the 2 lemons, 4 cups of sugar, 1 pint of orange juice and about 2 qts of cold water. Chill now, turn into a bowl containing a big single lump of ice, and point up with 4 bottles of really good ginger ale or ginger beer. It is an aromatic, pungent and tart drink, with a lovely colour. . . . It may also be poured into glasses or goblets half filled with cracked ice, and drunk through brightly coloured straws.

MANDARIN PUNCH, a RECEIPT GARNERED away BACK in 1931, from LADY BREDON, for a WHOLE GENERATION SOCIAL DICTATOR of PEKING'S LEGATION QUARTER SET

There are rare occasions when a Peking host or hostess has to produce a temperance punch, and this species makes a welcome relief for the usual. Actually this punch is more or less of an essence with fruit juices, and is usually served exactly like raspberry vinegar—poured to taste over cracked fine ice which almost fills the glass, with water added to suit final ideas of strength and flavour.

Melt out 2 cups of sugar with 2 doz whole cloves, 2 sticks of cinnamon bark, add ½ cup of water and cook for 10 minutes; draw from the fire and let cool. At that point stir in 2 cups of orange juice, and about ½ cup of lemon or lime juice. Strain through cheesecloth, let stand for ½ hr and mix in the following: 3 drops of spearmint oil, buyable at any pharmacy, 1 tbsp finely chopped candied ginger root, 1 bunch of green mint tips snipped fine with scissors. Mix to taste with cracked ice in tumblers or goblets; stirring with each spoonful so as not to miss the solids in this syrup. Fill up with plain water or soda.

A DELICIOUS & PRETTY BEVERAGE MADE from FRESH GRENADINES, or POMEGRANATES, which WILL BE GOOD NEWS to DWELLERS in all SUBTROPICAL or TROPICAL CLIMATES; ONE from CITY of JAIPUR, in INDIA

The lovely roseate tint of pomegranate juice is what makes grenadine syrup so attractive in mixed drinks, and here is a secret from Rajputana, and the city ruled by the Maharajah of Jaipur, mentioned elsewhere in this volume. For centuries the pomegranate's coral-coloured blossom and low-hanging, blushing fruit have been immortalized by poet and tale teller throughout the fantastic courts of Persia, Arabia, Egypt, and further East. Here from our window we can see some ½ doz bushes bending low under their burden of fruits—yet no one we have ever known in America—except ourself—ever does anything about them, even though they seem to grow in every other southern back yard! . . . Simply break open the fruit, over a big bowl as the ruby coloured, pulp-bound seeds tend to fly this way and that as the main rind breaks. Discard every bit of rind as it is bitter as gall, and turn seeds into a fruit press or a potato ricer.

Press out the magenta tinted juice, and mix with *gomme* syrup in ratio of about 2 tbsp of the syrup to every cup of juice. Now pack glasses with fine ice, pour in enough of this luscious fresh juice to fill, stir in the juice of ½ a green lime. Garnish brightly with red cherries, sticks of fresh pineapple, and serve with brightly tinted cellophane straws. Again, sugar syrup as to taste; also the lime juice—depending upon size of the latter fruits.

BLACK TEA PUNCH, from KANDY, in CEYLON, which REFRESHED Us after a MOTOR DRIVE up through the MOUNTAINS from COLOMBO, by WAY of the VASTLY INTERESTING TROPICAL GARDENS at PERADEYNIA, in the YEAR 1931

Sir Tommy Lipton's chief bailiwick was out there in the incredibly rich mountain soils of Ceylon, which many believe to have been the Garden of Eden—even to an imprint of Adam's foot in gigantic size on a table-topped mountain we have seen, winding up through the steep hills. It is only natural, then, that being both British and near some of the finest tea gardens in all the world, that this punch should have been served for benefit of those who did not believe in alcoholic liquids for inner decoration.

Take 3 cups of quite strong, freshly brewed, black tea. Add 1 qt of strained orange juice, 1 cup of strained lime or lemon juice, 2 cups of raspberry syrup and 1 cup of crushed—fresh if possible—pineapple pounded to a pulp in a mortar, or better still, in The Blender. Add sugar, now, to taste; pour over a single large lump of ice in a bowl, and add 2 qts of good sparkling water.

RASPBERRY VINEGAR, MADE from the FRESH FRUIT ITSELF; from a VERY, VERY OLD ENGLISH RECEIPT WE FOUND in ST. ALBANS, HERTFORDSHIRE, in the SUMMER of 1932

One of our earliest and most delightful memories during summer vacations from school was our spring visits every other year to the home of our favourite Aunt Josephine Leaming, either in Philadelphia, or at her country place out on the Main Line in Wayne, Pennsylvania.

Not only was she one of the most beautiful ladies ever born in America or Europe, but one of the most elegant, the most up-to-date even in her seventies; one of the most understanding of cryptic small-boy likes and dislikes; one of the most considerate of all those about her court—for that, actually, was what it really was. . . . And so amid a swarm of Leamings, and Heckschers, and Carsons and Storks, she would entertain in her lovely garden—and for the youngsters would be ginger beer, or more unusual still, great tumblers of thinnest crystal, filled to the brim with pale rose raspberry vinegar, with a bouquet of mint raising its fragrant emerald head in the center. . . . Raspberry vinegar!—How far we drifted apart during the hectic days of the Late Attempted Drouth! . . . How we missed you. How glad we are now and then to go sensible once more, and sip one of you, instead of a Tom Collins, or similar grownup acceptances. . . . Of course good raspberry vinegar may be bought in any fine delicacy shop, but try making your own. It's lots more fun, and saves purse strain.

Raspberries, dead ripe, 1 lb
White *wine* vinegar, 1 qt
(Or failing this, diluted white vinegar)
Raspberries, 1 lb (again)
Raspberries, 1 lb (again)
Sugar, just over 1 lb per pint of resultant juice

Put the 1st lb of raspberries in a bowl, and bruise well. Pour white wine vinegar over them—wine vinegar has a much more delicate flavour than either cider or malt vinegars, and can be bought from Italian shops, or made by exposing any good sweet domestic wine to the air by simply pulling the cork, adding 1 tbs. of vinegar, and letting it stand for a short time in that state.

Next day strain liquor through a cloth onto another pound of well-crushed raspberries. Stand overnight, strain, and pour onto the third batch of crushed berries. . . . *Do not squeeze the fruit* overmuch as this will cause it to ferment, which is not desired. . . . Wet a canvas bag with a little of the raspberry vinegar, and strain the whole business into a stoneware or glass container onto one pound of white sugar—lump sugar is recommended—per each pint of juice. Stir until dissolved. Put jar in pot of water, bringing latter to a simmer. Skim now and again until it grows clear and no further scum rises. Let it cool and bottle. . . . When cold it will have a consistency like heavy syrup, and a teaspoon or so diluted in water with cracked ice makes one of the most delicately flavoured summer thirst-quenchers in the world. . . . Fine for children, invalids; non-alcoholic, and one of the few non-alcoholic drinks worth touching besides water, milk, tea and coffee.

REPULSE BAY "RHUBARB HIGHBALL," from the SUMMER RESORT of HONGKONG, in CHINA, SPRING 1926

The drive up over the mountains, with its view of the Harbour and a maze of little islands dotting steel blue water amazingly like Puget Sound in certain aspects, from Hongkong to Repulse Bay, is one of the most inspiring anywhere. Repulse Bay is a beautiful setting, and small beach bungalows dot the horseshoe curve on either side of the big hotel there. One of the most amazing things we saw, surprising, at least, was a Chinese town on the way where our car exploded a flock of chickens dyed brilliant crimson, rose, cobalt blue and chrome yellow—just why, God only knew.

The Chinese have used rhubarb for countless centuries, both to eat and in specifics for varying ailments not apt to mention in this work. It was not strange, then, that the No. I Boy of our host of the day had converted the temperance members of his household to this drink. . . . Dice 6 cups of pink-stemmed rhubarb. Mix 4 cups of sugar with 2 of water, heat in a double boiler, and add rhubarb before it boils. Simmer until tender, then rub through a sieve and mix in the ratio of 1 cup of rhubarb syrup to the same of orange juice. . . . Pack glasses with fine ice, fill 2/3 full or so, with this business, and top off with club soda. A sprig of fresh green mint adds zest, and bright straws also. As before, the amount of fruit syrups and juices, to ice and sparkling water, is to individual taste; there is no safe, set, formula for every race and climate!

THE NASSAU TEA SHAKE, from a TRIP to NASSAU RECENTLY, and SERVED to THOSE WHO PREFERRED NOT to GAZE upon the CUP when IT WAS red with WINE

This is an invigorating drink and we wonder why it has not been more generally known and appreciated in the States. Simply take ½ cup of strong black tea, sugar to taste, and a whole—very fresh—egg. Pop in a shaker with lots of fairly large cracked ice; shake, then strain into a sour glass, or small tumbler—with or without ice, and with or without a topping of chilled club soda.

WEST INDIAN "TEMPERANCE" SHRUB, which MAY BE MADE from VARYING SPECIES of FRESH FRUITS, BERRIES, or what NOT —to SEASON & to TASTE; NOTED during a STAY in BERMUDA NOT too LONG AGO

This cooling summer thirst-quencher may be made out of wild or tame cherries, raspberries, strawberries or blackberries—any such northern fodder; and likewise of sun-ripened sea grapes, pineapple, mangoes, Surinam cherries, carissas, and a host of other tropical fruits and berries such as the *Eugenia Jambolina*. . . . Mixed with finely cracked ice and sweet water, it recalls the days of bronze-faced planters —well, sipping their real Shrubs or Planter's punches, while the women-folk, the children, sipped their "Temperance" Shrubs!

All we need is a crockery pot large enough to hold the fruit; a metal pot large enough to hold the crockery affair. Extract the juice by dredging fruit well with sugar, adding a stick or so of cinnamon, placing in crock, and this in turn in metal pot. Fill latter, now, with water—making a glorified sort of double boiler. Simmer until juices are pretty well drawn from the fruit, covered. Strain through a jelly bag, and strain again if any amount of sediment is still in sight. Add more sugar, to taste, to make a fairly sweet syrup; stir in the juice of 1 lime for each cup of syrup. . . . Fill tumblers with fine ice, then pour in as much of this fruit syrup as they will take, garnishing with bright red or green cherries, and sipping through brightly tinted straws. . . . The true West Indian Shrub has already been given on Page 124.

CERTAIN PROVEN FORMULAE for the HOME CONSTRUCTION of SUCH FLUID NEEDS as BITTERS, BOUNCES, & BRANDIES; WINES, MEADS, & CORDIALS; to SAY NOTHING of a ROSE LIQUEUR BRANDY by a VICOMTE, & the SIMPLE INSTRUCTION for MAKING GUM—or *GOMME*, or BAR—SYRUP

FIRST a BRIEF DISCOURSE on the HEALTH-GIVING TRIBE of BITTERS, INCLUDING THREE RECEIPTS for THEIR COMPOUNDITION—BEING an ALLEGED FORMULA for ANGOSTURA, ONE for ORANGE, & ONE for HELL-FIRE BITTERS—sometimes CALLED "CAYENNE WINE."

Let us wave our white bar towel in a good-natured plea for truce right at the outset, and affirm that this receipt for Angostura bitters makes no claim to be the one hundred per cent, unchangeable, priceless and violently kept secret formula. By the same token, if we breathed our last in tonight's sleep, the heirs and assigns of Dr. Johann Gottlieb Benjamin Siegert—one-time surgeon in Bleucher's army (we trust the Angostura receipt booklet means the Blücher who, aged and infirm, made that incredibly severe forced march to aid Wellington, and even though he was "late," nevertheless added the vital crushing effect against Napoleon at Waterloo)—should lower all house flags at half mast for the vats of their liquid we have consumed, or caused to be consumed in our warped and intermittent career.

Let it never be said that so starry-eyed a devotee at the Angostura shrine would ever claim that their "world's best kept secret" had ever crept out into light of day, in spite of the 7 people—all members of the Siegert family—who have courted insomnia and shattered nervous tone guarding it from profane eyes of a mercenary and covetous world all those 115 years since 1824! According to the book of Angostura, 3 of these are still alive and active, and we hope our favourite male actor Frank Morgan is one of them—as the rumour goes.

Angostura was originated as a tonic, a simple to ward off fevers, miasmas, tropical swamp mists, and the general assortment of mauve willies that beset Nordics under the equator—and the content of quinine or cinchona definitely had virtue along this line. However, as is so often the case with truly worth-while ventures, fate stuck her tongue in cheek, and decreed that the bitters invented for health should prove not only to be one of the best titillaters of the jaded appetite, but by far the best priceless ingredient in all sorts of cocktails and mixed drinks; as well as in many of the tastiest exotic food receipts we have sampled around the world.

Actually there are 8 main kinds of bitters sold on the open market:

Angostura, orange, Peychaud's, Calisaya, Amer Picon, Abbott's, Sazarac, and Boker's. Hell-Fire Bitters or Cayenne Wine are local semi-amateur tropical creations. Peach bitters, Boonekamp's and others, may be found in first flight provision houses catering in hard-to-find, and usually imported oddments of drink and good food. Of all these Angostura is by far the most important. . . . No Amateur worthy of name can have a bar of note without a large bottle of these peerless bitters at elbow. They are absolutely essential to creation of scores and scores of the world's best mixed drinks: drinks which without such aromatic pointing-up would be short-lived, spineless and ineffectual things.

NOW A FORMULA for the HOME COMPOSITION of ORANGE BITTERS by the AMATEUR

Here's another relatively expensive item as now priced in small bottles for the American market; and easily made at home. In view of the incredible gallons of Dry Martini Cocktails consumed every hour throughout the world—each one requiring a dash or so of Orange Bitters—this thought appears to possess valence. Dried orange peel, ½ lb, chopped fine. Burnt sugar, about 4 tbsp. Good grain alcohol, 4 cups; cologne spirits is best if possible. Cardamon, caraway and coriander seeds, ½ drachm each. These last come from the corner drug store.

First chop the orange peel very fine, add herb seeds and pour on alcohol, then stand in a sealed jar for 15 days, agitating every day. Pour off spirits through a cloth, and seal again. Take the seeds and peel, put them in a saucepan, crushing with a wooden muddler. Cover them with boiling water, simmer 5 minutes; put in covered jar for 2 days, then strain this off and add to the spirits. Put in burnt sugar for colour. Filter again, let stand until it settles perfectly clear, then bottle for use—being careful not to agitate the slight precipitation or sediment during this final operation.

HELL-FIRE BITTERS or CAYENNE WINE, another RECEIPT from the ISLAND of TRINIDAD, in the BRITISH WEST INDIES, and Now and AGAIN USED in GIN-and-BITTERS, & OTHER SIMILAR SHARP DRINKS instead of routine BITTERS by STOUT ENGLISHMEN with BOILER PLATE GASTRIC LININGS

This is an old, old receipt dating to 1817 in print right here before us—and likely long before that, because the British knew Port of Spain a century and a half before. In fact we have just been diving up coins, cannons, shot, crystal goblets and other miscellaneous relics from *HMS WINCHESTER,* 60 guns, 933 tons, commanded by one John Soule, and while bound from Jamaica to England, sank in a gale on a certain coral barrier reef, 24th September 1695—and have the loot to prove it! And photographs; and cinema film.

This Hell-Fire Bitters is an excellent cooking and seasoning sauce for fish, salads, soups and meats, when mixed half and half with strained lime juice and stood for 2 wks, in an uncovered bottle, before using—a fact which has been disclosed in *Volume I.*

Pound up 2 cups of scarlet round bird peppers, or small chilis or cayenne peppers. Put in a saucepan with 1 cup of tart white wine; simmer up once and turn everything into a pint jar, add 1 cup of cognac brandy and seal jar tight. Let steep for 14 days, strain through several thicknesses of cloth and bottle for use. *When used solely for seasoning food,* put everything through a fine sieve. These peppers have a vast amount of flavour in their scarlet skin and flesh, entirely aside from the intense heat of their oils. Seeds for their home growth in ordinary window boxes, flower pots, or rusty tin cans!, may be bought at any half-way seed store.

If no fresh peppers are possible simply stir ¼ oz of ground cayenne pepper into the wine-brandy mix. Claret and brandy, claret alone, sherry and brandy, sherry alone, and brandy alone, are also authentic steeping fluids. Actually it is not a "bitters" at all unless a little cinchona bark is added—and ½ drachm or so is plenty, strained out at the last along with the pepper pods.

BAR SYRUP, KNOWN as GUM, or *GOMME* SYRUP, & which Should Be on Every Bar

There is a reason for bar syrup to the practical eye of the professional, for in many iced drinks—especially those wanted in a hurry, ordinary sugar seems to take an age to dissolve. Remember all the Tom Collinses that were double sweet in the last sip? Well, *gomme* syrup dissolves evenly and quickly. It isn't quite so romantic, perhaps, but is far saner.

Many receipts call merely for sugar and water, but we supply the true old formula with egg white to clarify the syrup to the desired crystal limpid texture so necessary. . . . Dissolve 2 lbs of sugar—about 4 cups—in 1 cup of water. Stir in the well beaten white of 1 egg. Boil up briskly, and when scum rises take the skimming spoon and skim diligently. When the syrup is clear the job is done. Let it cool and bottle for future use. It may be coloured or not, according to the whim of the host. We must confess that a little light green colouring matter in Tom Collins syrup is mighty pretty!

FIRST ONE BOUNCE, then the BRANDIES

This Cherry Bounce receipt is to all intents and purposes a form of cherry brandy, or liquor, made more frequently than not from wild, or other small, dark, highly flavoured cherries not suitable for the table market. It would make a valuable agent for flavouring many cocktails, or served as a cordial to be taken with coffee. . . . Simply take a sizeable jar, having an absolutely tight cover. Half fill it with cherries that have been washed, and if possible with stems snipped half way off so stems will bleed, and bruise the fruit with a muddler. Dust with a little sugar, then fill up with brandy. Put on cover loosely and let stand for 4 weeks, then mash up fruit thoroughly but in this case don't break any seeds. . . . Strain through a thick jelly cloth, or folded cloth. Sweeten with *gomme* syrup to taste. Bottle tightly and stand another 4 weeks before sampling.

AN OLD ENGLISH CHERRY BRANDY RECEIPT, that AFFORDS a SPICED & DELICIOUS LIQUEUR as FINELY FLAVOURED as any of the BEST IMPORTED AFFAIRS, & FAR KINDER to the CHEQUEBOOK; from BOXMOOR, HERTFORDSHIRE, in 1932

Take 6 lbs of wild, or other small black cherries—but never the red "pie cherry" variety, please, and after washing them with clipped stems on add to 2 lbs of ripe fresh strawberries. Add 2 to 3 lbs of sugar, 1 doz whole cloves, 1 tsp cinnamon—or 2 whole sticks—2 tsp of nutmeg, a bunch of fresh green mint tips. Put fruit and spices in a small wood cask and bruise slightly with a wooden stick. Add 6 qts of brandy and let stand with bung very slightly open for 10 days—or until fermentation has stopped. Now siphon off the liquid, filter into a clean container. Empty out keg and scald—then refill with the fluid, driving in the bung. It is cricket to start sampling in 60 days. . . . A few cracked cherry pits are also suggested to add their characteristic bitter taste, and which were not suggested in the Cherry Bounce just noted. A fairly good average of sugar is to allow a scant ½ cup of sugar to each pound of fruit. Smaller amounts require their relative proportions.

VICOMTE de MAUDUIT'S ROSE LIQUEUR BRANDY

If there is a more charming, instructive and altogether delightful book on food and drink than Vicomte de Mauduit's *The Vicomte in the Kitchen,* it does not stand on our shelves. Possessing, as we do, every book in English and many translations, dealing with foods, and many dealing with spirits and wines, the issue we take with amateurs usually is their opinionatedness on the one hand, and their lack of travel—except in Western Europe—on the other. Their volumes are works of art when it comes to what they actually know, have cooked and eaten; but when it comes to many exotic foods and drinks, they are hoist by the petard of their credence for what others—travelers—have written on those unfamiliar subjects. The result is often a slight cloud of ridiculous misinformation blighting an otherwise sound book.

Vicomte de Mauduit, however, sticks to what he personally knows, or has himself originated, or has known to have been originated by gourmet friends. He is charmingly frank about his own information on wines, claiming "a brilliant training and a consummate experience," on the subject. Above all, however, it is the bright clean blade of his originality which pleases us most. He is not content to stick to eternally traditional variations of this or that, but with the wit of an angel or an amiable devil, figures out trimming all his own! This rose brandy receipt we quote from his volume, rendering a respectful homage and credit for its loveliness. We have tried it ourself and find that the fastidious guest who silently judges his host by the not-too-complicated excellence of his food and drink, obtains a fanatical and delighted gleam in the eye when it passes his lips. We cannot say why, but Monsieur le Vicomte's further thoroughness in listing the names of the red roses best suited for this liqueur, also satisfies us wholly. Just why we cannot say, but we are vastly uplifted, packed with a toast-warm and intimate titillation at the thought that the fragrant rose-brandy cocktail we sip was yielded up by the willing death of Lady Helen Maglona. This plane of reasoning is somewhat baffled however, should we become fragrantly swacked on a quartet brewed from the rufous petals of a General McArthur, or a George Dickson!

TO MAKE THE ROSE LIQUEUR BRANDY

Take 8 big red roses—and don't go around under the fond misconception that because no one is checking up, that yellow, white, or pink roses will do. The Vicomte says red roses are *en regle,* and *au fait*—and that means red roses! These furthermore must be picked *after a rainless night and before the morning sun strikes them,* for, like tender herbs to be dried, much of the fragrant volatile oil dissipates itself on the morning air as soon as the sun beats down on blooms or leaf tips.

Separate the petals, discard dewdrops, and inferior petal specimens, and snip off yellow or white areas around the stamen region. Now put petals in a jar with 1 qt of really decent cognac poured over them. Be sure it is covered tightly, and agitate it with a gentle and considerate hand every week. After a month of this scented bath add a *gomme* syrup generated from the wedding of 3 cups of sugar with 2 cups of *distilled water,* and handled as follows. . . . Boil briskly for 20 minutes, skimming off scum, then put in the selected petals of 1 doz more red roses, dusted and tossed first with powdered sugar. Let the saucepan boil up again, then simmer gently for 1 hr tightly covered.

Now filter the 1st rose petal-brandy infusion from the jar, and rack it into a large sterile bottle. A filter paper is of course best here. Then add the rose petal syrup, likewise filtered through a tammy or several thicknesses of cloth, working it through with a spoon. Stir the final mixture, then let stand uncorked except for a bit of cloth over bottle neck for 12 hrs, then cork and seal with wax. . . . Our experience has been that there is a very slight sediment which settles out of this blend, and if the bottles are once more filtered after a couple of weeks standing undisturbed, the result is all the heart could desire. . . . Receipt for the *Vicomte's Cocktail,* made of this rose brandy, may be found on Page 135.

NOW to CREATE a WORTHY CIDER—which Is Certainly as Important an Event as Fabricating a Profitable Mouse Trap, or Hot Water Bag, or Hair Tonic

The Normandy chateau country is famous for its apples, for its Calvados apple brandy, for its cider; for its cider champagne which, if properly made and aged, is as fine in its own manner as champagne made from Rheims grapes, for instance. This is an old French receipt we picked up in Paris 12 years back, and although cider making differs in its finer trimmings between France and—let's say—the Yakima

Valley, which, incidentally, is in Washington, and is pronounced *Yack*-a-maw and not ya-*Key*-ma, the basic fermentation principles are forever the same. Cider has been made for thousands of years and due to the fearful, muddy hogwash our rural folk insist on inflicting upon their customers, it is widely neglected by those who should know better.

As a matter of fact, and with all due credit to our Pacific Northwest stalwarts, the tart, more flavourful Eastern apples really are better for fine cider—apples like the favourite winesap, for instance. The rules are really quite simple.

1. Use apples not quite ripe, if we want sparkle, snap and finest flavour in cider.
2. Don't be both lazy and stingy by gathering up a bin of wormy windfalls, unless we really admire that sad bruised-apple taste. Cider is an important business and deserves first grade fruit, not something we wouldn't dare feed to swine. Science has not yet been able to announce any virtue in crushed worms, entirely aside from their distinct lack of *distingué*. Inferior fruit is what ruins most ciders.
3. Mellow these apples for 10 days to 2 wks, depending on briskness of weather—the colder the longer—by spreading them out on dry straw in a dry barn. This permits mucilage to break down, and perhaps the starch, for all of us!—and starts development of carbonic acid which insures that delightful sparkle so lacking in almost all professional, and most amateur, ciders.
4. The apples are now ground to a pulp and juice pressed out through coarse strong cotton bags. A small hand cider press is used in small amounts, filtering the juice well.
5. Put juice in open tub or vat at a constant temperature of around 60° Fahrenheit, covered with a cloth to prevent entry of dust, entomological specimens, and general rural addenda. . . . Allow 2 days for weak cider; 8 to 10 days for strong; or in latter event, when sediment has subsided. Beyond this point the vinegar trend develops apace—abortive and acid beverage, at best, and not one to be admired.
6. Rack off into clean wooden kegs and store in cellar where fairly cool, even temperature is assured.
7. Drink now if we cannot wait, but remember it will really be a divine nectar by the coming spring!

NOW a CAREFULLY CHOSEN LIST of PLEASANT WINES, FIRST of which Is a SIMPLE NORMAN TYPE of CHAMPAGNE, which REQUIRES No YEAST

Take cider that still has a very slight sparkle—about 5 or 6 days old, on the above scale. Rack it off through a filtering cloth, or paper, into a sterile keg that has been rinsed with scalding water. To a 10 gallon keg allow 3 cups of the finest grain alcohol, or about 2 bottles of brandy, whisky, or gin—if nothing else, and 3 lbs of sugar. Stir and let stand for 10 to 12 days with bung in loose. Now "fine," or settle, the wine by the routine given just below, and let settle 4 days longer —about 14 days in all. Rack carefully into champagne bottles, filtering again if at all cloudy. Cork with sound corks, and if we don't wish the risk of bombardment from inner bottle pressure, wire them or tie them on very tightly.

Under no condition use ordinary wine or other bottles. They are not made to stand high pressure, and the cellar will be filled with flying glass, and very untidy explosions. We know!

HOW to "FINE," or CLARIFY WINE the PORTUGUESE WAY, a RECEIPT DATED 1736, and FOUND in GIBRALTAR STARTING a VOYAGE THROUGH the MEDITERRANEAN, via MALLORCA, VILLEFRANCHE, NAPLES, & ATHENS, to HAIFA, which Is in PALESTINE, in the EARLY SPRING of 1931

Allow 5 egg whites and 1 tbsp of salt to each 10 gals of wine. Beat these together into a froth; draw off 1 pint or so of the wine and add to the eggs. Stir well and add this to the container of wine to be clarified. In a few days it will be "fine"—from 3 to 5 usually does the trick. The egg mixture settles out, carrying finely suspended bits of lees and sediment with it.

ENGLISH BLACKBERRY WINE, No. I, from NEAR WHIPSNADE, HERTFORDSHIRE, 1932

This receipt is a time-tested one and has been in use to our knowledge since 1832. Contrary to the *U. S. A.* country style, fermentation is started *before* adding any sugar.

Blackberries, any amount
Boiling water, enough to cover
Granulated sugar, 1 lb for every gallon juice
Brandy or gin (brandy preferred), ½ cup per gallon mash

Blackberries should be fresh and "gathered on a fine dry day." There is no mention of washing, and we presume that the dust and various impedimenta of the region (as in the Spey-side Scotch whisky distilleries) are left intact to aid in fermentation and to donate special flavour. . . . Cover with briskly boiling water and stand all night to draw out juices. Strain through sieve into crock or cask, and let ferment for fifteen days in a place not too warm, nor yet with any chill. Here you add your pound of sugar and pint of spirits to every gallon juice. This presumably halts all further thought of fermentation, and the potion is bottled for future uses. Or practically immediate use.

ENGLISH BLACKBERRY WINE No. II, a Receipt from Bicester, through which We Journeyed on the Way to Banbury, to See an Old Lady about a White Horse, Summer of 1932—and which is Exactly 101 Years Old: the Receipt, not the Lady—& to Get Some Banbury Cakes

Gather fruit dead ripe on a dry day. Have a crock, or wood keg without head, and a tap or faucet a couple of inches above bottom. Mash berries well, pour on boiling water enough to cover. Let them stand with a cloth cover, for 3 or 4 days, where temperature is fairly steady and not too chill. Pulp will then rise to surface in a crust. Open tap and draw off wine into another container, and add one pound of sugar per gallon. Mix well and put into a scalded keg, let stand with bung out until it stops working. Have keg almost full. When wine stops working drive in the bung. Rack off in six months and bottle, or scald out keg again, return wine and let stand tightly bunged for another six months. The latter is much better, but virtually impossible to the average amateur, lacking patience.

OLD ENGLISH DANDELION WINE, Being a Formula Fetched across the Atlantic in the 17th Century, by Sailing Ship, and Dated from Saybrook, Connecticut, *CIRCA* 1677

Water, 2½ gallons
Dandelion blooms, 6 qts (dry measure)
Ginger, 1 tbsp, ground
Raisins, 3 cups, chopped
Lemons, 6, juice and grated peel, yellow part only
Oranges, 6, juice and grated peel, as above
Yeast, ¼ cake fresh; ½ cake compressed, or 1 tbsp brewer's type
Two and a half gallon keg, 1, scalded out

We remember one of the high spots in our *"Advanced" Biology V* Course in college covered the enzymatic action of fruits and so on—and in case that word sounds puzzling it simply means what ferments such items usefully—and otherwise. . . . And at one point we were sent out to gather dandelions, which were fixed in a big glass laboratory crock of glass, and bottled as wine, and tested as early as commencement. So much for the liberal arts courses. . . . This ancient receipt is much better and more elaborate, although every bit as easy to brew.

Mix dandelions with water and boil for thirty minutes, timed after boiling starts. Strain, and mix in ginger, sugar, and grated peel of lemon and orange, simmering for another half hour. Pour into stoneware crock, and then add lemon and orange juice. When lukewarm, spread yeast on toast and float on, or stir in compressed or brewer's yeast. . . . When fermentation has stopped, siphon and strain off into keg into which raisins have already been put. . . . Rack off after four months or so, and bottle.

OLD ENGLISH ELDERBERRY WINE, also an Old English Specification

We lived that summer of 1932 in Hayward House, Box Lane, Boxmoor, Herts.,—all of that, and in cruising the hedgerows in one of those animated chafing dishes with right handed drives that true

Britons laughingly call "motors" we collected many interesting things —including this one extra fine elder wine. The spicing is what makes it so good.

Two and a half gallon wooden keg, 1, scalded out
Elderberries, 5 qts (dry measure)
Pale brown raw sugar, 2 cups per qt of juice
Ginger, ½ tsp
Allspice, 1 tsp
Cloves, 1 tsp
Brandy, 1 pint
Yeast, ¼ cake fresh; 1 cake compressed; 1½ tbsp brewer's

Crush fruit and pour on water. Put through a sieve. Measure juice and add 2 pounds of raw sugar (brown will do but not so well) to each liquid quart. Add spices and simmer for 15 minutes. Pour as-is into your stoneware crock, spread yeast on toast (if fresh) and float on, or moisten compressed with a little sugar, and stir in. . . . Elderberry wine must be in a warm place as it fails to ferment as promptly as other fruit juices. . . . When it stops working, strain into our keg, adding 1 pint of good cognac, and drive in bung tight. Rack off and bottle in 4 months—longer if we can wait.

ANCIENT BRITISH WINE OF MULBERRIES, CIRCA 1757, from the COTTSWOLD

Here is another classic wine which is not only simple to make but cheap as may be for anyone with even a single mulberry tree.

Mulberries, 10 qts, dry measure
Spring or rain water, 4 qts
Sugar, 6½ cups (pale brown raw is best)
Two and a half gallon keg, 1, scalded out
Spring or rain water, 2½ gallons
Sugar, 8 lbs or trifle less
A little isinglass to clarify

If isinglass is used make as follows: crush mulberries in a granite basin, add water and stand all night in a warm place. Strain through a sieve, and add sugar. When thoroughly dissolved, barrel. Break up isinglass in small bits, dissolve in juice, stir into barrel, adding the second batch of sugar and water. When it has stopped working, bung up tight—and leave a little air space in the keg. . . . Rack off in four to six months, and bottle.

CORDIALS, or LIQUEURS, to Grace any Cellar & Compounded by the Amateur Himself

Please let us explain on this page that there are many, many superb liqueurs which cannot under any stretch of imagination be assembled in the home by amateur mixers, no matter how sincere and diligent. In the first place the very best of these fragrant potions are firstfruits of varying secrets, guarded for generations—hundreds of years, even—which presumes knowledge of certain herbs or ingredients which guarantee their celebrated flavour. Also age is a definite factor, both in the character of ingredients, and subsequent mellowing of the cordials themselves. This factor too is a discouragement in our impatient era!

In other words, we do not claim to be able to make benedictine, chartreuse, and like immortals for all of these reasons. But we very definitely do claim knowledge of certain secrets gathered in Europe, mainly, whereby several delightful liqueurs may be made by the amateur—some of which are *not* at all available in the open market today; and furthermore their accomplishment insures tariff impossible under our existing ad valorem import duties which our lawmakers impose on foreign spirits whether or not they compete at all with American industries they rush to "protect" long after the industries themselves are out of their swaddling clothes.

We therefore offer this dozen or so of receipts, formulae, for making cordials that won't require infinite patience, aging of product, or ingredients too expensive or foreign for practical employment.

A BRANDY of ROSES, which We Have Called "Rose Liqueur Brandy, *au VICOMTE de MAUDUIT*"

This fragrant and delicate bit of genius has already been entered on these pages, being a Brandy as well as a liqueur, and we suggest turning to Page 155, for the formula.

GREEN *CRÈME de MENTHE,* an Excellent Receipt We Collected for this Volume in Paris Some Years Ago

This is delightfully simple, and as all *Crème de Menthes* are essentially synthetic mixes—in other words assembled and not the result of special distillations all their own, the amateur can do as well as the professional.

Oil of peppermint, in any pharmacy, 1 drachm
Good spring or well water, bottled or otherwise, 2 qts
Best grain spirits; or cologne spirits, better still, about 2½ cups
Gomme syrup, to taste
Green colouring, to emerald shade

Blend peppermint oil and spirits, then stir into the sweetened water. The amount of sugar in this last should be determined by tasting good *crème de menthe,* and matching it. Now add colouring, stand covered tightly in a wide-mouthed jar for 5 days, then take a new white blotting paper and carefully skim off all excess peppermint oil. The 2½ cups suggested for spirits content is 20 oz, or roughly 33 1/3% alcoholic strength, by volume.

OTHER CORDIALS of Similar Essential Oil Construction May Be Made Easily

Liqueurs of anis, caraway (which parallels kümmel), clove, and other liqueurs may be made in exactly the same way, and in the same approximate ratio. Essential oils are available, and much simpler to use than by infusing seeds or peels in spirits.

THE CELEBRATED RECEIPTS of Dr. William Kitchiner, & Dated 1817, for Orange Curaçaos No. I, & No. II

Dried Seville Orange peel, pounded fine, 5 oz
(Or the fresh peel of a Shaddock, Grapefruit, ditto)
Best rectified, or cologne, spirits, 1 qt
Gomme Syrup, See Page 154, 1 qt

Pour 180 proof spirits on peel; cork and stand for a fourtn't; strain through cheesecloth first, add syrup, and filter once through a chemical filter paper (obtainable at good drug stores).

NOTE: About the only decent curaçao on the American market now has to be imported from Holland—where most of it is made, despite the Island of Curaçao, off the Venezuelan coast, being nearer to America. Our import duties on such delectables are so ridiculously high that one would think them a roundabout way of collecting the much-publicized War Debt.

ORANGE CURAÇAO No. II

The easier of the two, in modern times.

Sweet oil of Orange Peel, 2 drachms (¼ oz)
Best rectified, or cologne, spirits, 1 pint
Gomme Syrup, See Page 154, 1 pint

Simply add orange oil to spirits. Add the sugar syrup, shake well, and stand overnight. Line a funnel with muslin, strain, then put through filter papèr three times until it is quite "bright," as Dr. Kitchiner calls it. . . . The Doctor states: "This Liqueur is an admirable cordial, (with coffee), and a tea-spoonful in a tumbler of water is a very refreshing Summer Drink, and a great improvement to punch."

MARIGOLD LIQUEUR, from the *COTE d'AZUR,* which Is in FRANCE; 1932

Here is a delicious adventure for those in the country with plenty of marigold blossoms coming along faster than we know what to do with them.

Marigold petals, ½ peck
Water, 6 qts
Strained honey, 1 lb
Sugar, 3½ lbs, brown
Raisins, chopped a little, scant lb

Petals may be gathered, with dew off, over a few days' period. Mix sugar, honey, raisins, and water, let boil up for fifteen minutes, then after clearing with white and shell of an egg, strain well, heat up to boil again and pour over petals. Stand in tightly covered crock or enamel kettle around 70 degrees Fahrenheit for twenty-four hours. Stir, and cover once more, and repeat for three days. Strain, put in wood keg; add grated rind of three oranges and another pound of sugar. Add a yeast cake and cover bung with cloth and when fermentation stops add a pint of brandy, stir in half an ounce of dissolved isinglass, or other clearing agent, and bung tightly. After four months rack off carefully into bottles; cork tightly. Ready for use in six months.

ORGEAT or ALMOND SYRUP, from a RECEIPT DATING back to 1817

This syrup is used in flavouring certain delicate and oddly conceived cocktails. The receipt may be compounded as follows:

Jordan almonds, blanched, 1 lb
Bitter almonds, blanched, 1 lb
Rose-water, 2 cups
Orange-flower water, 1 tbsp (½ gill or so)
Spring or rain water, 2 cups

Pound almonds very fine in a mortar or bowl, first adding the orange-flower water to keep from oiling. Then add rose water and spring water and rub through a fine sieve until the almonds are dry.

ROCK and RYE

All of us have seen this eye-titillating array of goodies imprisoned in spiritual bliss in a large squarish bottle. How many of us have thought to assemble a bit for ourselves. It's very simple indeed.

Rye whisky, 1/5 gallon, not a full quart
Jamaica rum, jigger
Rock candy, ½ cup, leave in large lumps
Whole cloves, 1 doz
Quartered small California orange, peel left on
Quartered seedless lemon, peel left on
Stick of cinnamon, or two

Put ingredients in jar, cover with rye, and stand for a fortnight. Strain out spices through fine cloth or filter paper. Put back on fruit until needed.

To serve: Cut spiral orange rind, also one spiral lemon rind, put in whisky glass, and pour liquor over. . . . Can be served hot with excellent effect to fight off colds, influenzas, miasmas, megrims, swamp mists, and blackwater fevers. In fact any sort of excuse seems to work.

ENGLISH MEAD, from THREE VERY OLD RECEIPTS

Far back in the dim past when thick-armed giant Saxon kings dined in raftered halls, with flaxen-haired ladies below the salt, at the lower tables, mead has been drunk in England. Huge horns washed down haunches of venison, and the bones were tossed over shoulder to the stag-hounds clamouring on the rush-strewn floors. Then more flagons were brought, the minstrels sang, the cooking fires were poked up so that sparks flew upward through the murky rafters, and another haunch of deer meat was skewered on the black iron spit. The Saxons were mighty men, mighty in battle, mighty with food trencher and wassail bowl.

OLD ENGLISH MEAD No. I, the Cottager's Delight

From a receipt dated 1677

Strained honey, 2 cups
Water, 4 quarts; rain water or spring water is best
Sugar, brown or white, ½ cup
Lemon, peel, 1 chopped fine; and juice 1
Yeast, ½ cake spread on bit of toast, floating; or 1 tsp of brewer's
(Or 1 oz compressed baker's yeast)
Egg, whites 2, beaten well

Mix honey, water and sugar; add eggs, simmering slowly. When scum stops forming, add lemon peel, juice; and yeast when it has become just lukewarm. Stand in a crock in a warm spot until it stops working, then bottle as we would beer—either with caps or corks, tied down for luck.

SAXON MEAD No. II, Approved Method of Brewing, & Older than Eld

Eggs, whites 6, beaten well
Water, 12 gallons; rain or spring water best
Honey, 20 lbs
Ginger, nutmeg, cinnamon, powdered clove, 1 tbsp each
Rosemary, 1 sprig if you can find it; or 3 tbsp dried needles
Yeast, 1 cake, worked into a cream with warm water; or 2 tbsp of brewer's

Mix egg white with water, and add the honey. Boil for an hour, skimming now and then; and add our spices and herbs. When cool, add yeast, and put into cask not closed, so it may work; keeping in a warm place at even temperature. When fermentation ceases, seal the bung, and let stand six months in a cool place of even temperature. At the end of that time it should be racked off and bottled.

STRONG OLD ENGLISH MEAD No. III, Dated A.D. 1736

Back in the year 1736 one E. Smith, in his *Compleat Housewife*—of London imprint—saw fit to list various noble dishes and potations of the time, among which was one for Mead, which appears to be among the accepted best of that time.

Spring water, 10 gallons
Honey, about 20 lbs
Mace, 8 blades to 10 gallons
Whole cloves, 24 to 10 gallons (We should say 48)
Ginger root, 2 roots to 10 gallons; or 1½ to 2 tbsp, ground
Cayenne pepper, ¼ ounce to 10 gallons
Cinnamon, 4 sticks
Nutmegs, 3, quartered or grated; or 3 tbsp, ground
Lemons, 4, sliced thin with rind on
Rosemary, 2 sprigs
Yeast, 1 modern cake spread on toast, or 1½ to 2 tbsp brewer's yeast

Heat spring water until nicely warm to the hand, then add enough honey to float a small *Fresh!* egg. Boil it gently for an hour, skimming as necessary. Then add the other ingredients—and after simmering for half an hour, discard the rosemary—turning the whole business spices and all into a large earthenware crock. . . . Float a piece of toast spread with a cake of yeast. Strain it into a clean scalded cask. After three months take out the spice bag, rack off and bottle it. In six weeks, then, our Englishman recommends to start sampling.

PERRY, BEING CONCEIVED from the JUICE of PEARS, and ONE of the MOST ANCIENT & DELICATE of THEM ALL, an ENGLISH RECEIPT of 1817

Perry is pear cider, and one of the early European drinks. It makes a delicate and delicious beverage, especially in summer when refreshing tastes are a help to fight humidity and other complaints following hot weather.

Pears should be sweet, and just under-ripe when picked for perry. If too sweet and ripe, and not astringent at the start, they will develop too much vinegar taste when juice is matured into full age.

Grind up pears exactly like apples, and press out juice. The fermentation is the same as cider, except there is no great amount of scum, and for this reason it is hard to tell just when fermentation ceases—a point coincidental with the stronger variety of this drink. . . . Just before fermentation stops in perry, draw it off from the main part of the lees, or dregs. Scald out the lees. Put it back into the tub or crock again until the fermentation is done—about the same as cider. Put it in kegs, and bottle it next spring—if there is any left at that late date!

A FEW TIMELY KERNELS of ADVICE for THOSE THREATENED with IMMINENT DEPARTURE for the BARS; or HAVING ARRIVED, HAVE, through this CRISIS or that, BECOME FACED with ANY of DIVERS EMERGENCIES

We have already lightly mentioned that plenary intoxication is contrary to lasting solvency, happiness—either during the final stages of becoming swacked, or on the morn after. The dividing line, however, between quitting a brightly pleasant stimulation and this sad estate is actually finer than we know; and until we find a proven way of regulating our liquid absorption as this condition approaches, any pleasant drinker may be betrayed by his own enthusiasms, or in proving his balance or his manhood as a 2-fisted bottle-man!

Particularly is this true on large and involved congregations, such as country weekends, trips on yachts, and other divers sequences—especially if liquors are visible in large supply and amateur mixers among the guests are given carte blanche to explore and blend to their heart's content. Therefore, should the barometer tend to forecast such alarming possibility, and we—through real or false pride, weak mind, fallible stomach, to cash a bet, revenge a rival, or impress a lady—feel certain of liability ourself, there is always one tried and true way of minimizing subsequent toxic effect, which is vastly gratifying to the party of the 1st part, mystifying to rival, and impressive to the girl. It is a drugless way, and incidentally in actual practice we find that the farther an inebriate keeps away from stiff drugs, the better for all concerned.

So, therefore, before the 1st stirrup cup take a scant 2 tsp of olive oil —gingerly, and repeat at 15 minute intervals, to a total of 6 tsp in all. Take these gingerly, and in no event try to take all 6 at once without having proved it harmless in the past. We once, in vasty youth, tried taking 2 oz of the oil in one gulp. To our collective sorrow the effect upon our timid and shrinking gastric unit proved far more violent than any man-made emetic.

TO ALLAY a MILD, or EVEN SEVERE, SYNCOPE, sometimes CALLED FAINTING, from POTATION

Should any guest, male or female, through any form of miscalculation fall upon this evil estate they should—in mild cases—be speedily placed upon a seat with knees spread. Then with the hands clasped behind the nape of the neck, urge the patient to draw his head down in that position as far toward the floor as physically possible. This forces some of the blood back into the brain, and the seizure may pass. . . . If not, and after 5 minutes, the condition still obtains—get him into a recumbent position; loosen clothing, especially at the throat.

Be sure there is an open window close by, present an uncovered bottle of smelling salts intermittently beneath the patient's proboscis, and bathe his, or her, temples with eau de cologne or rubbing alcohol. Lacking this, bathe temples with a lump of ice, ice water, ice water and vinegar.

In extreme cases remove the shoes from feet, and apply a very hot hot water bag thereto; watch the pulse and if it really becomes weak or gives any tendency toward flutter, do not hesitate to arouse the nearest physician. Above all, especially if hysterics are a by-product, forcefully refuse aid from any inebriate or amateur hands, no matter how willing. Bustle, hustle and hysterics are contagious; calm and good-natured sympathy works wonders. Where the patient can swallow, 30 to 40 drops of *sal volatile* in strong black unsweetened coffee is a vast help.

TO ALLEVIATE APPARENT DEATH from TOXIC POISONINGS, & ESPECIALLY SHOULD, in any HAPPENSTANCE, the QUALITY of the LIQUOR BE SUSPECT

Happily enough, while there are a good many comparatively youthful distillations of American gins and whiskys, their production, the reputation of their manufacturer, and a rigid government ruling and inspection make adulteration at the source impossible. However, there are in rare cases certain people who do illegal adulteration to make an unholy profit at the risk of others. And in such case the symptoms are usually sudden and violent enough to publish the emergency. In any case where a violent illness is felt, or apparent, administer an emetic at once. It is better to tax a patient-guest unnecessarily than to chance severe conclusion, and anyway, since the patient quickly regains a feeling of exhausted well-being no one will ever be the wiser.

There are 3 species of emetics that are usually possible in any household at a moment's notice:

1. *Mustard.* . . . Mix 1 fairly heaping tsp with 1 glass of warm water, or warm milk. Drink it all.
2. *Salt.* . . . The same, or slightly stronger mixture; also in warm water.

3. *Ipecacuanha.* . . . This simple is an emetic, a diaphoretic, and an expectorant. Mix from 10 to 20 grains of the drug with ¼ cup of water—depending on patient's ruggedness of physique. Repeat every ½ hr until gastric evacuation is accomplished. After 3 doses stop, and call a physician. Ipecacuanha is poisonous in overdose.

TO SALVAGE A GUEST from the EFFECTS of HANGING—by ROPE, not the MORNING AFTER

This is, we are happy to say, a most unlikely emergency; but we surmise, on occasion, that an amateur mixer—either through remorse at the horror of his concoctions, through self-induced intoxication and a weariness of life and life's problems, may seek to take his own life by knotting one end of a bar towel, or cocktail apron, over the nearest chandelier and noose it about his own neck. . . . In any such case we quote an ancient English routine which should kill or cure.

1. Don't dawdle or joke. Hanging is no fun and must be handled quickly or not at all.
2. Cut him, or her, down.
3. Carry the patient to the nearest open space on the floor, and strip off clothing; or if still breathing, take to the bedroom for this process. Wrap him in hot blankets with hot water bottles. Apply hot water bottles, hot bricks, hot bags of sand, or hot glass bottles—Ah those Britishers are a hardy race!—to the armpits, to the soles of the feet, between the thighs; and especially along the spine.
4. Rub the surface of the body with hands enclosed in wool gloves, Aunt Aphasia Fittich's red flannel shorts, or dad's golf stockings. . . . Under no condition use alcohol, either rubbing or drinking, on the body's surface.
5. Where respiration has ceased, don't go in for all this routine but place patient face down fully clothed on the living room rug, head on one side, tongue pulled free—and proceed with drowning 1st aid, see any Boy Scout Manual. . . . Or, briefly: kneel astride patient's hips, facing his head. . . . Place both palms on either side of spine, over the lower ribs; then gradually throw our weight forward on them until virtually supporting the whole weight of our upper body. Release pressure at once, but release it slowly. This whole pressure and release routine should take 4 seconds. Only 1 person is needed to save life by this so-called Schäffer Method. It really supplies almost as much air as normal respiration.

CONCUSSIONS & VIOLENT SHOCKS

This is a civilized and free country, but now and again men, being nothing but great big boys at heart, lay themselves open to this form of violence or that—either from barging into ½ open doors in the twilight, or through audible or secret notice of the lovely blonde creature at the next table. Now whether this sad eventuality come through a water carafe bent across the victim's head by a disciplining wife or sweetheart, or the lady's male escort at next table executes a purge, we advise prompt first aid as follows: remove to seclusion and quiet; expel all curiosity seekers, candid camera fiends, reporters, ex-wives or sweethearts, enemies, friends or partisans.

In severe shock and concussion, the face is pale, the body surfaces cold; the forehead often clammy, the pulse weak, the breathing slow and very gentle, the pupils contracted to pinpoints. . . . 1st try to arouse by shouting at patient. Give a jigger of brandy and water, if able to swallow, and either before or after this thoughtful act, subimpose an open bottle of smelling salts at nostrils. Loosen clothing, remove shoes, and chafe the feet—applying hot water bottle or other heating agency to the soles. Chafe the surface of the body generally. Keep in a prone position until revival. Then stop ears to all postmortems.

TO ALLEVIATE the EMBARRASSING EVENTUALITY of a RUDDY & BLOODSHOT EYE

There are many very fine and new-fangled collyriums for this silent confession to one thing or another, but nothing is much better than the old yeoman's simple: simmer 3 sprigs of snipped parsley in enough water to cover for 5 or 6 minutes. Strain, let cool, and apply with cup or eye dropper. In 15 minutes the danger signal has vanished!

TO ACCOMPLISH DEFEAT of the HICCOUGH, HICCUP, or HIQUET*

This, dear friends, is a spasm of the diaphragm caused by acidity,

* As these unpleasant spasms almost always result from a too-acid condition, half a teaspoonful of bicarbonate of soda (of Arm & Hammer Brand) in a glass of water will positively effect a cure. The Publisher.

indigestion, a pungent liquid or solid having been in recent contact with the inner lining of throat and stomach; from spleen and vapours of both general and special nature. . . . There are probably more old wives tales about such cure as there are spinsters on earth. Sipping water while standing on the head is allegedly effective; so is sipping water through a napkin—especially when the patient holds his, or her, own nose, while another sympathetic friend stops the ears. . . . Vinegar, to the amount of 2 tsp, taken undiluted, has salvaged many. The same faith is also placed in a lump of sugar with 4 drops of oil of peppermint on it. . . . In the days of our grandfather, a pinch of snuff was offered. Personally we always munch a cube of ice, continue the campaign along original lines if it takes all summer, and don't worry.

In other words any shock of sorts may, or may not, solve the riddle. We recall hiccoughs being promptly cured once in Seattle, by a resourceful husband who became mildly intolerant of all the 1 doz or so friendly suggestions to his thus-afflicted wife, all of which had failed, and who emptied a siphon of well-chilled seltzer water down the front of his wife's newest evening frock. The hiccoughs were promptly cured, but we regret to report the lady almost immediately departed for a brief residence in a certain well known city in Nevada.

AN ALLEGED WAY TO SAY "BOO" TO THE GOUT, NOTED BY VICOMTE DE MAUDUIT

We have referred to this aristocratic Amateur previously in this volume, under the receipt for Rose Liqueur Brandy. And here again we quote from *The Vicomte in the Kitchen*—to wit:

"Melt some beeswax and when still liquid, but not unbearably hot, apply it on the affected limb under any non-absorbent material. Leave it for three-quarters of an hour, then you will find the pain gone. Remove the application, and you may then drink more port."

THE BENGAL HOT DROPS, sometimes KNOWN in SINGAPORE as "RAFFLES' QUIET RELIEF"

Even though we may be careful and lucky enough to avoid the curse of amoebic alimentary disorders in India, or anywhere in the

Near or Far East, or in the Tropics generally, we sometimes become a prey—through nourishment on too-ripe fruits, or from other cause—to what the old British medicos loved to call "coliks, grypinges, spleenes, vapours, and other flatulencies, or scours." It is a sorry plight indeed, and no remedy handy, so we append this proven simple as one of the most valuable we have ever known, and administered as it is a sort of drink, it is far more pleasant to take internally than the maze of usual hot drops, blackberry cordials—so called—and other remedies.

Take 1 jigger of cognac, the same of blackberry brandy, turn into an Old Fashioned glass. Add 1 dash oil of peppermint and 3 dashes Jamaica ginger. Stir, dust nutmeg on top, waft up a prayer to any patron saint, and hope for the best. Not only is the uncertainty, the restless tendency done, but the mental and physical system is pleasantly toned into a new and more solid foundation of cheerfulness.

FOR *MAL de TÊTE,* a Proven Remedy which Will Probably Call Down the Anathema of All Graduate Physicians yet which Has on More than One Occasion, Saved Our Own Life

Take 2 Tom Collins glasses. Into 1 put 1 cup of water, 3 dashes of aromatic spirits of ammonia, 2 dashes of phosphate. Into the empty glass put 1½ heaping teaspoons of bromo seltzer. Mix back and forth, and when ½ subsided, drink.

WORDS to the LIQUID WISE No. XIX, on a TRIED and TRUE METHOD of PICKING UP the SAD REMAINS of OUR BEST CRYSTAL WINE GLASSES, SHATTERED by the ACCIDENTAL or CARELESS HAND, & without INDUCED HEMORRHAGE through SURFACE CUTS on the HANDS

Moisten a wad of common cotton very slightly, and after picking up the larger pieces, employ a blotting motion to the areas infested with tiny sharp bits. They will come away on the cotton.

MISCELLANEOUS BAR EQUIPMENT without which the Blender is Pointedly a Lame Duck

1 paring knife costing not less than seventy-five cents, and a small cutting board.
1 lemon squeezer
1 pair of lime tweezer-squeezers

1 medium coarse strainer about 1 pint size
1 long-handled bar spoon
1 corkscrew—a decent one with a comfortable handle
1 bottle cap opener
5 quill or squirter tops, for bitters and grenadine bottles
1 ice shaver or very fine crusher for juleps, and so on. This can either be electric, or manual. . . . A heavy canvas bag and wood mallet is as good as any. . . . If getting one of those gadgets which grind up ice cubes finely, don't try to beat the game by getting one for seventy cents; go to a decent place and get one big enough to hold more than one cube at a time, and conserve sanity.
At least 2 doz cherry picks for Manhattans, and so on.
1 big bar glass with strainer and a pouring type of top, and very long-handled spoon for stirring. This for Martinis, and allied, stirred drinks.
1 hand or mechanical shaker of around two quarts capacity.
1 small hand shaker holding two large or four average cocktails, for the *occasion à deux.*
1 pair mittens with jingle-bells on them, for feminine shaking to protect the hands from chill—and saving squeals and complaints.
1 apron. The field is as wide as the Pacific on this—varying from the white professional "sarong" type, to fancies like we get given now and then, of pied-piper colours, and printed thoroughly all over with various cocktail receipts.

Containers needed:
1 each for lump, granulated, brown, and powdered sugars.
1 bottle, cruet, or what not for *gomme* syrup.
3 attractive and not too large glass containers for red and green maraschino cherries, small pearl onions, or other garnishes.
1 glass or glazed pottery honey pot.
1 smart cream pitcher, and silver is handsomest.

These are all needed for any half way complete bar, so don't procrastinate about getting them.

Spice jars needed:
1 each for whole cloves, grated nutmeg, powdered cinnamon, and the covers should fit well to keep aromatics from dissipating in the air.
Small bars need only cloves and nutmeg; very small bars, cloves only.
1 swizzle stick, either the wooden West Indian type, or the smart modern metal kind all good household supply stores stock. This for frosting West Indian Swizzles and similar colonial thirst-quenchers.
1 egg beater for egg noggs and similar fancies.
1 package of *short* straws for juleps, and that society of sweet, creamy

affairs, which for known reasons are called "ladies" drinks. These come in bright colours of cellophane, and so on.

At least 2 doz small bar napkins, of paper, linen, or what not.

As many of the following list of glasses as the traffic will bear.

A PLEA for LARGER GLASSES, and a Lower High-Tide Level of Pouring

Use a larger glass rather than a smaller one. Much as we admire some of the liquids in Sloppy Joe's and in other places attracting trade through pouring drinks so full they slop over, a sound cocktail should *never be poured more than three-quarters full*. . . . Skimpy cocktails are an insult—hence graduate to oversize glasses.

STEMMED COCKTAIL GLASSES ARE BEST

Except for the Old Fashioned, all cocktail glasses should have stems. Heat of hand takes chill from drink if no stem; something certainly not to be desired. Now that the mad ignorance of the recent drouth is happily past, let's get back to some of the historic niceties of our national drinks, we urge. This is also why we invariably serve all Java Head Mint Juleps in big-stemmed goblets; for not only does the drink stay colder longer, but no careless, humid Philistine palm can melt the lovely white jacket of outer frosting!

NINE, or so, SHAPES OF GLASSES NEEDED for Proper Mixed Drink Equipment

Many people hold that all cocktails can be served in the usual two ounce Manhattan type glass; and just as rightly we contend that anyone can wear a crimson bow tie with tails.

1. The standard 2 oz Manhattan type glass, with stem. Must be on all bars.
2. Tall, slender type with stem, holding around 3 oz; for Daiquiris, Alexanders, and so on. . . . Should be on large and average bars. Omit for small bars.
3. The squatty, thick bottomed old fashioned glass, holding about 4 oz. . . . Should be on all bars, regardless of size.
4. The tumbler-shaped sour or "star" glass, holding about six ounces. Needed for large bars, mainly. Not needed for small ones.
5. Tall goblets for New Orleans and allied fizzes. They should be around

10 to 14 oz to our way of thinking. . . . Only needed for elaborate and fairly complete bars.

6. Highball glasses, thin, tumbler shape, and holding 8 oz minimum, 10 is better, and 12 will save a lot of pouring labour. . . . Some of these are needed even on the smallest bars, which can find use for Tom Collins work as well.
7. Tall taper-sided goblets for champagne, and other really important items like the Peking Tiger's Milk on Page 130. . . . These should not be less than 10 ounces we hold, and can go all the way up to 16, depending on glass source and host's generosity. . . . Only needed on pretty elaborate bars. Big rounded goblets will also do, but the taper side is what the world expects.
8. 16 oz straight-sided Tom Collins glasses, which are also used for mint juleps when hosts do not have silver cups. . . . These must not be less than 12 oz under any circumstances, 14 better, and 16 just about indicated. . . . The 16-oz Collins handles 1 pint of club soda or sparkling water.
9. Those overgrown Old Fashioned Glasses (but *double* normal size) in which to serve The Sazarac Cocktail. . . . Or your brandy sniffers will do.

SHAKERS in GENERAL

We've had all sorts of shakers from the aluminum ones they give away at Gosling Brothers in Bermuda and Soccony & Speed, Gibraltar, to case customers—through gigantic lighthouses, nickel silver jobs we took over one year for outside lacquering in Kyoto, Japan, and picked up the next, to sterling ones made up for us on Silver Street, Peking.

We have always felt that other metal than sterling reacts badly to liquor and acids, and aluminum especially lends a "brassy" taste. However, the newer chromium jobs appear unaffected. . . . In other words, if we cannot afford silver, get one chromium-plated inside and out, or glass with chrome top. . . . Certain cocktails like dry Martinis, should always be stirred in a bar glass, never shaken—and this routine is always given under the drink receipt. . . . The new electric cocktail shaker—known as The Blender—is treated on Page 6.

THE MEASUREMENTS ARE SIMPLE, & Apply to All Mixed Drinks Mentioned in this Volume

1 DASH . . . This means what comes from a bottle with a quill or

"squirter" top, with an average hard movement of the hand. . . . *Approximately 3 drops.*

1 PONY . . . 1 oz, level full.

1 JIGGER . . . 1½ oz, level full . . . However, here at Java Head a 2-ouncer is the admired standard.

1 BARSPOON . . . This is a long handled spoon used for measuring or stirring. . . . *Approximately 1 tsp.*

1 PINCH . . . What we can pick up between thumb and forefinger—such as grated nutmeg, cinnamon, and the like. . . . *Approximately ⅛ tsp, or a trifle less,* depending on how well we pinch.

PLEASE MEASURE EXACTLY, not CARELESSLY, LAVISHLY, or STINGILY!

Just as in cookery, the amateur often fails because he approximates measurements. *All amounts given here are level full, unless otherwise noted.* . . . No matter what certain skeptics may say good cocktail and other fancy drink mixing is an exacting chemical art—just as modern music is an art. If we are lemonade squeezers at heart better not bother to mix at all, or else be graceful enough to approach the subject in a professional manner.

A FINAL NOTE, *en PASSANT,* on the QUANTITY USE of ANGOSTURA BITTERS, as well as SOME SLIGHT ADVICE on ITS GENERAL EMPLOYMENT

Most amateur mixers, including ourself, squirt in bitters more or less by the touch system. We know too that whereas 1 dash does for a single cocktail, what to do for a gallon? Standing before a large container making 60 dashes would be rather silly, and slow, and would send the usual mind to psychopathic wards before the night was pinned back. The answer is, allow 1 tsp of Angostura per 1 qt of mixed cocktails or drinks.

LIQUIDS NECESSARY to BRIGHT BARRING, either on a SMALLER or a LARGER SCALE

There are two sides to this business. If we go and list what an elaborate outfit can afford, those with a 3 by 6 alcove equipped to brew 8 or 10 of the simple standbys, and with neither inclination nor gold to play with more, will shout bloody murder. . . . Those readers with increment enough to stock a fair to unusual bar also have their say.

And if we *can* buy things why not get money into circulation and really make an elaborate cocktail book something to use, not merely to read and skip between Old Fashioned, Martini, and Manhattan?

The first-chop bar should have every single thing on this list; the cost should run in the neighbourhood of two hundred dollars, depending on geography.

The average bar amateur should run through the list and pick out those in most general use throughout the receipts.

Small bars should stick to the following. Dry, sloe, and old Tom gin; bourbon, rye, Scotch; orange and angostura bitters; French and Italian vermouth; grenadine and plain bar syrup; and a little each of the following:

Absinthe, benedictine, apricot brandy, cognac brandy, crème de menthe, cointreau, curaçao, maraschino, port, dry sherry, Rose's lime syrup, raspberry syrup, honey, orange-flower water, and a Sparklets siphon.

Even this small-bar list looks lengthy, and totals around seventy-five dollars without the Sparklets. But let's look at it this way:

Any mixing spot will serve a given number of potations per annum. If we only have gin, bourbon, and rye, with grenadine and angostura, that doesn't mean we'll consume any less cubic centimeters of alcohol than with the above assortment—which actually is capable of an amazing number of permutations and combinations. . . . The first investment is larger, but the yearly outgo in dollars will remain the same. . . . In one case we may gain name for pecunious and uninteresting assortments to offer a guest—in the latter we straightway become mighty clever and interesting fellows indeed. Good reputation is so rare, it would seem a canny gesture to cotton on to what little is going around through this simple expedient of stocking two dozen active ingredients in plain sight.

Of course many exotics and oddities are lacking, but if we include those given here nothing will be found wanting, believe us.

NOW for the LIQUIDS THEMSELVES

ABSINTHE . . . Needed both for frappés, drips; but mainly in tiny quantities to fetch out the other tastes in cocktails—importantly, picker-uppers.

Now made principally in Switzerland, being banned in France. It is a highly toxic beverage based on wormwood elixirs, with a very odd and intriguing taste. It is an absolute essential for every well-stocked bar—mainly as a flavouring agent.

ANIS . . . A potent Spanish liqueur made of aniseed and other simples. *Anis del Mono* is the old favourite. Needed oftener than the average mixer believes. A fine morning eye-opener indeed.

ANISETTE . . . A French aniseed cordial. Not only good as a liqueur, for the various tummy aches which beset humanity, but often commanded in cocktails. Sweeter and milder than Spanish.

APPLE BRANDY, or APPLEJACK . . . Needed these days for several excellent cocktails and taller drinks, but not necessary for the small bar except on special occasions. . . . Don't get Jersey Lightning that some friend has put down in the wood since last fall, get it at least four or five years old. It is a very deceiving fluid, and when not watched will induce a happy state from the waist down, closely approaching voluntary paralysis. We speak feelingly.

APRICOT BRANDY . . . Invaluable both as a cordial and for certain cocktails such as the Grande Bretagne. . . . The best imported dry type is indicated, as overly-sweet attempts spoil the drink entirely, unless used as a straight cordial. Eschew American brands.

AQUAVIT . . . A clear potent spirit from the Scandinavian countries, and drunk in tiny thimblefuls, with a toss of the head. Aside from being a kind gesture to visiting Danes, and so on, it is practically uncalled-for in mixing. The general flavour is reminiscent of caraway. Say *sköl.*

AROMATIC SPIRITS of AMMONIA . . . No bar should be without this morning after saviour, as well as such itinerant feminine emergencies such as faintings, swoonings—either real or assumed. . . . Chemically it is NH_3, distilled from a pungent gas, which in its former state is of scant interest to mixers.

ARRACK or RACK . . . A distilled, variable, and erratic spirit found throughout the Far East; without enough flavour to attract western palates. It may be made from fermented palm toddy, from *muohwa* flowers, fermented sugar cane refuse, rice mash. Some cocktails indicate it, and like tequila, if aged it has merit. . . . Only for large bars; and only decent brands are recommended.

BENEDICTINE . . . One of the most important liqueurs, and made for centuries out of sugar, herbs, spirits, and divers secret elixirs by the French Benedictine monks at Fecamp. . . . French copyists among the laymen state that it is compounded by blending the essences of angelica root, arnica blooms, lemon peels, thyme, cardamons, peppermint, cassia, hyssop, and cloves, blended and aged with pure water, sweetening, and the finest cologne spirits. . . . Everyone knows the squatty bottle with the D.O.M. label, and the big seal of scarlet wax. . . . Not too good as a mixing agent, as it lacks character, and loses its delicate flavours. . . . Best for cordials with coffee or without. . . . Not often indicated for cocktails, in spite of unjustified activity along this line by the manufacturers and importers, we've found it unremarkable except in pousse cafés. It is too sweet for most cocktails, and isn't vigorous enough in flavour to overcome the strong spirits and bitters.

THE EIGHT MAIN BITTERS . . . Angostura and orange bitters must be on every bar shelf, be it ever so humble. Next in importance are Calisaya —made on a quinine base and sometimes used in considerable quantity in cocktails—or quinine bitters; New Orleans Peychaud, Abbott's, Sazarac—this last a special New Orleans-made affair designed as an all-purpose bitters for mixing the Sazarac Cocktail: claims to eliminate bar work by supplying the combined virtues of Peychaud Bitters and Absinthe, or Pernod, at one fell squirt. . . . We find the classical Sazarac mix method far the better plan; see Page 121 this book. . . . Final two types of bitters are: Boker's and Amer Picon.

BRANDY, COGNAC, and *CHAMPAGNE FINE,* sometimes CALLED *"FINE"* . . . Brandy is simply distilled grape wine, aged in wood casks. Cognac is brandy from the finest possible region for its excellent construction—the Cognac region of France. No brandy not from Cognac is permitted to use the word on labels. . . . *Champagne fine is* merely very old, very fine, and very excellent brandy. *Fine* is only used in one cocktail to our knowledge, being entirely too precious and delightful in itself to be outraged by admixture with less aristocratic spirits. . . . Napoleon brandy is probably the best-known *Fine.* It runs about thirty dollars per fifth, and the finest is dated around 1832 or slightly later. Its price advances with age and rarity of vintage. Brandy was discovered through the keenness of a Dutch apothecary who, when seeing that the Cognac grape region, through a huge bumper crop, was producing more wine than could be shipped, thought up the idea of reducing the freight by extracting water by heat,—the same to be put back later at the consumers' end. . . . Although this didn't prove sound as to wine handling, the distilled wine turned into a new and mellow fluid of bouquet and potency which the original could never hope to equal—and thus brandy was given to the world, of which the well-known Hennessy cognac is a typical example founded in 1765. . . . Beside all the fancy tests tasters apply to brandy, the main one for laymen like ourselves is as follows: Poor brandy when sipped neat burns harshly on the tongue, and flavour vanishes quickly. Sound brandy, on the contrary, does not burn sharply and leaves a flavour and bouquet which lingers pleasantly. . . . Sip it slowly, roll it on the tongue—and the result should be like ripe grapes under warm harvest-time sun. . . . The bouquet of good brandy lingers in the glass long after the liquid itself is gone.

Brandy is taken in three principal ways: Mixed with other things, and alone, either in a small brandy glass, or in the large globe glasses. In the latter case the globe should be warmed between palms. This bodily warmth startles the perfumes into wakefulness, and they arise to greet nose as well as lip—and the brandy is then sipped slowly, a very tiny bit at a time.

Almost beyond all other spirits brandy requires enough aging, as only in this way can the delicate qualities be properly brought out, and rawness mellowed. Brandies from certain years are blended with other years, so that an even quality may be maintained. The colourless, raw distilled wine becomes mellowed and darkened from the wooden casks. Actually 1 bottle of aged brandy requires the distillation of about 10 bottles of wine.

Brandy out of wood never ages, and 1 bottled in 1900 after 10 years in wood is still 10 years old in 1939. Remember to check on this when buying rare brandy.

CRÈME de CACAO . . . Needed in at least one important cocktail, and a favourite with the ladies as a cordial with coffee. Naturally has a potent chocolate flavour from cacao beans from which cocoa and chocolate come.

CRÈME de CASSIS . . . French black currant syrup, useful with vermouth as an appetizing cooler. Also used at rare intervals in special cocktails. Good with soda for non-alcoholic summer beverages.

CERTOSA . . . No one who has ever been outside Florence to the lovely little monastery with its old gardens and the one privileged Padre who is allowed to speak that day, will ever forget Certosa. . . . We have half a dozen of their brightly painted and glazed bottles, shaped like globes in eagles claws, Della Robbia bambinos and Virgins in flat bottles. . . . And within yellow and green liqueurs much like Chartreuse, only Italian. Their strawberry Certosa is especially, and oddly delicious. . . . Never used for cocktails, just as liqueurs, and with coffee. Pronounced Chair-*toes'*-a.

CHARTREUSE . . . One of the cordial immortals of all time. Like Benedictine and Certosa, Chartreuse is the product of monks—this time of the Carthusian Order, and formerly only at their establishment in the French Alps called Grande Chartreuse. . . . Unfortunately this order was banished from France to Spain just after the turn of the century and, at Tarragona, they again set up with their secret formula compounded of elixirs from odd and rare herbs, water, sugar, and fine spirits. . . . Naturally all of France sprouted imitations. Clever chemical folk pronounce it made up of the following essences: Sweet flag, orange peel, peppermint oil, dried tops of hyssop, balm, leaves of balm, angelica seeds and root, wormwood, tonka bean, cardamons, as well as well known spices such as mace, cloves and cinnamon. Nice, simple little formula, this!

Green is most pungent, expensive, and a bottle will run as high as forty dollars alleged gold per quart, in the older supplies. . . . Yellow is just as good, and more aromatic; and is not only invaluable as a liqueur with coffee, in *pousses cafés,* but is the final decoration for a Gin Daisy, and other delicate drinks. . . . White is sweetest.

CHERRY BRANDY . . . Danish *Kirseboer* is best, and may be one hundred years of age! In more recent vintages it is widely used in many cocktails, as well as a liqueur and *pousse café.*

COINTREAU . . . Can't do without. Not only is it one of the six favourite liqueurs of the world, but is indicated in several very important cocktails like Between the Sheets. . . . Triple-Sec, another good French liqueur, approximates Cointreau; both as a cordial and in mixing drinks.

CORDIAL MÉDOC . . . Not used often in cocktails, but with coffee, and alone. It is one of the most delicate liqueurs extant, giving a rich after-taste hinting at peach pits, and bitter almonds—very, very far away, but pleasantly there.

CURAÇAO . . . Made from special undisclosed spices, and from the peel of oranges grown in the rather barren little island of that name belonging to Holland off the Venezuelan coast. The best is made in Holland, although we've had some interesting green Curaçao on the island itself, in Willemstad, the tiny Capital. . . . Yellow is most used, and has the most helpful flavour, both as a liqueur, *pousse café,* or in cocktails.

DAMIANA . . . One of those indeterminable French liqueurs made for scant reliable purpose, and indicated in a few *pousse cafés,* and those cocktails intended for profitable feminine absorption. As mentioned elsewhere, the label is worth the price of admission. . . . Should be on elaborate bars, mainly; otherwise it is strictly a bedside table liquid.

DANTZIGER GOLDWASSER . . . Purely a matter of swank, but always effective when with a handsome lady. It is also called *Eau de Vie de Dantzig,* and is a cordial with a pleasant but unimportant taste, in which flecks of real gold leaf flutter and swim about when it is only slightly shaken. The gold does no harm and no good.

DUBONNET . . . A French creation based on wine fortified with herbs, and this and that. Universally accepted in France for years, it is just becoming appreciated again in America. There are a few cocktails calling for it. Only needed in the more elaborate establishments.

FIORI ALIPINI . . . The tall attractive bottle of delicious liqueur in which a rock candy tree rears its realistic trunk and branches. A fine liqueur, but never indicated for cocktails.

FOUR GINS MUST BE IN EVERY BAR

DRY GIN . . . A white spirit flavoured with juniper oils, and too well known to describe here. All we can plead for is to get a decent grade, and stick to it. No bar can be without dry gin, and be called a bar.

HOLLAND GIN, or HOLLANDS, and sometimes *SCHNAPPS* . . . This is a vigorously flavoured gin which must appear on all sizeable bars. It has a very potent juniper taste, aids digestion, promotes appetite, and is needed in several important cocktails like Death in the Gulf Stream.

OLD TOM GIN . . . Old Tom has an oilier texture and a slight orange taste. Indispensable.

SLOE GIN . . . Totally unlike other gins, being flavoured with the astringent blackthorn fruit, or sloe berry. It is ruby red, sweetish, and makes delightful and mild fizzes, rickeys, and so on. . . . Should be on hand in all well-appointed bars of average type and above.

GRAND MARNIER . . . A delicious French liqueur and useful as a *pousse café,* but never specified for cocktails. Tastes faintly like a combination of curaçao, cordial médoc and Benedictine—with orange basis predominant.

GRENADINE . . . This, as the name indicates, is a syrup flavoured with the juice of pomegranates. No bar, regardless of its modesty can be without this need. . . . Don't be deceived by inferior American imitations of the real thing. Be sure and get the imported.

HONEY . . . This man-stolen product of bee's industry is, in its strained state, useful now and then in special cocktails. A small, cup-size, covered porcelain or china container should be on every thoroughgoing bar.

KIRSCHWASSER, or KIRSCH . . . This odd liqueur is made principally in the Black Forest sector of Germany, in France and Switzerland from small black wild cherries. These are fermented in wooden containers, stirred at intervals, and probably a few of the cherry pits are crushed with the cherries—which imparts the faint hint of bitter almonds. . . . Taken as a liqueur it is somewhat of an acquired taste, but in punches or in cocktails the flavour intrigues everyone who tries them. Kirsch is, of course, the same as *Kirschwasser.* No bar can be without a bottle.

KÜMMEL . . . A white, pungent liqueur made from cumin and caraway seeds, with the latter taste dominant. A great favourite with the Russians of royal days as most of it was made in Riga, pre-Soviet. Now

Germany produces most of it. . . . Like *anis* and anisette, kümmel is a great stomachic, relieves pains, collywobbles, aids digestion, and is specified in enough cocktails that it should be on the shelf of every average bar. . . . Swans, bears, and what-not, determine the shape of the bottles, and those with sugar precipitated on the bottom are held to be best—one brand having a sugar-frosted sprig of edelweiss in the swan's neck.

ROSE'S LIME SYRUP, and LIME CORDIAL . . . The former is a pungent oil-of-lime syrup coming in tall, slender, decorative bottles so often seen behind good soda fountains. It is indicated in the Gimlet Cocktail, Page 37, and bears a lot of experimentation. . . . Lime Cordial can be made by mixing this about half and half with *gomme* syrup, see Page 154. . . . Lime syrup of soda fountain type also approximates the result. These should be used more by American mixers!

MADEIRA . . . A bottle indicated for the well-stocked outfit. It is called for in one special cocktail, and used as flavouring in others. Especially delicious taken with desserts, or cakes.

MARASCHINO . . . Another delicious cherry derivative, fermented and distilled, then flavoured by the bruised cherry stones themselves. Maraschino is so essential that no fairly equipped bar can afford to be without it.

CRÈME de MENTHE . . . Two kinds of peppermint flavoured liqueurs; green and white. The former for flavouring special cocktails, for frappés; the latter for Stingers; both for cordials. . . . Must be on every complete amateur bar shelf.

CRÈME de NOYAU . . . A very sweet but potent apricot liqueur. Wise men take it with coffee, and only one or two. In peach and apricot pits there is a cyanide influence which most people don't know about, and over dosing will definitely become injurious. In small amounts it is perfectly safe. . . . In France they also frappé it in a glass of fine ice, livened up with a little seltzer or soda.

OJEN . . . The so-called Spanish Absinthe. Needed by larger bars, and used like ordinary Absinthe. For many years this was made in New Orleans. Still is.

ORANGE-FLOWER WATER . . . A delightful flavouring agent for many delicious drinks like the immortal Ramos Fizz and the Golden and Silver New Orleans Fizzes. Not used in everyday practice, but necessary for the average complete mixer. . . . But don't try to use just any old thing tagged "Orange Flower Water." Get the real French product: Eau de Fleurs d'Oranger Bigarade, by Warrick Frères, Grasse, France. (Solari Brothers, Royal Street, New Orleans, stock this.) . . . Also used by the Russkis in their tall sweet glasses of hot tea.

ORGEAT SYRUP . . . One of the needed bar flavours, compounded from almonds, orange-flower water, and sugar, see Page 166. Every well-stocked bar must have it; small bars ignore it.

PARFAIT AMOUR . . . Another of those highly coloured cordials hatched in the fertile and agile brain of France. It is also erroneously conceded improbably persuasive powers, but is very pretty in *pousse cafés,* and many ladies prefer it with coffee.

PEACH BRANDY . . . Mainly domestic. It makes a nice, although very sweet, business to take with coffee. . . . Used in Georgia Mint Julep, as on Page 66.

PORT WINE . . . Needed in enough unusual cocktails to make it necessary on any fairly well stocked shelf. Also an essential after coffee in any civilized community.

ROSE WATER . . . Used very rarely; only for the most elaborate bars.

RUM of THREE BASIC TYPES . . . Bacardi, *Carta de Oro,* and *Carta Blanca;* which are light brandy-type rums. . . . Barbados, St. Croix, Haitian, or Demerara rum, which are the darker, medium type. . . . Jamaica, the dark, richly flavoured type. . . . All three are needed. . . . All rums are distilled from fermented sugar cane products. . . . Watch Demerara rum! We've run into some nice gentle types from there that run 160 proof—or 80% alcohol! The strongest bourbon is only 50%.

SAKI . . . Japanese rice wine, and much like Chinese rice wine. It is mild, useless for cocktails, but heated quite hot makes the proper accompaniment for *Suki-yaki,* the Japanese classical dish. Saki service sets with thimble cups and porcelain bottle are obtainable in larger cities or from Japanese or Chinese restaurant folk.

SHERRY . . . The dry type makes the finest cocktail known, served as-is with a dash of bitters. All bars must have a bottle, for there are still essentially sane people who prefer it to any chilled, mixed drink.

SLIVOVITZ . . . A playful and potent brownish-tinted plum brandy hailing from Hungary, Rumania and Jugoslavia. An exotic variation from usual brandy. It's dry, not sweet: now made here in the States.

SWEDISH or CALORIC PUNCH . . . A much overrated affair, and which always stands neglected on our shelves for long. Drunk mainly by folk who expect a stout blow, and get a pat instead. Hints palely at rum and no one knows what else.

THE SIX CHIEF SYRUPS . . . Plain *gomme* sugar, or bar syrup—as on Page 154; grenadine as on Page 186; lime, pineapple, raspberry and strawberry—the latter quartet being those used at better soda fountains. Average to big bars need all five; small bars, plain syrup and grenadine.

TEQUILA . . . An exotic from Mexico which impressed us enough to run in three or five mixed drinks and cocktails. It is buyable in most average American towns, on slight notice—and everywhere in the Southwest. . . . Distilled from the *Maguey* plant, see Page 127.

TRIPLE-SEC . . . See COINTREAU, Page 184.

VANILLA . . . *Crème de Vanille* is usually specified for cocktails but there are a very few exotics which indicate the extract, and in this case a raid on the kitchen shelf will probably bear fruit.

CRÈME de VANILLE . . . Indicated in a few cocktails, but rarely. Only for large bars.

VERMOUTH . . . There are two basic types: The dark, more richly flavoured Italian variety imperative in many cocktails, as well as alone, with soda, and with cassis, as an aperitif; the light, or "dry" French vermouth, without which a Dry Martini would be a wet, old-fashioned Martini. . . . Both are wines fortified, and stepped up with various secret herbs. They aid digestion, promote appetite. . . . No bar can be without both, and better have two bottles of each. They go fast!

CRÈME de VIOLETTE, and *CRÈME YVETTE* . . . Made with violette flower essence and of a rich violet hue used to colour certain few cocktails; much preferred by girls who think they are being sophisticated in ordering something out of such a funny shaped bottle, and by gentlemen who erroneously think it possesses congressional powers little short of miraculous.

VODKA . . . This, although for a time banned by the Soviet, is still easily to be had. Theoretically it should never be sipped, but tossed off with a flip of the head, like Aquavit, which in many ways it resembles. It is a potent white liquor which should be on every complete bar shelf, but unnecessary to medium or small bars. Formerly made from rye and barley malt it is now made from corn and potatoes. The proof runs as high as 120, which means 60% alcohol, so take care.

THE COMPANY of WHISKIES, which ARE BOURBON, IRISH, RYE, and SCOTCH . . . Bourbon and rye are needed for very many important cocktails, besides a host of mixed drinks. . . . Irish is indicated for a few cocktails, hot toddies, and highballs. . . . Scotch is not a happy cocktail mixer, unfortunately, and its main value is in a highball called "whiskysoda" around the civilized and uncivilized world.

The smallest bars need bourbon *or* rye, and Scotch. Medium require bourbon, rye and Scotch. . . . Large require Irish as well.

Bourbon, Irish, and rye run close to 100 proof or 50% alcohol. Scotch a trifle milder, around 40%. . . . All are distilled from malted or fermented grain: corn, barley, rye, and so on, and flavoured by the waters, minerals, dusts, pollens and what-not native to their place of origin.

Due to the same mysterious natural factors which make the Spey River Valley good for Scotch—just so the water, climate, and so on of Maryland prove toward good rye, and Kentucky toward sound bourbons. . . . This is no argument against the location of the immense modern distilleries everywhere—but a simple statement of proven history. . . . There are peanut-fed smoked hams outside Virginia—but Virginia is known to the world; there are crabs and crabs, but the Florida and West Indies stone or Morro Crab is something else; there are soups and soups, but a New Orleans gumbo is super—just like brandy from France's Cognac region, scuppernong wine from our own North Carolina, Angostura bitters from Trinidad. . . . Bear this in mind when American whisky stocks get decently aged and within range of a sane man's bank balance again. . . . As they will!

Taken sanely and in moderation whisky is beneficial, aids digestion, helps throw off colds, megrims, and influenzas. Used improperly the effect is just as bad as stuffing on too many starchy foods, taking no exercise, or disliking our neighbour.

WHITE MULE, CAWN LIKKER, SHINE, MOON, et al. . . . Regardless of alias this sequence simply means the raw, new, colourless, distilled product of fermented corn mash, sugar and water. . . . If well made, of decent materials, in a proper still, with the fusel oil rectified out, and aged in wood it starts to be bourbon whisky after not less than four years in the wood of charred oak casks. . . .

None of the manufacturers of bourbons should have any right to call any corn whisky "bourbon" until it has aged at least four or five years, but the demand so exceeded supply that all rules were off.

As far as corn likker goes we have drunk it from a fellow quail and turkey shooter's still in the Big Swamp country of Central Florida—made in a copper wash boiler, run through an old shotgun barrel, and a length of iron pipe into a galvanized washtub covered with a cotton blanket; drunk it in the "dry" mountain sections of Nawth C'hlina last summer. We have drunk it straight, with water, with juices, and disguises. We have drunk it scalding hot on chill October evenings, with cloves, brown sugar, and lemon peel. We've drunk it cold.

In spite of hades and elevated water that old cawn bouquet comes shearing through like a rusty can opener to smite us between the eyes. . . . Hot with cloves, and so on is best; drowned in grapefruit juice is about the only cold method possible. . . . No matter what, that cawn has a scent of decaying vegetation blended with the fluid men used to put in old ship lanterns; and taken neat it burns with all the restless fires of hell.

As you may gather we don't recommend cawn—mentally, morally; or for general wear and tear and declined insurance risk, physically. We certainly don't—until after at least five years in charred oak casks.

A FEW NOTES on the CARE & SERVICE of OUR BEST USUAL WINES, as THEY AFFECT the AMATEUR

WE ALWAYS have believed that one reason most Americans know nothing about wines except champagne, claret, port, and sherry, is due to a practical non-existence of a truly leisured class within our shores. Everyone who doesn't leap out of warm sheets at command of an alarmclock daily, rush through a shave, a hurried breakfast and a dash to an office is—for reasons no sane soul has ever been able to explain to us—viewed as not quite Worth While, and lacking the proper attitude toward life. Any young person under fifty who stops work when he has enough worldly wealth to eliminate the daily grind, is a butt for whispers, raised eyebrows; he is considered not quite Worth While.

What we mean is that nothing about wine can be hurried. It takes an allotted length of time for grapes to grow and ripen, more time to ferment, still more to age properly in barrels and later in bottles. It takes a man time to learn about wines, time to drink them, a lifetime of appreciation to value them. The chap who is Worth While, and who spends half his life sprinting to offices, naturally hasn't time in all that milling about to slow down enough to notice wines. He wants quick action from his spirits, not leisurely sipping and pauses for appreciation. Few Americans have ever learned to play. There is nothing sadder than most American Big Business out of the office. We have seen a lot of it lately in that predicament, and a more restless, half-lost bunch of sagging muscles, golf alibis, and short breaths we've never seen.

Abroad, in all the wine lands, men have learned to play—at least after a fashion—leisurely, calmly; not fiercely, as though it were a matter of grim life and death. Our Britisher starts his week-end Friday noon, often as not. A whole French family will lie under trees throughout a Sunday, doing nothing in particular—a form of relaxation which would have the American Man Who Matters in a padded cell from sheer triple-distilled boredom.

Our great outdoors inheritance in conquering the great west has left us with story and song about two-fisted, two-gun, five-fingered drinkers of raw likker—who tossed off a tumbler full of red eye without a blink. All this sort of thing has got us to thinking we are a stout race of monstrous manly fellows, and the thought of dallying with a cobwebby wine cork, and sipping such meek and mild fluids out of a tiny and delicately stemmed glass, appears just the slightest bit effeminate; something grown men left to the companions of older women and visiting alleged foreign titles.

In other words America has always consumed hard liquor. She always will, but we are delighted to see the recent renaissance of interest in proper wines, along with that renaissance in good cookery we mention through *Volume I*—and most encouraging of all, interest in our truly fine American wines, of the type made by our friend Paul Garrett's family for well over 100 years.

Actually our first experience with wine service is utterly simple, easy, and without any more problem than a little chilling if, and where, indicated.

THE FIRST A B C of WINE SERVICE

White Wines: go with seafood, light-meat poultry; with fruits, sweets, and desserts. . . . Champagne, although white, is traditional with game or throughout any meal, if and when desired.

Red Wines: go with meats generally, and dark meats in particular; with entrée, game, and roast. . . . Port goes with cheese.

Not with Salad: as a general rule wine is skipped during the salad course, the acid dressing interferes with the true wine taste.

WINE TEMPERATURES

White wines must be chilled, except of course the tawny fortified types like sherry, Madeira, Marsala and so on.

Red wines should never be chilled, except what we buy as Sparkling Burgundy. . . . Bordeaux red wine should be served a trifle higher in temperature than the dining room. . . . Burgundy red should be slightly cooler, or as it comes from cellar.

The easiest way to handle a red claret wine is to decant it and let stand in the dining room for three or four hours before pouring, see Pages 195 & 196.

Serving a red wine really chilled would hamper its taste and flavour severely. For further thoughts on red wines in the Tropics, turn to Pages 197 & 198, and not too distant, below.

SIP WINE, DON'T DRINK IT

Somewhere the fiction got about that wine was made solely to quench thirst. So it may be, beside the hearth of our worthy and horny handed son of toil, perhaps, but no amateur worthy of the name ever gulps decent wine. Water is for satisfying thirst, wine is to be sipped and enjoyed.

First twirl a half filled glass, and watch the lovely jewel-like colour fan up on the empty inner side; then sniff it in leisurely fashion to catch the bouquet.

Sip, twirl the tongue, and enjoy each succeeding nuance of taste as it strikes the taste buds, palate, and rebounds through a renewed sense of smell from the posterior section of the nasal cavity. Then swallow, and catch the final after-taste.

Americans can't get used to having restaurants put bottles away for clients to call on later. Some wines, of course, do not keep for more than a few hours after being opened, but most regular patrons of any given spot have their bottles labelled, corked tightly, and properly cared for until their next visit. For this reason, and possible Scotch instincts through not wishing a waiter to get an unused half bottle, Americans gulp all their wine to the last drop—thereby not only drinking too fast but surfeiting themselves with so much vinous fluid that true appreciation, after the first brief introduction, is impossible.

WORDS to the DRINKING WISE No. XX, on the OPENING of GLASS STOPPERS of DECANTERS if and when STUCK
Dr. Kitchiner, 1823

"With a feather rub a drop or two of salad oil around the stopper, close to the mouth of the Decanter, which must then be placed before the fire . . . not too close . . . the heat will cause the oil to insinuate itself between stopper and Neck.

"When Bottle or Decanter has grown warm, *gently* strike the Stopper on one side, and then the other, with any light wooden instrument; then try it with the Hand; if it will not yet move, place again before the fire, adding another drop of oil. After a while strike again as before. . . . However tightly it may be fastened in, you will at length succeed in loosening it."

This is a sound bit of advice, for we remember the sad experience of breaking a specially fine cut crystal decanter stopper in a brandy decanter we'd just picked up in London. The sweetness of the spirit had sealed the stopper in tight as glue, and we were impatient. . . . The quickest modern way is to put the outer neck of the decanter under quite hot water from the spiggot; tap stopper lightly with something made of wood—anything not metal, and a twist of the wrist will usually loosen it—the heat having expanded the neck to a size larger than the still chilled glass stopper.

THE CEREMONY of STORING and UNCORKING any WINE WORTH the EFFORT

Immediately below we give routine for opening and decanting fine claret, which is a ceremony in itself, and here we will list briefly the strict rules. Neglect of any indicates the same lack of courtesy toward a discriminating guest as would be consequent to appearing in a soiled linen collar.

1. Store in cellar on racks with necks slightly up. This eliminates the risk of sediment on the cork.
2. A truly fine wine should be gently lifted from rack, wiped off and put carefully in buffet or wine-basket three or four days before serving, so that any disturbed sediment can settle once more. . . . Wine bottles worth opening are always dusty. Take them up gently so as not to stir up; carry them like new born babes, put down gently.
3. Carefully wipe off the neck, then remove foil, sealing wax, and such. . . . But *don't overdo* and wipe all the signs of age from the bottle—it is a happy picture to the epicure.
4. Use corkscrew precisely, don't shake bottle; drawing cork with a gently slow action, if the self-drawing corkscrew isn't on hand—don't yank it out for the dramatic effect of the pop.
5. It is good form to hold bottle in white napkin or cloth, and when cork is out, to wipe out neck carefully—being very careful that no old cork falls into the wine. A speck of cork in a glass is almost like a fly in soup, *Messieurs*. The final gesture is to offer cork to guest of honour for his inspection, who shall murmur audibly his appreciation.
6. If wine is to be decanted at this point, do the job against any sort of strong light, pouring steadily, gently, and stop precisely when the first film of sediment rises to a point where the next cubic centimeter will cause it to flow out into the decanter. . . . Better waste an ounce of wine than chance spoiling what we have decanted.
7. If not to be decanted, have a little poured first into the host or hostess's glass. When we see this done on foreign ships or restaurants it isn't just an idle gesture. . . . From the Borgia regime it indicated the host's willingness to prove to guest that the usual dram of poison was omitted as a special favour! . . . In more kindly times it indicates that the host pours the first few drops for a preliminary sniff and taste. Poor bouquet, or "corked" flavour is then detected before subjugating the guest to this embarrassment, and the bottle can be replaced. It is merely a courteous gesture worth keeping alive.

A PROPER CARE & HANDLING ROUTINE for the Most Tweaky Wine of All—Claret

1. Claret must always be handled like a new born babe.
2. Remove claret from the cellar at least 1 day ahead of time.
3. Stand *uncorked* in a slightly warmer than dining room temperature, but *do not heat.*
4. If fairly young wine stand uncorked for one hour, if older, for up to eight hours. This process is called *"chambre,"* or fetching it to "room" condition.
5. Draw corks ourself, carefully. Sediment kills claret, and ninety American bottles out of a hundred are killed, my friends. . . .
6. Have decanter a couple of degrees warmer than dining room, and put wine into it slowly but continuously from bottle to decanter—*against the light.*
7. When we see sediment flowing toward bottle neck, stop pouring. That lost glass of wine may pain us, but will ruin the rest.
8. Put decanter on dining room sideboard with the *stopper out.*
9. Drink claret out of large, *thin,* plain glasses.

A new or young claret will show a purplish bubble as it first strikes the glass, and is unrecommended for internal consumption. If the bubble is a rich red, it is matured, ripe and sound. If bubbles are rich tawny brown it is over twenty years old, perhaps more. We may then sit back and brood upon the delicacies of a truly worthwhile wine.

This simple routine actually takes only a few moments of our time. The reason we never do it properly is that it requires the mental effort of thought about a fine point of good living, which many otherwise important and influential people think foppish, fussy, European, and highly unnecessary. . . . These above 9 rules must be observed if our claret is worth the bringing home from the shop. Think it over. How many of us have ever had decent claret, either in a restaurant, or at home.

The average American restaurant's technique on wine is crude and brutally simple. It is snatched off the rack when ordered, and either served cellar (or rack) temperature for most red wines, or chilled more or less. It is handled roughly, carelessly. The cork pops, curious, envious, heads raise at neighbouring tables at this wide display of lavishness, lower again. The wine is hastily poured out—and there we are gentlemen—we are drinking wine, and God help us!

EXPLODED OLD ALEWIVES' TALE No. III, IMPROPRIETY of HEATING CLARETS

No matter what nice old Aunt Peola Fittich remembers about claret in London's famous inn *The Cheshire Cheese*.* never heat claret artificially. Place it in the room where it is to be served, in the forenoon, properly decanted, with the stopper out. Pour at night without further treatment.

A WORD on the CORRECT SERVICE of WINES with MEALS, GIVING FOUR EXAMPLES, or so, of WINE SEQUENCES & SIMILAR ADDENDA

THIS CHAPTER on wines makes no pretense to go into types, qualities, traditional vintages, and the like. This information, often the life work of gentlemen far more qualified than ourself to speak of such matters, is readily available from hundreds of sources—one of the most charming being a small pocket-size volume by a gentleman and a gourmet in his own right, Julian Street, entitled *Where Paris Dines;* and no amateur should be without it on his shelves.

But many of these books by experts fail to remember that the average American amateur, not conceived in a wine-drinking land, may need a helping hand to guide him over the first barriers. Not being primarily able to concern ourself with extravagant vintages, Americans generally prefer peace and mixed drinks rather than wars and rumours of wars, and infinite wine knowledge. What we note below are just about all the needful service essentials.

Let us explain 2 points which have always struck us as not usually made clear to the amateur. In the first place Game can be a relatively unimportant course, technically an Entrée, or it may be the whole focal point of a meal—like a vast platter of wild duck, or wild turkey, and there may be no conventional Roast course included in such a meal. The other is: where we live in the tropics and dining room tem-

* A tear stands in our eye as we report relayed news that this grand old institution was destroyed by a Hun bomb in the London blitz. Author.

perature may, on infrequent summer days, be close to 80 or 85 degrees Fahrenheit, we consider it proper to chill all still red wines gently to around 60 degrees—and we don't give a worm-eaten fig what long haired Gallic gentleman may tear his bangs out by the roots when he hears of this heresy.

We haven't drunk as much wine as a Frenchman but we have drunk about as much—probably a great deal more—red wine in the tropics, the Oriental hot countries, than the average Frenchman. Therefore, bearing in mind there are no cellars in such *pays chauds* that maintain a temperature around 65 degrees, even at 70! anywhere, we cry that too-warm red wine is just as bad in its way as too-warm white wine; and we earnestly recommend that readers think over this point in summer. We feel that red wine should be cool—not warm, not chilled. This goes for sherry too, which we find tastes infinitely better here in Florida when slightly cooled. It is a simple matter of reason, and not letting ourself be bound and swept away by what we've read about red wines, what some lame-wit, conceited ass has screamed at us after his first and only 5 day stay in Paris; all the fuss and fume that people kick up about a subject which is far worse than any mild mishandling of wine could ever be!

A SIMPLE FRENCH WINE SEQUENCE with MEALS, No. I

WITH OYSTERS or SEAFOOD COCKTAIL, and SOUP . . . White wine; Chablis, or Pouilly; chilled.

WITH the ROAST . . . Red wine; still Burgundy at cellar temperature; claret at room temperature.

WITH DESSERT . . . Chablis or Pouilly, as at the start; but better still would be a somewhat sweeter wine of the average Sauterne type.

NOW a SIMPLE EUROPEAN SEQUENCE of WINE with MEALS, No. II

WITH OYSTERS or SEAFOOD COCKTAIL, and SOUP . . . Dry white wine; Rhine or Moselle; chilled.

WITH the ROAST . . . A sound glass of any good red wine, not sweet;

room temperature if claret; cellar temperature if Burgundy; Spanish dry red wine, or Chianti.

WITH DESSERT or FRUIT . . . A good glass of cool Sauterne, well-chilled champagne; or the same white wine as at the start.

A SIMPLE YET PLEASANTLY EFFECTIVE EUROPEAN SEQUENCE No. III, to GRATIFY a PARTICULAR AMATEUR GOURMET

WITH HORS d'OEUVRE . . . Pale dry sherry and bitters. Vermouth or Dubonnet, or Amer Picon; room temperature.

WITH OYSTERS or SEAFOOD COCKTAIL . . . A good Chablis, vintage Rhine, or Chilean White *Undurraga*, chilled.

WITH SOUP . . . Old dry sherry, room temperature.

WITH FISH . . . Still white *Montrachet* Burgundy, chilled.

WITH ENTRÉE . . . Light Bordeaux claret, room temperature.

WITH GAME . . . Champagne of good vintage year, chilled well.

WITH ROAST . . . Red Burgundy, or Château bottled claret; former cellar temperature, latter room temperature.

WITH DESSERT or PASTRY . . . A sound Madeira, room temperature.

WITH CHEESE . . . Port of a good year, room temperature.

FRUIT . . . Tokay, or Malaga, room temperature.

COFFEE . . . *Champagne fine*, green Chartreuse, Drambuie, room temperature.

In this latter list the service of white Burgundy, of a good year, instead of the usual white Bordeaux, brands any host as being gentleman and scholar, and deucedly stout fellow as well. . . . It is a touch which some true amateur is bound to remark, and one quiet word of praise on our *Montrachet* is worth all the parrot-like praise of casual champagne, from a multitude. . . . Chilean Rhine type *Undurraga* we discovered four years ago on a Grace Line boat on a Panama trip. It is as fine as most Rhines, and greatly approved by connoisseurs, we now find. Comes in a cute squatty bottle.

A SPECIAL OCCASION SEQUENCE No. IV, & GOOD ENOUGH for ROYALTY

WITH HORS d'OEUVRE GENERALLY . . . Be sure and don't

serve too rich hors d'oeuvre before a fine dinner; skip mayonnaise types. . . . Serve a fine dry sherry, with or without bitters, or a Daiquiri, not too sweet, see Pages 30 & 31.

WITH CAVIAR . . . Vodka or *kümmel* in liqueur glasses, or a really good Dry Martini.

WITH OYSTERS . . . Chablis, *La Moutonne* or *Grenouilles,* of good year. *Schloss Johannisberger* Rhine, or *Berncasteler Doktor* Moselle, of excellent years, chilled.

WITH SOUP . . . Fine old dry sherry.

WITH FISH . . . Still white Burgundy like *Meursault Perrières,* a white *Côtes-du-Rhône Hermitage,* or dry white Bordeaux *Château Haut-Brion Blanc,* or *Château Margaux Pavillon Blanc*—choosing a good year; chilled.

WITH ENTRÉE . . . A fine light claret like *Château Carbonnieux Rouge* of good year, or *Château Haut-Brion Rouge* might be better still, to tie up with its white sister accompanying the piscatorial friend above; room temperature.

WITH GAME . . . Vary the procedure with a white still champagne, instead of the usual sparkling champagne which would do well with game—all this provided the game be fairly light like pheasant, and not dark like hare, wild duck, or venison. . . . In former case a good white still champagne would be a *Verzenay* of *Sillery;* for darker game try a red still champagne like *Château Montflaubert* or *Ay.* In the case of still white champagne, chill; in serving red still champagne it can be chilled slightly, or served like Burgundy from a cool cellar.

WITH ROAST . . . *Grand Vin Romanée Conti,* or *Grand Vin Clos de Vougeot,* choosing a vintage year for red Burgundies, and serving cellar temperature not over 65 degrees Fahrenheit.

WITH VERY SPECIAL VEGETABLES . . . A good Tokay is in order. Room temperature.

WITH DESSERT or SWEET . . . Choose a fine Sauterne, of which *Château Yquem* is finest of all, or *Château Guiraud,* or *Château Rieussec;* or a glass of fine Tokay or Madeira—all should be of good years. Sauterne may be cooled; the others room temperature, of course.

WITH CHEESE . . . A fine old ruby or tawny port, of good vintage, but if the cheese is of a strong type omit wine altogether.

WITH COFFEE . . . A fine liqueur Brandy, or *champagne fine;* Cordial Médoc, or Green Chartreuse.

WORDS to the DRINKING WISE No. XXI, on the EXCELLENCE of SERVING THE CHEESE BEFORE the DESSERT

The French they are a canny race. Knowing that only a sip of red wine can possibly harmonize with cheese, then change our order, and serve it before the sweet—thus enabling a guest to use his final few sips of Burgundy in proper fashion. Otherwise it means an extra wine course like a good port. Try it some time. No one will notice until the thing is done, then they will see the logic.

WORDS to the DRINKING WISE No. XXII, on the BEST MOMENT for SERVING CHAMPAGNE at a MEAL

Just note the sequence above. If other wines precede it, always serve the champagne with the *first hot meat course,* in this case the game. If sparkling wine is served after too many hot courses, gases are released more potently, causing a tendency toward heartburn, for those who tend. A great many tend.

A THOUGHT on SERVING ONE WINE THROUGHOUT the MEAL

Many gourmets often and connoisseurs who know whereof they speak, claim that all this business of having four or five varieties of wine with a meal is sheer boasting, and that if a wine is sound enough to deserve to serve at all, it is good enough for the whole meal. . . . Usually this means some white wine—Rhine, Moselle, Bordeaux, still Burgundy white, or something similar. A white wine will go with the meat whereas red wine simply doesn't seem to suit caviar, oysters, delicate boiled fishes, and seafood like shrimps and lobsters—and with sweets or dessert a white wine fetches out the flavours better. . . . In fact there is one school which calls for a dry champagne of decent vintage now and then for a complete meal, claiming that with fruits and desserts of all sorts the harmony is particularly gratifying.

Sometime when we elect to serve champagne right through a meal make the added gesture of serving a dry type with the meal up to the dessert, then changing to a slightly sweeter kind—as dry wine does not march quite so well with sweets, and sweet pastries.

WINE at TEA TIME

The smartest people in America used to serve sweet wine—Catawba, or Virginia Dare scuppernong, with cake or tiny small cakes, just as in France a sweet Bordeaux or champagne was often served with cakes in the late afternoon. . . . Ports, sherries, Malagas, Madeiras and Marsalas were also offered. . . . The old custom has merit. Why not offer favoured callers a nip of decent wine and handsome small cakes, to relieve the eternal tea and macaroons, or cocktails? We've tried it and the combination tastes so good it's well worth consideration.

EXPLODED OLD ALEWIVES' TALE No. IV, OVERRULING the COMMON BELIEF here in AMERICA, that a TRULY MAGNIFICENT RED VINTAGE WINE—such as an ANCIENT PORT, a PRICELESS *HOSPICE de BEAUNE* BURGUNDY, or a *CHÂTEAU LAFITE* CLARET—CAN BE OPENED by DRAWING the CORK

Let us hasten to explain this does not apply to average wines, but to the priceless citizens in bottles; to those grand seigneurs whose name and dating should be mentioned only in bated breath. . . . In such ancient affairs it is just as ruinous to spoil the excellence through agitation—even with the greatest care—in cork pulling. An agitated great red wine becomes an average red wine, immediately. There is no more sanity in such spoilage than there is in checking a Raphael madonna, uncrated, in a baggage van.

Go to the nearest good hotel or club and get a pair of bottle tongs. Heat them quite hot and fasten about the bottle neck just below the lower cork end. Count 10, take tongs away, and touch the spot with a pad of cloth soaked in cold water. The neck cracks all around in a clean break—no fuss, no splinters. . . . Even during this slight activity a fine old red wine should be lifted gently as a babe, and carried so; no sudden jolts, no agitation whatsoever. Only in this way can the ancient sediments remain in their undisturbed position, and be kept from clouding, injuring the whole bottle.

"Gloomy or depressed people should never be given good food, or any sort of wines or alcoholic beverages, as neither will go down well. The first quality a gourmet must possess is *joie de vivre* which implies a sparkling, natural satisfaction with life, a genuine appreciation of all good things in life, a disregard for the bad things, and the creation of happiness all around him.

". . . *Bons vivants* do not overeat or overdrink; they leave the table with room for further gastronomic enchantments. . . . Indigestion and intoxication are the two worst punishments a gourmet could receive. . . .

". . . Speaking of intoxication, it is curious to note that it embraces five stages: jocose, bellicose, lachrymose, comotose, and morotose. The first two are not only respectable, but very, very nice; the third not quite so respectable and not quite so nice; the fourth not respectable at all, and not a bit nice. As for the fifth, well, it finishes one."

The Vicomte in the Kitchen,
By Vicomte de Mauduit,
1933

INDEX OF DRINKS

END

CPSIA information can be obtained
at www.ICGtesting.com
Printed in the USA
BVHW03s2122160718
521663BV00010B/65/P